CONCEPT OF GOD AND RELIGION

TRADITIONAL THOUGHT AND CONTEMPORARY SOCIETY

CONCEPT OF GOD AND RELIGION

TRADITIONAL THOUGHT AND CONTEMPORARY SOCIETY

Editors

K. Jose SVD, Gautam K. Bera

Birinchi K. Medhi, R.P. Athparia

ABHIJEET PUBLICATIONS

NEW DELHI 110002

ABHIJEET PUBLICATIONS
4658-A, 21 Ansari Road, New Delhi 110002
Phone: 011-22960492, 65698474
E-mail: abhijeetpublication@gmail.com

CONCEPT OF GOD AND RELIGION

First Published 2012

ISBN 978-93-81136-52-2

PRINTED IN INDIA

Published by J.K. Singh for Abhijeet Publications, New Delhi-110002, Lasertypeset by Gaurav Graphics, Delhi and Printed at Himanshu Printers, Delhi.

Introductory Preface

Science and religion argue all the time, but they increasingly agree on one thing: a little spirituality may be very good for your health.

Jeffrey Kluger

Human beings as they advance in knowledge and excel in various sciences accumulate a sense of self confidence. This does not amply establish that religion has in any substantial way given way to science. Rather, it only affirms that both science and religion have their crucial roles in advancing the contemporary society. We are only too aware of the fact that especially the young people find great satisfaction in disassociating themselves from the age old traditions. However, students of human cultures admit that religion is one of the most important ingredients in culture. We know that every known human society has given an envious place to it as it interacts with other cultural institutions. It finds expression in material culture, in human behaviour, in value systems and in morals and ethics. No other cultural institution has so perverse a range of expression and implication as religion finds arena to interact with systems of family and clan organization, marriage, law and politics. It so elusively enters into the formidable realms of medicine, science and technology too.

As we know India is always and has been a deeply religious country, in spite of its secular constitution which enshrines not the absence of religion but a profusion of religions. Yet, concept of God and concept of religion seems to be becoming more abstract. Is it because religions belong less and less to every life? Or since politics, commerce, law, education, medicine and other spheres of life are becoming increasingly more significant to day to day life in our contemporary society? The point is how can this multi-religious and pluri-cultural country be genuinely engaged in making long lasting contributions to build a just, peaceful and a more humane society? Or how does the concept of God and Religion which is traditionally handed down to us by our parents, elders and others make its presence felt in our contemporary engagements in the society today. Many believe that the most compelling reason for studying religion today is to reach a better understanding of contemporary society. Without the study of religion, ignorance in this subject would create more global conflicts and prejudices. There is still a great need for more study into religion as there is still a lot of ignorance in the subject and in today's society, with the amount of different religions/faiths; understanding is the key to a cultured social wellbeing. There are still too many racial and religious prejudices in the world through lack of vital knowledge in this subject.

We are sure no one will have the ultimate answer to these and many other related problems. But based on the papers which will be presented and discussed in this national seminar, we are happy to note that a good number of authors make a clarion call to translate the fundamental values of religions from the prevalent ones to more relevant ones reading the signs of the time. There seems to be a strong and pointed opinion that the moving from closed to open religions and from authoritarian religious institutions and bureaucracy to participatory democracy is the way to make religions relevant in contemporary India. Our religious atmosphere must gather confidence to engage in fundamental debates on the major issues confronting our country. Because there is a need to foster this ongoing communication, which ensures that all religions open up to the concern of over a billion of our brothers and sisters irrespective of their religious affiliations. We are happy today our esteemed professors, scholars and friends have joined us to debate on these and many other vital and related issues, to balance the spiritual needs confronting everyday with a combination of scientific temper.

While fundamentalist groups are found in every religion it is important that all people of goodwill need to come together in the promotion of shared human and spiritual values. As Pope John Paul II of happy memory addressed the leaders of religions saying 'as we open ourselves in dialogue to one another, we also open ourselves to God… As followers of different religions we should join together in promoting and defending common ideals in the sphere of religious liberty, human brotherhood, education, culture, social welfare and civil order. Human beings pray everyday. They pray for peace, for serenity, for wealth. Some travel to Lourdes in search of a miracle; some go to Mecca to show their devotion; some gather in the church to praise and worship God, some chant *mantras* to realize that they are part of the Brahman, some ask for the grace to follow the eight fold paths in all honesty and simplicity. So there are many ways people pray, many needs they pray for. However, there may be nothing we pray for more than health. If we have health everything else becomes meaningful. So at the end of the day though our medicines are powerful, produced by a branded company, our physicians are well trained and trustworthy, we also pray for healing as well'.

God should be worshipped in "Truth and Spirit" especially in our days because all other ways of worship tend to sow the seeds of division and discord. We are also aware that every religious scripture has unfathomable teachings and if they are followed in spirit and truth there will be great harmony and amity between people of various religious affiliations. Even though there is arguably no harm in having a high regard and respect for the religion of one's faith and adherence, it should rather lead us to tolerance and a spirit of appreciation for the other who takes a path different from mine. After all, we are all children of the one God whom we call by different names based on the cultural-historical-theological parlance.

Many people today look at religion as a divisive force. This is all the more reason for us to invite people to think of religion as a resource, an energy inspiring ethical living and a motivating force for the welfare of individuals and communities. Then it soon becomes a mighty resource human growth and enrichment. For we know only religion can plant those profound and all encompassing convictions on which values for human sustenance can take root and flourish. Religion and religious sensitivity are the factories that manufacture morality that society and business both need to function. It is religion alone that can impose inwardly binding laws from within. F.W. de Clerk of South Africa was asked whether there was international sanctions that brought apartheid to an end. His quick reply was, "It was not sanctions, but a deep analysis on our knees before God." Religion is an unfailing resource for human growth, and for peace.

Anthropologists who specialize in the study of preliterate societies have always been faced with the difficult problem of defining what kind of phenomena can be called religious. There are special places for the pursuance of religion – temples, churches, mosques, etc and special people to officiate in it – *purohits, priests, imams,* etc. Even in these cases, however, the matter is much less simple. The problem is even more complicated in the case of traditional societies, not only because phenomena which are easily referred to by the English word 'religion' are part and parcel of activities which would not so label, but also because people in such societies, unlike the participants in a world religion, have no concept of 'religion' as a distinct phenomenon. This has led social scientists to try a whole range of definitions, usually settling with little convictions, on formulae such as: religion involves the belief in supernatural forces. The problem with this type of definition is in the difficulty of distinguishing between 'natural' and 'supernatural' knowledge.

Durkheim called all religious beliefs and practices which were believed to be right of themselves, not merely right because they were the best way of doing something according to practical criteria. The first type of beliefs and practices were, according to him, 'sacred'; the second 'profane'. Weber, however, thinks that in practice it is impossible to distinguish on the basis of any criterion, as it separates what is not separated in ordinary life. The only solution seems to be to abandon the notion of religion as an analytical category and to look at social reality in terms less closely tied to a particular cultural tradition. It is implicit in the work of Marx where religion is subsumed under the wider label of ideology. Even if we reject the notion of religion as an analytical tool, we can retain it as a general indication of an area of study. Taking this perspective, we may explore topics that seem to recur in the discussion of religion, we have here three of the typical ingredients of religion: 1) philosophical or intellectual speculation; 2) the denial of the validity of experience; and 3) the legitimization of authority.

It is apparent that in the world of religion there are also professional theologians trying to organize and systematize beliefs and their ideas seem curiously distinct from the everyday religion of people. Accordingly some anthropologists distinguish between two types of religion, a folk religion and an official theological religion. It is partly as a result of these problems that anthropologists and sociologists have found it almost impossible to agree about the notion of 'belief'. Religion, in order to be powerful and to perform its right role, must have the appearance of deep truth, and explanations of religion must not only explain how it maintains authority but also why it is so apparently necessary and comforting to the participants.

All of our religions have rich scriptures that contain profound thoughts and teachings. One would certainly find at least a few believers in every religion who, out of interest or out of love for God's word, have learnt whole or parts of scriptures by heart. The scriptures, if read in their original languages such as Sanskrit, Arabic, Hebrew, Pali and so on, pose difficulties in comprehending their meaning. We then look at the translations or consult a commentary or even turn to a *guru* to understand the deeper meaning hidden behind the words.

All the religions in the world have rich holy books that contain profound thoughts and teachings. These scriptures give profound themes to the seekers of truth and they also call them to make their life in tune with the religious traditions of the given book. Anyone who observe the contemporary rhythm of life in our country will have often asked a fundamental question, as to why despite our chanting, reading of scriptures and devoutly praying, the lives of many of us remain unaffected. This question is more pertinent for us as we live in a country where religiosity is practiced quite seriously in public as well as in private and where much importance is attached to the word of God.

This brings us to the various papers presented in this comprehensive volume.

II

Birinchi K. Medhi in his Key Note Address made an attempt to portray some aspects of socio-religious life of the indigenous Sikhs of Assam, usually referred to as the 'Assamese Sikhs', who are principally distributed throughout the Brahmaputra valley of the state of Assam in North-East India. The Assamese Sikhs are one such ethnic group who identify themselves with Assam, their homeland, and Assamese, their language. These Sikhs identity with the common culture shared with the Assamese people. The present day Assamese Sikhs appear to be the descendants of different groups of people like the Sikh disciples of Guru Tegh Bahadur who settled at Dhubri and Chaotala in the seventeenth century; the Sikh soldiers who were brought to Assam in connection with the secret maneuver in the eighteenth century, and those Sikh soldiers who were brought to Assam to fight against the Burmese army in the nineteenth century; and those Sikhs who migrated to Assam from Punjab during the 1830s for trade and gradually mingled with the Assamese people .

R.P. Athparia through his paper delivered as **St. Arnold Janssen Foundation Lecture** establishes that the people of Assam are broadly divided into four categories, namely general castes, scheduled tribes, scheduled castes, and the immigrant communities. Assam is the meeting ground of ethnic streams from the west, north and east. The different communities have contributed the ethno-religions fabric of ancient Assam since time immemorial.

Gautam K. Bera in his **Mother Teresa Centenary Lecture** brings into light the theme of religious diversity in India while observing that Indian civilization is characterized with the phenomenon of unity in diversity as a consequence of harmony of contrasts. He argues that in India, the term religion refers to aspects of India's cultural traditions, which, however, portray diverse concepts that emanated over the ages. This diversity of religion occurred through both ways of fission and fusion of ideas which designated the country to be the land of diverse religions.

Joy Thomas in **Prof. Stephen Fuchs SVD Memorial Lecture** poignantly observes that though anthropology is a very young science, it studies the questions of human origins, present day life and the journey onward to the future. In this technological age though it only gives a glimmer of guiding orientations, visions and hopes from the myths, religious symbols, folklore and history, the author says that we need to focus on the emerging trends in the anthropology of religions, which is moving in the direction of cosmo-theandric anthropology.

Vijoy S. Sahay in Prof. Wilhelm Schimdt Memorial Lecture mentioned that in Anthropology, maximum attention has been drawn in the pages of anthropological literature for the subject matter of Religion. As a theoretician he has delineated in detail the perspectives of religion in global context and the practices thereof by different communities living across the globe. He brought into light the concept of animism as proposed by Edward Burnett Tylor in contrast to the different forms of tribal religion as subscribed in India.

K. Jose SVD and **Manoj Anthony SVD** in their joint paper bring to light the various dimensions of religion in a society while calling for a greater engagement of religions considering the contemporary needs of the society at large. They observe that in north east India tribal religions are in no uncertain terms come under their own cultural traditions, yet they are in the process of change in tremendous speed and agility. Anthropological knowledge makes it amply clear that they belong to indigenous tribal religions each in its own right, identity and beauty. In the twenty first century religions will have to work against social exclusion, and to bring the cause of the poor to the forefront and provide the spiritual nourishment *vis-a-vis* promote harmony between peoples and cultures.

Pushpa Anbu observes that the Islamic traditions teach every Muslim is to be endowed with this ability to find God in oneself and in the other. The content of Prophet Muhammad's teaching was centered on the concept of God as One who is all powerful. He is the creator of the Universe. The paper also deals with the Sufi (Islamic mystics) concept of God, which is very relevant today. Their concept of God makes people come closer to God and their very principle of life is to love God, serve God and serve humanity. The author elucidates the whole idea of God in Islam from philosophical and anthropological perspectives.

Surojit Sen Gupta studies the place of religion in a society. The history of mankind shows that religion is one of the deepest and most intimate urges of mankind which, in one way or another, is found everywhere. The tendency to reduce it to a particular instinct or drive, conscious or unconscious, is not substantiated by modern scholars who rather look upon religion as a spontaneous impulse of the whole man embracing thought, will and emotions, whereby he perceives his internal limitation and contingency and aspires to achieve his perfection and happiness in permanent union with God. Kingsley Davis is of the view that, "so universal, permanent and pervasive is religion in human society that unless we understand it thoroughly, we shall fail to understand society".

Tom Mangattuthazhe gives a clarion call for peaceful co-existence when he observes that religion has long been used to fuel conflict, but it can be an effective way to bridge divides, promote reconciliation, or advocate peaceful coexistence. The challenge for modern society is to engage the powerful religious forces that run so deep in many countries around the world to preach a love of peace, understanding and respect. The first part of the paper will examine what some of the religions say on coexistence, the role of religious leaders in promoting interfaith dialogue and peaceful resolution of conflicts and what needs to be done to promote an active role of religions in peaceful coexistence The legacy of religions and religious leaders who made a valuable contribution to peace is lessons plans for coexistence.

Paul Pudussery in his paper on Indigenous Spirituality writes that each indigenous group may have a unique spirituality, yet there is one thing that is common, the interconnectedness among all the living and inanimate objects around them. Indigenous spirituality is strongly connected to their habitat and their societal values are adopted to bring harmony among all the living. It is the summation, the signifier of both concrete and non-material existence. The author observes that when one is spiritual, it is much easier to feel connected with, and have compassion for, and serve our families, companies, governments, and the environment.

Nishikant Kolge and **Roshani Rai** in their joint paper observe that Gandhiji finds the compartmentalization of human life at the centre of most of the human problems which also constitute core of our secular age. As an alternative to this he proposed a holist way to life where religious, political, economic and other aspects of life are seen as different aspects of one whole reality, and not different watertight compartments. It is known that his numerous public prayers were part of his political struggle and for him his political struggle was part of his search of God amidst 'religious pluralism'.

Samita Manna argues that simple religion with its various belief patterns and practices are still preponderant in different tribal societies. Traditionalism still persists in terms of animism, spiritism and bongaism among them. Side by side they also share their mind with other dominant culture through cultural transmission. Gradually they have developed a mixed culture consisting of elements of primitive religion and a complex religion developing a sacred ecology, sacred specialists and sacred roles and performances.

Francis Pereira SVD argues that the tribals believe in a supreme God who is the creator of all that exists. They also believe in benevolent and malevolent spirits. But supreme God has control over all the spirits. According to the their understanding, God's work of creation does not end with the creation of heaven and earth and everything in it but continues, especially in making our crops grow and bear much fruit. Tribal concept of God is anthropomorphic. According to some myths, God has also a female counterpart, a wife who plays the role of giving advice to him.

Rajib Chatterjee based on the empirical data collected from the Muslims of Darjeeling Himalayas analyses the cultural life and assimilation of the Muslims with the greater society of their habitat. This harmonious coexistence thus enriched the secular environment which helped the Muslims in adapting to the social environment of their habitat. Islam has a distinct presence in the Himalayas though historically the region is predominated by Hinduism and Buddhism.

Luke Daimary eloquently brings out the system of Bodo society while he observes that this society is an egalitarian society. It does not give any special position or status to any group on any ground. It concedes equal social standing to all religions that the Bodos follow. Therefore the author suggests that for progress and integrity of the Bodos egalitarian values should be upheld. Since recent time some followers of the Bathou religion have been making concerted effort to revive the originality of their religion under an umbrella organization called - All Bathou Religious Union. The organization is trying to cleanse Bathou religion of its sanskritic influences and engages itself in researches and holds seminars and symposiums at intervals with a sole objective to make the Bathou religion a unique and independent religion like any major religion in the world.

Binita Basu discusses the multi-ethnic composition of sundarbans along with poor economic condition of the people forces them to visit forests for collecting forest produce for their daily living. The author brings to our notice that the ferocious animals the village folks confront leads them to take shelter in the religious observations. This is elucidated by the writer through explaining the myth of Bonbibi cult.

An important point which is mooted here is that *Bonbibi* in Sundarban has assumed a new dimension with a new social meaning in the changed socio-political environment. Hence, the case of sundarbans is the poly-ethnic mosaic where one finds as essence of assimilation, secularization, syncretism and universalization of culture while delineating the cults as a cultural process.

Janet Tellis SSpS While delving deep into the religious and cultural realm of Riang, one of the seventy five Primitive Tribal Groups of India, observes that as each indigenous group has its own worldview, depending on its habitat, history, and resources, the Riang seek to establish harmony and integration with all life including the spiritual, natural, and human domains. The author concludes that the essence of religion is the concept of the sacred which unites all religions.

Arifur Zaman writes that Death and disposal are integral element of each culture and it has an indispensable relation with religious belief system of the society. Elaborate ethnographic study of a particular community regarding the customs, rituals, taboos, etc., related with death and disposal were carried out by different scholars. The present author brings to light elaborate rituals integral to death and the disposal of the Tengapania Deoris who have maintained a lot of traditional elements in their day to day life.

Sumitabha Chakraborty portrays the picture of Kinnaurese society while observing that if any discipline which can bind humans in a lucid way, is religion. It is not mere belief but behaviour; nor mere conviction but conduct; not mere faith but functioning. In religion, the whole of human being's personality is involved. At the end it may be inferred that a type of religious pluralism exists among the Kinnaures as a cohesive amalgamation of Hindu-Buddhist elements. The amalgamation of these two religious strain have got a stronghold in the people's mind and it is implemented at the right time to seek remedies to the problems posed from the external forces and urge to seek *moksha*.

Ravi Khangai in his paper Neo-Viashnavism and Social harmony in Assam argues that Bhakti, i.e., devotion to God is inherent in the growth of every religion. When human mind fails to solve the intricacies of life, we turn to God, either to help us in our mundane affairs or to get peace of mind. Like any other religion, the feeling of devotion was prevalent in Indian religious tradition since antiquity. Bhakti Movement was one such bridge which tried to bring harmony in the Human relations. In fact the Bhakti saints were more focused on creating Harmony within the individual. But after all, it is harmonious individual that creates harmonious society.

Bikash Bhargab Sarma describes that tribal religion is one of the many aboriginal forms of Religion. Indian traditional religion is more noticeable in remote interior areas. Here we are mainly concerned with the tribes of Tripura, and these tribes have imbibed the religious concepts of surrounding peoples besides their own. Living an isolated life they have retained their primitive tribalism almost intact, though remaining in close contact with the non-tribal population. As a result the tribals here are a step ahead of other tribals in respect of assimilation with the main religious stream of the country.

Lincoln Reang writes about tribal religions. The most distinctive characteristic of tribal religion is that it does not have any specific sacred scripture(s). The religious ethos is contained in the people's hearts, oral history and in rituals. In the tribal religion of Tripura there is a close interaction of the people with the nature in relation to rocks, forests, serpents or even the belief in the transmigration of soul and spirit. The paper will cover various tribal religious traditions and beliefs with relation to socio-religious changes in the lives of the tribals of Tripura.

Paulami Chattopadhyay writes on the Mech people and their new found religious belief *Ultapani*. They do not offer liquor and does not sacrifice any animal. They offer fruits, flowers, milk, flattened rice, sun dried rice, *Batasa* (one type of sweet) and water. Agriculture is their main economy and for agriculture, they depend upon the nature where human has no control over circumstances. They think animal sacrifice bears the uncivilized identity. Their intention is to uplift their social position and they think the *Ultapani* way of life can raise their social position. It is clear this new religious belief has brought change in their ideology, faith and religious practices. They have consciously organized an attempt of social reform within the fold of their tribal identity.

Sumitabha Chakraborty elucidates that the religious beliefs provide shape and meaning to one's perception of the Universe. Religion also provides understanding and meaning for inexplicable events such as a loved one being killed in an earthquake or some other unpredictable forces of nature. The purity of their belief towards nature is diverted with Tibetan Lamaism, which was introduced into Sikkim three centuries ago and is regarded now as the official religion. It is difficult to determine the extent Buddhist influence has had on Lepcha psychology, but it is clear that the pre-Buddhist religion is not entirely dead.

Satyadeo Poddar and **Nirmalya Karmakar** feel that Christianity and Ramakrishna Mission used the terrain of North East India for bringing revolutionary changes in the mind and heart of the people. Through social service universal approach of humanity was achieved which has brought Christianity and Ramakrishna Mission to work together in this region. The Ramakrishna Mission made their beginning by opening a high school for adults. Under the dynamic leadership of Swami Prabhananda it successfully expanded the activities in the Khasi Hills. Through the educational institutions of the Ramakrishna Mission, Khasi children received their education without any danger of their religious beliefs and traditions being undermined.

Prof. Saroj Chaudhuri, Eminent Scholar, Agartala, in his **Valedictory Address** observes that religion has a functionary dimension as well as a cultural dimension. In its functionary dimension it contains in it the process of socialization. It is the source of ethical codes and morals. The aberrations are to be removed; the spirit of generosity in religion has to be made perceptible and priorities are to be determined on the basic of rationality. The religious leaders have to be pro-active. He believes this seminar is a beginning - beginning of exploration of other areas like the social psyche.

III
SANSKRITI INSTITUTIONAL AWARDS 2010.

Sanskriti - **The North Eastern Institute of Culture and Religion,** Guwahati has selected Dr. Luke Daimary, Silchar, Assam, Mr. Rajib Chatterjee, Siliguri, W.B., Ms. Binita Basu, Kolkata, W. B., Sr. Janet Tellis SSpS, Agartala, Tripura as ***Sanskriti* Fellows**. This year's awards are given as an encouragement to potential scholars who are called to contribute to the cause of research and publication, to promote goodwill and social advancement among the people of our country with special reference to poor and the marginalized.

SANSKRITI EMERITUS FELLOW LIFETIME ACHIEVEMENT AWARD, 2010.

An important event of this seminar was conferring upon Lifetime achievement award. This award was given to a senior scholar who has contributed for a prolonged period of time to the formation of a large number of young and creative scholars through his writings, teachings and above all lifetime commitment to innovative and vibrant scholarly pursuits. The selection committee chose **Prof. Saroj Chaudhuri** for the ***Sanskriti* Emeritus Fellow Lifetime Achievement Award for the year 2010.**

ST. ARNOLD JANSSEN SVD FOUNDATION AWARD.

As the previous year was the concluding year of the death centenary of St. Arnold Janssen who is the founder of Oisho Bani or Divine Word Society (SVD) International, we have instituted an award in his name. In 2010 the award was given away to **Dr. R.P. Athparia,** a well known anthropologist who served as the Superintending Officer in the ASI-NERC, Shillong for a long period of time.

PROF. WILHELM SCHMIDT SVD MEMORIAL AWARD.

Late Prof. Wilhelm Schmidt is the Founder of SVD anthropological tradition as well as the founder director of *Anthropos International,* Germany which has given a great leadership in anthropological and ethnological research world-wide. *Sanskriti* has instituted an award to honour this great personality and **Prof. Vijoy S. Sahay,** Head of the Department of Anthropology, University of Allahabad and Editor-in-Chief of *THE ORIENTAL ANTHROPOLOGIST* received this year' award.

PROF. STEPHEN FUCHS SVD MEMORIAL AWARD 2010.

Late Prof. Stephen Fuchs SVD, well-known among anthropologists, folklorists, and other social scientists across the globe was born in Austria in 1908 and dedicated himself to scholarly activities for the cause of Indian people, particularly the dalit and tribal people. Leaving behind his career in teaching in Anthropology in Bombay, he founded the Research Institute 'Institute of Indian Culture' in 1950, in India and he worked among the Chamar, Korku, Balahi, Gond, Bhil, Bhumia and also on reformistic social movements. Stephen Fuchs has been a source of inspiration to a large number of scholars who have undertaken research on the marginalized people of India. As a mark of tribute to this great scholar, *SANSKRITI*, NEICR, had instituted an award – 'SFMA' from 2008, the centenary year of this scholar, to be given away to a scholar of eminence. So far **Prof. S.M. Michael SVD** and **Dr. Gautam Kumar Bera** have been the recipients of this award for the years 2008 and 2009 respectively. The **SFMA 2010** was presented to **Prof. Joy Thomas SVD**, Director, Ishvani Kendra, Asian Institute of Social Communications and Missiological Research, Pune, Maharashtra.

BLESSED MOTHER TERESA CENTENARY AWARD.

This year marks the Birth Centenary of Mother Teresa who through her loving and dedicated life long service has made a difference in the life of the poorest of the poor in India. To honour this great soul, *Sanskriti* has instituted an award to be given away to a prolific writer who has written most of his acclaimed works with a touch of simplicity, originality and profound sense of social concern. **Dr. Gautam Kumar Bera** received this coveted award in the Centenary year.

We hope this volume based on a slightly uncommon yet a vital theme of today will be immensely useful for the social scientists and others who have undertaken studies on religions and its various ramifications. The host of scholars deserve our gratitude for they not only presented their papers but have updated their manuscripts with great promptness. The views expressed in various papers are entirely of the authors who have researched for prolonged period of time in the vast ocean of religions with special reference to their contemporary applications for the present day society. At this point of time we place on record the various agencies that have come to our aid in partially sponsoring this three day national seminar. Specially we are grateful to our parent body *Oishobani* (SVD) Society, Anthropological Survey of India, Shillong and Indian Council for Social Science Research – North Eastern Region Centre, Shillong. We appreciate the endeavour our good old friend, Mr. Jitendra Singh of Abhijeet Publishers, Delhi for bringing out this volume elegantly and within the shortest possible time. Thanks to ASHA Holy Cross, Agartala, the venue of our seminar, who provided us their hospitality, Manoj Anthony SVD (Assistant Director) and John Bosco SVD (Research Associate) who worked tirelessly for the arrangement of this National Seminar in a meticulous way.

K. Jose SVD & Gautam K. Bera

SANSKRITI-NEICR

February, 2011.

Contents

SECTION-IV

SECTION-I

1

Religious Life of the Assamese Sikhs

Birinchi K. Medhi

Prelude

An attempt is being made in this paper to portray some aspects of socio-religious life of the indigenous Sikhs of Assam, usually referred to as the 'Assamese Sikhs', who are principally distributed throughout the Brahmaputra valley of the state of Assam in North-East India. The Sikhs are a religious community of India who followed Sikhism, one of the indigenous religions of India founded by Guru Nanak (1469-1539). They claim Punjab as their homeland. The Sikhs comprise only 1.96 per cent of India's population, which is less than the percentage of the Christians (2.43%). They have played a significant role not only in the history of Punjab but also that of South Asia. The Sikhs occupy a distinctive position in the national society due to various historical, religious, socio-political and ethno-demographic factors. They are readily noticeable and they appear to be more numerous because of their turbans and other traditional garb. Many of them never cut their hair and all are supposed to be teetallers, non-smokers and not supposed to use any tobacco product.

The Sikhs are found in large numbers in Punjab, Delhi, Haryana, Rajasthan, Uttar Pradesh, Jammu and Kashmir and Maharashtra. They are also found in other states of India.

Many Sikhs have moved away from Punjab and adjacent areas and have often abandoned farming for urban life and various wage-earning occupations. Helweg (1979:20) has stated 'Migration is part of the Punjabi heritage'.

The Growth of Sikh Population in Assam

Assam is a land of wide ethnic diversity which may be viewed as a localized manifestation of the ethnic diversity of North-East India. There have been migrations of peoples from the past to the present to North-East India including Assam who belong to different racial stocks and languages and varied socio-cultural traditions. Such migrations of peoples to this region have not only contributed towards the growth of ethnic diversity but also resulted spectacular social transformation. Furthermore, a few ethnic groups have come into existence as a consequence of prolonged interaction between the cultures of the migrants and those of the autochthones. The Assamese Sikhs are one such ethnic group. The Assamese Sikhs identify themselves with Assam, their homeland, and Assamese, their language. These Sikhs identify with the common culture shared with the Assamese people.

The rise of Sikh population in Assam is not a recent phenomenon. Some of the Sikh disciples of Guru Tegh Bahadur settled at Dhubri and Chaotola in the 1670s after the Guru left Assam for Patna. These Sikhs have come to be known as 'Damdamiya Sikhs'. Allen (1905:95) mentions that the Sikhs who came to Assam with Guru Tegh Bahadur had intermarriages with various indigenous Hindu castes like the Kalitas and Keots and thus mingled with the Assamese people. It was nearly a century after the visit of Guru Tegh Bahadur that a batch of Sikh soldiers came to Assam. They were recruited along with some other soldiers by two brothers. Hardatta and Birdatta, in connection with a secret maneuver to expel the Ahoms from Guwahati during 1790 A.D (Bhuyan, 1947: 272-273). Hunter (1897:46) states that some of these Sikh solders also married women belonging to the Rajbangshis and the Rabhas. The majority of the Sikhs had taken to agriculture. Robinson (1841:313) observes that during the 1830s, the trade of Nagaon district was exclusively in the hands of the Sikhs, who had migrated from Punjab. The British, who came to occupy Assam in 1826 A.D. had also recruited a number of Sikhs from Punjab and employed them in various departments of the state. Allen (1905:46) commenting on the increase of the Sikhs in Assam writes that their increase was no doubt due to the employment of the Sikhs as military policemen in the Assam Bengal Railway.

The present day Assamese Sikhs would, thus, appear to be the descendants of different group of people: (a) Sikh disciples of Guru Tegh Bahadur who settled at Dhubri and Chaotala in the seventeenth century; (b) The Sikh soldiers who were brought to Assam in connection with the secret maneuver in the eighteenth century, and those Sikh soldiers who were brought to Assam to fight against the Burmese army in the nineteenth century; and (c) Those Sikhs who migrated to Assam from Punjab during the 1830s for trade and gradually mingled with the Assamese people.

The overwhelming majority of the Assamese Sikhs are rural inhabitants and agriculturists by occupation. The Assamese Sikhs of Barkola in Nagaon district make up the largest Sikh community of Assam. Besides Barkola, the Assamese Sikhs are distributed through three other villages in the district, viz., Chaparmukh, Hatipara and Lanka. The Assamese Sikhs are also to be found in various places of undivided Goalpara district including the town of Dhubri. They are also to be found in Rampur-a small town in Kamrup district and in Helem, another small town in Sonitpur district.

The Village Scenario

The presence of the Sikhs at Barkola is made felt by the attire of their men folk, who wear turban and keep their hair uncut and beard long. This attire distinction and their clustering mainly in one hamlet of the village make them clearly distinguishable from their non-Sikh neighbours. They are also noticeable at Barkola because of their having three gurdwaras. The gurdwaras can be recognized from a distance, because each of them has tall flag poles, wrapped in yellow socks and triangular flags with the Sikh symbols consisting of quoit *(chakra)* with double edged dagger *(khanda)* in the centre and two daggers *(kirpan)* crossing beneath. This symbol is called *khanda*. Another striking feature of the Sikhs of Barkola is that in the case of most of the Sikh houses, the top of the front wall of the front house is decorated with the *Khanda*.

The first Sikh who had come and settled at Barkola was Subedar Ram Singh. Though he was a Sikh, he married two Assamese Hindu women and the present generations of Assamese Sikhs of Barkola trace their descent from Subedar Ram Singh. Subedar Ram Singh gradually became attracted towards Hinduism, presumably because of the influence of his Hindu wives. This helped Subedar Ram Singh to mingle with the Hindu neighbours. Because of his isolation from his co-religionists, Subedar Ram Singh was more associated with the Hindu neighbours. It is said that though Subedar Ram Singh was not formally a Hindu, he practiced a number of Hindu rites and rituals. Thus, during the early period of the nineteenth century, the Sikhs of Barkola had nothing of the Sikh religion except the names. It has been gathered that Subedar Ram Singh had erected a shrine for the Sikhs near his house at Barkola and worshipped Hindu goddess Durga at that shrine. Even animals like goat, duck, pigeon were sacrificed to the goddess in that shrine. Since Subedar Ram Singh performed puja (worship) in the shrine, he was nicknamed by the villagers as pujari (priest). Even to this date Subedar Ram Singh's direct descendants at Barkola are referred to by others as members of pujari family.

During the 1830s quite a number of Sikh traders migrated from Punjab to parts of Nagaon district (Robinson,1841: 313). A few such traders used to visit Kampur and Barkola on business tours. The Assamese Sikhs, who had chosen to marry the Assamese girls, behaved in the manner of their Hindu neighbours and they were ignorant about Sikh religion. This way of life of the indigenous Sikhs baffled the Sikh traders from Punjab. These Sikh traders persuaded the Assamese Sikhs to discard Hindu customs and to take to Sikh religious practices instead. Their contact with the Sikh traders made the Assamese Sikhs realize that their way of life was far from the Sikh way of life. A few Sikh villagers also met some learned Sikhs from Punjab who had come to Assam to pay a visit to the gurdwara at Dhubri. These learned Sikhs also tried to introduce the local Sikhs to the doctrines of Sikhism.

In 1921, Atma Singh of Barkola, who was in service in Punjab, returned to his native village and tried to introduce his co-villagers to the doctrines of Sikhism and also tried to teach them Gurmukhi. As a result of the persuasion of the Sikh traders and learned Sikhs, the Assamese Sikhs of Barkola removed the idol of goddess Durga from the shrine erected by Subedar Ram Singh and placed the Granth Sahib on the altar. Afterwards, the shrine was shifted to its present site and was converted into a gurdwara towards the middle of the nineteenth century. Another gurdwara was constructed by the Sikhs of Barkola following a few years of the establishment of the first gurdwara. The latter gurudwara was constructed by those Sikhs of the village, who considered that the former was constructed on the plinth of a Hindu shrine. The third gurdwara has been constructed recently by the side of the main road of the village.

The Sikh villagers of Barkola refer to the former gurdwara as Purana (old) Gurdwara and the latter as Natun (new) Gurdwara. The new gurdwara is also referred to as 'Barkola Bari Sangat'. The third Gurdwara is known as Gurdwara Nanaksar. It has been observed that in their day-to-day life, while they chat among themselves, the Sikhs refer to their gurdwara as namghars, the Granth Sahib as Bhagavata (a greatly revered scripture of the Hindus) and the granthi, i.e., the keeper of the gurdwara, as pujari (priest). But when the villagers discuss religious matters with an outsider, they refer to their temple as gurdwara, their principal holy scripture as Granth Sahib and the keeper of the gurdwara as granthi. Only five elderly Sikhs of Barkola including the two granthis can laboriously read Gurmukhi in which the scriptures of Sikhism have written. But none of these Sikhs can write well in Gurmukhi. Their ability to read Gurmukhi rarely couples with an understanding of the language. The Sikh villagers who can read Gurmukhi are proud of their abilities. There is no Assamese version of the Granth Sahib which the local Sikhs could read and thus learn about their religion. On the other hand, there are a number of books in Assamese on Hinduism and Vaishnavism. These books have influenced the local Sikhs in imbibing elements of Hinduism into their socio-cultural life. Moreover, the Assam Vaishnavism has many parallels to Sikhism. That is why the earliest Sikh settlers in Assam were absorbed into the local population (Neog 1984: 163-173; Singh 1967:242).

It appears that the present generation of the Assamese Sikhs of Barkola has not been able to completely wean themselves away from the Hindu social life. The Sikh villagers of Barkola practice many rites and rituals and observe taboos prevalent among their Hindu neighbours. It has been gathered that during the early part of 1950s a few Sikhs from Punjab, who were well versed in the Sikh religion, paid visit to the gurdwaras at Dhubri and in other places of Assam. During their stay in Assam, they also visited Barkola, met the local Sikhs and persuaded them to observe Sikh religious beliefs and practices. It may be mentioned here that Giani Jail Sing, the then chief minister of Punjab, Mr. Surajit Singh Barnala, the Union agricultural minister, visited Barkola in 1975 and 1977, respectively. Both these dignitaries addressed public meetings at Barkola which were attended by the Sikh and non-Sikh villagers. Later on as a result of their efforts the SGPC (Shiromani Gurdwara Prabandhak Committee) deputed a sewadar (worker) to teach Gurmukhi at Barkola. Giani Jail Singh also ensured the establishment of a library at Barkola. The SGPC has contributed books on Sikh history and Sikhism to this library. Later on, in 1985 the Government of Assam donated some books to this library. At present this library is known as Guru Nanak Library

The Village Gurdwaras

All three gurdwaras at Barkola are situated towards the south of the village and are located within the hamlet predominantly populated by the Sikhs. The old gurdwara is smaller and less spacious in comparison to the new gurdwaras. Each of the gurdwaras possesses a well in its compound. The old gurdwara building consists of two rooms. In one room the Granth Sahib is kept and prayers are offered, and the adjacent small room serves as a store-room. The new gurdwara building has a big hall. This hall is used for prayers. The Granth Sahib is kept in the adjacent small room. All the gurdwaras have their own flags, triangular in shape and yellow in colour, surmounted with the *khanda,* the Sikh religious symbol.

In each of the gurdwaras of the village, the Granth Sahib is placed on a wooden pedestal *(asana)* covered by white silken or cotton clothes. The walls of both the gurdwaras behind the asanas are decorated with a number of *sarudoia japis* (traditional head-gear of the Assamese females). Articles like *sarudoia japi, sarai* (platter on stand) and *gamocha* (hand woven Assamese towel) are integral parts of Assamese culture. These articles are used by the Assamese people in a variety of formal and social functions and these have important social significance. In each of the two old gurdwaras a *daba* (large kettle-drum) is kept inside. The *daba* is beaten, whenever required, to call the Sikhs to the gurdwaras for congregation. It may be noted here that in each of the namghars, the village prayer house of the Vaishnavas of the Hindus, at least one *daba* is kept which is beaten regularly in the morning and in the evening and also whenever necessary to call the Hindu villagers for congregation. In all three gurdwaras colourful canopies (chandratop) are tied beneath the ceiling over the Granth Sahib. Each of the gurdwaras possesses a harmonium and a *dholok* (drum). It has been observed that when festivals like Holi, Diwali, etc., are observed in the gurdwaras, the Sikh villagers sing religious hymns playing the harmonium and *dholok.* The division among the Sikh of Barkola in terms of their association with the gurdwaras has, however, little significance in their day-to-day life. All the gurdwaras of Barkola has a committee to look after the affairs of the gurdwaras. This committee is called Gurdwara Committee. Each committee is made up of adult male members chosen unanimously by the people of a particular group.

Everyday prayers are held in the morning and in the evening in the gurdwaras. The granthis recite the prayers. Not all the Sikhs attend such prayers regularly. Large number of Sikhs comes to the gurdwaras on Sikh festivals. Almost all the Sikhs attend the gurdwaras during the birth and death anniversaries of Guru Nanak, Guru Arjan, Guru Tegh Bahadur and Guru Gobind Singh and during the festival like Holi and Diwali.

The Sikh villagers pay their respect by saluting to the

gurdwaras whenever they happen to pass alongside or reach the entrance of the gurdwaras. Both male and female Sikhs of Barkola visit the gurdwaras. They put off their shoes when they enter into the gurdwaras. No Sikh can enter into the gurdwara without covering the head. The Sikhs of Barkola also allow non-Sikhs to enter into the gurdwaras. Women neither enter the gurdwara nor touch the Granth Sahib during menstrual period. A person under the influence of intoxication is not allowed to enter into the gurdwara. There is no distinction in the sitting arrangement in the gurdwaras. The gurdwaras have mats and carpets for this purpose.

Before entering the gurdwara the Sikhs take off shoes and after entering they kneel down before the Granth Sahib. Then they stand up with folded hands *(hat jor kara)*, bow their heads and salute the congregation by uttering once in the following way:

Waheguru ji ka khalsa,

Waheguru ji ki fateh.

(The khalsa are the chosen of God; victory be to God)

Though all the Sikh villagers of Barkola can utter this greeting fluently, only a few elderly Sikhs could explain the meaning of the greeting to this investigator.

The *karah prasad* (food offerings) is distributed among the congregation after the prayer. It is a kind of pudding prepared in an iron vessel from wheat flour *(chuji)*, sugar and ghee mixed in equal quantities. Following the recitation of the thanks giving short prayer, consisting of six stanzas, the man who officiates the function stairs the *karah prasad* with an iron sword. Before distributing it among the people, the officiating person set apart a small quantity from it for *panj-piyare* (the five original khalsa members). Then it is distributed among the congregation.

In the morning and at night, earthen lamps (chaki) with ghee, prepared from the milk of cow, with a wick of cotton yarn placed inside the lamps or candles are lighted inside the gurdwaras. Joss sticks and incense are also burnt in the morning and in the evening.

The village gurdwaras are the nerve centre of socio-cultural life of the Sikhs of Barkola. The Sikh villagers loyalty to their gurdwaras is very strong. They go to the gurdwaras not merely to offer prayers. The gurdwaras also provide them ample opportunities to meet one another, exchange views, and discuss matters relating to the developmental activities of the village, agriculture, marriage, politics and so on. The gurdwaras may also be considered to some extent as agencies of social control among the Sikhs of Barkola. Whenever the Sikhs assemble in the gurdwaras to offer prayers, they generally chat with one another before and after the prayers. The village gurdwaras are the centers of various activities like discourse, teaching, scriptural reading and story telling of the Sikh Gurus in which many of the Sikh villagers participate.

The Granth Sahib

Like other Sikhs, the Sikhs of Barkola also pay utmost respect to the Granth Sahib. They do not touch the Granth Sahib without taking bath, and washing hands and feet. The Granth Sahib is daily opened in the gurdwaras in the morning and close in the evening by the granthis. When the Granth Sahib is opened for the first time in the morning, the first stanza on the left page is read by the granthi. If the passage be in continuation to that on the previous page, the page is turned over and the granthi reads from the beginning of the stanza on that page. That is the passage must be read as a whole. A *chowor* (fly-flicker) is always waved over the Granth Sahib by a villager deputed for the purpose while it is recited. Except the Granth Sahib, no other scriptures are kept in the wooden pedestal in the gurdwaras.

According to the Sikh villagers of Barkola, the Granth Sahib has life and it feels cold or warm like any other living being. The villagers never refer to the Granth Sahib as a book, because they say that 'a book has no life, but the Granth Sahib has'. The Granth Sahib is wrapped in a white cotton cloth in summer and in a warm cloth in winter. During summer, the villagers, one after another, use to fan the Granth Sahib with a big fan. Apart from the warm cloth, a small quilt is spread over the Granth Sahib during winter. Three small cotton pillows with white satin covers are placed on the pedestal. When the Granth Sahib is opened, two pillows are placed on sides and the third one in the front.

During the rituals relating to birth, marriage and other functions such as after the completion of the construction of a house, getting a job, etc., some villagers sometimes carry the Granth Sahib from the gurdwara to their homes. When the Granth Sahib is carried from gurdwara to the house of somebody, a person walks alongside all the way sprinkling water from a small metal-pot *(ghati)* to purify the path through which the Granth Sahib is carried, followed by anther person carrying the Granth Sahib on his head on a cot. Another carries a fly flicker in his right hand fanning the Granth Sahib. All these three persons go along bare foot. The cotton clothes (1.35 cm. x 1.35 cm. in size) with which the Granth Sahib is covered, is generally offered by the Sikh villagers. Such clothes are offered by the Sikhs following the weekly reciting-session *(saptahik path)* of the Granth Sahib. Such clothes are also offered following an akhand path (non-stop recitation) by the Sikhs.

To the Sikhs of Barkola, the Granth Sahib is the most sacred scripture. To them the Granth Sahib is animate. The Vaishnavas (the followers of Vaishnavism founded by Sankaradeva) of Assam also consider the chief works of Sankaradeva and Madhavadeva as objects of worship. Like the Sikhs treating the Granth Sahib as the Guru and equating it to the Guru, the Vaishnavas of Assam have also made the chief works of Sankaradeva (Kirtana, Dasama and Gunamala) and Madhabadeva (Bhakti Ratnavali and Nam Ghosa) the objects of worship. The Vaishnavas also consider these chief works standing for these two Gurus. The kirtan ghar or namghar, the Assamese Vaishnava temple, is an ordinary house having rectangular space like the inside of a Sikh gurdwara and in it the object of worship is not an idol but a large pedestal containing one or more of the works of the Gurus. This is called asana (a seat) or Guru asana (the seat of the Guru) and it has striking parallel in the worship of the Granth Sahib.

God, Guru, Prayer and Pilgrimage

In Sikhism, God is known as Waheguru, the wonderful Lord. The Sikhs of Barkola refer to their supreme being as Waheguru. But in their day-to-day life, they also refer to their God by the name of Bhagaban, very much like their Assamese Hindu neighbours. When asked the Sikh villagers to describe their God, most of them describe God in the following manner. He is the epitome of all virtues; He is Karta- purukh (creator of all things); Sayambhu (shelf created , self existent); Ojoni-akal (not subject to birth or death); Ananta (infinite); he is Sat (pure), all-knowing, all-giver, all-adorable, all-pervading, omnipotent and omniscient; He is Satnam (the eternal and absolute truth); He is an anuvab (inner feeling); He is the father of all created beings; He is not subject to time; He lives inside human bodies forming part of the atma (soul); He is Jagannath (Lord of the universe); He sends rain and sunshine Most of the descriptions of God given by the Sikh villagers fit in well with the definition of God given in their religion.

The Sikh villagers of Barkola refer to the name of God as Guru. When asked the villagers about the attributes of a Guru, most of the villagers pointed out the attributes similar to those of God. The common notion of the Sikh villagers about their Guru is that, they are the adorable Supermen who lead man on to good life-ways and help them attain salvation. A Sikh villager, Bijay Singh, aged 35 years, a shopkeeper, has said that a Guru is not an avatar (incarnation) of God. He is the messenger of God who asks to pray God. It has been observed that most of the middle aged and elderly Sikh villagers of Barkola know that there are ten Sikh Gurus, but not all of them know the names of all the Gurus. They only know the names of the first, fourth, ninth and the tenth Gurus, i.e., Guru Nanak, Guru Arjan, Guru Teg Bahadur and Guru Gobind Singh, respectively. Guru Nanak is known to them as the founder of Sikhism. Some of the villagers are also aware of the historical fact that Guru Nanak visited Assam. They know about Guru Tegh Bahadur, because he established the gurdwara at Dhubri. Most of the Sikh villagers have visited the gurdwara, which they consider as a pilgrimage. They know about Guru Arjan, who founded the

Sri Akal Takht Sahib (Golden Temple or Swarna Mandir) in Amritsar. Guru Gobind Singh is known to the villagers for his enterprising heroic deeds. All the students, including the Sikhs and non-Sikhs of Guru Nanak L.P. School, know the names of the ten Gurus. One of their teachers, who hail froın Punjab, has narrated to them about the Sikh Gurus. However, the educated Sikhs of Barkola by and large have a fair knowledge about the Sikh Gurus.

Prayer is an indispensable part of the Sikh religion. The Sikh prayers are both personal and congregational. The Sikh villagers of Barkola offer four different types of prayers: *nitnam* (daily prayer), *akhand path* (continuous recitation), *khola path* (free recitation) and *saptahik path* (weekly recitation). According to the Sikh villagers the hymns to be recited at each of these prayers have been prescribed by the Sikh Gurus. The prayers consist of repetition of the name of God and chanting hymns in his praise. Those who are baptized in Sikhism are expected to recite daily prayers three times a day, in the early morning, in the evening and at night before going to bed. At Barkola among the Sikhs, there are only 12 adult male Sikhs, who perform the prescribed daily prayers regularly.

On occasions like marriage and also sometimes at birth, success in examination, getting a job, etc., the villagers perform akhand path. *Akhand path* is held in gurdwaras and at the residences of the desiring parties. During *akhand path,* the Granth Sahib is recited non-stop from the first page to the last page within 48 hours. Such recitations are undertaken by adult-male Sikhs one after another. *Khola path* or free recitation is generally performed by a single person. During *khola path,* complete recitation of the Granth Sahib is completed by a person within a period which may vary from seven days to one month or even more. The recitation of the Granth Sahib during *khola path* is not continuous. *Saptahik path* is also organized among the Sikhs of Barkola. Like *akhand path* and *khola path, saptahik path* is also organized on the occasions like birth, marriage, and so on.

The Sikh villagers of Barkola put emphasis on pilgrimage. To them, there are three principal Sikh pilgrimages which they feel that they should visit as and when possible. These three pilgrimage-centres are Gurdwara Mataji of Chaparmukh,

Gurdwara Sri Guru Tegh Bahadur Sahibji of Dhubri and the Golden Temple of Amritsar. The granthis of the gurdwaras and a few educated Sikhs of Barkola have informed that the Sikhs in general consider the four principal gurdwaras as the four places of pilgrimage for the Sikhs. These are known as takhts (thrones or seats of spiritual power) situated in Amritsar (Sri Akal Takht Sahib), Anandpur (Takht Sri Keshgarh Sahib, birth place of the Khalsa, the soldier-saint brotherhood of believers adhering to Sikhism, initiated by Guru Gobind Singh), Patna (Takht Sri Patna Sahib, birth place of Guru Gobind Singh) and Nander (Takht Sri Hujur Sahib), where Guru Gobind Singh was cremated. The Sikh villagers of Barkola frequently go to visit the gurdwara of Chaparmukh. Every year during the death anniversary of Guru Tegh Bahadur, groups of Barkola Sikhs pay homage to the Gurdwara Sri Guru Tegh Bahadur Sahibji of Dhubri. This investigator has met at Barkola some adult male Sikhs, who had visited the Golden Temple of Amritsar. Whenever a Sikh from the village determines on visiting the Golden Temple, the other Sikh villagers give him money to buy some articles like *kara, kangha, kirpan,* lithographed pictures of the Golden Temple and the Gurus, etc. Any Sikh villager of Barkola, who visits Amritsar, generally brings such articles for distribution among the Sikh villagers. A large number of Sikh villagers of Barkola have also visited the Kamakhya temple situated in Guwahati. The villagers consider the Kamakhya temple as an important place to visit, because the temple was also visited by Guru Nanak and Guru Tegh Bahadur. They have also pointed out that the descendants of the propitiatory priest who had accompanied Guru Tegh Bahadur live at Kamakhya. This priest is said to have come from Punjab and was a Sikh. However, in due course of time the descendants of the priest had adopted Hinduism and became Assamese.

Sikh Religious Practices and Observances

Generally all the Sikh villagers lay stress on wearing *Pancha-kakar* (five Ks), viz., *kangha,* (comb), *kara* (bangle), *kachha* (specially designed under shorts), *kirpan* (sword), *kesh* (uncut hair) and sporting *paguri* (turban) by the males. However, all the Sikhs of Barkola do not follow this practice strictly.

Only 6 elderly male Sikhs of Barkola regularly wear *kachha,* while other grown up boys and adult males wear general type of underwear. The two granthis regularly carry kirpans of 6 inches in length. Most of the male Assamese Sikhs keep a special kind of comb on which a small symbolic sword is inscribed and is kept under the bun of hair. There have been a few instances among the Sikhs of Barkola of trimming hair and shaving beard. One of the Sikhs who has trimmed his hair and beard has, however, re-grown his hair and beard. A person who trims his hair or shaves is known as *patit* (apostate) among the Assamese Sikhs. Generally, a Sikh who does not observe Sikh religious taboo is considered a *patit* by the villagers. The Sikh villagers are of the opinion that, a *patit* is a person with whom other villagers should not keep any social contact. However, the practice seems to be in abeyance.

To the Sikh villagers of Barkola the wearing of *pancha-kakar* (five Ks) is dependent on age. The children are expected only to keep long hair and wear the bangles. The wearing of *kachha, kirpan* and *kangha* is expected only after the initiation ceremony, Male and female Sikh villagers immediately before marriage go through the initiation ceremony. Once a person is initiated he or she is supposed to maintain five symbols of Sikhism throughout his or her life. It has been gathered that all the married Sikhs of Barkola have gone through the Sikh initiation ceremony. According to the Sikh villagers, if a person is not initiated before marriage, during marriage he or she will have to take a vow in front of the Granth Sahib to go through the initiation ceremony at the earliest possible opportunity following marriage. Those married males, who have gone through initiation ceremony, do not keep their head uncovered. While at homes, even when do not wearing turbans, such males cover their heads with gamochas (hand woven Assamese towels). Taking tobacco, smoking and drinking liquor are considered by the Sikhs as religious offences. A Sikh, they say, strictly supposed not to take tobacco and drink liquor, especially after going through the initiation ceremony.

Beliefs in Hindu Gods and Goddesses

The Sikhs of Barkola have been in contact with the neighbouring Hindus since long back. Such contact has facilitated the percolation of a number of Hindu beliefs and customs into the Barkola Sikh society. Besides, the Assamese Sikhs have been, since long back, establishing marriage relations with the Hindus. It has been already mentioned that the first Sikh settler of Barkola, Subedar Ram Singh, married two Assamese women. An analysis of the community background of total 205 married Assamese Sikh women (including the widows), distributed through 100 Sikh household of Barkola, shows that 45.85 per cent of the married women were Assamese Hindus before their marriage. Thus, the marriage among the Sikhs has been one of the significant factors in paving the ways for the percolation of Hindu beliefs and customs into the Sikh households. Besides, they live in face-to-face relations with the Assamese Hindus in the village, due to which also good number of factors from Assamese culture percolated to the Assamese Sikh society.

Among the Hindu gods and goddesses, the Sikhs worship mainly Ai-bhagabati (goddess of pox), Krishna (the eighth incarnation of Lord Vishnu), Lakshmi (goddess of wealth) and Siva (god of prosperity and destruction). Almost all the Sikh villagers of Barkola know the stories of the Mahabharata and the Ramayana –the two great Hindu epics. In the same manner they also know about gods and goddesses like Rama, Lakshmana, Krishna, Saraswati, Durga, Kali, et al.

It has been observed that most of the Sikh villagers of Barkola, both males and females, can sing Assamese devotional songs as are generally sung by the Assamese Vaishnavas. In almost all the Sikh households of Barkola, there are small plinths in one of the corners of courtyard in which a sacred basil (tulasi) plant is carefully planted. The Hindus, especially during the whole month of Kati (October-November), light a clay lamp by the side of the sacred basil plant. The Assamese Sikhs also follow this custom throughout the month of Kati. The Sikhs of Barkola do not consider it irreligious to believe in Hindu gods and goddesses and to show respect to Hindu shrines, temples, etc.

Prevalence of Folk Beliefs

The Assamese folk cultural traditions have exercised an appreciable influence on the Assamese Sikhs. Like the Assamese people they too believe in a number of benevolent and malevolent spirits (*deo* or *bhut*). They have a clear-cut idea about the sex, appearance, nature and abode of these spirits and demons. All the villagers of Barkola including the Sikhs believe that a large number of spirits and demons reside in different places of the village like the morass land near the village, the tanks within the village, in the trees allegedly planted by Subedar Ram Singh and in some other big trees (wood apple, peepal, etc.) near the Siva shrine of the village. It is believed by the villagers that such demons and spirits are more harmful to women and children. It has been found that the Sikh villagers like other people of the village, approach the village *bej* (folk medicine man) for *tabij* (talisman), and *dol-phohati* (knotted-thread believed to have magical power, given by the folk medicine man) to protect persons, particularly the women and children from spirits and demons. There are two Assamese Hindu medicine men of Koch caste at Barkola.

Like the Hindu neighbours, the Assamese Sikhs also observe various taboos connected with agriculture. One comes across the prevalence of a large number of folk beliefs and customs concerning cattle, plant, cosmic body, sex, virtue, auspicious day, luck, house building, food, etc., in rural Assamese society. Such beliefs and practices are also prevalent among the Sikhs of Barkola.

Festivals

The Barkola Sikhs observe a number of festivals. Some of the festivals are observed by the Sikhs only and some other are celebrated both by the Sikhs and the Hindu villagers. To the Sikh villagers of Barkola, their Gurupurbs are the most important festivals. Gurupurb is the anniversary of the birth or death of a Guru. They celebrate the birth days of Guru Nanak on the full moon day of Kati (October-November) and Guru Gobind Singh on the month of Puh (December-January), the martyrdom of Guru Arjan in the month of Kati and Guru Teg Bahadur in the month of Aghon (November-December). They also observe Baisakhi, one of the great Sikh festivals, corresponding to the Assamese calendar month Bohag (April-May).

The other two festivals- Diwali (festival of light) and Holi (festival of colour) are celebrated by the Sikhs of Barkola with much enthusiasm. Diwali is celebrated in the month of Kati and Holi is celebrated in the month of Phagun (February-March). These two festivals are also celebrated by the Hindus in general. The Hindus of Barkola also observe these two festivals. All the Gurupurbs are celebrated in the gurdwaras of the village. Two days before each of the festivals akhand path is organized in the gurdwaras. During the whole day of akhand path the Sikh villagers visit the gurdwaras at different hours of the day and join the prayer. On the day of the festival, two processions are taken out from the old and new gurdwaras by the Sikh villagers. All the male Sikh villagers and mostly the Sikh girls join the processions. Each of the procession is lead by an elderly male Sikh villager who carries the Granth Sahib on his head on a pedestal held aloft. Whenever possible, a truck is hired to carry the Granth Sahib during the processions. The Sikhs, who join the processions raise slogans like 'Waheguruji ka Khalsa, Waheguruji ki fateh', 'Bole so nihal, Sat sri akal', (whosoever speaks 'God is true' will ever be happy), etc. Both the processions from the two gurdwaras proceed to Guru Nanak Library, join there and all the Sikhs in one procession move about through the main lanes and by lanes of the village. Afterwards, the procession bifurcates and Sikhs proceed to their respective gurdwaras, where they seat and take roti and vegetable curry. In the evening janam-sakhis (biographies of the Gurus) are read by the granthis of the gurdwaras, which is mostly attended by the male Sikhs. During the Gurupurbs, the gurdwaras are decorated with coloured papers and flowers. In the evening, the gurdwaras are illuminated with candles and clay lamps. The Sikh villagers also illuminate their houses with candles and earthen lamps during the Gurupurbs.

On the day of Baisakhi also processions are taken out from the village gurdwaras. The Granth Sahib is also taken out in the procession. During this festival 5 younger male Sikhs are selected by the villagers to represent the panj piyars. These men who wear pajamas and loose shirts of yellow colour, kachha, kangha, kirpan and kara, lead the procession. During this festival also the gurdwaras are illuminated and prayers are also held there.

During the whole month of Bhada (August –September), the Sikh villagers assemble in the gudwaras in the evenings, where the granthis read the janam-sakhis. They consider the month of Bhada as a sacred month. But none can explain, why this month is a sacred month. It may be pointed out here that the Assamese Vaishnavites also consider the month of Bhada as sacred because on the 9th day of Bhada, 1568 A.D., Sankaradeva, the founder of Assamese Vaishnavism, and on the 26th day of Bhada, 1596 A.D., his principal disciple Madhavadeva died. During this month, the Assamese Vaishnavites in their namghars and kirtanghars recite the devotional songs composed by Sankaradeva and Madhavadeva. The Hindus and the Vaishnavite Tiwas of Barkola village also follow this practice.

The Bihu is the principal festival of Assam. It is celebrated all over the state by the Assamese people with varying rituals and customs. There are three Bihus : Bohag Bihu, Magh Bihu and Kati Bihu. Bohag Bihu, the most popular and colourful of the three, is celebrated from the last day of Chot through the first 7 days of Bohag (mid-April). Bohag Bihu is also called Rongali Bihu because of its association with merry making through singing and dancing. The Sikhs of Barkola also, like their Assamese neighbours, celebrate Bihu with much enthusiasm. Like their Assamese neighbours, the Sikh womenfolk also prepare varieties of cakes to entertain guests during the festival. Like the Assamese women, the Sikh women of Barkola present home made gamocha known as bihuwan (present of Bihu) to relatives and friends, especially prepared for Bohag Bihu. The Sikh villagers, like their Assamese neighbours celebrate the first day of Bohag Bihu as Garu (cattle) Bihu. On this day, they smear paste of turmeric and black-gram and mustard oil on the bodies, hooves and horns of the cattle giving them a wash in the nearby river. The Sikh boys in small groups visit the households singing Bihu songs and playing drums (dhols), bamboo clappers (takas) and small cymbals (tals) during Bohag Bihu. Magh Bihu is celebrated in the middle of winter after the harvesting with bonfires, social gatherings and feasts. Magh Bihu is also known as Bhogali Bihu (enjoyment through feasting). Kati Bihu is the most insignificant of the three Bihus. It is celebrated from the last day of Ahin (September-October) to the first day of Kati (mid-October). Kati Bihu is also known as Kangali Bihu (literally 'the poor Bihu'). In this Bihu clay lamps are lighted near newly planted sacred basil plant (*Ocimum sanctum*) in the corner of the courtyard near the granary and in the paddy fields. The Sikhs of Barkola like their Assamese neighbours also lit clay lamps in Kati Bihu. During each Bihu in the evening the Sikhs assemble in the gurdwaras and the Granth Sahib is recited by the granthis.

Conclusion

To a large extent the quality and content of social life of the Barkola Sikhs epitomize that of the Assamese Sikhs as a whole. In other words, it can be stated that the wider Assamese Sikh social situation is expressed in the localized framework of Barkola. The basic values of the Assamese Sikhs are derived from Sikhism. But there are significant regional and syncretistic variations. The indigenous Sikhs observe Sikh rituals and practices, but not as rigorously as the non-Assamese Sikhs. The socio-religious life of the Assamese Sikhs tends to be guided by the doctrines of Sikhism. But at the same time the influence of indigenous folk beliefs and customs is quite appreciable in their life. Elements from both Sikhism and indigenous folk tradition co-exist in the social life of the Assamese Sikhs. In the village context their Hindu neighbours interact in a variety of social and economic levels. The identity of being a Sikh or a Hindu is of little import in day-to-day interactional fields. They interact as equals, as members of a wider village community. The ritual distance and religious difference between the Sikhs and their non-Sikh neighbours should have created a sort of barrier in the fields of inter-community relations. But the sharing of a large number of common elements of socio-economic life by the two groups has considerably reduced the social distance emanating from religious differences. The situation obtaining among the Sikhs of Barkola is, by and large, similar to that of the Sikhs of Daleke, a small village, situated at a distance of nearly 8 km from Tarn Taran in Amritsar district in Punjab which is known as the 'cradle of Sikhism'. Singh (1961: 91-219) has observed considerable impact of different religions on the Sikhs of Daleke. These Sikhs also worship different tribal and Hindu gods and goddesses and Muslim pirs and fakirs.

The philosophy and doctrines of Assamese Vaishnavism and Sikhism exhibit many similarities. To quote Neog (1984: 173):

'.......... Sikhism and Assam Vaishnavism are happy parallels. That is why the earliest Sikh settlers in Assam were absorbed into the general population and those who came within the last two centuries had no difficulty in living in great amity with the local people.'

There are a number of ways in which the Sikh doctrines and indigenous cultural values and beliefs co-exist and interact in Assamese Sikh social life. It is a kind of social life which is a meeting point of two sets of factors: the religious ideology of Sikhism and the indigenous socio-cultural mores. While the former prevails in the obligatory ritualistic domain, the latter prevails within the social, cultural and economic spheres. The two sets of divergent factors influence each other, exist in mutual association and interact in a way as to make each adaptive to the other. Thus, the Assamese Sikh social life, in Redfield's (1965) terms, shows a combination of influences from two different sources. A part of Assamese Sikh social life is derived from Sikh socio-cultural tradition while another part is derived from the indigenous folk cultural tradition.

References

Allen, B. C., 1905, *Assam District Gazetteers, Goalpara District*, Calcutta, Vol. III.

Bhuyan, S. K., 1947, Lachit Barphukan and His Times, Gauhati, Govt. of Assam, Department of Historical and Antiquarian Studies.

Helweg, Aurther Wesley, 1979, *Sikhs in England,* New Delhi, Oxford University Press.

Hunter, W.W., 1897, *A Statistical Account of Assam,* Vols. I and II, Delhi, B. R. Publishing.

Neog, Maheswar, 1984, *Religions of the North-East,* New Delhi, Munshiram Manoharlal Publishing Pvt. Ltd.

Redfield, Robert, 1965, *Peasant Society and Culture,* Chicago, Chicago University Press.

Robinson, William, 1841, *A Descriptive Account of Assam,* Calcutta.

Singh, Indera, P., 1961, *'Religion in Daleke : A Sikh Village'*, in Aspects of Religion in Indian Society, L. P. Vidyarthi (ed.), Meerut, Kedar Nath Ram Nath : 191-219.

Singh, Trilochan, 1967, *Guru Tegh Bahadur: Prophet and Martyr,* Delhi, Gurdwara Prabhandhak Committee.

2

Ethno-Cultural and Ethno-Religious Scenario of the People of Assam Through The Ages

Dr. R.P. Athparia

I

The ethno-cultural identity of the territory now known as Assam emerged very early in legends and history. Pragjyotisa, the land of tantra, magic and incantation is mentioned in the epic history of Mahabharata, as well as in Kalika-Purana, a work of the 10th century A.D. Its city called Pragjyotisa Pura, the city of eastern astrology, is described as the city equal to the city of Indra. Pragjyotisa is interpreted to mean the Eastern Land where the sun rises or the land where the sun rises early. The land was inhabited by the Kiratas who are described in the earliest literature as the people dwelling in caves or in the hills, occupying the lower slopes of the Himalayas living in forests as hunters and gatherers, and having knowledge of herbal medicines. In the Mahabharata again this region is mentioned as the inhabitants of gold coloured (yellow skinned) Kiratas. In later literature, the Kiratas are described as people shinning as gold. Later, in Kalika Purana, the Kiratas are described as yellow skinned, strong, ferocious and addicted to meat and drink. In fact, the Kiratas had occupied the eastern region of India. Later, the territory was referred to as Lauhitya and Kamrupa.

Assam is not a Pre-Ahom word. According to some scholars the word Assam is derived from the Sanskrit word "asom" which means "of uneven terrain" in contrast to the plains of Bengal, which is an even land. The Bodos have the word "ha-com", the low level land. Assam also denoted "unparalleled" or "peerless", and was as such applied to the mighty Ahom which gave an identity to the land where they settled in the 13th century. The Ahom had the Tai word "ocham", the "undefeated", of which "asam" is the sanskritised form. The Ahoms built up agricultural economy of the valley, a powerful state that repulsed the Mughals, and a cultural system that synthesized diverse elements. It was during the medieval mid-Ahom period that the word Asham gained momentum and was mentioned in *Ain-i-Akbari*. The celebration of the anniversary of Su-Ka-Pha, the founder of the Ahom dynasty, and now described as the father of the Assamese identity is currently on. The word Assam is of colonial origin. The foreign travellers in the 17th – 18th century used the words Assen or Asam, Achem etc. The Kachins in Yunnan and Myanmar call the Tai people by the name of Asama or Lasem. The 18th century copper plate inscription of Ahom king have three forms- Acham, Asam and Ahom (Phukan, 1989). The presence of Negrito stream in Assamese populations particularly of the frizzly forms of hair have long been suspected but it has now been rejected. The Australoid were no doubt the earlier settlers, and the Australoid traits are reportedly present among the Bodos and some "lower" Castes. The two major streams which have mingled in Assam are those of the Caucasoid and the Mongoloid, which explain the preponderance of the mixed type in the two valleys. The claim of the Kalitas to belong to Alpine stream of the Caucasoid has almost been rejected (Das, et-al 1988) as the Kalitas do not seem to differ from the other upper caste groups of Assam, and in fact, form along with the Brahmans, a sub-cluster.

The identity of the people of Assam has evolved over the historical period. Asomia identity today is marked by inter-alia by language, territory, dress, food, festivals, folklore and rituals. Assamese language emerged from the tenth century onwards and spread as the language of trade and economy, the language of communication between tribals and non-tribals. The American Baptist Mission introduced the Printing Press in Assamese in mid 19th century and demanded recognition of Assamese language which had a distinctive script and started a journal, *Arunodoi*. In 1873, Assamese became the language of courts, school and administration. The Asom Sahitya Sabha played a pivotal role in the development of Assamese language and Assamese consciousness.

The Indo-Mongoloid of North East India speaks different languages of Sino-Tibetan linguistic group. Their group of languages has been divided into two broad branches: Tibeto-Burman and Siamese-Chinese. The Siamese-Chinese includes Siamese, and it connects speeches or dialects like Davi or Thai. The Ahoms, the Khamyang, the Aiton, the Phakial, the Turung etc. living in different parts of North East India speak languages belonging to the Thai sub-division. The other Indo-Mongoloids of North East India except the Khasis and the Pnars of Meghalaya speak languages of Tibeto-Burman family. One of the sub-divisions of the Tibeto-Burman is North Assam groups of languages spoken by the tribes of Arunachal Pradesh and some parts of Assam. These tribes are the Aka, the Adis, the Mishings, the Nishis, the Mishmis etc. Another sub-division of Tibeto-Burman family formed by Assam-Burma group, which includes the speeches of North and East Bengal, Assam and Burma. These include – 1) the Bodo speeches- Bodo, Mech, Rabha, Garo, Tripura and few more; 2) the Naga dialects like Ao, Angami, Sema, Tangkhul, Sangtam, Konyak, Lotha, Mao and Kabui; 3) the Kuki-Chin speeches of Manipur, Tripura and Mizoram. In the southern Manipur and Mizoram, we encounter with Lushai-Kuki tribes, which are closer to Chin and Burma. The Meiteis or Manipuri show intermediate characteristic between the Naga and the Lushai-Kuki.

Thus, Assamese is the meeting ground of three major language families – the Austro- asiatic, the Indo-Aryan and the Tibeto-Burman. Assam is linguistically heterogeneous with as many as forty five languages spoken by the communities. Twenty four communities to the Tibeto-Burman language family, twelve languages to the Indo-Aryan language family and five languages belong to the Austro-Asiatic language family, namely, Kharia, Khasi, Kherwan, Munda and Santal. The rest four languages belong to the the Siamese-Chinese includes Siamese, and it connects speeches or dialects like Davi or Tai. The Ahom, the Khampti, the Khamyang, the Aiton, the Pakial, the Turung etc. living in different parts of North East speak languages belonging to this Tai sub-division.

II

Assam is the meeting ground of ethnic streams from the west, north and east. However, the archaeological findings in the North East suggest that the movement of the people could also have been the other way round i.e. from the North-East to South-East Asia. Assam received waves of migration from Madhyadesa (Kanyakubja), from Mithila (Dware bang), from North Bengal and northern India which is traced to the first century A.D.. The Brahmans were lured by land grants. They legitimised the rule of the indigenous chiefs and settled down in and around the royal seats, Kamrupa and Sivasagar. Besides performing priestly functions, they also emerged as landlords, warriors, administrators, etc. Their progeny and also those locally recruited Brahmans constitute 6 percent of the total Hindu population. Next to Brahmans, the other communities described in the epigraphic records are the Kayasthas, Karanas, Lekhakar, Daivajnas or Ganaks, Vaidyas, Kumbhakaras and Tantuvayan. There are no references to the present day local tribal communities such as Kalitas, Koches and Deoris. The Kayasthas in Assam were also called Kath derived from the Aryan root Katho to write or from Kaithoh to keep accounts. The Karanas and Kayasthas merged and the first became a section of the secend. The ancient texts also speak of professional castes such as the Kumbhak (Potters) and Tantuvay (Weavers). The Kumars are today separated into two endogamous groups, one who use the wheel (Kumar) and the other produce handmade pottery (Hira).

The Brahmans were indigenised despite attempts were made occasionally to purify Brahmanism by imposing "pure" Brahmans. Rules of gotra exogamy were not rigidly followed. The Kalitas are today a heterogeneous community, consisting of peasants and artisan groups, whether or not the Kalitas were originally Alpine Aryans, who immigrated to Assam or were "degraded" Kshattriyas, that they emerged as a dominant group in the country east of Bhat and north west of Sadiya is evident from their description in Shihabuddin Talish's "Fathiyah-i-Ibriyah" in 1662 as one of the "Powerful nations". The other powerful group was the Ahoms, have attained a "high degree of advancement and civilization". It is obvious that the Kalitas, its core represented by the peasant Barkalita, absorbed many other groups such as the fisherfolk (Saru Kalita), potter (Kumar), blacksmith (Kumar Kalita), Duliya (Palki bearer), Katani (silk weaver), Sonari (goldsmith), Barber (Napit), Mali and Nat. All these groups are endogamous and they owned land. In the Brahmaputra valley, the Kalitas claimed the status of the Kayasthas.

Many other communities also appear in the medieval history of Assam. Some communities founded states and formed aristocracies. The mighty Ahom, as mentioned above, came from the east, and with them came Khampti, Phakial, Naras followed by the Aitonias. The Morans, the Barahis and the Chutiyas all belonged to the Bodo-Kachari group. The first two groups supplied elephants to the Ahoms. The second two groups were also engaged by the Ahoms in different occupations. The Ahoms created mighty state machinery with military, administrative, diplomatic and other posts with high sounding titles that survive as surnames of present day among the communities. Among the high officers were the Bura Gohain, Bor Gohain, Borpatra Gohain, Bor Barua and Bor Phukan. There were paiks, over which were placed such as Borah, Saikia, Hazarika and Raj Khowa.

Another major Assamese group was the Assamese Muslims who came from Gaur (Goria) and elsewhere in Northern India integrated with Ahom polity and Assamese language, culture and economy. They were also the carriers of technology in making guns and agriculture. The Maria Muslims are still bell metal workers. They were also local converts. The Assamese Sikhs were also integrated with Assamese language, culture and economy and also integrated with the Namgarh tradition of neo-vaishnavism. Another major group of Assam was the Kaibartta or the present day Kewat or Keot. The Kaibarttas and the Keots are two distinct communities today. In Upper Assam, all Kewats are agriculturists, in lower Assam (i.e. the undivided Kamrup) they have two major endogamous divisions – the agriculturists or ploughmen (nalore) and fishermen (jalore), besides small artisan groups such washer men, barbers, florists, net weaver and oil pressure. The Ganaks emerged as a dynamic community enjoying a higher status in the Brahmaputra valley next to the Brahmans, while the Ganaks of Barak valley occupy a lower position in Bengali society.

In the colonial period, the pace of migration picked up of the labourers who came from the tribal areas of Bihar, Orissa, Chotanagpur and Andhra Pradesh to work in tea estates. By 1921, the tea garden labourers accounted for one-sixth of the population of Assam. The fertile land of the Brahmaputra and the Barak valleys attracted the Muslim peasants from East Bengal (Bangladesh) who reclaimed wet land. They came to form about one-tenth to one-sixth the population by 1951. The Bengali Hindus also came to Assam from East Bengal along with the Britishers to work as government servants and professionals.

III

Many scholars who studied Assamese society in the colonial period noted that traditionally, there were no professional castes in Assam. Hutton (1931) also studied that the caste in Assam valley was a racial division, not a functional division and that the functional castes were few. Assam, today has a mixture of both ethnic (tribal) groups and of "functional" castes. Hutton further said that the notion of exterior castes was imposed on Assam that was applied elsewhere in the country. "Exterior castes" were defined as "unapproachable", whose touch necessitates purification who are not allowed to read in the schools along with other castes. "An unapproachable caste is unknown here and boys of all castes are not freely admitted into all schools and colleges, nor are they have any differences of drawing water from public tanks and wells". However, Hutton who was the Census Superintendent of 1931 was compelled to place a few castes in the new constitutional category as "those beyond the social pale of Hindu society". Those included were the Kaibartta,

Brittial Bania/Bania, Hira, Mali and Namosudra. However, he added that it was possible in the Assam situation for an exterior caste to become interior as happened in case of the Kaibartta.

There was also the weak notion of clean and unclean in the Brahmaputra valley like that of jal-chal or jal-achal in Barak valley and Bengal. These norms were not rigidly followed. The unclean castes occupy a higher position in the Brahmaputra valley, The Doms of Assam were fisherfolk. Endogomy was the rule for the higher castes but others could intermarry. The Dhobas, a trading caste in the Barak valley was originally a jal-achal, enjoyed power and prestige. In Assam, the jatis do not exactly fit into the varna order. Except the Brahmans, there are neither indigenous Kshatriyas, nor indigenous Vaishya. The status of the Sudras is much better than elsewhere in the country as mentioned above. Sanskritization of the indigenous tribal groups of Assam such as Koch, Kachari, Mishing, Rabha and Lalung is well documented. In the colonial era social mobility of many communities or that of their segments, through the mediation of the Vaisnavite Gurus in the Brahmaputra valley has been documented at length.

The people of Assam are broadly divided into four categories. First, there are general castes which include the upper caste groups mainly agriculturists including the Mukihi, who recently shifted from traditional lime making to agriculture. Secondly, there are scheduled tribes which in Assam are called the hill tribes and plain tribes. The hill tribes are Chakma, Garo, Hajong, Hmar, Dimasa, Khasi, Jaintia, Kuki, Karbi and Nagas in the two hill districts, namely, Karbi Anglong and North Cachar Hills. The plain tribes are Deuri, Lalung, Mishing, Rabha, Boro-Kachari, Sonowal Kachari, Barman and Hojai. It is interesting to note that some of the hill tribes living in the plains are not notified as scheduled tribes such as Nocte, Sema, Rengma, Kanyak, Khampti, Singpho, Halam, Tripuri etc.while some of the plain tribes living in the plains and hills are not notified as the scheduled tribes such as Aiiton, Dowaniya, Khampti, Khamyang, Singpho, Turung, Tai-phake etc. Further, there are some tribes which are not scheduled tribes but they claim the status of the scheduled tribes such as Madahi, Thengal, Saraniya under Kachari and Nocte, Sema, Konyak, Rengma under Naga tribe.

Thirdly, there are scheduled castes. It is interesting to observe that the scheduled caste in Assam consists of all artisan groups as well as the fisherfolk. They are Bania (goldsmith), Hira (potterfolk), Jal Keot (fisherfolk), Kaibartta (fisherfolk), Mali (flower garland maker), Namosudra (fisherfolk), Patni (boating, fishing), Jhalo-Malo (fishing and infantry).

The fourth category consists of the immigrant communities who form a sizeable portion of Assamese population. The largest segment is made up of the tea garden community which again consists of many small "tribal" communities such as Bhumij, Kharia, Kherwar, Koya, Munda, Oraon, Santal, and others recognized as Scheduled Tribes in their native places and also of non-tribal groups such as Rajputs, Goala, Tanti, Mushahar, and so on.

IV

It is already mentioned above that the different communities have contributed the ethno-religions fabric of ancient Assam. One element of the religious heritage is fetishism, a belief in crude magic, associated with objects, such as stones and trees. Fetish worship constituted the foundation of tantricism in Assam, with its centre at Kamakhya, the temple of the Yoni, developed by the Austric and other such elements. The worship of both linga and yoni is proved by the Kalika Purana. The Yogini Tantra refers to the existence of a million lingas in Kamrupa. Idol worship is likely to have originated from the worship of the phallus. Fetishism, in fact, part of animism, has laid the root of various cults in Assam. This was contributed by the non-Aryan people. This is based on the attribution of spirits to all things, with which man had a close relationship for which he felt awe and from which he sought to derive benefit through rites and rituals. All elements of the cult of fertility, head-hunting, human sacrifice, faith in reincarnation, ancestor worship and the rites converted with the dead, belief in heavenly bodies, magic and sorcery were derived from the same animistic belief. These animistic belief practices have contributed to by the Austric and Tibeto-Burman people and formed the basis of tantricism in Assam, which passed on into the Hindu fold and later into the Buddhist faiths.

The disposals of the dead, ancestor worship and funeral rites of the Hindus are connected with the cult of fertility and the idea of incarnation. These elements were also the legacy of the pre-Aryans and non-Aryans in Assam as they were elsewhere. There is no evidence about the mode of disposal of the dead in ancient Assam. The practice of burial, particularly observed by the Khasis and the Jaintias, Garos, Karbis and others, is attested by some megaliths of Khasi-Jaintias and North Cachar Hills where human remains were found. The practice of stone cist brurial of the skull, and urn burial of the remains parallel the local Aryan Hindus practice of keeping the bones in an earthen pot for ten days or at least for some time after cremation. The different practice of keeping the bones, as is done by some of the Kuki tribes, throwing these into water as done by some Kachari groups, burial of bones as is followed by the Garos and the Karbis or digging of graves in a rice field or near water all have parallels in similar Hindu practices; all these are associated with the cult of fertility and ancestor worship. Whatever the ideas associated with these practices, the custom of offering food to the dead, like the erection of memorial stones by the tribals, suggest that besides the cult of fertility and ancestor worship, they had a belief in life after death. The Hndu Sraddha ceremony, in fact, may have arisen from the same idea of feeding the dead.

Like the tribals, an Assamese household undergoes a period of pollution during childbirth, after the death of an inmate and during the menstruation of a women member of the family certain rules are followed by the individuals or the family concerned at these times. Even today, a person suffering from smallpox puts the household under taboo. The worship of the goddess Sitala(smallpox) by the caste people has a parallel in the tribal worship of snakes. The stoppage of agricultural work on certain days by tribal people compares with the Hindu restriction on days like Ekadasi or Sankranti. In fact, most of the tribal agricultural rites and rituals lie at the foundation of the Assamese Hindu harvesting festival "Bihu" which in its origin was nothing but a combination of a solar cult and a cult of fertility, contributed alike by the pre-Aryan and non-Aryan, such as Austric, Alpine and Tibeto-Burman elements. In spite of the prevalence of so many Aryan, and non-Aryan cults, there was much tolerance among their adherents. The temple ruins indicate that at a single place, images of different deities were set-up and temples dedicated to deities of different sects were erected on the same site. The glaring example is furnished by the shrines at Kamakhya in Guwahati and Haigribha Madhava temple at Hajo (near Guwahati). Another notable feature of the ethno-religious history of Assam is that many non-Aryan ruling families and tribes, particularly of the plains, were gradually inducted into the Hindu fold and many of them had been given divine ancestry. The Koch kings trace their origin from Lord Shiva and have gradually became completely Hinduised. The Kacharis were also converted and their rulers trace their origin from Bhima and Hidimba of the epic story of Mahabharata. The Chutiyas, who established their kingdom in the Sadiya region of the Upper Assam not later than the 13th century A. D. claimed Hindu origin after conversion to Hinduism. The mighty Ahoms trace their origin from Indra and converted to Hinduism. As a result of this conversion and assimilation of the culture of the plains, the Hindu population increased, and this resulted in the fusion of different communities. Even though the people of the plains and the hills continued to profess different faiths, the followers of all the sects prospered equally. The rise of the neo-Vaishnavism could not dislodge or wipe out the influence of tantricism in Assam.

Srimanta Sankardeva (1449-1569) was the fountainhead of the Vaishnavite movement in Assam. He has left a deep impression on the culture, literature, religion and lifestyle of the people of Assam. Srimanta Sankardeva propogated Vaishnavism at a time when ritualism was gaining ground with occasional intrusions of ultra-religious animism and occultism. In order to do away with the mushroom growth of gods, he proceeded against the theology of Polytheism. He emphaised the unity of godhood. In the cosmology of

Sri Sankerdeva, God is absolute reality. Sankardeva's neo-vaishnaism has many institutional aspects and even today these exercise tremendous influence on the people of North East in general and Assam in particular. As an institution, the neo-vaishnavism has two major aspects: the Satras and the Namghars. The Satras are like medieval monasteries or 'maths'. The first Satra was set up by Sri Sankardeva near his ancestral village at Bordowa, Nowgaon district. Later on, Satras grew at all places where Sankardeva stayed during his journey from Bordowa to Madhupur in North Bengal. The first Brahman seceders who established independent Satras were Damodaradeva and Harideva.

The Satras founded by the Brahman preachers usually follow the pattern of the Bamuniya sub-sect like the Auniati or Dhakhinapat of Majuli of Jorhat district. The others follow the setup of the Mahapurushiya sub-sect of Bordowa or Barpeta Satra. They derive inspiration from Mahadeva, the chief apostle of Sri Sankardeva. The followers of Mahapurushia sub-sect do not worship any other god and goddesses except Vishnu. The Mahapurushia followers surrender to the one, Vasudeva Krishna, also known as Vishnu, Narayan, Rama or Hari and therefore, his creed is known as Ekasaraniya naam dharma. The followers of Bamuniy sub-sect worship other gods and goddesses apart from Vishnu. Altogether there are four sub-sects or samhati, namely, Purush samhati, Brahma samhati, Nika samhati and Kal samhati. These sub-sects have developed after the death of Srimanta Sankardeva and Madhavdeva.

The Namghars or the prayer halls are public institutions and their affairs are conducted on a democratic basis, every householder in the village having an equal voice in the management of the affairs. The villagers with their combined labour and resources build and repair the namghars, provide necessary articles, and look to their upkeep, and thus in diverse ways foster social solidarity and discipline. One notable contribution of the satra institution is their work towards the upliftment and betterment of the downtrodden people of the society. It can be said that the Vaishnavism in Assam was not confined only to the upper caste people but it spread among the tribal and lower caste Hindus as well. The disciples of the Satras no doubt preached the cult of devotion and universal love but it opened the door of salvation to all people irrespective of caste and tribe. They also introduced an element of gentleness in the unusual and often harsh rites of tantric worship that were prevalent in the society.

The Buddhism practiced by some of the groups like Khamyang, Turung, Aiton, Mann, Khampti and Singpho are identified as separate group in the society. It is said that the Kalitas were once followers of this religion. There are others who believe the Banias and Kaibarttas were originally Buddhists. It is due to the proselytising influence of Hinduism that the influence of Buddhism slowly diminished from the society. It is believed that the Haigribha Madhava Temple at Hajo in the district of Kamrup was originally a Buddhist temple. It was only later that it came to be a place of worship for the Hindus. The temple deity is known as Mahamuni, another name of Lord Buddha. It is a place of pilgrimage not only for Hindus but also for the Buddhists.

Muslims constitute the second largest group of people of Assam. Husain (1987 A:21) states that though the Muslims of Assam belong to the religious faith, they reflect significantly different from other Muslims. Unevenness is observable among the Muslims of Assam in terms of caste, clan, culture, language, occupation, education, geographical distribution, political participation and ideology. The Assamese Muslims are divided into three distinct groups, namely, Syeds, the Shaikhs or the Goria and Maria. They all belong to the Sunni sect. The Assamese Shaikhs are numerically the largest group among the Assamese Muslims. Their position comes next to Syeds and above the Maria Muslims. The Maria Muslim are mainly the bell-metal workers. Below the Marias another Muslim group known as Julaha occupy a lower position in the hierarchy among the Assamese Muslims.

Assam had come into contact with the Muslims in 1203 (Husain 1987). The systematic and serious propagation of Islam started only in the early part of the seventeenth century by a Muslim saint, Shah Milan, popularly known as Azan Faqueer. This saint compased Zikirs and Zaris, devotional songs embodying the fundamental tenets and spirit of Islam suited the local conditions and helped in taking Islam to the masses in Assam. Saint shah Milan and his disciples contributed significantly in propagating Islam and educating the dominant non-Muslim Assamese population about the spirit and significant of Islam. Of the Christian missions that came to spread the Gospel of Christ in Assam and win converts to it. The American Baptist Mission is the most popular. They first set foot in this land in 1826. Surya Kumar Bhuyan (1954) opined that they came to Assam at a time when the older regime was fast disappearing from the view. Christianity has not spread on any large scale in this state, specially in the plains. Besides the American Baptist Mission there were other missionaries that were also engaged in similar work.

During the days, after the treaty of Yandaboo in 1826, the American Christain Missionaries brought light to revive the Assamese language. Their main mission was to spread Christianity could spread only through the people's own language i.e., Assamese. With it began once of the crucial chapters in the history of modern Assamese Literature. Any discussion on Modern Assamese literary history has to begin with a reference to the journal *"Orunudoi"* (1846) edited and published by Dr. N.Brown (1807-1886), Dr.M.Bronson ((1872-1883) and O.T. Cutter. also associated with it were some names like Anunda Ram Dhekial Phukan (1829-1859), Gunabhi Ram Barua (1837- 1998), Hem Chandra Barua (1835-1896) and others. This way, the Christain Missionaries contributed the Assamese literature and at the same time they propagated the Christianity among the people of Assam. Inspite of all their endeavours, the progress of conversion to Christianity was slow in the plains but it was high in the hills.

REFERENCES

(Phukan,1989).

(Das, et-al 1988)

Hutton (1931)

Phukan, J.N., 1989. Presidential Address: Proceedings of North East India History Association.10th Session, Shillong.

Das, B.M. et-al.,1988. Biological Variation in the Kalita Caste of Assam, Guwahati: Department of Anthropology, Gauhati University.

(Husain 1987).

Husain (1987 A:21)

Surya Kumar Bhuyan (1954)

"Orunudoi" (1846).

3

Perspectives in Religion and Religious Diversity in India

Gautam Kumar Bera

Indian civilization is characterized with the phenomenon of unity in diversity as a consequence of harmony of contrasts. This harmony is based on the following arbitrarily drawn principles, viz.:

I. a sense of unity of all life as the expression of an unseen reality which is both immanent and transcendent;

II. a desire for synthesis;

III. an adherence to mystic perception;

IV. recognition of root causes of sorrows and sufferings;

V. a feeling for the sacredness of all life; and

VI. the tolerance for all other beliefs.

The harmony based on the above principles embodies the higher thought of Hinduism in its three forms of Brahminism, Buddhism and Jainism; the later development of other religion like Sikhism and various sectarian faiths; the Sufi form of Islam as it developed in India, heocentr through the hands of Fakirs, Pirs and Darveshs after taking shape in Mesopotamia, Iran and Central Asia; Zoroastrianism as it was established in India; the Indian Christianity in some of its aspects, and so on. All of these manifested highest expressions of human spirit through the languages of Sanskrit and other Aryan languages of India, Tamil and other Dravidian speeches, Persian and English.

The intermingling of different ideas taking place in varying proportions under local conditions in different areas of India formed a composite type with more or less common characteristics. Many indigenous communities retained their purer forms owing to either safeguard their identity or for lateness of contacts. It is understood that since time immemorial various forces of cultural immigration took place in India. After an initial phase of hostile contact in some cases these cultural forms settled down in a peaceful manner with an attempt for fusion of ideas, thoughts, beliefs, practices and so on. On the whole, during this process of fusion of the culture-worlds of the Austric, Dravidian and the Aryan peoples, there has been a continuous and general development of Indian civilization at large and an extension of it through the arrival of later comers.

One can find a glimpse of this fusion in the poem Bharata Tirtha composed by the Nobel laureate Rabindranath Tagore who sees merger and unification of humanity in all its diversity. This poem sums up in a noble poetic language the main trend of India's history in the past and of India's destiny in the future.

To transliterate this one understands that 'no one knows at whose call so many streams of men flowed in resistless tides from places unknown and were lost in one sea; here Aryan and non-Aryan, Dravidian, Chinese, the bands of the Sakas and Hunas, the Pathan and Mogul, have become combined in one body. The door to the West has also been opened, and they bring presents from there; they will give and they will take, they will unite and be united, and will never go away, in this ocean-shore of the Great Humanity of Bharata or India'.

From the above mentioned part of the note one can find a glimpse of the trend of participation of various elements of culture and people in the formation of Indian history and their contribution in the evolution of Indian civilization for over three millennia. The study of this aspect of the evolution of Indian culture and history demands closer look with great introspection through the various human sciences like Anthropology, Linguistics, Sociology, Comparative Religion, Comparative Literature, Political History and so on. Through the cross-cultural study, as an example, one can find the instance of Buddha, one of the most outstanding international personalities of both India and the world, who is considered among the greatest thought-leaders and teachers of mankind. He has been seen to embody in himself the principles of ahimsa (non violence), karuna (mercy) and maitri (charity) that are characteristic to India. He was of pure or mixed Indo-Mongoloid origin and through him one could establish a material and spiritual kinship with the Buddhist Mongoloid world.

II

George Peter Murdock's (1945:124) list of universal aspects of culture reports that all societies have the custom of propitiating supernatural beings and have religious rituals. These universals apply to cultures rather than to individuals. Nineteenth century writers who wrote about 'primitive religion' hoped to figure out how religious beliefs originated that became characteristics of the earliest primordial religion. Edward Burnett Tylor's two-volume work on Primitive Religion (1877) is devoted to religion finding out a minimum definitión of religion that applies to all religions in different parts of the world and different stages of development. Theologians considered this aspect stemming from revelation, a view Tylor rejected. Tylor developed the concept of monotheism from animism in the evolutionary scale and elevated the concept of one God dominating over others. Emile Durkheim, who emphasized the social, collective nature of religion in his book, The Elementary Forms of Religious Life (1912) claimed that religion is a collective enterprise that involves a church or community or fellow believers. Bronislaw Kasper Malinowski (1954) referred to that religion is an end in itself and religious belief is more complex, involving pantheons of supernatural beings. To him, religion gives humans the confidence to carry on, but on a more long-range basis, establishing positive attributes and values.

While dealing with ecclesiastical institutions, one comes across two forms, namely Olympian, which recognizes a pantheon of Gods; and monotheistic, in which there is worship of one Supreme Being. As examples of monotheistic cults one finds references of Hindu-Buddhist, Judeo-Christian, Islamic, and Chinese monotheism. But the characterization of Hinduism as monotheistic is questionable; in so far as traditional village practices are concerned it is better characterized as Olympian. An evolutionary sequence of forms of religion has been proposed by Robert N. Bellah (1964) who sees five stages: Primitive Religion, Archaic Religion, Historic Religion, Early Modern Religion, and Modern Religion. The classification of Bellah (ibid) merits little explanation. His Primitive Religion has two main features: (i) the high degree to which the mythical world is related to features of the actual world, and (ii) the fluidity of organization. In Archaic Religion there is a more definite distinction between humans and Gods and more distances between them. The Historic Religion is relatively recent and found in more or less literate societies. It stresses the theme of world rejection; it is dualistic and transcendal and has a pessimistic view of the human condition but a potentially better (or worse) conception of the afterlife. Salvation is regarded as the main purpose of life, and religious elite, priesthood, is committed to helping people attain it. The Early Modern Religion is the state of Protestant Reformation, when salvation no longer needs to be mediated but is potentially open to anyone. There is stress on faith rather than on ritual behaviour, and there is more individualism. In Modern Religion the tendencies set in motion during the preceding stage are carried further. There is a collapse of orthodoxy, and there is still more individualism. Indeed, freedom increases at each of these five stages. However, psychoanalysts like Sigmund Freud, Abram Kardiner, Cora Du Bois and others have developed the notion of God as a part of pantheism based on different religious beliefs.

All these put an anthropologist, who specializes in the study of preliterate societies, to face the difficult problem of defining what kind of phenomena can be called religious. This has led social scientists to try a whole range of definitions, usually settling with little conviction on formulae such as: religion involves the belief in supernatural forces (Goody, 1961). But the problem lies in the line of demarcation to understand: what is 'natural' in contrast to 'supernatural' knowledge. Durkheim (ibid), on the contrary, referred to religion as all beliefs and practices which are believed to be right of themselves, not merely right because these were the best way of doing something according to practical criteria. The first type of beliefs and practices are 'sacred' and the second 'profane'. However, in practice it is impossible to distinguish on the basis of this criterion, as it separates what is not separated in ordinary life. On this issue Weber (1930[1905]) stresses how particular religions are coterminous with particular ways of acting, particular ways of life; as a result the 'sacred' and 'profane' are ultimately inseparable.

This, however, does not help in defining what religion is, and the only solution seems to be to abandon the notion of religion as an analytical category and to look at social reality in terms less closely tied to a particular cultural tradition. This is implicit in the work of Marx where religion is subsumed under the wider label of ideology, which also includes such ideas as the 'rightness' of competition in capitalist systems (Marx and Engels, 1939[1845-6]).

Through the famous theory of ideas in The Republic, Plato argues that all one apprehends through his senses is in fact a necessarily compromised and misleading shadow of a clearer, simpler and eternal reality which he may not see but which governs what he sees. The intellectual speculation about metaphysical questions is well illustrated by Claude Levi-Strauss in *An Introduction to the Science of Mythology* (1970-81) through his work on the mythology of South and North American Indians.

In the world of religions there are also professional theologians trying to organize and systematize beliefs, where their ideas seem curiously distant from the everyday religion of people (Tambiah, 1969; Geertz, 1960). Accordingly, some anthropologists have distinguished between two types of religion, a folk religion and an official theological religion (Srinivas, 1952). It is partly as a result of these problems that anthropologists and sociologists have found it almost impossible to agree about the notion of 'belief' (Leach, 1966). What seems to matter above all in religion is the declaration of the limitations, if not outright pointless, of conscious human action.

III

The country named India had been the home of all religions that have a worldwide presence today. Here one refers to the term 'religion' as aspects of India's cultural traditions. Indic religions namely, Hinduism, Buddhism, Jainism, and Sikhism originated here. Other religions like Christianity, Islam, Judaism, Zoroastrianism and the Bahai faith arrived here from abroad at different points of time during the last two millennia. The plurality of religions in India is often obscured by the fact that Hinduism is not only culturally characteristic but also hegemonic in nature. It is a federation of faiths which has a horizontal as well as vertical distribution, rather than depicting homogeneity. The celebrated French anthropologist, Louis Dumont (1970), attested Hinduism as basically a religious or ritual expression of caste relations as modified by the goals and values of world renouncers. He argues that, the man in the world, the householder, possesses an identity primarily defined by membership in groups, pre-eminently castes. The renouncer leaves this social world behind; he now pursues his own liberation (moksha), and in doing so defines himself as an individual. Hence, he is an individual, outside the world, for the world of the caste has no room for the normative (as opposed to the empirical) individual. He is Indian civilization's greatest creative force, a speculator, discoverer, and the inventor of India's great soteriologies. His religious outlook provides a civilizational alternative to caste-based (and ascribed) religious values. Hence, religion in the Indian cultural setting traditionally permeates virtually all aspects of life, not through mechanical diffusion, but in an integrated, holistic perspective (Radhakrishnan, 1927).

The other factor concerning religion is divinity. The Abrahamic religions characterize monotheism which is absent in Indic religions. In the latter case one finds other conceptions like the abstract notion of 'Essence' or 'Being' as the source of all that truly exists, for e.g., the Brahman of Vedantic Hinduism, polytheism in Puranic Hinduism, and the exuberant 'spiritism' of folk Hinduism. One may note here that the most widely used appellation to the term religion is dharma, originating from the Sanskrit root dhṛ or its Pali equivalent dharma, which denotes the ideas of maintenance, sustenance or upholding, steadfastness and moral virtue. It rather opposes the dependent bonding of the human being with supernatural powers conveyed by the term religion, borrowed from the Latin derivation religio meaning obligation or bond. Incidentally, religio also denotes reverence.

Hoping to provide the posterity with a treasure of knowledge on the concept of dharma several scriptures were scribed all of which conceived dharma as the fulcrum of Indian civilization, since it is not affected by any linguistic, sectarian, or regional differences. Being a semantic, cultural and religious determinant, the term itself is untranslatable for it has several connotations. Having an Indo-Aryan origin the term dharma or dharman evolved through various phases finally occupying a position in the intellectual history of India. Its Iranian equivalent in old Persian is 'remedy', which is totally different from the Indo-Aryan conception. In *Rig Veda*, the term is not considered central to the lexicon, although it occurs as many as sixty three times. In Dharma Shastra and Smritis the whole corpus of dharma can be viewed as a record of custom. Since dharma is the power of supporting the cosmos and sustaining life, it is a common feature in all ritual and socio-ethical spheres and, for that reason, the diachronic changes in custom and convention are often overlooked. Therefore, it is felt that dharma is derived not from the Vedic literature but from achara. There is also a reasonably well established definition which holds dharma as an injunctive verbal force (codana), a Vedic enactment that has to be judiciously implemented. As a concept and idea, it is different from Dharma Shastra, which contains the textual reflections on the concept of dharma. Hinduism is the religion of Aryan cultural community and it is often denoted by the word dharma, which encompasses all those practices that represent Aryanness. In the Ramayana, the term connotes a sense of propriety or morality. In the Mahabharata, the term is chiefly associated with action. In Buddhism, the concept of dhamma (dharma) is mentioned in the Nikayas, which stands for something sublime, peaceful, subtle, and trans-rational. It is used in Sarvastivada Abhidharma highlighting its relationship with other terms such as bhava, swabhava, dravya and swalaksana in the inter-traditional context. The Buddhist scholastism shows that the concept is, at once, stable enough for any sectarian debate and elastic enough for further refinements. In Jaina literature, it is interpreted as virtuous behaviour, behaviour in accordance with intrinsic nature, and behaviour in terms of *pravrittii* (activity) and *nivritti* (non activity), and of cosmic order.

The religious diversity in India gave birth to various Indic religions at different points of time. The diversity was more internal centering on social, theological and scholastic divisions. The earliest of the knowledge concerning religious life was Vedism based on a body of sacred literature called the Veda meaning knowledge or wisdom, which is believed to be ever-existent *(sanatana)* and therefore lacking any human author *(apaurusheya)* stretching over almost a thousand years. The earliest of these, the *Rig Veda* containing ten books of hymns in praise of divinities presumably represent ten family traditions among the Brahmans or ritual specialists. The *Sama Veda* and *Yajur Veda* extend the scope of the Rig into music and ritual respectively. The fourth and the final of these, the *Atharva Veda* is believed to represent the absorption of folk religions into the Vedic corpus, which is said to be based on Shruti[1] that which had been heard and constitutes the first source of dharma understood as righteous conduct. These formed the basis for an immense textual efflorescence, comprising manuals of ritual performances like Brahmanas and Aranyakas, and discursive speculative treatises like the Upanishads, also called the Vedanta, the culmination of Veda. Later, Vedism gradually made way for the emergence of Hinduism, which produced more texts like the Griha Sutras dealing with performance of domestic rituals, the Dharma Sutras depicting social ethics and law, and the Shrauta Sutras as technical treatises on the correct procedures for the performance of Vedic rituals of public significance. The Sutras provided the second source called Smriti that which is remembered and these texts are credited to human authors. Later, Dharma Shastras came into being, the best known being Manav Dharma Shastra, attributed to the seer Manu, and thereupon known as Manu Smriti.

The philosophical concerns of the Brahminical tradition based on the Vedas were ascribed as orthodox thought or jnan and were termed visions or darshana referred to paramarthika (extra-referrential knowledge) and vyavaharika (transactive knowledge). These six schools of thought are; (1) Samkhya (enumeration) asserting the ontological duality of prkrti (matter) and purusha (self); (2) Yoga (joining, mixing) constituting a pair with Samkhya in terms of its metaphysics; (3) Mimamsa (Vedic exegesis) taking a pluralistic view of reality; (4) Vedanta (culmination of Veda), grouped with Mimamsa, denying the reality of many; (5) Nyaya (logic); and (6) Vaisesika (dialectics), considered a pair, dealing with logical, ontological, and dialectical issues within an empiricist, pluralist (more precisely atomist) framework (c.f. Hiriyana, 1949).

The Vedic rituals, called the Shrautas (Shruti, revelation) were the first to provide space to Smartas (followers of the Smritis or Dharma Shastras) or the Pauranikas (followers of Puranas). Non-Vedism probably first appeared with Tantras, which reveal considerable variety specially with secret rituals performed at special sites such as cremation grounds, preferably at night time. The worship of Vishnu, Devi (the goddess) and Shiva is combined in Smartha-Pauranika traditions, which also derived many cults and sects at different times in different parts of the country. Since the fifth century A.D., the Vaishnavas were divided into the sects of Pancharatras and Vaikhanasas. Similarly, the Shaivas incorporated Pashupata, Kapalika and Kalamukha sects (Lorenzen, 1972). Almost since the seventh century A.D., the Vaishnavas and the Shaivas began to generate distinctive liturgical texts called the Samhitas and Agamas respectively, each of which claimed superiority over the other.

With the passage of time these theistic traditions started fusing with Sanskritic as well as folk religious traditions. As a result of this, the Bhakti cult developed with an expression in emotionally charged poetic devotionalism. The expression in anthropomorphism or through abstract formulations constituted a speculative thought of different religious traditions ranging from advaita (monism) philosophy of Sankaracharya (c. 788-820), to qualified vishishtadvaita (non-dualism) of Ramanuja (c. 1017-1137) and dvaita (dualism) of Madhava in the thirteenth century. The thoughts and philosophical teachings of Ramanuja and Madhava combine the metaphysics of the Upanishads with the theism of Vaishnava and Shaiva cults. Along with these, the cult of Devi emerged independently as the Shakta (from Shakti, power) tradition. She manifested herself in manifold manner like Lakshmi as the divine consort of Vishnu representing the Goddess of wealth, prosperity, and auspiciousness; as Uma-Parvati, the divine consort of Shiva depicting mother of the Universe; as Durga and Kali, the destroyer of evil or the victorious image of good over evil. It is apparent that the religious traditions as is prevalent in India manifest pluralistic tendencies emanating from various sources and inspirations. At the same time there had been a binary tendency of both fission and fusion at various levels of thought. This dyadic nature depicted a strong sense of religious diversity in India as far as Hinduism is concerned.

Buddhism is the most widely prevalent religion in whole of Asia though it is a minority religion in India with an almost negligible frequency of followers in the human surface of the country. With an etymological origin from the title Buddha of its founder Gautama (c. 563-483 B.C.) it opposed the Vedic view of supernaturalism and its association with ritualistic beliefs and practices. With his own awakening to knowledge and wisdom called 'His enlightenment', he taught his disciples 'the four noble truths' that forms the basis of all schools of thought of Buddhism (Harvey, 1990). According to Gautama Buddha the first truth of life is sorrow and suffering; followed by the second truth that the source of sorrow is ignorance and desire; the third truth that sorrow can be ended if desire is overcome; the fourth and the last truth that the path to nibanna (blowing out) of both desire and sorrow lies through 'the noble eightfold path' comprising right views, resolve, speech, conduct, livelihood, effort, mindfulness and concentration encapsulated in path of dharma (righteousness).

Buddhism attaches no function to God. Man's actions can make or mar him. A man full of lust and worldly pleasures is bound to fall in bhavachakra (cycle of birth and death), which entails endless agony of birth, old age, disease and death. Only nirvana is the way to get rid of agony and suffering, when all vasana (lust) dries up; all trisna (thirst) is satiated. In Buddhism jiva or atman is not an eternal being; rather it is a flow of consciousness.

With Buddhism there emerged sangha (monastic community of monks and nuns) practicing rigorous vinaya (regime) as the ideal for the pursuit of true knowledge. After a century of Buddha's death the faith split into Sthaviras (elders) holding Buddha as an enlightened human preceptor; and the Mahasanghikas (upholders of the Great Community) claiming His status as a transcendent being. These two later came to be known as Hinayana (little, lesser) and Mahayana (great vehicle or approach) respectively. Around the seventh century A.D. a third school of thought in the name of Vajrayana (thunderbolt vehicle) emerged as a result of confluence of Buddhism and Tantrism especially in the northern Indian sub-Himalayan region where it later absorbed shamanism under its fold. Half a century ago in some parts of central India specially the Vidarbha region the Mahars (a community of Dalits) mobilized themselves under the charismatic leadership of Dr. Babasaheb Bhimrao Ambedkar (1891-1956) and got converted themselves to Buddhism finally to rename themselves as Neo-Buddhists, which, however, has explicitly politicized Buddhist identity.

Originating almost at the contemporary time of Buddhism, Jainism has also made little strides in India with a much below frequency in the Indian population strength. With the etymological origin in the word jina meaning the conqueror of one's physical self and thus of action of karma, the title of Jainism is bestowed on prince Vardhamana Mahavira (c. 599-527 B.C.) to whom the basic teachings of faith are attributed. He is regarded as the last tirthankara (ford maker), who recovered the perennial 'three jewels' of right faith, right knowledge, and right action. The faith accommodates both ascetics (monks and nuns) and the householders. The Jain ideal is forever engaged in self-purification and ahimsa (non-injury). During Mahavira's lifetime only heresies and sectarian schisms began and later there emerged the mainstream followers and the breakaway groups, the Shvetambaras (clad in white cloth) and the Digambaras (clothed by the sky; naked) (Dundas, 1992). The attribute of clothing refers to the ascetics only. Among the Digambaras the nuns wear clothes; only men remain naked. The Shvetambaras receive and eat food in a bowl while Digambaras receive food and eat in cupped palms. The two sects follow different scriptures. Territorially the Shvetambaras occupy the north and western regions of India while the Digambaras are found mainly in the south.

Jainism and Buddhism are homocentric religions. Jain religion proceeds with certain ontological assumptions like (i) the world has no creator with no beginning and no end, which ever existed and will ever exist; (ii) everything changes with the passage of time where things appreciate and depreciate; and (iii) in spite of changes, continuity is also there, where change has a continuity and continuity has a change. Jain philosophy does not believe in the existential entity of time. Time is regarded here as devoid of entity. Jainistic assumptions make God redundant. In the world view of Jainism cosmos ever exists, which does not require any creator. Moreover, a man's actions can elevate him to the stature of God for which he does not require any help from outside. On his own initiative jiva can rise to the height of God; can get the results of their good and bad deeds without the mediation of God; and can attain kaivalya (oneliness) through his own efforts of samvara and nirjara (checking the inflow of pudgalas and weeding out the already deposited pudgalas). Attainment of kaivalya makes a jiva *arhat* (equivalent to God) or *nirgrantha* (knotless), which transcends the cycle of birth and death.

During the sixteenth century A.D. Sikhism (Sikha, disciple) developed through Nanak Dev (c. 1469-1539), who discarded ritualism, idol worship, magic and miracles of the existing faith of Hinduism spearheaded by the Brahmans (McLeod, 1968). With a positive view of worldly existence he rejected caste distinctions and took a path to divinity through nam simran (name remembrance) with recitation and singing of hymns. He emphasized upon dharma as moral duty, karma as human effort, spiritual knowledge, truth, and divine benevolence. In reality, it was an effort to carry forward the medieval Sant tradition of syncretic religious devotionalism that had given rise to many panth (path) or sects. This formed the basis of Sikhism and the followers were called Nanak Panthis. Over the next two centuries there were changes and dilutions of dogma and practice which brought the core form of the religion under mist. The tenth guru (preceptor) of the Sikhs, Gobind Rai (1666-1708) merged effectively the theological, practical, social and the political fronts and institutionalized *pahul* (ritual of initiation) comprising norms of conduct and injunction to retain bodily hair unshorn. He also voiced for suffixing Singh (lion) and Kaur (lioness) after names of men and women respectively.

With the institutionalization of such norms there emerged sectarian groups with independent nomenclatures like (i) the Amritdhari (bearer of nectar, the baptismal water), also called Khalsa (pure, chosen of the God), who passed through *pahul* and later played a hegemonic role in the second half of the nineteenth century in defining Sikh identity; (ii) the Keshdhari (bearers of hair) who kept bodily hair; and (iii) the Sahajdhari (bearer of spontaneous, inner light) who affirmed Sikh identity without new injunctions. Several reformistic movements also shook Sikh identity of which the notable ones were the Nirankari and Namdhari (or Kuka) movements. The former one took to the path of divinity as nirankar (formless) and the latter rejuvenated Khalsa identity.

It is apparent that Indic religions comprising Hinduism, Buddhism, Jainism and Sikhism depict pluralistic tendencies with a concern for unity in diversity and absolute transcendence of expressions of thoughts and beliefs. Along with that there is an attempt for metaphysical foundations of the key issues like dharma and karma. However, unlike the others, Hinduism lacks a founder or a set of fundamentals of belief and practice. It is rather an agglomeration of diversified ritualism, idolatry, magic, miracles of faith under the stranglehold of Brahminic traditions. There is also a tendency to Sanskritize, secularize and universalize some of the local traditions, and also parochialize elements of greater Sanskritic canopy.

Contrary to Indic religions, Abrahamic religions originated outside India but found a home in this land. Christianity being the oldest entered this soil around the sixteenth century and formed its base in Kerala by the Apostle St Thomas under the patronage of Nestorian Church. The Thomas Christians also called Syrian Christians owe their origin to the jurisdiction of the Syrian Patriarch of the East in Damascus (Syria) and their liturgy was in Syriac. It subscribes to the various fundamentals of Christian faith – such as Immaculate Conception, the divinity of Jesus, and the status of the Bible as revealed scripture – and practice like the celebration of the Eucharist. Later, with the advent of Jesuit missionaries in Goa under the patronage of Rome, a section of the Thomas Christians affiliated themselves to the former (Jesuits) while the other half reaffirmed their loyalty to the Syrian Patriarch of Antioch. It took another three centuries or so to form the Anglican diocese of Calcutta (1814). Meanwhile there was an interflow between congregations, and the Anglicans, Protestants, and non-conformist societies produced a plurality of Churches. In 1947, the Anglican, Methodist and other Protestant Churches formed together the Church of South India. Subsequently in 1970, such efforts in north India formed the basis of a United Protestant Church. However, in India, there is a predominance of Roman Catholics (about 60 per cent). In Indian Christianity there is an attempt to retain Indian idioms of expression of pre-conversion beliefs, attitudes, and ceremonies. However, Evangelicalism has not waned away since it is a cherished goal (Gibbs, 1972).

Zoroastrianism has its own cosmology where Ahura Mazda is the supreme Lord of everything; the pure eternal omniscent and powerful Creator of the world, out of whom everything proceeds, depends, and is ruled. In Zoroastrianism, virtue and vice, good and evil are seen as interlaced dyads. The idea of inseparable dyad of good and evil can be explained with the help of an analogy. Evil, belonging to cosmic dynamism as a person, as a concrete object, rules the universe with the same energy as God has. God remains beyond the destructive, which can not rise above the level of existence itself. It is a theocentric religion, where God has two functions: (i) Creation, maintenance and dissolution of the cosmos, and (ii) Guiding man to his goal, rewarding and punishing him for his good and bad deeds. It is also considered as henotheistic religion since faith is put in one supreme deity.

Judaism, the religion of the Jews, was founded by Moses. The supreme deity of this religion is Yahveh, also called Jehovah, who releaved this faith to the most pious member of the chosen people on the earth. He revealed to him the secret of divinity, along with the codes of the proper conduct. Yahveh gave Moses the rules of social life in the form of Ten Commandments. Judaic God is just and merciful. He is the perfect one, who created the world in six days. Jews believe in the continued existence of soul, after the death of man. Judaism is monotheistic religion opposed to idolatry at least in principle if not in practice.

Scripturally speaking, Judaism and Christianity are very much like Siamese twins. The Holy Bible has two sections namely, the Old Testament belonging to Jewish faith and the New Testament belonging to Christianity. Judaism is regarded as the parent faith of Christianity. If not a Siamese twin, Judaism and Christianity may at least be seen as a dyad bound by the common lace of historicity. Whereas Lord Moses is called Kaleemullah, Jesus is called Roohallah (the soul of the supreme deity).

Islam, derived from the world Aslam (submission to the will of God) emerged as the youngest member of the family of Abrahamic religions in the chain of Semitic religions dating back to A.D. 622 when its originator Prophet Muhammad (A.D. 571-632) migrated from Makkah (in Arabia) to Madinah. His accommodation included resident Jews and Christians since they too followed books of divinely revealed knowledge. Affirming oneness of God under guidance from Quran (the holy book to be read and recited) a follower is supposed to recite kalimah (word of creed), perform five namaz (daily prayer) a day, observe annual rozah (fasting by day) for a month to burn away sins, give zakat (alms) and visit the pilgrimage to hajj (at Makkah) during Idu'l-Azha, if situation permits.

Islam spread across the country accommodating much of the pre-Islamic practices where Sufis and saints played a great role in preaching the doctrines. Partitionism also occurred in Islam and as a result the Sunni (from Sunnah, customary way of life) and the Shiah (followers) sects emerged. The former group acceded to Prophet's words and deeds and the latter followed Ali (the Prophet's cousin and son-in-law) as khalifah (legitimate successor) and imam (leader) (Rahman, 1979; Mujeeb, 1967).

Some scholars believe that there are syncretic elements underlying Sufism in India since it has borrowed many idioms of expression of Brahminical philosophy of Yoga or the magical Tantra. Hence, one can find an essence of Indic elements in Sufism in India where there are orders namely, Chisti, Naqshbandi, Quadiri, and Suhrawardi who represent both classical and folk traditions. Apart from them, there are Pirs, Fakirs, and Darveshs as serious devout. These groups of people contributed enormously to the religious diversity in Indian Islam.

IV

It is apparent then that religious diversity and pluralism operates at two levels in India. One is at the inter-religious level and the other at intra-religious level at which sectarian and quasi-sectarian movements operate. As an outcome of the Enlightenment and Renaissance, the centuries immediately preceding the twentieth century witnessed the growth of philosophies that excessively emphasized the power of human reason not only to reach truth unaided but also to ensure a better life for those deprived of it.

Along with that there have been instances of end numbers of reform movements both at the pan-Indian level as well as at the local level where only particular communities were involved. One can find an essence of such ideas of reformism in the Brahmo Samaj movement initiated by Raja Ram Mohan Roy in 1829 against casteism, untouchability, child marriage, polygamy, bride price, purdah, idolatry, etc. that had a bearing in Hinduism. After his death his ideas were carried forward by Maharshi Debendranath Tagore. But it too suffered schism and in 1869 Kesab Chandra Sen formed Naba Bidhan Brahmo Samaj (also called Bharatiya Brahmo Samaj) which later broke again when Sadharan Brahmo Samaj was formed by Shibnath Shastri in 1878. Another example of such reformism was Aryya Samaj movement founded in Bombay in 1874 by Dayanand Saraswati which not only rejected post-Vedic forms of Hinduism but also denied the views of Christianity, Islam, Buddhism, Jainism, and Sikhism. As a fundamentalist believer of Vedic Hinduism it tried to reform the society along its own lines in colonial India, which probably could not make much dent at the pan-Indian level. Of late, there were other attempts too namely, Lingayat movement, Shankaradeva Vaishnava movement in North East India, Veer Shaiva movement, Neo-Buddhist movement and so on.

On the whole, religion can be classified into two categories, namely, proselytisive and insulative. In proselytisive religions, adherents propagate the messages of their religion among the people and induct them into their fold. On the contrary, in insulative religion, adherents concentrate on the quality of their native fold. The three proselytisive religions are Buddhism, Christianity, and Islam. Votaries of these religions have crossed almost all geographical boundaries to spread the message of their God and their religion. The remaining religions come under the fold of insulative category, where Zoroastrianism contains the maximum insulatory tendency. Hinduism does not believe in proselytization but keeping in view the accelerating pace of proselytization by other religions, it is resorting to reconversion. Further, of late, it is trying to assimilate different tribal religions into its fold in response to the challenges posed by proselytisive religions. But this has long back been attested by the eminent Gandhian anthropologist, Nirmal Kumar Bose, as the 'Hindu method of tribal absorption' (Bose, 1941).

The brief historical overview might seem simplistic, yet it enables one to understand that no theology has developed in a vacuum. Even when it assumes to be unaffected by the intellectual climate of a particular period, it can not but be influenced by the popular philosophies and ideologies of that time. In reality, theology necessarily deals with metaphorical, analogical and symbolic language, and it is always insufficient to fully express, much less, exhaust, the divine mystery.

Every religion imagines a special kind of relation between God and the World as well as God and the Man. On this basis, religious and social ideas and morality are well systemized. While religion is meant to foster peace, harmony and community-building, it has, sadly, of late, been a cause of division and strife. Moreover, God and religion have been used as a shield to shed blood. This seems to be a fratricidal war. Called by any name and worshipped in any form, the ideas of God must lead one to promote Life for all peoples everywhere. If religionists can come together and respond to the larger problems of life based on their experiences of God, and only later, as a second step, articulate their theologies and conceptions of God, one might have a more harmonious society, and religion would have played a pivotal role in fostering peace.

All religions accept the concept of God, but all philosophies do not agree on God as the highest manifestation. The mystery of God can neither be encapsulated in some doctrines nor shackled in the confines of some sanctuary. Through the acceptance of a religion theologians and philosophers, both in the East and the West, have tried to prove God's existence and his nature by appeal to scriptures, as also arguments, although among themselves they are not in complete consensus. The cosmological, teleological, and ontological proofs, in various forms, have been interpreted to assert the reality of God.

After having articulated so much, one can put it all down in the following Vedic hymn, which seems to provide a rational explanation.

NOTES

1. Shruti is the highest authority; next in importance is Smriti, or the tradition set up by human beings; and it is authoritative in so far as it is not repugnant to the Veda from which it derives its authority. Practices or customs (achara) are trustworthy if they are adopted by the cultured. Individual conscience is also authoritative. (S. Radhakrishnan, *Religion*

and Society, London, 1947, p. 111). The term Shruti is used for Vedic literature which consists of the four Vedas and Brahmanas, Aranyakas, Upanishads, and Sutras. Only the Vedas are revealed by God while the others are commentaries, and the former's authority is therefore superior to the latter's. Of the Vedas, the Atharva, containing as it does magical spells, and so on, is inferior in authority to the others – it was not even recognized as a Veda till about 300 B. C. Yajur and Sama Vedas are later than the first and highest Veda, Rig. Some of the material in Yajur and Sama Vedas is a repetition of what is in the Rig Veda.

REFERENCES

Bellah, Robert N., 1964. 'Religious Evolution', *American Sociological Review,* 29:358-74.

Bose, N. K., 1941. 'The Hindu Method of Tribal Absorption'. *Science and Culture,* VIII: 188-194.

Dumont, Louis, 1970. 'World Renunciation in Indian Religions'. In Louis Dumont, ed., *Religion/ Politics and History of India,* 33-60. Paris/The Hague: Mouton Publishers.

Dundas, Paul, 1992. *The Jains,* London: Routledge.

Durkheim, Emile, 1915 (1912). The Elementary forms of Religious Life. London. Translated into English by Joseph Ward Swain in 1965. New York: Free Press.

Geertz, C., 1960. *The Religion of Java*. Illinois: Glencoe.

Gibbs, M.E., 1972. *The Anglican Church in India, 1600-1970,* Delhi: ISPCK.

Goody, J., 1961. 'Religion and Ritual: The Definitional Problem'. *British Journal of Sociology,* 12.

Harvey, Peter, 1990. *An Introduction to Buddhism: Teaching, History and Practices,* Cambridge: Cambridge University Press.

Hiriyana, M., 1949. *The Essentials of Hindu Philosophy,* London: Allen and Unwin.

Leach, E. R., 1966. 'Ritualization in Man in Relation to Conceptual and Social Development'. In J. Huxley, ed., *A Discussion on Ritualization of Behaviour in Animal and Man,* London.

Levi-Strauss, C., 1970-81 (1964-1972). *An Introduction to the Science of Mythology,* 4 vols. London. (Original French Edition, Mythologiques, Paris).

Lorenzen, D.N., 1972. *The Kapalikas and Kalamukhas: Two Lost Shaivite Sects,* New Delhi: Manohar.

Malinowski, Bronislaw Kasper, 1954. *Magic, Science and Religion and Other Essays,* New York: Doubleday Anchor Books.

Marx, K. and F. Engels, 1939 (1845-46). *The German Ideology,* Part 1 and 3. New York (Full text first published in 1932 as Die Deutsche Ideologie).

McLeod, W. H., 1968. *Guru Nanak and the Sikh Religion,* Delhi: OUP.

Mujeeb, Muhammad, 1967. The Indian Muslims. London: Allen and Unwin.

Murdock, G. P., 1945. 'The Common Denominator of Culture'. In Ralph Linton, ed., The Science of Man in the World Crisis. New York: Columbia Press.

Radhakrishnan, S., 1927. *The Hindu View of Life,* London: Allen and Unwin.

Rahman, Fazlur, 1979. *Islam,* 2nd edn. Chicago: The University of Chicago Press.

Srinivas, M. N., 1952. *Religion and Society among the Coorgs of South India,* Oxford: Clarendon Press.

Tambiah, S. J., 1969. *Buddhism and the Spirit Cult,* Cambridge.

Tylor, E.B., 1877. *Primitive Culture: Researches into the Development of Mythology, Philosophy, Religion, Language, Art, and Customs,* 2 vols. New York: Henry Holt and Co.

Weber, M., 1930 (1905). *The Protestant Ethic and the Spirit of Capitalism,* London. (Original German edition Die Protestantische Ethik und der 'Geist' des Kapitalismus, Tubingen).

4

Cosmo-Theandric Anthropology: Emerging Trends in Anthropology of Religions

Dr. Joy Thomas SVD

Traditional cosmologies presented before us a worldview of nature, humans and spirit based on their understanding and knowledge systems. At present with the advancement of modern science our knowledge of the world and the cosmos has expanded its grasp and become more complex in its understanding of reality and life. In this context anthropology has to rethink the traditionally accepted worldview, as this emerging knowledge gives us new understanding of the origin of human beings and how civilisations and cultures are changing today. We shall, therefore, try and focus on the emerging trends in the anthropology of religions, which is moving in the direction of cosmotheandric anthropology.

Anthropology in Search for Sacred Horizons

Anthropology is a science that studies humans and their behaviour and works. It is a very young science with a history of about 200 years. It is a study that delves into the questions of the origin of human beings, from where they come, who they are and where have they arrived at present? The questions of where they are going and what is the purpose of life are left incomplete, but none the less, we get a glimmer of their guiding orientations, visions and hopes from their myths, religious symbols, folklore and history.

Somewhere in all these fragments we can trace the contours of the transcendence that animate them into a people, nurturing a culture of life as opposed to death and forming a civilisation. It is the sacred quest of being 'Human' that is life enhancing. Zizioulas claims that being a human person is basically different from "being an individual or 'personality' in that the person cannot be conceived in itself as a static identity, but only as it relates to. Thus personhood implies the 'openness of being,' and even more than that, the ek-stasis of being, i.e. a movement towards communion which leads to a transcendence of the boundaries of the 'self' and thus to freedom" (Zizioulas, 1975:408).

As anthropology moves ahead in the 21st century, I am concerned with the urgency of this task of sharing and communicating the need for this sense of the sacred, transcendence, ultimate-concern, the mystery and meaning of life, and the story of the cosmos. Hence this heuristic effort of cosmotheandric anthropology lends a holistic integrity to the anthropological vision. Victor Turner's anthropological studies on the 'rites of passage' the 'liminal person' have encouraged this search in anthropology.

All the same, the mentality of modern rationality and the scientific method has camouflaged the religious quest for being, it has closed us to the quest beyond ourselves, to an endlessly fascinating mystery of what makes us live, with faith, hope and love. Huston Smith says that "archaeologists have discovered no founding city of a civilisation that does not have a sacred centre" (Bryant, 1992:11).

Anthony Giddens has sensed that this present globalising world is "the runaway world", where we do not have a shared sense of direction of our history which appears out of control, and we do not know where we are heading. This "runaway world" needs a shared vision and spirituality – a sense of the holy (whole) without which it will perish by the weight of its own arrogance and "manufactured risk": global warming, overpopulation, pollution, unstable markets, and unforeseen consequences of genetic engineering. We still do not know the consequences of what we are habituated to do. What this world seeks for is not just knowledge but wisdom of humanity's ultimate destination that will liberate it from its deep anxiety and hopelessness (Giddens, 1999: 1-6). Hence, the role of religion in the globalised world is yet to be explored.

The utopian promise of a material paradise promised by the new economic social order has not brought any tangible result especially for the poor. On the other hand, the negative effects of globalisation have led to exploitation of labour, job insecurity, reduction in wages and consequently lower standards of living. The utopia of better life for the developed nations and promise to the poor have ended in the rich continuing to get richer and the poor becoming poorer. Worse still is the increasing influence of multinational companies and corporations on political decisions, especially of developing nations.

James A. Overtone notes that in such critical liminal times: "throughout most of the world the shaman fulfils, the roles of a healer, master of spirits, guardian of psychic and ecological wellbeing of his community...intermediary between the natural and supernatural, the liminal figure who occupies the central place in traditional cultures, who guides the way to the future" (Overtone, 1988:151-170). Jojo M. Fung, after his field studies on indigenous shamanism, says, "These healing rituals have humbled me, for the sacredness of the scene bespeaks the presence which has already preceded me," as it is the overshadowing presence of the Divine Mystery. The cultures of the indigenous people are sacred grounds where God (the ultimate) has chosen to dwell amongst a simple marginalised people forging a new beginning for a greater human completion. This indigenous logic of "many in the one" as opposed to the rationality of "many into one" subsumes the theological understanding that God is God of all because God who is Spirit is omnipresent in all cultures and the many worlds, in the one seamless creation (cf. Fung, 2002:2-31).

In the present times we need such shamans, 'liminal personalities', communities and cultures that will enlighten and orient humanity to the larger vision of life that beckons us. We cannot exist as a people without a trans-cultural maturity which is far beyond just social adjustments, no longer limited by the culture in which one has grown, it is giving birth to a comprehensive self, who is a peacemaker going beyond violence, primitive perceptions of the other as a threat, and lives in the insight of this inner freedom of life (Gorman 1985:162). "The only thing you have to offer another human being, ever, is your own state of being, as Meister Eckhart had said that there is no being except in the mode of being" (Dass 1974:6) This state of being is a trans-cultural maturity sustained by the new Shamans (liminal figures) of our age that's in transition to a planetary society.

Thus, the Cosmotheandric Anthropology attempts to study religion in a new way in the problem centred 21st century, trying to give meaning to the meaningless world. This seeking of meaning is in the context of the new knowledge of the cosmic world.

Anthropological Quest for Origins: Where Have We Come From?

a) Story of the Material Universe - Is there a Design? Is There a Purpose?

The scientific discoveries of the last two centuries have changed the horizons of the way we look and perceive the universe and tell its story. This changes the way in which we think and relate to the universe. A native North American tradition believes that human beings do not arrive at its maturity without making room within themselves for the immensity of the universe.

Our universe is very immense in its expanse and depth both at the macroscopic and microscopic levels. At the microscopic level the matter in the universe devolves to atoms, electrons, protons, neutrons, particles and then energy (radiation) that behaves both in a wave and particle form, paradoxically complementing each other.

At the macroscopic level we are in the spiral shaped Milky Way galaxy. Our solar system with its earth is nested in one of the spirals of the Milky Way. Our Milky Way is one hundred thousand light years across and ten thousand light years deep, with between two hundred and four hundred billion stars. Our Milky Way is not the entire universe, besides there exist billions of other galaxies, each with billions of stars. The nearest galaxy to our Milky Way is the Andromeda galaxy which is 2.5 million light years away. This is not the only extent of the universe. It has been discovered that our universe is continuously expanding in all directions. Scientists in the 1920's found that the stars within our Milky Way are moving away from each other as the other galaxies are doing. The ones furthest away are hurtling away at 60,000 miles-per-second! Edward Hubble the astronomer in 1929 made an astounding statement: "The universe itself is expanding!" If that was the case then the universe must have had a beginning at some point in time.

Our observable universe has burst from an unthinkably hot and infinitely small and dense, hot singularity, about 14 billion years ago. It rapidly expanded and within the first seconds, particles in their plasmic state interacted with other particles and going out of existence (particle with anti-particles). By the end of the first second a billionth of the original matter survived and stabilised. The fundamental forces of the universe emerged (gravity, electromagnetism, and strong and weak nuclear forces). The universe continued its expansion and cooling the soup of elementary particles such as electrons, neutrinos and photons. From the first second, protons neutrons were able to bond together to form the nuclei of hydrogen and helium. It was too hot for them to form into atoms. By the end of the first three minutes, the universe existed as expanding and cooling plasma of nuclei of hydrogen and helium. When it was just 300,000 years old it cooled enough to form the first atoms of hydrogen and helium and for matter to be separated from radiation which means, photons were set free and seldom interacted with matter and it became transparent to light, the universe then was filled with the universal sea of radiation. This is the origin of the cosmic microwave background detected by Arno Penzias and Martin Wilson in 1965. Its radiation comes from all direction of the sky and has a temperature of about three degrees Kelvin.

These evidences gave birth to the Big Bang theory which remains the most accepted explanation of its origins. The theory was confirmed in 1964 by the discovery of the 'microwave background radiation', energy consistent with an explosive origin. According to their calculation, the Big Bang must have occurred approximately 14 billion years ago; this is the age of the universe.

In the final analysis some physicists have come to the conclusion that from the very first moments of the Bing Bang there has been the thrust towards life. Suppose the universe had unfolded one trillionth of a trillionth of a percent slower, the gravitational force would have been too great and the universe would have imploded before anything of significance had occurred. If however the universe had unfolded one trillionth of a trillionth of a percent faster, matter would have been flung apart before anything could happen. It makes us to wonder if there is some inbuilt intentionality towards life woven in the very fabric of the universe all along. Three hundred million years after the Big Bang when the universe started to cool the first stars and galaxies emerged, forming clusters as the universe began to expand away from its singularity (centre). Some galaxies continued to create stars while others turned cold. It was in the first generations of stars that the primary elements were formed: carbon, oxygen, nitrogen, copper, silver, silicon, magnesium, calcium, sulphur and iron – all the elements which make organic life-forms.

Everything in the universe is so intricately interconnected, what happens to the stars and what happens in the evolution of life on earth has a deep relationship. All ninety-two elements (except for hydrogen and helium were formed in the Big Bang's plasmic state) have been made in the stars. The living creatures are made of the molecules composed of atoms of carbon, hydrogen, oxygen, nitrogen, and phosphorous; they have all been made by nuclear fusion in stars. With each generation of stars, the chemical elements of the galaxy were transformed from lighter to heavier elements. Astronomers calculate that it takes about three generations of stars to form these elements. The resources for life are found in abundance in the interstellar clouds of the Milky Way. Astronomer Martin Rees speaks of a 'galactic ecology' of the Milky Way. He says that the galaxy resembles a large 'ecological system' in which the pristine hydrogen is transformed into the basic building block of life such as carbon and oxygen, and then some of it is returned to the interstellar space to be recycled in new generation of stars. To conclude Rees says, "No element in the universe, including ourselves, can be ultimately understood, except in relation to the whole" (Rees, 1997:3).

The birth of our solar system – sun, earth and planetoids– came also as a result of a supernova explosion that occurred about five billion years ago in one of the spiral arms of our Milky Way galaxy and in another billion years, life forms began to appear on earth. Anthropology of Religion must ask serious questions with regard to the above cosmological knowledge. Is there a purpose to the universe? Is there a Design in the universe? These are vital questions human beings are seeking for answer. Anthropology of Religion must take them seriously.

b) Story of the Biological Universe: Is it Biogenesis or Spontaneous Generation?

It was four billion years ago that life on earth began to emerge in the form of prokaryotes – primitive cells without a clear nucleus; tiny lifeless particles of matter became alive and began to interact with the environment, with themselves and amongst itself. From the very beginning the direction of evolution of the universe has been towards life and ever greater complex life forms.

One of the most awe inspiring moments of earth's evolution came three billion years ago when the simple primitive cells mutated and began to capture the light of the sun in a process called photosynthesis, tiny chlorophyll molecules able to capture solar energy in the form of light and convert it into food and oxygen which is beneficial to life. In the process of photosynthesis carbon-dioxide is converted into oxygen and later released into the atmosphere. Virtually all oxygen we breathe is a result of the photosynthesis. Almost all forms of life from simple to complex depend on the tiny yet extraordinary mutation that occurred three billion years ago, creating photosynthesis.

At some point in time, four million years ago a small mammal stood erect, with a brain capacity a bit larger than chimpanzee, this hominid (the australopithecines) was *Homo sapiens'* distant but direct ancestors of the present humans. Grace filled evolution preceded further until some 2.6 million years ago, that the first species that we recognise as the humans, the first genus Homo erectus (humans) emerged. *Homo erectus*, used fire, could run like modern humans and made stone tools they evolved into various bands including the Neanderthals between 25,000 and 30,000 years ago. Just as photosynthesis was a breakthrough moment in the relationship to the earth and the sun, so the emergence of the first human species was a breakthrough moment in the living world.

In about 150,000 years ago our species Homo sapiens emerged. Their brain size increased from about 826 to 1250 grams. As far as we know for the first time in 14 billion years history of the universe there was a kind of birth of a consciousness that we call self-awareness. Unlike other species, Homo sapiens had the capacity to know what they know. Homo sapiens could reflect upon their own experiences and begin to ask questions about its origin, meaning and purpose. In evolutionary terms the 'universe had become conscious of itself'.

About 100,000 years ago this new species developed the capacity for language, an ability to communicate in signs and symbols, to be able to share and exchange information and experiences of events or entities that were not immediately present: Language, signs-symbols, from conscious memory was to set the species apart from all others in a definitive way. The species before long made the connections that there was something larger than themselves, some other, like in nature and life, where power could be witnessed. Even earliest humans knew intuitively that there was some mysterious force or forces, intricately involved in their lives. Call it God or gods, they began to use the capacity for language to create myths and rituals to explain and celebrate conscious connections with the divine other, that we are not alone in the universe and that gracious power or energy is at the heart of all life.

As evolution continues, our self-awareness too increases to the point of self-transcendence to become a new species Homo Universalis (universal); humans with the capacity to integrate with the larger whole. We are at the cross roads of an evolutionary breakthrough, one that requires conscious participation as co-creative agents of altruistic love itself or bury ourselves with the gravity of the self-centeredness of our own self-consciousness. Barbara Marx Hubbard in her book: Emergence: the Shift from Ego to Essence says that humans have to transit from being Homo sapiens (wise ones) to Homo Universalis (universal ones). She says that at the present evolutionary stage we must engage our consciousness and respond to the issues that threaten the very survival of the earth: materialism, political geocentricism, religious fanaticism and human ignorance have created a political and environmental crisis of a colossal proportion. Sooner than later we will have to respond to these issues or else we will not exist as a human species. We need to connect to the totality of life, and the deeper intelligence of the universe.

The major scientific findings discussed here are from the fields of astronomy, physics, and evolutionary biology. There is now another significant development contributing to the present telling of the story of the universe from the field of Geology (Earth Sciences). The main question which is unresolved is whether the whole universe and living beings including humans, did they evolve spontaneously or is there a purpose and direction? The answer to this question will make all the difference. There are divided opinion between pure materialists and spiritualists. Anthropology of Religion must deal on these questions to make sense of our universe.

James Lovelock and Lynn Margulies in the 1960's postulated that the earth is a self-regulating ecosystem, a biological organism in its own right. Lovelock named this concept the Gaia hypothesis. They pointed to the fact that the 'Earth' has maintained a steady temperature over hundreds of millions of years as any biological system does. The salt of the seas remains below the saturation point so the oceans do not become poisonous to plants and animals. Rain forests act as lungs and rivers as arteries. Earth, they maintain, is alive as an organism with systems that support her life and ours.

These amazing discoveries of the magnitude of our cosmos have displaced our notions that human beings are the centre of the fixed universe. These new findings make their way into our lives and minds. The way in which we think and feel about who we are and God is, will surely change. Neither human beings nor God are the machines of a mechanistic worldview. Our existence is characterised by our relationships and connectedness. The language of some scientists engaged in the new cosmology often sound like mystics and shamans who acknowledge that our lives are rooted deeply in the universe with an ability to reach far beyond ourselves and touch the ultimate. We are rooted in mystery and on the level of mystery we are all one.

Denis Edwards in his book Breath of Life: A Theology of the Creator Spirit, reflects that "Human beings, along with all other life forms of the earth are intimately related to and dependent on the long history of the universe..., the astronomers George Coyne and Alessandro Omizzolo, speak of a social character of the universe (2002:125). They conclude that no element in the universe including ourselves can be ultimately understood, except in the relation to the whole" (Edwards, 2004:15). Stephen Hawking at the end of his book, *A Brief History of Time,* asks: "What is it that breathes fire into the equations and makes a universe for them to describe?" (Hawking, 1988:174).

c) Anthropological Quest for Meaning of the Contemporary World

The contemporary reality of the world is that though the standards of living for more than half the world's population has actually become better the dark side is that half the global village still lives in dire poverty, social evils and obscene inequality even though we may boast of the advances in science, technology, industry and wealth accumulation. The United States and Europe spent nearly ninety times as much on luxury items as the amount of money that would be needed to provide safe drinking water and basic sanitation for those in our global village who do not have these necessities now.

In one day's military spending; we could virtually eliminate malaria in Africa. What we spend in two days on the military, we could provide the health care services necessary to prevent the deaths of three million infants a year. For less than a week's military spending, we could educate each of the 140 million children in the developing countries who have not gone to school. Poverty and gross inequalities throughout the world waste human potential, weaken the entire community and put the whole family at risk, diminishing their hopes for better lives, and makes them insignificant (c.f. Groody, 2007:1-30).

Mother Earth produces enough to feed all human beings. But more than one third of members of human family do not get to eat one square meal a day because 80% of world's resources are consumed by mere 15% of human population. In the Indian context 15% of the population controls and consumes 85% of the nation's resources. The money spent by the so called 'advanced nations' on weapons of mutual destruction in one year is more than sufficient to feed the entire humankind for 5 years! One man's greed can prevent others from fulfilling their basic needs. The father of our nation has said it many years ago; "We have enough for the needs of people, not for their greed."

Globalisation today has created possibilities for local, regional and global integration, but it has left waves of disintegration in its wake. It has given us more of a free market, but unmasked human and structural 'unfreedom' that contribute to making a few so wealthy while many remain so poor. It has given us a new technology such as global positioning systems, which help us to find our way in time and space, but in other ways it has made us less able to find the ethical coordinates and the spiritual vision that would help us find a place in human solidarity.

Civilisation, as we know, is undergoing an unprecedented process of integration; the World Wide Web making a global community, development of transportation, communications and technology, coupled with dismantling of trade barriers. The current global business arena, trade marked as it is by liberalisation, universalisation, westernisation and modernisation reach every political border. Thomas Friedman, describing this situation in his book *Longitudes and Attitudes: the World in the Age of Terrorism*, says: "In globalisation system we reach for the internet, which is a symbol that we are connected and nobody is quite in charge" (Friedman, 2003:4). Since no one is in charge of major decisions to have any accountability for the welfare of the planet as a whole, it becomes less clear where we are going as a global village.

Today our free market economy alone is insufficient to bring genuine human liberation and may result in enslaving us in our inordinate desires. The strength of the free-market must be evaluated alongside of the weakness of human nature. In our current predicament, we are losing sight of people in pursuit of profit, responsibility in the face of new freedom, and common good in the search of self-interest. If we have to be veered off course and correct today's abuses as a human family, it requires more than 'market-logic', to overcome the economic polarities that negatively affect the global village. The world today is crying out for moral and spiritual wisdom that can help us navigate the path to peace.

Scholars of various academic disciplines have helped identify and analyse the terrain and some have even offered a course of action to steer in the right direction. History helps us understand our place in the unfolding course of world events, but it cannot help us understand the relationship within and among nations, but it has not given us insight into the values needed to make us a better global village. Economics helps us understand the complexities of financial transactions, but it has virtually ignored the human costs that stem from the current market system. Sociology helps us grasp human behaviour, but it has not helped us address the deeper disorders of the human heart that affect it. Psychology helps us understand our relationship with ourselves, but it has stopped short of helping us understand better our relationship with God. For the ones who have a sense of the sacred, globalisation offers a new hope for human solidarity and interconnectedness, which coexists against the re-emergence of age-old human constants like greed, selfishness, and sinfulness. I would like to quote from a website entitled, A Paradox of Our Times:

The paradox of our time in history is that we have taller buildings but shorter tempers, wider freeways but narrower viewpoints. We spend more but have less. We buy more but enjoy less. We have bigger houses and smaller families, more conveniences but less time. We have more degrees but less sense, more knowledge but less judgement, more experts yet more problems, more medicine but less wellness.

We drink too much, smoke too much, spend too recklessly, laugh too little, drive too fast, get too angry, stay up too late, get up too tired, read too little, watch TV too much, and pray too seldom. We have multiplied our possessions but reduced our values. We talk too much, love too seldom, and hate too often. We've learned how to make a living but not a life. We've added years to life, not life to years.

We've been all the way to the moon and back, but have trouble crossing the street to meet a new neighbour. We conquered outer space but not inner space. We've done larger things but not better things. We've cleaned up the air but polluted the soul. We've conquered the atom but not our prejudice. We write more but learn less. We plan more but accomplish less. We've learned to rush but not to wait. We build more computers to hold more information to produce more copies than ever, but we communicate less and less.

These are the times of fast foods and slow digestion, big men and small character, steep profits and shallow relationships. These are the days of two incomes but more divorce, fancier houses but broken homes. These are the days of quick trips, disposable diapers, throwaway morality, one night stands, overweight bodies, and pills that do everything from cheer, to quiet, to kill. It is a time when there is much in the showroom window and nothing in the stockroom (http://onespiritproject.com/paradox.shtml (accessed on August 18, 2006).

The economically prosperous parts of the world live with the modern illusion that we are more 'advanced' than the previous generations, but the paradox of our present moment comes from a spiritual emptiness. It makes us realise the paradoxical relationship between economic development and spiritual development, between the cravings of the body and the hunger of the soul, between the invisible hand of the economy, and the invisible heart of the human person. It teaches us the simplicity which has more to do with the clarity of the heart and intention than with simply having 'things'.

d) Cosmotheandric Anthropology of Religion in the Mass Technological Society

It has become obviously clear that our own culture has fallen into a dangerously unbalanced state, and now producing warped and unbalanced minds. Technology claims priority in human affairs and the whole biological world is now being supplanted by technology and that man/woman will either become a willing creature of this technology or cease to exist. Humanity has forgotten its central task of becoming human. The failure to perform that humanising task even for a single generation might set the erring community back, a whole geological epoch: indeed, there is reason to suspect that this has actually begun to happen in our time. Humans are thus losing hold on any personal life that can be called their own: they are now being turned into a 'thing' destined to be processed and reconstructed collectively by the same methods that have produced the atomic pile and the computer.

This technological age has to slow down, without this slowing down of the tempo of all activities the positive advantages of plenitude could not be sufficiently enjoyed for the congestion of time is as threatening to the good life as the congestion of space or people, and produces stresses and tensions that equally undermine human relations.

The inner stability that such a slowdown brings about is essential to the highest uses of the mind through opening that second life which one lives in reflection, and contemplation and self-scrutiny. The means to escape from the noisy crowding up of things and whatsoever wars on the divine was on the visible offerings of the classical religions: hence their emphasis was not on the technological production but on personal poise. For its effective salvation humankind will need to undergo something like a spontaneous religious conversion: one that will replace the mechanical world picture with an organic world picture, and give to the human personality, as the highest known manifestation of life, the precedence it now gives to its machines and computers. Of one thing we may be confident. If humankind is to escape its programmed self-extinction the God who saves us will not descend from the machine: he will rise up again in the human soul (c.f. Mumford, 1964: 283, 285, 393, 409).

Hence, all thinking worthy of the name now must be ecological, in the sense of appreciating and utilising organic complexity and in adapting every kind of change to the requirement not of humans alone, or of any single generation, but of all their organic partners and every part of their habitat, which is a new organic model of ecological association and self-organisation today.

Most of us who inhabit mass technological society find it difficult to understand technological impact on social reality, let alone our psyches. At this point in history, it is essential that we ask difficult and searching questions about the place of technology in our lives. What is the essence of modern technology? How does it structure our lives, our perceptions and our politics? How does it shape our psyche? What does it say about our relationship to our humanness and to the earth?

It is not a new idea that we live in mass technological society and suffer psychological addiction to specific technological products. But the picture is bigger and more complex. The social philosopher, Morris Berman, says in The Re-Enchantment of the World, "Addiction in one form or the other characterises every aspect of industrial society...dependence on alcohol, food, drugs, tobacco...is not formally different from dependence on prestige, career achievement, world influence, wealth, the need to build more ingenious bombs, or the need to exercise control over everything" (Berman, 1981).

Gregory Bateson the evolutionary philosopher, in Steps to an Ecology of Mind, points out that addictive behaviour is consistent with the Western approach to life that puts mind against the body. He concludes, "It is doubtful whether a species, having both an advanced technology and this strange polarised way of looking at its world, can survive" (Bateson,

1972:472-3). The technological revolution has developed in size and complexity to the point of cancelling our very ability to grasp their impact upon us. The socially structured scientific-technological reality that now threatens to determine every aspect of our lives, and encases the entire planet is in an out of control situation. Total immersion, loss of perspective, and loss of control tip us off to the link between psychological process of addiction and the technological system. It leads to changes in perception, behaviour, and life-style, and then to total breakdown. The hallmark of this process is out-of-control, often aimless compulsion to fill a lost sense of meaning and connectedness with substances like alcohol or experiences of fame.

Vine Deloria in the book, *We Talk, You Listen,* asserts that we technological people 'have no idea' about much of anything residing outside 'the artificial technological universe with which (we) are familiar.' Human beings evolved over the course of some three million years and a hundred thousand generations in synchronistic evolution with the natural world. We are creatures who grew from the earth, who are physically and psychologically built to thrive in intimacy with the earth. A mere three hundred generations ago, or 0.003 percent of our time on earth, humans in the Western world began the process of controlling the natural world through agriculture and animal domestication. Just five or six generations have passed since the industrial societies emerged out of this domestication process. Our experience in mass technological society is indeed 'outside the range of human experience' and by evidence of psychological distress, ecological destruction and technological control, this way of life has been 'markedly distressing' to almost everyone (c.f. Deloria, 1970: 185-7).

Though largely ignored, evidence jumps from the pages of anthropological texts suggesting that the very psychological qualities so earnestly sought in today's recovery, psychological, and spiritual movement; the social equalities for which today's social justice movements struggle valiantly; and the ecological gains sought after by today's environmental movements, are the same qualities and conditions in which our species lived for more than 99.97 percent of its existence. As human life comes to be structured increasingly by mechanistic means, the psyche restructures itself to survive. The technological construct erodes primary sources of satisfaction.

Once found the primary needs, such as physical nourishment, vital community, fresh food, continuity between work and meaning, unhindered participation in life experiences, personal choices, community decisions, and spiritual connection with the natural world. We will not be healthy in the absence of them, because these are needs we were born to have satisfied. In their absence, bereft and in shock, the psyche finds some temporary satisfaction in pursuing secondary sources like drugs, violence, sex, material possessions, and machines. While these stimulants may satisfy for the moment, they can never fulfil primary needs. And so the addictive response is born. We become obsessed with secondary sources as if our lives depend on them.

We as a society have become addicted to technology (techno-addicts); it is also an addiction to a way of perceiving, experiencing and thinking. As the world has become less organic and more dependent on techno-fixes for problems created by earlier techno-fixes, humans have substituted a new worldview for one, which once was filled with clean rushing waters, animals, constellations of stars, tales of ancestors, and people working together in sacred purpose. But the ancestors from Western world took on crucial task of redefining their worldview in a state of psychic dislocation, and so they ended up projecting a worldview that reflects the rage, terror, and dissociation of the traumatised state. They dreamed of a world not of which humans are fully part of, but one that we can define as compartmentalised and controlled. They created a linear perspective, the scientific-technological paradigm, instrumentalised reason, and created the mechanistic worldview disembodying the human self.

It will now require a collective psychological process to heal us technological people who, through a mechanistic culture, have lost touch with our essential humanity.

Discussion

After half a century of communism the previous Soviet Union, Eastern Europe and China are looking to be saved from the results of stagnation by a change to liberal capitalistic market economies. Meanwhile the United States, Germany and Japan are beginning to realise that success has created an underclass of homeless and unemployed, and massive pollution of the environment. On the psychological level, the shadow of our success, the flip side of our affluence, is the increasing problem stress and burnout, on the sociological level, it is the anomie, homelessness and fragmentation to individualism. But finally, stress cannot be dealt with by psychological or socio-economic tricks because, for the most part, it is philosophical/spiritual rather than a psychological problem, a matter of the wrong worldview.

When we live within the horizon of the economic myth we begin to consider it honourable for one to do whatever he must to make a living. Gradually we adopt what Eric Fromm called a 'marketing orientation' towards ourselves, moulding ourselves into commodities. Our success, our industry, our habit of work has produced our economic mimeses. In our current economic crisis we are lamenting our falling productivity and spending our inflated money in an environment polluted by industry. Work made modern humans great but now it usurps our souls, to inundate the earth in things and thrash, to destroy our capacity to love and wonder, somehow humans got so lost in doing that we forgot to ask, what is worth doing? What of value, are we creating – and destroying – within the economic order? Today we need to stop the world for a while and look carefully at where our industry is taking us. Our dignity as humans lies not in exhausting ourselves in work but in discovering our vocation (Keen, 1991:61-6). In this context, Anthropology of Religion must ask new questions with regard to the very purpose and meaning of life. This is very vital for the future of humankind.

Dr. Stephen Fuchs SVD who spent more than 60 years of his life in India was a student of Prof. Wilhelm Schmidt SVD. Schmidt is known for his nine volumes of the "Origin of the Idea of God". He took lot of interest in the field of religion. Dr. Fuchs SVD who inherited this tradition continued this interest in his research on Dalits and Tribals of India. His volume on the "Origin of Man and His Culture", "Social Origins", "The Aboriginal Tribes of India" and many other of his research deals with the question of Anthropology of Religion. You had the privilege to hear more on this last year during the inauguration of the research seminar by Dr. S. M. Michael SVD. The lecture which I deliver now in Dr. Stephen Fuchs' honour is still further tribute to his memory and his hard work and research contribution in the field of Anthropology of Religion. I hope that this seminar will throw many more new insights in the field of Anthropology of Religion for the contemporary world.

REFERENCES

1. Bateson, Gregory, 1972. *Steps to an Ecology of Mind*, New York: Random House.
2. Bryant, M. Darrol, (ed.), 1992. Huston Smith: *Essays on World Religion*, New York: Paragon House.
3. Cannato, Juddy, 2006. *Radical Amazement: Contemplative Lessons from Black Holes Supernovas, and other Wonders of the Universe*, Notre Dam, Indiana: Sorin Books.
4. Chomsky, Noam, 2003. *Hegemony or Survival: American's Quest for Global Dominance*, London: Penguin Book.
5. Coyne, George V., SJ, and Allessandro Omizzolo, 2002. *Wayfarers in the Cosmos: The Human Quest for Meaning*, New York: Crossroad.
6. Dass, Ram, 1974. *The Only Dance There Is* (He is not to be confused with the great Indian mystic saint Swami Ramdas 1884-1963. This present Ram Dass is Richard Alpert), New York: Anchor, Doubleday Publications.
7. Davis, Paul, 1998. *The Fifth Miracle: The Search for the Origin of Life*, London: Penguin.
8. Deloria, Vine, 1970. *We Talk, You Listen*, New York: Delta.
9. Edwards, Denis, 2004. *Breath of Life; A Theology of the Creator Spirit*, Maryknoll, NY: Orbis Books.
10. Friedmann, Thomas, 2003. *Longitudes and Attitudes: The World in the Age of Terrorism*, New York: Anchor Books.

11. Fung, Jojo M., 2002. "Towards a Paradigm Shift in Mission amongst the Indigenous People in Asia," FABC Papers, No.105.

12. Giddens, Anthony, 1999. *Runaway World: How Globalisation is Reshaping our Lives*, London.

13. Gorman, Margaret (ed.). 1985. *Psychology and Religion*, New York: Paulist Press.

14. Groody, Daniel G., 2007. *Globalisation, Spirituality and Justice*, Maryknoll, NY: Orbis Books.

15. Hawken, Paul, 2007. *Blessed Unrest: How the Largest Movement in the World Came to into Being and why No One Saw it Coming*, New York: Viking Publications.

16. Hawking, Stephen, 1988. *A Brief History of Time: From Big Bang to Blackholes*, New York: Bantham.

17. Hubbard, Barbara Marx, 2001. *The Emergence: The Shift from Ego to Essence*, Charlottesville, VA: Hampton Roads Publishing Company Inc.

18. Zizioulas, John, 1975. "Human Capacity and Human Incapacity: A Theological Exploration of Personhood," *Scottish Journal of Theology*.

19. Karokaran, Anto, 1978. *Evangelisation and Diakonia*, Bangalore: Dharmaram Publications.

20. Keen, Sam, 1991. *Fire in the Belly: On Being a Man*, New York: Bantam Book.

21. Morris, Berman, 1981. *The Re-Enchantment of the World*, NY, Cornell Univ. Press.

22. Mumford, Lewis, 1964. *The Myth of Machine: The Pentagon of Power*, London: Seeker and Worburg.

23. Overtone, James Alexander, 1988. "Shamanic Realism: Latin American Literature and Shamanic Perspective" in *Shaman* 6 (Spring).

24. Radhakrishnan, S., 1968. *Religion and Culture*, Delhi: Orient Paperback.

25. Radcliffe, Timothy, 1987. "A Theological Assessment of Sociological Explanation". In Robin Gill (ed.) *Theology and Sociology: A Reader*, New York: Paulist Press.

26. Rees, Martin, 1997. *Before the Beginning: Our Universe and Others*, London: Touchstone.

27. Roszak, Theodore, (ed.), 1995. *Ecopsychology: Restoring the Earth Healing the Mind,* San Francisco: Sierra Club Book.

28. Sorokin, Pitrim A., 1954. *The Ways and Power of Love,* Templeton Foundation Trust Publications.

29. Swimme, Brain, 1997. *The Hidden Heart of the Cosmos: Humanity and the New Story,* New York: Orbis Books, Maryknoll.

30. Toynbee, Arnold, 1979. *An Historian's Approach to Religion* [2nd edition] New York: Oxford University Press.

5

Anthropology of Religion

Vijoy S. Sahay

In Anthropology, if any topic could be said, to have drawn the attention of maximum number of internationally acclaimed anthropologists in the world, ever since the inception of the discipline, and has covered the maximum number of pages in anthropological literature, it is, with little doubt, the subject matter of Religion. To quote Paul Bohannan (1963) " There is probably no single subject with which Anthropology concerns itself today on which the literature is larger than that on religion, specially, the Tribal Religion." It is also the only anthropological topic, on which, there have been dozens of monumentally original minds at work, such as, that of Edward Burnett Tylor, Sir James Frazer, R.R. Marret, R.H. Codrington, Max Muller, Father Wilhelm Schmidt, Bronislaw Kasper Malinowski, Levy-Bruhl, Emile Durkheim, Max Weber, Robert Redfield, Mckim Marriot, M.N. Srinivas, L.P. Vidyarthi, and many more.

Etymologically, the English word "religion" is derived from the Middle Age English 'religioun', which, in turn, has derived from Old French 'religion.' However, the root word seems to have come from Latin word 'religo', which means "good faith." A yet another explanation is that the word has derived from Latin word "religâre", which means 'to tie fast.' Whereas the definitions, meaning, and concept of religion has differed from time to time and from space to space, which we shall briefly discuss in the proceeding paragraphs; at the very outset, I take this opportunity to submit that the Sanskrit or Hindi word 'Dharma', also called 'Dhamma' in Buddhist and Pali texts, has been very wrongly translated into English as 'Religion.' As per the ancient Hindu scriptures, Dharma has two-fold meanings; first, the law of nature, and secondly, one's duty. In order to make clear my point of view, I would like to furnish only three simple sentences that would precisely reveal the inherent and succinct meaning of Dharma in ancient Indian scriptures, such as: It is the Dharma of fire to burn and provide heat; it is the Dharma of ice to cool everything; it is the Dharma of a King to protect his subjects. In the first two sentences, the inherent meaning of Dharma is 'the law of nature', and in the last sentence, it points to 'one's duty.' In any case, in this lecture, I would not go into the details of the meaning and implications of the term Dharma, as enunciated in the ancient Hindu texts, which I have discussed in some of my articles earlier (Sahay 2008, 2009). Instead, I would confine my discussion only to the very concept of 'Religion' as held by the western scholars, chiefly the anthropologists and other social scientists.

The earliest concept and definition of religion in the western dictionaries was that Christianity alone was a religion, and the rest were pagans. Later, the western scholars considered Christianity, Judaism, and Islam as the World Religions, and the rest were, according to them, irreligious and hedonistic. Clubbing together of Christianity, Judaism, and Islam was because all the three sought their origins from Abraham, the first of the great Biblical patriarchs, father of Isaac, and the traditional founder of the ancient Hebrew nation. Abraham is also considered by Muslims as Prophet and ancestor of the Arab peoples through his son Ishmael; therefore, some people preferred to call the above three religions, also, as Abrahamic religions.

Problem of Definition

Though the famous Canadian anthropologist, Irving Hexham (1993) from the University of Calgary, Alberta, in his famous book *Concise Dictionary of Religion*, prepared a list of definitions of religion furnished by various authors and theologians, however, defining the term 'religion' has always been fraught with difficulty. Many people in the past have focused on a very narrow definition that matched the individual's own religion. In western world, some equated 'religion' with 'Christianity', and thus, considered that two, out of every three human beings in the world, as non-religious. A humorous case could be cited from Henry Fielding's novel *Tom Jones* (1749), where one of its characters speaks, "By religion, I mean Christianity, by Christianity, I mean Protestantism, and by Protestantism, I mean the Church of England as established by law."

Some definitions have focused too narrowly on only few aspects of religion, and have tended to exclude those religions that do not fit well in their scheme. In this context Kile Jones has very aptly wrote in his Essay on Defining Religion, "It is apparent that religion can be seen as a theological, philosophical, anthropological, sociological, and psychological phenomenon of human kind. To limit religion to only one of these categories is to miss its multifaceted definition" (source: from the website).

While in perfect agreement with Kile Jones, I also deem it pertinent here to refer to some of the definitions of 'religion' furnished by social scientists in general, and anthropologists in particular. To begin with, Immanuel Kant (1898), in his Critique of Practical Reason, suggested that in essence, religion is "the recognition of all our duties as divine commands."

Edward Burnett Tylor (1871) in his monumental book Primitive Culture defined religion as "belief in supernatural being",

For James Frazer (1922), religion is "a propitiation or conciliation of powers superior to man which are believed to direct or control the course of nature and human life."

Emile Durkheim (1912) elucidates religion by making distinction between the domains of 'sacred' and the 'profane.' According to him, religion is "a unified system of beliefs and practices related to sacred things." Durkheim considered religion as 'sacred', and differentiated it from 'profane.' Sacred was that which generated either fear or reverence, and profane was that which was not sacred.

For Brownislaw Kasper Malinowski (1948), religion "relieves anxiety and enhances social integration."

William James (1902) in his book Varieties of Religious Experiences suggested that religion is "the belief that there is an unseen order, and that our supreme good lies in harmoniously adjusting ourselves thereto."

For Karl Marx (1884) "Religion is the sigh of the oppressed creature, the heart of a heartless world, and the soul of soulless conditions. It is the opium of the people."

For the noted American Essayist and Critic, H.L. Mencken, "...single function (of religion) is to give man access to the powers which seem to control his destiny, and its single purpose is to induce those powers to be friendly to him" (source: from the website).

According to Jerry Moyer, "Religion is a system of beliefs by which a people reduce anxiety over natural phenomena through some means of explication" (source: from the website).

Anthony Wallace in his book Religion: An Anthropological View (1966) defined religion as "a set of rituals, rationalized by myth, which mobilizes supernatural powers for the purpose of achieving or preventing transformations of state in man or nature."

Clifford Geertz in his article Religion As Cultural System (1966) defines religion as "...a system of symbols which acts to establish powerful, pervasive, and long-lasting moods and motivations in men by formulating conceptions of a general order of existence and clothing these conceptions with such an aura of factuality that the moods and motivations seem uniquely realistic."

Thus, we observe that there is no unanimous definition of religion; though Tylor's definition that "religion is belief in supernatural being" is held as a classical definition, in that it covers both, the world religion as well as the tribal religion. There is little doubt that in both the religions, there is belief in supernatural being.

Theories on Religion

If we examine the definitions and concepts of various scholars, it emerges that there are three schools of thought with regard to religion, which are as follows:

1. Theories related to origins.
2. Functional theory.
3. Psychological-functional theory.

E. B. Tylor, Sir James Frazer, R. R. Marret, and Max Muller are the chief exponents of the origin theory. Tylor's concept is known as 'Animism'; Frazer explains religion in term of evolutionary sequence of Magic, Religion, and Science; Marret calls his concept as 'Animatism'; and Max Muller's theory is called 'Naturism.' The most elaborate Functional explanation has been furnished by Durkheim; and the Psychological Functional theory is represented by Malinowski.

In his concept of Animism, Tylor (1871) said that the origin of religion took place because of people's belief in 'soul', i.e. anima in Greek. Primitive man could not distinguish between the death and sleep; he did not understand the cause of 'echo' of his sound, nor did he know the cause of his shadow; he could not explain the cause of 'dreams' while asleep, and in dreams he often met his 'ancestors', and travelled to far off places. All this generated in his mind the concept of 'soul' and its 'immortality.' Thus, Tylor presented his scheme as such: that the origin of religion took place from the concept of Soul to Ancestor Worships to Polytheism to Monotheism.

Frazer, in the Golden Bough (1893-1912) suggested that primitive man was quite ignorant of the causal explanation of catastrophes and various natural calamities that he witnessed in his daily life; and thus, lived in constant fear and periods of crises. This gave rise to the concept of a 'supernatural power' in the mind of the so called 'savage'. According to Frazer, magic, religion, and science are the three gradual stages in the growth of human culture. They are, in essence, the three ways of tiding over the crises. In the course of development of human culture, the first stage was that of magic, when man attempted to control that supernatural power by organizing certain rituals, and thus grappled with the crises. The method of magic was the method of 'coercion.' After long experience, man learnt that the supernatural power could not be controlled; instead, that should be appeased and propitiated through the methods of prayer and sacrifice. Thus was the emergence of religion. And when man began to understand and unfold the causal explanations of the mysteries of nature, including all natural catastrophes, the era of science began.

Marret, a disciple of Tylor, in *The Threshold of Religion* (1909) suggested that primitive man believed that 'supernatural power' existed in every animate and inanimate being and things, and that too in different quantum as per the size and/or the magnitude of the object. Following Marret, Codrington coined the term 'manaism'. He said that the Melanesians believed in 'mana'; accordingly, the stronger and bigger the object, the more the mana, and smaller and feebler the object, the lesser the mana. However, Tylor's animism gained more acceptance, endurance, and popularity in the anthropological and academic world than Marret's animatism.

Max Muller's Naturism suggested that throughout the world, in all time and space, man has propitiated natural objects, such as the Sun, the Moon, the Stars, the Rivers, the Mountains, the Trees, et cetera. Therefore, the origin of religion has to be sought in 'nature'. He further explained that in all ancient religions and civilizations, the gods and goddesses had anthropomorphic forms, sheer because of 'error of language.' We use the same verbs for the natural and inanimate objects that we use for ourselves or any living being, such as, the Sun rises, the rivers meet, water falls, or the tree stands, and likewise. Thus, the use of such verbs, unconsciously and un-deliberately, gave rise to the anthropomorphic forms of natural objects.

Of all the functional explanations on religion, Durkheim's concept holds utmost prominence. In the Elementary Forms of Religious Life (1912), he took up the case of Arunta Totemism as his starting point. The Aruntas, an aboriginal group of Australia, were considered by Durkheim as a people living at the lowest level of technology, hence the most primitive. He believed that their religion would be the earliest form of religion. For Durkheim, society was 'super organic.' He proclaimed, society sui-gereris i.e. society has a life of its own. In his personal life, Durkheim was an atheist; however, on account of his over emphasis on 'social fact' and 'social solidarity', he is supposed to regard society as his 'deity.' He said that individuals merely constituted the society. Society ensured its own survival. He stressed upon 'collective consciousness '

Arunta religion was also the result of collective consciousness, according to Durkheim. He said that the Aruntas were divided into twelve totemistic groups. Each totem was an edible item. Each group refrained from eating its own totem; thus, the Arunta society, living in difficult ecological setting, ensured its survival by regulating the supply of food to its members by imposing self restrain; and thus, they maintained a counterbalance between their ecological set up in which they lived, and procurement of foodstuff that they received from that set up.

Malinowski's concept on religion is a mix of Frazer's and Durkheim's. His concept, as a matter of fact, emerged out of exigency and his own personal experience. This has been very succinctly discussed in the book *They Studied Man* (1961) by Abram Kardiner and Edward Prebble. Once, Malinowski accompanied the Trobrianders on their ceremonial voyage of Kula. Midway, they were trapped in a storm. The waves were very high, and the voyagers on primitive type of canoes were struggling hard to save the canoe from getting overturned or capsized. While all the voyagers were busy in protecting the canoe and their lives, the Shaman on board the canoe was continuously trying to invoke the spirits, supposedly under his control, to protect the life of all, and help them fight the crisis. Malinowski observed that the very presence of the Shaman infused lots of confidence among all; and they were confident that in the presence of Shaman, howsoever strong might be the storm, no mishap would occur. Such was the psychological effect of mere presence of the Shaman and his effort to invoking spirits for protection of all. Malinowski says, "then and there I came to know what the function of magic and religion was."

Of all the anthropological studies on religion, Anthony Wallace's (1931) study also deserves mention. Instead of seeking either the origin or the function, Wallace discusses about the organization of religious beliefs and practices. He has arranged them into four categories, viz. Individual Cult, Shamanistic Cult, Communal Cult, and Ecclesiastical Cult. Without going into details of each with examples, his ideas could be summed up as follows:

In Individual Cult, he says that every individual in a society, practising any religion, is a religious practitioner in his own way. In Shamanistic Cult, a Shaman is a part-time religious practitioner. There are times, when all the members of a group become religious practitioners for a specific time and occasion. This he calls Communal Cult. And in Ecclesiastical Cult, full-time religious practitioners are appointed, and hierarchy of such practitioners could be found there, such as found in the organized World Religions.

Tylor's Animism Vis-à-vis Tribal Religions of India

Edward Burnett Tylor, no doubt, is considered to be one of the most influential personalities among the mid-19th century anthropologists. Though, not even a graduate, but because of his scholarship, he was first appointed as a Lecturer in 1884, then Reader, and finally, occupied the Chair of a Professor of Anthropology in Oxford; and thus, became the First Teacher of Anthropology in the world. We remember him for his following significant contributions:

1. For his classical definition of culture.
2. For his minimal definition of religion.
3. For his concept of Animism
4. For his statistical analysis of couvade as a 'Cultural Survival.'

In the following paragraphs, I would like to discuss Tylor' Animism only. Tylor's animism was subjected to criticism during the fag end of the 19th century itself; and finally, the school of evolutionism, to which Tylor was one of its chief exponents, itself was completely denied, dumped, and buried for next several decades, until V. Gordon Child dug its grave, and re-established it in 1936 with the publication of his book of *Man Makes Himself*. Besides a number of criticisms, it was alleged that Tylor made primitive man a philosopher. Tylor was, unquestionably, one of the most erudite thinkers and scholars of his time. What in fact, he did was, that he put himself in place of a primitive man, and thus, began to seek the causal explanations of differences between sleep and death, meeting one's ancestors in dreams, the echo of one's sound, et cetera. Although, he had first hand experience of the Mexico and the Mexicans, he was also, one of the arm-chair anthropologists of his time. Had he witnessed the contemporary 'savages' that how barely they managed their meals both the times in a day, I believe, Tylor would have furnished a different explanation. Tylor assumed that primitive man must have thought, as he (Tylor himself) did. But he forgot to assume, first, that the entire mental faculty of the primitive man was directed towards procuring daily and regular food for their survival, either by hunting or by gathering, than leisurely analysing the philosophical problems; secondly, in comparison to primitive man, Tylor's mental faculty was highly developed and enlightened. Tylor's Animism in general, and evolutionism in particular was rejected on the grounds, interalia, that all its exponents depended on conjectural history, over emphasized upon Psychic Unity of Mankind, were ethnocentric, and depended upon Comparative Method.

I do not intend here to go into the details of criticisms, either of Tylor or of the school of evolutionism. However, I deem it necessary to affirm that in my personal view as an anthropologist, Tylor's Animism has misled the Indian scholars and administrators for over a century; and very tacitly, it has done irreparable damage to the fabric of Indian society in general and the tribal society in particular. It is unfortunate that even to this day; the tribal religion in India, is very wrongly, referred to as 'Animistic.' The starting point in Tylor's Animism is 'belief in soul.' Belief in soul is not exclusive with the so called 'primitive man', or the 'savages', as the simple societies ere referred to in the 19th Century. In all the world religions, be it, Christianity, Islam, Hinduism,

Buddhism, Jainism, et cetera, the followers believe in soul. Then why do we say that only the tribesmen believe in soul?

Tylor's concept of Animism is also diametrically opposite to the concept of Father Wilhelm Schmidt. Schmidt categorically asserts with empirical examples, that the so called 'primitive' or the 'savages' man, practiced Monotheism first; and had the idea of a supreme God. He explained in his theory of Primitive Monotheism that primitive religion, among almost all tribal peoples, began with an essentially Monotheistic concept of a high god – usually, a sky God- who was a benevolent creator. Professor Schmidt theorized that human beings, first believed in a God, who was the First Cause of all things and Ruler of Heaven and Earth, before men and women began to worship a number of gods. Thus, Father Wilhelm Schmidt professed that Monotheism was the earliest religion of this planet. According to him, there had been a primitive Monotheism before men and women began practicing Polytheism. The concept of Sing Bonga among the Mundas, and several other tribes of the State of Jharkhand is a testimony of this. Religion of the Mundas, the Oraons, the Santhal, the Kharia, the Hos, and almost all the 32 tribal groups living in the state of Jharkhand is referred to as 'Animistic'; whereas, empirical studies suggest that they all consider the Sing Bonga as their 'Supreme Deity' or 'Supreme God.'

Let us examine who did Tylor referred to as 'Animists'? Ever since the days of explorations during the medieval period, the travellers, the explorers, the missionaries, and the colonial administrators discovered new lands and new people, and their cultures. The cultures of newly discovered people were diametrically opposite to the medieval European culture that was technologically most advanced then. Such explorers, travellers, missionaries and colonial administrators also wrote about the land, the people, and their cultures. The most striking thing that attracted the attention of the Europeans was the uncommon, and sometimes strange beliefs and rituals of such people whom the Europeans referred to by such obsolete terms as, the 'savage', the 'exotic', or the 'natives'. Thus, the literature on the beliefs and rituals of the so called 'savage' people began to accumulate; and within a period of two to three hundred years, it turned out to be exhaustive to behold.

All the mid-19th Century evolutionists, including Tylor, based their concepts and theories on the basis of study of such literature. Barring, L. H. Morgan, who had at least some knowledge of the Iroquois, none had ever studied any primitive group. Interestingly, it is said that James Frazer, who wrote volumes after volumes, particularly on 'savage man and his mind', was once asked whether he had ever seen a savage. He replied, "God forbid, I haven't ever...and I don't ever want to..."

Why I want to draw the attention of the readers to all this is that during the days of exploration, the new lands, and particularly the new people, who were discovered by the explorers, travellers, and the colonialists, had mostly lived in complete 'geographical and social isolation'. Barring their neighbouring tribesmen, they had little contact and interaction with the outside world. When the account of their cultures, beliefs, rituals, customs, et cetera, which were completely different from the European's, were studied by the mid-19th Century scholars, their fertile mind began to speculate; and each such scholar, like Tylor, Morgan, Frazer, Henry Main, McLennan, Bachofen, Adolf Bastian, Theodore Waitz, et cetera, also began to make conjectural history of human culture in general, and that of such institutions like family, marriage, kinship, religion, totemism, political organization, economic organization, et cetera in particular. Their basic premise was that all cultures in general, and all the social institutions in particular had independently developed because of 'psychic unity of mankind' from simple to complex forms; and that the cultures of the contemporary savages represented the past savagery.

Tylor called the religion of such people as Animism. In principle, I have little objection to the animistic theory, except that Tylor was also, like other evolutionists, ethnocentric, in that he believed that Monotheism was the most developed form of religion. Every scholar has the liberty to think and interpret the social and cultural phenomena in his own way, as did Tylor, or Morgan, or Frazer, or any of the classical evolutionists of the mid-19th century. However, the greatest anomaly that I find is that whereas Tylor's Animism was already rejected by the end of the 19th century itself; the Indian scholars still carry this obsolete concept of animism in their mind, and refer to the Tribal Religion of India as 'Animistic.' Moreover, if we agree to what Father Wilhelm Schmidt said with regard to the origin of the idea of God in his book *The Origin and Growth of Religion* (1931), then we have to agree that Monotheism was the earliest form of religion, practiced by the so called 'savages.' Thus we find a direct contradiction between Tylor and Father Schmidt. According to Tylor, Monotheism developed lastly in human history; and according to Father Schmidt, Monotheism was the earliest form of religion on this planet, and practiced by our earliest ancestors.

Anyway, I wouldn't like to join this debate whether polytheism or monotheism appeared first in human history and culture. My central point is that in no case, the Indian tribesmen could be called Animists. Unfortunately, to the best of my knowledge, as early as in 1881 Census, when the popularity of Tylor and his *Primitive Culture* was at its peak throughout the length and breadth of the British Empire, the colonial administrators in India dubbed the religion of the Indian Tribes as Animists, as they did with the tribes of Africa, Australia, Oceania, et cetera. I hardly believe that the enumerators of the 1881 Census ever knew the complexities of the concept of Animism. I also wonder that during the last one hundred and thirty years since the first Census in India was conducted, and at least, particularly after independence, none of the Indian anthropologists also, ever raised this problem of tribal identity. To call the religion of the Indian tribesmen as Animists is misnomer, and quite misleading, at least to the academic world.

If believing upon 'anima', i.e. 'soul'/'spirit' is Animism, then I would very firmly say that people of all the religions in the world are Animists first, thereafter they may be monotheists or polytheists. Everyday we watch in Television in Discovery or History Channel about the haunted houses or places in America, which is, scientifically and technologically, the most developed nation in the world. The Americans, the British, and others too believe in 'spirits' or 'souls.' Then, why are they not called animists? Why only the Indian tribesmen are called Animists?

Secondly, all institutions in a society, whether it is family, marriage, kinship, or religion, largely emerge and develop commensurate with its ecology. Accordingly, if we examine the social and geographical conditions in which the tribes of Africa, Australia, Oceania, Papua New Guinea, and even the 'natives' of the North and the South American Continents lived before the advent of the Europeans, we discover marked differences between them and the Indian tribesmen. While the Indian tribesmen, though mostly lived in and around hills and forests, have never lived in that degree of social and geographical isolation, as did the tribes of Africa, America, Australia, or Tasmania. Did anybody know about the Australian aborigines, Tasmanians (who have become extinct now), Papua New Guineans, and the tribes of the South Seas before 1790, until James Cook first arrived in Tasmania? Did anybody know about thousands of American Indian peoples living in the North and South American Continents before 1492, until Christopher Columbus first set foot on the New World? Very simple answer is that nobody did know.

On the contrary the oral traditions of over 90% of Indian tribes suggest that despite living in inaccessible areas of the Indian Sub-continent, they have interacted not merely with the neighbouring non-tribals but with the Great Traditions of the Hindus, or the ancient Indian civilization. Could this fact of oral history be denied? One could only intentionally deny. Economic interaction of the Indian tribesmen with their neighbouring non-tribesmen has been an age-old phenomenon. During such interactions both have borrowed a number of cultural traits from each other, and imbibed them into their own culture. Examples are replete to refer to several tribal traditions and rituals having been adopted by the non-tribals. And, except perhaps a few parts of the Northeast, in the entire tribal region of the country, we may find the tribesmen propitiating and worshipping Mahadeva, i.e. Lord Shiva. There is hardly any tribal group in Central India, where the traditions of Mahabharata and the Ramayana have not entered into the life and culture of the people. There are folk songs relating to these epics among the tribesmen.

In addition to the above, let us take the example of the Tribal Religion of the state of Jharkhand, and its adjoining states. Almost all the tribal groups believe in one Supreme God, Sing Bonga, i.e. Sun God. Numerically, the largest tribal group in the country, the Santhals, believe in 'Thakurji', as supreme God. Where did this concept of Thakurji come from? All celebrate Karma and Sarhul festivals with great enthusiasm. Karma and Sarhul are concerned with nature worship, and not 'spirit' or 'soul' worship. Sarana is held sacred by all, not only the tribesmen, but even by the non-tribesmen. Sarana, in no case, is concerned with anybody's 'soul', but the benevolent spirits and deities reside there. A Sarana consists of a flock of trees in one corner of the village, wherefrom cutting even a branch of any tree is prohibited. Deep inside the forests and along the hills, there are sacred places called Mahadev Sthan (place).

I would also like to cite another example from the tribes of Bastar region. In times of crisis, the tribes of Bastar propitiate different kinds of Matas and Devas, as suggested by the Sirha (the medicine man). In one of my articles on Bastar (Sahay: 2000), I have referred to the names of 54 Matas and 65 Devas that the tribes of Bastar propitiate on different occasions. When faced with any crisis, one consults a Sirha, and at his advice, a tribesman goes to a Gharawa (a community expert in bell metal craftsmanship living in Bastar), and approaches him to prepare a statue/image of the particular Mata or Deva, referred to by the Sirha. Thus, the image is procured by the tribesman, who in turn gives it to the Sirha for propitiation with the belief that after propitiation by the Sirha, his crisis would be over.

I dare not challenge the very concept of Animism by Tylor, whom I regard as the 'Father of Modern Anthropology.' However, I categorically deny and reject dubbing the religion of the Indian tribes as Animists. Where do we find Animism among the Indian tribesmen? Do we find it in concept of Sing Bonga? Do we find it in the concept of Thakurji among the Santhals? Do we find it in the celebrations of Karma and Sarhul? Do we find it in the worship of Mahadev? Or do we find it in the concept and worship of the Matas and the Deveas in Bastar? Deep inside the forests in central India, ancient temples could be found dedicated to Shiva, Kali, Durga, or any of the Hindu pantheons. In many such temples the tribal priests could also be found. For example, in Dewari temple in Ranchi District, the priest belongs to Munda tribe, at Ramrekha temple in Simdega District, the priest belongs to a Bedia tribe, and in the temple of Hinglajin Mata in Bastar, the priest belongs to Halba tribe. Numerous such examples could be found from different parts of tribal India.

Conclusion

I do not intend to say that the Indian tribesmen are Hindus; because, a Hindu is always a born Hindu, otherwise not a Hindu. Hinduism is a closed social system. This is its demerit and merit as well. Its demerit is that it is based upon hierarchical caste order, under which a number of unprivileged groups have lived for over thousands of years subjugated and exploited by the privileged groups. And its merit is that despite physical and cultural onslaughts over centuries by invaders, sometimes Muslims and sometimes by others, it still survives and flourishes as majority population of the country.

There are fundamental organizations in the country, which for political reasons maintain that the tribesmen are Hindus. But, as an anthropologist, I completely disagree with them. Instead, I maintain that the tribesmen in India, despite living in comparative geographical and social isolation, from time immemorial, have also lived in close interaction with the non-tribals, which have necessarily been Hindus. And during this age-old interaction many of the Hindu cultural elements have been adopted by the tribesmen, and the vice-versa is also true. Originally, they were nature worshippers, as they lived in the lap of nature; forests and hills have always been necessary components of their eco-system. However, in no case, their religion could be called Animistic. After the advent of the Europeans, mainly the British and the Missionaries, the tribal situation in India began to change. Barring a few exceptions, proselytization to Christianity among the tribal groups started, which accelerated by leaps and bounds during the post-independence era. Well, India is a secular country. One may adopt any religion that suits him, his family, or his group. The tribesmen in India have of course converted to Christianity, to Islam, or in some parts to Buddhism.

However, regretfully, sometime back, I read a book written by a Christian tribal scholar of Jharkhand (I do not recall the reference), in which I found that on the basis of religion, the Indian tribesmen were divided into three categories, as such:

1. The Christian Tribal
2. The Hindu Tribal
3. The Animists

I am sorry to say that such categorization of Indian tribes on the basis of religion cannot be acceptable, at least to anthropologists. For, it is not only fundamentally wrong, but seems to be intentionally designed to encourage the divisive forces in society in general and country in particular. I wonder who the Hindu tribes are! A tribe is a tribe. Of course, during the thousands of years of continued interaction with the non-tribals, the tribesmen have absorbed some elements of Hindu life and culture in varying degrees. It is a matter of degree alone that some groups have adopted more and others less of a Hindu life-style. But can anybody find the demarcation line that wherefrom a group is called a Hindu tribe, otherwise he remains an Animist? Can anybody say that at what point of time and space an Animist tribe was formally converted to Hinduism? As an anthropologist, I deem it my duty to warn the academicians, planners, policymakers, as well as laymen to categorically reject such misinterpretation and misrepresentation of tribal situation in India. Therefore, if the Indian tribesmen have to be divided on the basis of religion, there could be only two categories, viz. first, the converted tribesmen (be it to Christianity, or Islam, or Buddhism), and secondly, the non-converts i.e. the indigenous tribesmen. The concept of a 'Hindu Tribe' and/or an 'Animist Tribe' is a myth, created either by ignorance or by design by some vested interest groups.

REFERENCES

Codrington, R.H. 1891. *The Melanesians: Studies in their Anthropology and Folklore,* Clarendon, Oxford.

Durkheim, E. 1912, *Elementary Forms of Religious Life,* Paris: Alcon

Fielding, Henry. 1749, *The History of Tom Jones, a Foundling*: Andrew Miller, Britain.

Frazer, J.G.,1922, *The Golden Bough* (Abridged Edition). London: Macmillan.

GeertZ, Clifford 1966. Religion as a Cultural System. In *Anthropological Approaches to the Study of Religion.* Ed. Michael Banton. pp. 1–46. ASA Monographs, 3. London: Tavistock Publications.

Hex-ham, Irving, 1993, *Concise Dictionary of Religion,* Regent College Publishing.

James, William, 1902, *The Varieties of Religious Experience: A Study in Human Nature,* Longmans Green & Company.

Kant, Immanuel. 1998 (Original 1788), *Critique of Practical Reason,* Longmans Green & Company.

Kardiner, Abram & I961, *They Studied Man,* Secker and Warburg, Edward Prebble.

Levy-Bruhl, Lucian, 1926, *How Nature Think.* Trans. by Lilian A. Claire. London: G Allen.

Malinowski, B.K. 1922, *Argonauts of the Western Pacific.* London: Routledge.

--------------- 1926, *Myth in Primitive Psychology,* New York: Norton

--------------- 1948, *Magic, Science, and Religion,* Waveland Press Inc.

Marret, R.R. 1909, *The Threshold of Religion,* Methuen, London

Marx, Karl, 1844, *A Contribution to the Critique of Hegel's Philosophy of Right,* Deutsch-Französische Jahrbücher,

Sahay, Vijoy S., 2000, Impact of Gharwa Art in the Tribal Life of Bastar: In *Contemporary Societies: Tribal World,*

Volume VI (Eds.) George Pfeffer and Deepak K. Behera, Concept Publishing Company, New Delhi

Sahay, Vijoy S. 2008, Anthropology in India: In Retrospect, Prospect, and in the Light of Globalizations and Postmodernism in *The Oriental Anthropologist*, Volume 8, No. 1 & 2, 2008.

Sahay, Vijoy S., 2009, Anthropology of the Buddha. *In Nidan-An International Journal for the Study of Hinduism*,Volume 21, 2009; Durban, South Africa.

Schmidt, (Father)1931, *The Origin and Growth of Religion*, New York: Cooper Square Wilhelm Publishers.

Tylor, E.B. 1871, *Primitive Culture*, London: J Murray.

Wallace, Anthony 1966, *Religion: An Anthropological View*, New York: Random House.

Weber, M. 1930, *The Protestant Ethic and the Spirit of Capitalism*, London: G. Allen Unwin. Translated by Talcott Parsons.

SECTION-II

6

Religions Today: Perspectives for the Contemporary Society

K. Jose SVD* & Manoj Antony SVD**

India had been the home of all religions that have a worldwide presence today. Every religion admits and promotes certain concern and correlation of the divine with the humans. Here one refers to the term 'religion' as an aspect of India's cultural traditions. Indic religions namely, Hinduism, Buddhism, Jainism, and Sikhism originated here. Other religions like Christianity, Islam, Judaism, Zoroastrianism and the Bahai faith arrived here at different points of time during the last two millennia. So all these religions together with other indigenous religions have impacted the lives of the people of the country for hundreds of years and continue their effect to this day.

Religions in India: Contemporary Perspectives

Our country's 'tryst with destiny,' as Nehru famously puts it, started in the shadow of the pain of partition. To safe guard this fragile multi-religious and pluri-cultural arena, the new nation chose to be a secular country. Scholars such

* Director, Sanskriti-NEICR, Guwahati – 781 014, Assam

** Assistant Director, Sanskriti-NEICR, Guwahati - 781 014, Assam as Andre Beteille, Dipankar Gupta, and T. K. Oomman continue to defend an areligious rather than anti-religious reading of the Indian constitution. From this perspective, the cause of communal violence is not that the state is too secular but rather that it is not secular enough, not that the state should use its influence to curb or end religion, but rather that the state should be neutral among contesting religious groups and concerning the larger question of religion versus nonreligion as a cultural desideratum (Demerath and Straight, 1997).

We note that religions often profess great values but in the realm of practice they fail to live by the profound teachings. As a result, often religious instead of being an opportunity to be at the service of humanity as a whole, strives to dominate and overpower the other systems of beliefs. The serious threat we encounter is the religious fundamentalism often because of its fanatical disapproval of the people who even narrowly disagree and deviate from the narrow definitions of a particular religion. It is time for us to learn to live in pluralistic society to guard against the tendencies of fundamentalist groups who are making religions sources of conflict and violence.

The religious community of North East India mainly comprises of Hinduism, Islam, Christianity, Sikhism and Buddhism. Apart from this, various indigenous groups also follow Animism, Tantricism, Brahminism and Vaishnavism. Despite such vast differences in their religious faiths and beliefs, all the people within the region live in perfect peace and harmony with each other. The understanding of a religion as an integral part of every human community is accepted in the region. Christianity or Islam, for example, has a basic characteristic which is the relationship of human beings with the Divine. These religions are, in fact, defined on their belief system or conceptualization. But, in the case of religions like Hinduism or Jainism religion is much more than a belief system. Religion, according to these faiths is a way of life in harmony with divine and human in its various dimensions.

These exceptions in secular state policy have festered and exacerbated over the years. From a neutral vantage point, religious personal obligations are fine as long as they do not contradict at least the minimal rights and responsibilities of the citizens at large. Rather than use religious status as a basis for reserving jobs, some argue that this should be based on more general socio-economic disadvantage of the individuals and communities. At any case, it is clear that India's recently increasing "communal violence" reflects the tendency for state leaders and state structures to become embroiled in religious conflicts. As concessions made to one group require concessions made to its rival, constructing state policy has come to resemble the uneven legs of a chair: and the seat of power becomes increasingly unstable.

Religion in spite of its many and apparent limitations can be an effective agent to purify the secular domain of its dehumanizing factors of poverty, fundamentalism, ecological degradation that have become a bane of contemporary Indian scenario. Hence, religion in the Indian cultural setting traditionally permeates virtually all aspects of life, not through mechanical diffusion, but in an integrated, holistic perspective (Radhakrishnan, 1927).

Faith Traditions and Sacred Scriptures

Faith tradition is the tangible and ultimate source of everyday observance of religion. When traditions are ratified by the written scriptures it becomes an authority to guide and teach the generations to come. We see in al the major and world religious traditions scriptures are revered as sacred and authoritative. In Hinduism the Rishis see the eternally resounding 'vac' (word). Traditions have that its holiest texts, the Vedas have been orally transmitted for three millennia or more – for most of the time, in explicit preference to writing them down. Sacred Scriptures are the sacred writings of a religion that usually have much claim to divine origin and have supreme authority in the religious and moral life of the adherents. Though every religion will name it differently, based on the historical and geographical-cultural context the reality itself is same. Ekam Sat Vipraha Bahudaha Vadanti (God is only one but the learned call it by the different names). The deepest and truest identity of any religion is fostering brotherhood and promoting friendship among peoples with the ideal of Vasudhiva Kutumbakam (the whole world as one family).

Islam speaks of the descent of the Word of God in the 'sacred night'. Every Muslim is to be endowed with this ability to find God in oneself and in the other. Every single birth of a child is a sign of God's presence in the world. He is the Sun without whom there is no sunlight, and a Tree without whom there is no shade (Muhammad Zia Ullah, 1984:5). But unfortunately today extreme form of materialism has buried the sacred seed of God's love and His very existence, in some of the societies and traditions. The Islamic spirituality that is to be practiced and lived by every Muslim is an invitation, all about knowing, loving and obeying God as revealed in the Holy Quran and promulgated and exemplified by the Prophet in hadith (traditions of the Prophet). When one comes to Buddhism it is the enlightenment bestowed on Gautama. He teaches this to the adherence through the eight fold paths. Hurt not others in ways that you yourself would find hurtful – this is an invitation to know the other and love the other following the eight fold paths.

Pope John Paul II said with reference to the events of Sept. 11: "We must not let what has happened lead to a deepening of divisions. Religion must never be used as a reason for conflict." Religious believers must take the lead in building a world in which all peoples can live together in peace and brotherhood. Thus each religion is a response of the believer of that religion to the divine self-communication. In fact the Biblical revelation undergirds three basic ideas: the unity of the human race; God's universal salvific will and the eschatological convergence of all sacred history in Christ.

Religions in the Tribal Cultures of North East India

North East India is well known for its tribal cultures. Each and every ethnic community has its own distinctive cultural and religious beliefs which are often associated with their day to day activities like festivals, rites of passage, birth, initiation, marriage, death, agricultural operations especially Jhum cultivation, sickness, natural disasters, spirits, gods and goddesses, magic sorcery, sin, taboo and so on. As there are no written scriptures for tribal religions they are passed on orally. These are expressions of human experiences in a given society. They are found in villages, beginning from the family, clan, and society. However, anyone who observes the practice of religion among the tribals will not fail to understand that tribal concept of God and Religion are very noble though in the tribal world view, one cannot make a clear cut distinction between sacred and profane an element of unity and continuity is necessarily seen. In North East India, religions may be categorized as wholly or partially influenced by great traditions of Hinduism, Christianity and Buddhism. Yet, some others belong to those communities who retain pristine tribal faith, and, still some others, a minority group of ethnic communities having affiliations to other religions are also seen. In all these forms of religious leanings people invariably nurture and cherish a sense of the sacred in their every day existence.

Verrier Elwin in his acclaimed book *A Philosophy for NEFA* (1964:222) observes: "the people of NEFA, and of all the tribal areas throughout India, are making rapid progress in material prosperity, but this prosperity may be positively dangerous unless there a parallel spiritual and ethical revival". Yet, anyone who critically studies the concept of God or religions among the ethnic communities of North East India will certainly note that among the tribes in general there is a profound sense of the sacred in spite of their pre-literate or semi-literate condition of living. We see Tribal religions of various kinds in each of the 8 states of north east India. We have ample evidences from north east India that tribal religions are in no uncertain terms come under their own cultural traditions, yet they are in the process of change in tremendous speed and agility. Many times a grave mistake is made to enumerate them as coming under the fold of Hinduism. Anthropological knowledge makes it amply clear that they belong to indigenous tribal religions each in its own right, identity and beauty.

Tribal Religions permeates all aspects of life in North East India. Therefore, it is basically a community religion that involves the active participation in the religious beliefs, ceremonies, rituals and festivals of the community. The most distinctive characteristic of tribal religion is that it does not have any specific sacred scripture(s). The religious ethos is contained in the people's hearts, oral history and in rituals. In the tribal religion of Tripura there is a close interaction of the people with the nature in relation to rocks, forests, serpents or even the belief in the transmigration of soul and spirit. Although the worship system/religion of the indigenous Tripuri revolved round 'agriculture', it catered to all aspects of human living. There were prayers and rituals to be performed at various stages in a person's life beginning with prayer for a child in its mother's womb. The Bhakti Dharma of Sankardeva is seen in Assam which is a religion of love that binds together all the peoples irrespective of caste, creed and colour. He says God is closer to the one who takes his name in great devotion. Sankardeva's vision was to create a society wherein people of all walks of life may be considered equal, loved and appreciated (Kuruvachira et al, 2007:43).

When we come to Arunachal Pradesh we have Donyi-Poloism adhered by all tribes of Tani group. Literally the words Donyi and Polo mean the Sun and the Moon respectively. According to them the Sun or Donyi is the symbol of strength, nourishment, justice and life giving force. Efforts are being made to evolve a religion and name it as Donyi Polo religion. In Meghalaya the annual Seng Kut Snem festival is celebrated to commemorate the Seng Khasi movement to preserve, protect and uphold indigenous Khasi religion and culture. For this they did a formal organisation of the indigenous religion, which was formed in 1899 with a view to safeguarding the Khasi tradition. The four cardinal principles underlying the objectives of the organisation are: Adherence to the tenets of kinship as specified by the ancestors; Righteousness through service; love and truth and a desire to improve both mind and body; Respect for one's own fellowmen and cultivation of humility; and to work for one's country with faith in God. This is clear evidence that the Khasis are intensely religious people as they stress on Kamai ia ka hok, which they can fulfill only by means of honest work, truthfulness in thoughts and word, and justness in all their transactions. Thus religion permeates the life of a Khasi-Pnar in all its aspects because he or she must work to live and honest work is worship.

In sum, not many efforts have been made to study the religious beliefs of the tribal communities; however, religions in north east India are variously described by various writers and labeled as animism, animatism, polytheism, nature worship etc. However, all of them are giving importance to living in harmony with a higher spiritual power, promoting eco-friendly attitude and fellow feeling among the human fraternity. It is noteworthy that religions in North East India have shown praiseworthy acceptance of each other and mutual appreciation for one another. This will necessarily promote diversity of religion – a call for worshipping God in spirit and truth.

Religions: Invitation to be More Relevant

The fact that religions do not always practice what they often preach is a truth that comes never as a surprise. However, the fact is that many historical painful scars still exist in the people's psyche due to the antagonism between religions, caste injustices, and the demolition of religious sites by zealots of one religion or the other. Sadly, this adds up to tremendous amount of fears, violence and ignorant prejudices. You and I surely find it ironic that we are living in a nation full of conflicts, violence and tensions whose origins can be found in with religious institutions and their traditions. Don't we? As a result, instead of being an opportunity to travel as fellow pilgrims we strive for dominion over others. We are only painfully aware of the evil of discrimination based on class and caste, race and other affiliations still prevalent in our society which are eating into the very fabric of our existence.

However, religion, for its pitfalls, has still an aura of grace to give one of the few compelling visions for our times. It has a tremendous energy to promote peace and harmony. It has a role to play as a catalyst as the nation tries to integrate the world through a process of globalization. To hold fast to that vision religions have to reconstruct, reformulate and reinterpret their present values with a more innovative and participatory democratic ethos.

Religion in Practical Life: Call for Intense Engagement

Every religion envisages a special kind of relation between God and the World as well as God and the human beings including the created universe. On this basis, religious and social ideas and morality are well systemized. While religion is meant to foster peace, harmony and community-building, it has, sadly, of late, been a cause of division and strife. Called by any name and worshipped in any form, the ideas of God must lead one to promote life for all peoples everywhere. If religionists can come together and respond to the larger problems of life which haunt humanity it will be the greatest contribution they can make to humanity and this surely bring honour to God. Through this one might have a more harmonious society, and religion would have played a pivotal role in fostering peace (Bera, 2010:12).

All the religions in the world have enriching scriptures that contain profound teachings. There are, however, times when, while the reader understands almost whole of the holy book, she is either unable to abide by it or fails to integrate its essence in one's life. One must time and again ask a fundamental question, as to why despite our chanting, reading of scriptures and devoutly praying, the lives of many of us remain unchanged or largely unaffected. This question is more pertinent for us as we live in a country where religiosity is practiced quite seriously in public as well as in private and where much importance is attached to the Word of God in Scriptures. In India one finds temples, mosques, churches, gurudwaras and other places of worship always full (Emmanuel, 2010:8). The Bible tells us that Jesus is very stern in saying that, scrupulous and dutiful observance of religious laws and taboos can become a cover up for the lack of true religion – practicing justice and the love of God and neighbour in our lives (ref: Lk: 11/47-54). Other religions too exhort practicing of true religion with great devotion and earnestness.

Thus religion is an ideology of social commitment and social engagement. This ideology calls us to pursue paths of social transformation whose aim is to create a better human community and nation at large. That is the reason why we need to have Intense engagement with religions so as to invite all the adherents of religions to transcend their self-restrictive mentality, form multi-religious organizations and take broader perspectives within national boundaries and even develop and expand the universe of 'thinking' and become more relevant whereby affect social transformation. Our society needs to shed apathy and for this our religions need to work with more inclusive policies and programmes taking the civil society also into confidence. This will make the people empowered to stand up to the values of the religions they profess. So Religions in Practical Life shall be not mere belief system but intense engagement.

Pluralism of Religions in India: Gift & Challenge

Indian openness to pluralism of religions is a gift and a challenge. A gift because it is the way we can take the lived experience of the followers of other religions in our day-to-day life in our neighborhood, work places, on travel, in celebrations and other areas of our presence. Further, the genuine practioners of all the religions lead a morally upright life. As the Christian Faith exhorts the human soul is naturally drawn towards the one true God (Dupuis, 1992:272). This existential situation also throws up challenges as religions understand the Divine as an inexhaustible ocean into which many rivers flow or as an immense mountain to which many roads lead. The rivers and roads are compared to different religions; none of them can claim the monopoly of the Reality. This also calls different religions not to be indifferent to the followers of other religions, but a commitment to one's faith vis-à-vis a profound respect for other faith traditions. We are only too familiar with this type of a socio-cultural, religio-political and economic scenario in our country wherein fundamentalism and intolerance raise their tentacles sadly too often than days past.

Concluding Thoughts

Living in the present day calls for a rediscovery of the essence of religions. That means all the religions of today and "of the future will have to survive and flourish in a multi-cultural, multi-religious India that simply will not be homogenized;

it will have to flow with, rather than against, the currents of modernization and globalization. It will have to open its doors wide to welcome change, for in any case, it is too late to shut them" (Doniger, 2009:34). In the twenty first century religions will have to work against social exclusion, and to bring the cause of the poor to the forefront. If they rise up to the expectations of people to provide the spiritual nourishment vis a vis promote harmony between peoples and cultures they will thrive and flourish beyond any doubt. In the meantime one has to be vigilant in the clandestine efforts of some religious groups to absorb traditional religions of any zone or region of India - may it be in Khasi hills, in Assam plains, or in Arunachal or else where in north east India. The variety of practicing religions is to be appreciated and promoted because God experience is unique for various cultures based on historicity, environment and scores of other factors. Religions are paths leading to the divine; so civilized society should enhance elements of spirituality in the religions to wean away religious fanaticism and intolerance and bring in mutual respect and dialogue between people of various religions as they are children of one and only God.

REFERENCES

Bera, Gautam Kumar. 2010. Perspectives in Religion and Religious Diversity in India, Mother Teresa Centenary Lecture, Agartala, p. 12.

Doniger, Wendy, 2009. Why the Gods Can't Fail, *India Today*, 24th August, pp. 32-34.

Elwin, Verrier, 1964. *A Philosophy for NEFA*, p. 222.

Emmanuel, D., 2010. *Asian Age*, New Delhi Edition, p. 8.

Kuruvachira, J., et al. (eds.) 2007. *Readings in Cultures of North East India*, vol. 1, Dimapur, Salesian Publications, p. 43.

N.J. Demerath and Karen S. Straight, Religion, Politics, and the State: Cross-Cultural Observations In *Cross Currents*, Spring 1997, Vol. 47 Issue 1 (web article, visited on 15th Oct. 2010.)

Radhakrishnan, S., 1927. *The Hindu View of Life*, London: Allen and Unwin.

Ullah, Mohammad Zia, 1984. *Islamic Concept of God*, London: Kegan Paul International Ltd.

7

The Concept of God in Islam

Pushpa Anbu SVD

Salaam alei kum!

The essential feature that makes a human person distinct from all other beings is his/her ability to think, to reason and to speak. At the same time, we also know that from time immemorial, human beings wondered at some unseen, unknown and mysterious power which continued to influence and generate their life. They pondered over the meaning and significance of life and their inquisitiveness to know more about life here and life after death lead them to wonder and find an answer to their innermost queries of life. Today with the help of religious and social scientists, through their research on the primal and primitive societies of the earlier periods, we understand that religion and some form of religious thoughts prevailed over humankind and formed integral part their life. This kind of religious ideas and forms led to the formation of various religious beliefs and rituals. It was the belief of many of the ancient civilizations that some places, persons or rituals were sacred and possessed some form of invisible supernatural power, such as: Huaca of the Incas of Peru, Mana of Pacific Islands and Taboo of Maoris (David Stent, 1983: 1-4).

In Africa, people used fetishes or lucky charms as bearers of good luck. In some parts of the world like Africa, North and South America, among the Eskimos and the Chinese, people believed in the shaman, a medicine man or a priest who had special power to heal and foretell the future. One of the responsibilities of the shaman was to guide the souls of the departed to the end of their journey and usually they acted under the influence of an ecstatic trance. Many tribal religions all over the world believed in totems - an animal or plant or object which they believed to have possessed a special power to protect them from all possible dangers and became important part of their worship. Sir James Frazer (1854-1941), a Scottish social anthropologist, considered totemism to be earliest form of religion. There was also the practice of animism, a belief that objects possess a kind of spirit or soul, as proposed by an English anthropologist Sir Edward B Tylor (1832 – 1917). These developments in religious thought prove the fact that human beings from the beginning of their existence had some form of religious identity and religious worship, which then became part of human identity.

With the preaching of Islam in Arabia by Prophet Muhammad, religion became the nucleus of the people. In the Islamic tradition, belief in God is one of the natural dispositions of man, where every Muslim necessarily finds meaning in life. It needs no scientific argument or logical conclusion to know if there is God or whether one has to have belief in Him. God in the Holy Quran affirms, 'On the earth are signs for those of assured faith, and also in your own selves. Will you not then see?' (51:20-21). It only proves that the existence of God is self – evident that God is found in the nature and in every individual. As a human being one needs to have the spiritual eyes to see the Reality. Every Muslim is to be endowed with this ability to find God in oneself and in the other. Every single birth of a child is a sign of God's presence in the world. He is the Sun without whom there is no sunlight, and a Tree without whom there is no shade (Muhammad Zia Ullah, 1984:5). But unfortunately today extreme form of materialism has buried the sacred seed of God's love and His very existence, in some of the societies and traditions.

The Quranic verse, 'He is the First and the Last, the Outward and the Inward' (57: 3), refers not only to God's Divine nature as the First, so that there was nothing before Him, as the Last so that there is nothing after Him. He is evident so that there is nothing above Him and He is hidden so that there is nothing hidden from Him. God is omniscient the supreme intellect who knows everything that is hidden and evident. The verse of the Holy Quran refers to God's role and function in the Islamic spirituality. For a Muslim God is both transcendent and immanent, both majesty and beauty, both One and the Source of the manifold, both Origin of Mercy and Judge of all human actions, both Originator and Sustainer of the cosmos and the goal to which all beings journey... whose will rules over all things, whose love for knowledge of Himself is the cause of all creation and whose Mercy is the very substance of which the threads of His creation are woven (Seyyed Hossein Nasr, 1985:311). The Islamic spirituality that is to be practiced and lived by every Muslim is an invitation, all about knowing, loving and obeying God as revealed in the Holy Quran and promulgated and exemplified by the Prophet in hadith (traditions of the Prophet). The very concept of God among the Arabians has undergone various stages of religious developments. In order to understand the concept of God in Islam, we need to have an idea of God and religions in the pre-Islamic period.

Concept of God in the Pre-Islamic Period

To understand the people of pre-Islamic period and their concept of God it is only proper that we get an idea of the socio-religious, political and economic situations of the period. From the geographical point of view, Arabian Peninsula has an overwhelming expanse. The Arabian land had always been full of life and activities. The civilization that was born, developed and flourished in the desert area was spread all over the world due to its economic and trade activities. The original inhabitants of the land were Bedouins, who were characterized by the absence of a place of settlement that could be a point of reference for identity and a source of unity among them (Paul Jackson, 1988: 6). It is said that most of the Arabs were pastoralists who were constantly on the move in search of pastoral grounds for their herds and flocks. Restless and rootless with no permanent habitations they were innocent of science and art and illiteracy was common among the people.

Socially they belonged to tribal organization. As Arabian tribes they were characterized by virtues of hospitality, generosity, fortitude, enthusiasm, manliness, chivalry, courage to fight and tenderness in love. Hospitality was considered to be one of the sacred duties of the Arabs. In the words of Arab Historian, P.K. Hitti, "To refuse a guest, such a courtesy in a land where no inns or hotels obtain or to harm him after accepting him as a guest, is an offense not only against the established mores and honour but against God Himself, the real protector" (Hitti, P.K., 1970: 25). Their generosity manifested in their readiness to sacrifice their camel at the coming of a guest or on behalf of the poor and the helpless. Such was the generosity of the pre-Islamic Arabs, who later embraced Islam.

The pre-Islamic period was generally known as the Jahiliyah (ignorance) period signifying their lukewarm and indifferent attitude to religious and social life. To spiritual impulses the Arabs had a tepid response and were even indifferent. Their religious identity was marked by idol worship, based on belief in polytheism. They worshipped the sun, stars, trees, wells, caves and stones. The heavenly bodies and other powers of nature were venerated as deities. As a tribal organization, each tribe had its own deities. The ancient Arabs believed in the existence of a supreme God called Allah. Their belief and their faith in the so called 'Allah' was rather vague and weak (Shariff MM, 1961: 128). At times of any danger they would invoke this god and when the danger was over, they would forget all about him. In the Arabic poetries and inscriptions of northern Arabia the name of Allah as a great deity was mentioned. The name also finds its place in many idiomatic phrases which were in constant use among them.

There are clear indications that the Arabs during the time of the Prophet too, did have the name of 'Allah' as their supreme deity. Prophet Muhammad's own father was

'Abudullah, which means 'Servant of Allah'. We read in the Quran, 'In times of difficulties they would invoke Allah but the moment they returned to their own land they would prefer to seek the local deity' (29:65). So the Arabs, though had acknowledge of Allah, He was ignored in favour of the local deities (Paul Jackson, 1988: 4). It only shows that the name 'Allah' was prevalent among the pre-Islamic Arabs as only one of many gods. Practice of kethnotheism seem to have prevalent during the pre-Islamic period.

The aspect of sacrifice was very common among the pre-Islamic Arabs. They sacrificed camels, sheep and goats. It was believed that sacrifices brought them into close relationship with the deity. They used the term qurba and qurban (derived from the root QRB, to be near) for sacrifice. At times they even had human sacrifices to appease their gods and goddesses. The most important deities of the time were al-lat, al-uzza and al-mana (goddess of fertility, goddess the almighty and goddess of fortune respectively) and were considered as daughters of Allah. These three principal idols of Pagan Arab idolatry are mentioned in the Holy Quran: "Have you seen al-lat, and al-uzza and another, the third al-manah?" (53: 19-20). According to one of the opinions al-lat was in the human form, al-uzza had its origin in a sacred tree and al-manah in a white stone. However, the Holy Quran denounces such forms of Allah, as it was believed by the pre-Islamic people.

Hubal (vapor, spirit) was the chief deity of kaba' and was represented in human form. According to the belief, kaba is a cube-like structure without roof, built by Adam himself and handed over to the prophets for the purposes of offering sacrifices and performing annual pilgrimage. Apart from a number of gods and goddesses that they believed in, they also worshipped nasr (vulture) and 'awf (bird), which were considered to be deities of the period. Some of the scholars are of the opinion that the presence of kaba and worship of birds was a sign of the existence of totemism during the era.

The Arabs too believed in the existence of demons. A shadowy beings of local spirits called jinn, was common among the people. Jinn mean 'covered' or 'hidden' so they were being invisible to the eye. The people were frightened of jinn and usually offered sacrifices to appease them. Jinn were different from gods in their relation to man. Gods were considered to be friendly and jinn were hostile. Jinn were considered to be the personification of the notions of the terrors of the desert and its wild animals. Gods belonged to the regions where people were inhabited while the jinn belonged to the unknown and untrodden parts of the desert. The Arabian deities had different categories, where some of them were personification of abstract ideas, such as jadd (luck), sa'd (fortune), rida' (good will), wadd (friendship, affection), manaf (height, high place) (Shariff MM, 1991: 129). Originally abstract in character, later were given concrete identities.

People of the age were not rooted in their religious fervor and enthusiasm. The religious sentiment of the Bedouins was just at their lip service and nothing deeper into their hearts. The Holy Quran bears witness to this fact, 'The desert Arabians are most confirmed in unbelief and hypocrisy and most fitted to be in ignorance' (9:97). Thus the socio-religious, cultural and social fervour of pre-Islamic period was rightly known as 'period of ignorance' (jahliya) and their notions of god had always been vague with paganism and idolatry.

Some of the towns of Arabia like Mecca, Medina and Tai'f had their own urban civilization. Mecca was an important commercial center as the city was on the crossroad of the routes from Yemen to Syria and from Abyssinia to Iraq – a commercial route. The presence of Kaba', a sanctuary made Mecca, a religious center. As a place of pilgrimage for the Arabs, it attracted many Arabs for the annual fair (urz). Medina too was an important place, which later became second most holy place for the Muslims, for the tomb of the Holy Prophet is located in the city. Tai'f was another commercial center of less importance than Mecca and it was the place of the shrine of the goddess al-Lat, giving religious importance to the place.

Apart from the polytheistic belief of the Arabs, there were followers of monotheistic religions such as Judaism and Christianity. A vague form of monotheism was present among the Arabs who were called as hanafiyya (seekers of the truth), who kept themselves detached from polytheism without joining any monotheistic religion. According to the Historians, Jews for the first time migrated to Arabian Peninsula during the persecution of Nebuchadnezzar (605 BC – 562 BC). Jews were devoted to agriculture, developed good system of irrigation, experts in metal work and production of jewellery. They fully got integrated into the life of Arabians. There were different sects of Christians in the Arabian Peninsula as Syrian Nestorians and Abyssinian Monophysites. Among the Christians, the monks and hermits became an integral part of the life of the Arabians preaching and organizing Christianity among the Arabs. The Holy Quran has reference to Jews and Christians: "Strongest among men in enmity to the believers will you find the Jews and Pagans. And nearest among them in love to the believers will you find those who say, 'We are Christians', because among these are men devoted to learning and men who have renounced the world and they are not arrogant" (5: 82). By the sixth century, Judaism and Christianity had made a considerable headway in Arabia extending their sphere of influence, leaving the pagan masses gradually preparing the way for Islam (Shariff, M.M., 1961: 135).

Concept of God During Islamic Period

A brief outlook into the biography of the Prophet would shed light on the Islamic period. Prophet Muhammad was born in/around 570 AD to the Quraysh tribe of Hashim family at Mecca, to Abdulla and Amina. His father died before he was born and his mother died when he was just six years old. Practically he grew up as an orphan. His grand father Abdul Muttalib took care of him first and later he was under the care of his paternal uncle Abu Talib. At the age of 12, when he accompanied his uncle on a caravan journey, he was predicted by a Christian monk, Bahira that he would become a Prophet one day. He married Kadhija in 595 AD. While in Mecca, his natural inclination to spiritual life led him for a regular meditation and prayer at a small hillock called 'hira. One day, while he was praying there in the year 610 AD, he heard a voice, "Recite (Iqra), thou in the name of thy Lord who created you." Not knowing what it was all about, he later realized that it was the revelation that he received from God. The night on which, he received the revelation for the first time was called as, 'Night of Power' (Lailat al-Qadr) (Hitti P.K., 1970: 112).

Again for the second time he received the revelation, but this time under the stress of great emotion. So he rushed home and covered himself in a blanket. The revelation came as: "O thou covered in thy mantle! Arise and warn my people." The voice came like a reverberating bell. Later it was identified as the voice of Injil Jibril (Gabriel). When the prophet received the revelation, his wife went and told her Christian cousin, Waraqah Bin Nawfal, who in fact confirmed it as the revelation from God. It is to be noted that in the early period of the life of Muhammad, there are two Christians who in fact influenced and confirmed the Prophethood of Muhammad: Bahira and Waraqah Bin Nawfal.

Prophet Muhammad realizing his mission and Prophethood began to preach and warn his people of their life of ignorance. The content of his teaching was centered on the concept of God as One. He is all powerful. He is the creator of the Universe. There is judgment Day. Those who do according to God's commandment will be rewarded and others will be punished. The Arabians failed to accept him and his teachings, for they were pagans and idol worshippers. His new message had only a handful of takers. His wife Khadijah, his cousin Ali and his kinsman Abu Bakr were the first converts to the new religion preached by Muhammad. Though he and his companions were persecuted by the Meccan enemies, he fearlessly continued to preach and convert people from the worship of many and false gods to that of One and True God (Hitti, P.K., 1970:114). Prophet Muhammad continued to receive revelations from Allah at various times and on a number of occasions. The revelations that the Prophet received at Mecca were short, crisp, expressive and impressive.

Due to the continued persecution of the Prophet and his companions in Mecca by the Meccan enemies, at the invitation of a few Medinese, Prophet Muhammad together with his two hundred followers quietly migrated to Medina in 622 AD. The year is called the year of Hijra (migration). This is an important year in the history of Islam for it divides the biography of Prophet from Mecca and Medina and it is also the beginning of the new Islamic era/calendar. Even after migration to Medina, the Meccan enemies continued to fight against Prophet Muhammad and his companions. Yet Prophet Muhammad stood determined in his teachings and firm in his faith in One God. Gradually he gave a new shape and orientation to the religion that he preached and practiced. In Medina he made Islam a distinct religion by introducing: Friday as the Sabbath day, adhan as the way of call for prayer replacing trumpets, gongs and bells, the month of Ramdhan was declared as the month of fasting, qibla (direction of prayer) was changed from Jerusalem to Mecca and pilgrimage to Kaba'h was authorized.

In 630 AD Prophet Muhammad and his companions made pilgrimage to Kaba'h for the first time ever since he went to Medina. As he went for the pilgrimage, he destroyed all three hundred and sixty idols around Kaba'h and declared, 'Truth has come and falsehood has vanished." (Hitti, P.K., 1970: 118). With this act, Muhammad declared Kaba'h and the place around Kaba'h as the place of holy of holies and made it forbidden for any non-Muslims to step into this area. Prophet made his last earthy pilgrimage to Kaba'h in 632 AD, and three months after his return to Medina he unexpectedly took ill and died.

With the birth of new religion in Arabia, we find a social organization that is knit together with religion as its foundation and basis rather than blood relation. The bond of Arab relationship was replaced by the new bond of faith. Life of piety was expected from all. All forms of vices were to be discarded and no more wine and gambling in the newly formed religious community. People believed in One God, creator and sustainer.

Prophet Muhammad as a messenger of peace, a Prophet, a lawgiver, a religious leader, a chief judge, a commander of the army and a civil head of the state, founded a democratic state in Medina on Islamic principles of love, joy, peace, brotherhood and justice. He made people to understand that Islam is a religion of peace and it is demanded from every

Muslim a total surrender and resignation to the will God. It reminds people of their imperative duty to God and His creatures. As a social reformer he brought out social order in the society. He gave sanctity to marriage and preached equality of people. Idolatry was removed and people with their new religion and faith, reached the highest standard in morals, spirituality and knowledge.

The Prophet preached about the Oneness of God, Allah. Allah is the name of God that he proclaimed. The precise meaning of the word, Allah comes from the Arabic form ilahu, meaning 'a god'. When used with the definite article, al-ilahu it means, 'The God'. When the 'l' consonant of the article coalesces with the same letter in the first syllable of the word eliding the 'I' sound, Al-lah is made (Kenneth Cragg, 1964: 37). According to some other sources, it comes from the root 'lah', meaning 'the secret one'. Thus Allah is the most secret one, whom we cannot just see with our physical eyes.

According to Abu Hanifah, just as the essence of God is unchangeable, so is His name and that Allah has ever been the name of the Eternal Being (Thomas Patrick Hughes, 1976: 140). God is known by ninety nine beautiful names, but the supreme Name by which he is best known is Allah. According to a tradition, Muhammad said: 'Verily, there are ninety nine names of God and whoever recites them shall enter into Paradise' (Thomas Patrick Hughes, 1976: 141). The ninety nine beautiful names of Allah are divided into asmau'l jalaliyah (glorious attributes) and asmau'l jamaliyah (terrible attributes). Attributes like, 'merciful', 'kind', 'forgiver' ... belong to the former while attributes like 'the strong', 'the avenger', 'the powerful' ... belong to the later category.

This indeed is the name of God's Essence as well as of all the Divine Names and Qualities as related to and 'contained' in the Divine Nature (Seyyed Hossein Nasr, 1985:312). All that is said about the Divine Nature pertains to Allah. In Persian and Hindustani, Allah is expressed by the word 'Khuda', derived from the Persian root khud, which means 'self' or 'the self existing one'. Another word frequently used to denote God is Rabb, which is generally translated as, 'Lord'.

It is normally understood by Muslims to mean 'the sustainer'.

The concept of God as preached by the Prophet of Islam is the essential belief of the Muslims today all over the world. The fundamental teachings are found in the five pillars of Islam. The first pillar is shahadat (profession of faith), which is expressed by the formula: "La ilah Ill'allah wa Muhammadun rasul-ullah" (There is no god but God and Muhammad is the prophet of God). It is indeed the faith formula with profound meaning. This is the supreme synthesis of Islamic doctrine, where God is One, beyond all duality and otherness and is the source of all reality, beauty and goodness. It clearly expresses the belief in the existence of God, His absolute Power, the Eternal and Almighty Being. The first part reveals the uncompromising affirmation of Monotheism and the second part highlights the unique position of Muhammad in Islam. Keeping in mind the background of the pre-Islamic religions, the mission of the Prophet was not merely to proclaim God's existence, but also to deny the existence of all gods.

In the pages that proceeded, we have dealt in detail about the pre-Islamic concept of God and the religion preached by Prophet Muhammad. People were so much involved in worshipping a number of gods and goddesses that they remained pagans and idol worshippers. It is against this background the first pillar of Islam is to be seen. It denies all deities and affirms One Unique God. Quran refers to the Arab belief in Allah as the creator of earth and heaven, as the one who has the knowledge of all things and as the one who sends rain (29:61-63). Muslims are taught to believe in God, Unique, and Self-Subsistent Creator of the universe. Belief in One God (tawhid) is the crux of the faith in Islam and associating any other gods with this One God is the most unforgivable sin in Islam, known as shirk. Literally it means associating or placing any other gods or goddesses at the same level as God. In fact this central belief of God shaped and sustained the life of future Muslims.

Every Muslim is to have the fear of God (taqwa). It is believed that every God fearing person belongs to the wider family of the Prophet. It is a reminder to the Muslims that

God should always be remembered and never to be forgotten. He should be always obeyed never to be disobeyed and always to be thanked. The taqwa of man is indicated by: good trust with respect to what has not been granted, good contentment with what he has been granted and good patience in the face of what he has lost (al – Qushayri, 2004: 27). Trust in God (tawakkul) is another prerogative of all Muslims. It means to cling to God at all times and to abandon oneself to God, the Most High. The constant remembrance of God (zikr) leads to perfection in his/her wayfaring. God is with such persons and protects them from all adversities.

In fact today, Muslims believe that everything that happens in the world, take place by God's will or by His permission. For a Muslim for example natural calamities are signs of God's displeasure while good events are signs of God's bounty. They feel the presence of God in their life and give importance to Allah's intervention in life. One of the oft repeated phrases of the Muslims is 'insha Allah'. It literally means 'if God so wills'. It in fact reveals God's power in His interaction with the human beings. Because everything happens by God's will, we must accept everything as from God. If ever, we enquire about the health of a Muslim, his immediate answer would be: al hamdulillahi, means 'praise be to God'. By this, he attributes his good health to God alone, for God is greater than anything in the world.

Quranic Concept of God

The Holy Quran is the inspired scripture of the Muslims and is the foundation on which the entire life is built. It is the most comprehensive and complete code of life for all Muslims of every age and place. They refer to the Quran on every aspect of life – be it social, political, economic or religious. According to the Holy Quran, it is the right guidance given by God to mankind, expressing it in clear language, in order that people may learn wisdom (12:2). Etymologically the word, Quran comes from the root words, 'Iqra' and 'Qarra' means that it is the best collection of all the books and that which should be read or recited or proclaimed by every one. The Holy Book is considered to be the communication on earth of the Eternal Word uttered by God and defined as "The Well-Guarded Tablets" (85: 22), which means that God's message is not ephemeral but eternal and preserved from any form of corruption. It is "The Mother of the Book (43:4), which means it is the Original Scripture, the Foundation of Revelation revealed by angel Gabriel as the mediator, is the core or essence of revelation, the original principle or fountain-head of God's Eternal and Universal Law (2:97) for the community. The Holy Quran was revealed to the Prophet, time to time over a period of 22 years from the first revelation in the year 610 AD.

The Holy Quran is a book essentially religious not philosophical, but it deals with all those problems which religion and philosophy have in common (Shariff, M.M., 1961:136). For example the Book expounds on topics related to the God, the world, individual soul and their interrelatedness; good and evil, free-will, predestination and life after death. According to Holy Quran God is the Ultimate and Absolute Reality, sole-subsisting, all-pervading and eternal (2:186, 31: 30, 2:115, 6:62, 20: 111). He is transcendent for the reason that human beings cannot comprehend His full Glory (6: 103) and because he is beyond the limitations of time, space and sense perception. He is so fine and subtle as to be invisible to the physical eye and imperceptible to the senses.

Human words may not suffice to describe fully the nature of God. However, Quran describes God as Cherisher and Sustainer (1:2, 6:164, 10:32), Protector (2:257, 3:150, 22:78), Helper (3:150, 4:45, 40:51), Most Bountiful and Merciful (96: 3, 4:26, 5:74, 6:12), Beneficent and Forgiving (52:28, 4:25 -26, 5:74, 15:49). To God belongs our birth, our faculties and affection (16: 77-78). He is the shelter to the orphans, satisfaction to the needy and guide to the wanderers (93: 6-7). God is the Light of heaven and earth (24: 34-36) all creation speak of Him and give praise and glory to Him (13:12-13, 17:44, 24: 41-46, 1:1, 17:111, 30:17-19, 34:1). He is the giver of life. The mystery of the development of life is in God, for according to the Quran, 'You were without life and He gave you life' (2:28). In Him human beings have life and unto Him everyone will return finally.

God is immanent both in the souls and in the universe. At the same time it is very difficult to know His exact nature. But in order to apprehend what we cannot comprehend, and to realize His attributes, certain similitude and parables from our human experiences are used. Even so, the highest that we can think of, falls short of the true Reality of God. For God is higher and wiser than the highest and wisest that we can think of. But at the same time, in this regard Quran reveals God as self-subsisting (2:255, 20:111), is eternal, all powerful, all knowing, all beauty, most just, most loving and all good. His attributes are connoted by His name, which could be summarized under a few essential heads: Life, Eternity, Unity, Power, Truth, Beauty, Justice, Love and Goodness. These are the essence of God. By this, human beings are to be faithful to represent this divine essence in their lives.

There is a close relation between God and His creatures. God interacts with His creatures and His creatures in turn enter into fellowship with Him through prayer, contemplation, mystic gnosis and good life. The Holy Quran again and again brings out the uncompromising concept of strict monotheism. God is One and only One (112:1) and there is no god but God (2:63, 3:18, 6:19). Therefore no gods should ever be associated with God.

God is omnipotent and the primal origin of everything is due to Him (10:4, 30:11). He is the creator (96: 1) and the one who began the process of creation (30:27). He created the heaven, earth and everything in it (7: 54, 10:3, 31: 10). There is nothing on earth to oppose His will, for when he says "Be" behold! It is (6:73, 19:35). His decree is absolute (6:34), He separated day and night. He created the sun, the moon, the stars and everything moves according to His command (7:54, 16:12, 36: 38-39). The rhythm of the universe is controlled by Him. 'He is Allah the creator, evolver and restorer of all forms on earth' (59: 24), brings down water from the sky and raises life on earth. The creative activity of God is continuous. Death is a phenomenal event. What comes after death is the process of recreation by God, who is both the source and goal of everyone on earth.

God is not only the creator, but also cherisher (1: 2, 6: 164, 10:32), sustainer (7: 54, 11:6), protector (2: 257, 3: 150), helper (3: 150, 4: 45), guide (6: 71, 26: 63), and reliever of distress and suffering (27: 62) of all His creatures, as God listens to man's innermost conscience and heart. He is the most merciful, most kind and most forgiving. God has created the world and His creatures with a purpose. Everything in the world has a purpose and the goal is to reach God Himself (53: 42). Human beings should fear none but Him because He alone can give life and death. Men and women are God's vicegerent on earth (2:30). The power of will and choosing bring human beings nearer to God-like nature. The perfect vicegerent is the one whose power of action reflects the will of His creator. Human perfection lies in his assimilation of God's attributes, for He is much closer to human beings than the jugular vein (50:16).

God is omniscient. Nothing on earth or in heaven is hidden from Him. He knows every word that is openly spoken (21: 4) and whispered in secret, there is nothing secret that He does not know (57: 6, 64: 4) and he knows the secret minds of every individual (2: 284, 3: 29, 4: 3, 16: 23). Justice and love are other attributes of God, prominently brought out in the Holy Quran. God is just ((4: 57, 10: 109). He is the owner of the Day of Judgment (1: 3), who judges everyone according to their deeds. The good deeds are to be rewarded and the evil doers will be punished ((3:173, 9:120). He also forgives the sins of His creatures (39: 53), as He is most loving and most merciful.

Islam is a religion of love. We have a number of references in the Quran stressing the value of love. There are many verses in the scripture mentioning God as love (4: 28, 6:17, 64, 77, 88, 122, 10: 57, 17: 20, 21). His love is shown in creating, sustaining, nourishing, sheltering, helping and guiding His creatures. Therefore it is fitting that His creatures love Him and are always thankful to Him for His love and care (26: 114). The Quran has ninety nine Beautiful Names of Allah. Muslims constantly recall to mind, these names of Allah with the help of 'rosary' or chain of beads in thrice thirty three beads, recollecting the ninety nine beautiful names of God. The most important Divine Names are: al-Rahman al-Rahim, 'The Compassionate, the Merciful.' The sequence is not mere repetition. The Rahman is the one who is in His character merciful and Rahim is He in merciful action. He who is merciful behaves mercifully. His mercy is of His essence and also of His deeds (Kenneth Cragg, 1964: 40). All the 114 chapters of the Holy Quran begin with this invocation, except surah 9 on account of stern warning against idolaters.

Concept of God in Sufism

Sufis are the Islamic mystics. Sufism has its origin in the Holy Quran and hadith (traditions of the Holy Prophet). Sufis themselves have explained the origin of the word 'sufi', which is quite interesting and instructive. Sufi Hujwiri wrote in his book, Kashf-ul-Mahjub (The Revelation of What is Veiled) that the word may have come from the word for 'wool' (suf), because they wore woolen garments as a mark of simplicity and poverty; some say that the word may have come from the word for 'bench' or 'platform' (suffa), pointing to their spiritual life on a bench or platform, spending their time in reading the holy Quran and engaging themselves in religious discussions; others say it comes from the word denoting 'first rank' or 'first row' (saff), because these people rank first with regard to their religious and spiritual life; others refer it to the word for 'purity' (safa), for theirs is a life of purity (Paul Jackson, 1988: 254).

One of the early definitions of a Sufi was: "One who wears wool over his purity; gives his lusts the taste of tyranny and having overcome the world, journeys on the path of the Chosen One (Muhammad)" (Valiuddin Mir, 1977: 3). It is a clear indication that Sufism is a lucid path of spiritual journey towards God, living a life of love of God, devotion to God and service to humanity. They belong to the world but not of the world or crave for money, pleasure, name or fame. They denote a spiritual thirst in man. Islam is the shell of Sufism, for Sufism is the secret teachings of Islam. According to Nizamuddin Auliya, a chishti sufi, the life of a Sufi lies in his perfection, for 'man's perfection lies in having little of food, a little of sleep, a little of rest, a little of talk and a little of association with people.' The main features of Sufism are: self-abandonment, self-mortification, poverty and quietism.

The life of a Sufi is marked by his relation to God, people and the world. According to Qushairi, Sufi's relation to God should not have any element of doubt. In his relation to God, he identifies himself with God, loosing his mortal self. In the process he realizes that his relation is pure, without any material link (Sharif MM, 1961: 317). The goal of the Sufis is to be united with God in total and full reliance on Him. The motive power of a Sufi is love and is a complete man. He is among roses a rose, among thorns a thorn, giving meaning to life. For him there is a valley of quest, valley of love, valley of intuitive knowledge and valley of detachment. Sufism is glory in wretchedness, riches in poverty, lordship in servitude, satiety in hunger, clothedness in nakedness, freedom in slavery, life in death and sweetness in bitterness.

The early form of Sufism was very simple in its teachings without much of philosophical or speculative ideas. For example Hassan of Basra (642-728 AD) in his teachings he focused on the consciousness of sin and danger of hell. The Sufis are to act in obedience to God, speak the word of God, keep the love of God in their hearts, voice of God in their ears and beauty of divine contemplation in their eyes. He said, "Beware of the world for it is like a snake, smooth to touch, but its venom is deadly.... Beware of this world for its hopes are lies and its expectations false" (Sharif MM, 1961: 335). Another early Sufi par excellence was Rabiah bin Basra. She was born in a poor home, was a slave girl but her devotion to a life of piety and prayer enabled her to gain freedom. She embraced Sufism and remained a celibate. Her main contribution was her doctrine of disinterested love of God, which served both as a motive and goal for her life. For the people of her time, the motive of asceticism and otherworldliness was the fear of hell and hope of paradise. But for Rabia, her only hope was for union with God. Once she was seen running with fire in one hand and water in the other. People asked her the meaning of her action. She replied: 'I am going to light fire in paradise and pour water on hell,' so that both veils may completely disappear and that the pilgrims may not live in the hope of paradise or fear of hell. Such were the simple teaching of the early Sufis. Some of the other early Sufis to mention were: Abu Hashim of Kufa (d 776), Ibrahim bin Adham (d 777), Shaqiq of Balkh (d 810), Dhu al-Nun Misri (706-856), Bayazid Bistami (d874) and al-Hallaj (857-922).

There are philosopher-Sufis who had their own intellectual idea of God that they tried to propagate. These Sufis who belong to later period of Sufism have such philosophical and speculative ideas in their teachings. It was Ibn al Farid of Cairo (1181- 1235 AD) who introduced the Logos doctrine into Islam, by which the theory is meant that God's vicegerent controlling the material universe is, "the Idea of Muhammad". The theory resolves the transcendent God with a theistic universe. Anyone who aspires to know God seeks this end by achieving union with the 'Idea of Muhammad' projected by God to be united in him (AJ Arberry, 1950: 93-94). The idea is to seek and find God, in following the teachings of Islam.

Ibn al 'Arabi (1165 AD – 1240 AD) is of the opinion that God is the 'Absolute Being', who manifests Himself in every form of existence and in the highest degree in the form of man (Shariff MM, 1961: 420). In Him alone Being and Existence are one and inseparable. His idea of 'unity of being' is of pantheistic tendency, though was rejected by the main body of Islamic believers. God is both Transcendent and Immanent. Another speculation of Ibn al'Arabi is that God created the world in order to contemplate on His attributes and names, thus bringing about mutual dependence. This idea was considered by many as ill defined theory. According to him, there is no such thing as union with God in the sense of becoming one with God, but there is the realization of the already existing fact that the mystic is one with God (AJ Arberry, 1950: 100). Each prophet is the Logos of God. The Logos is the Muhammad, the 'head' of the hierarchy of prophets. All the individuals are united in the Reality of Muhammad. The Reality (Idea) of Muhammad is the creative, animating or the First Intellect. It is also called as Reality of Realities and it finds its fullest manifestation in the Perfect Man. Perfect Man is the cause of the universe, being the epiphany of God's desire to be known. Such Perfect Man knows God, loves God and is loved by God.

For Al-Kindi (801- 873AD) God is immutable, simple, of invisible nature and the true cause of motion. He believes in the theory of causality that God is the efficient cause. God is the only true efficient cause for He acts and is never acted upon. Another proof for the existence of God, he derives from the perfect order observed in all natural beings, as we have the cosmological proof for the existence of God. For him God is the Perfect Being, who manages everything according to the greatest wisdom (Shariff, M.M., 1961: 430).

According to Ibn Sina (980 – 1037 AD), God is the necessary being, while, everything else in the world, are contingent beings. So He does not need any one else for his existence. God's essence is identified with His Necessary Existence. All the attributes like knowledge, creation, power, will ... are the facts of His existence. He is the Pure Intellect in which the subject and object are identical. God though being supra-temporal, changeless and incorporeal, not a particle remains hidden from Him in the heavens or on earth. So he is All-Knowing. God's creative activity and will for Ibn Sina means the necessary procession of the world from Him and His self-satisfaction through this process. The world as contingent depends entirely on God eternally and thus the world has eternal existence. (Shariff, M.M., 1961: 501-503).

Al-Ghazzali (1058 -1111AD) was a philosopher, theologian, jurist and a Sufi. He stressed on the Unity of God that He is the sole-existent and the ultimate cause and ground of all being and the only self-subsisting reality. All His attributes are spiritual. He is the perfect goodness and perfect beauty. He is the supreme object of love. He is the light of lights, the eternal wisdom, the creative truth and the eternal will, a will which is the cause of creation. The Ultimate Reality is essentially will. For al-Ghazzali God is both transcendent, beyond the limitations of space and time and immanent, where His eternal wisdom, eternal will and supreme beauty of the wonders and glory of His creation. But he does not accept God as Absolute, but a personal God, a living God. This God constantly interacts with His creatures through prayers, contemplation, meditation and mystical gnosis (Shariff, M.M., 1961: 618-619). For him the attributes of God and the eschatological terms such as heaven, hell, balance ... are to have allegorical interpretations, where spiritual or symbolic interpretations are equally valid. The orthodox Muslim thinkers have reproached him for having watered down the true Islamic beliefs for giving prominence to spiritual experiences. They objected his basic faith as 'God palpable in the heart' (Paul Jackson, 1988: 201). However, Al- Ghazzali is considered today as a thinker who has combined rationalism and spiritualism, who had catholicity of outlook and who made the Islamic theology acceptable, coherent and relevant today.

The Ultimate Reality is the ground of everything that exists. The appearance of multiplicity of forms and modes are only subjective. God and the world are two aspects of the same reality. The universe is the outward expression of God and God is the inner reality of the universe. Before the manifestation the world was God and God after manifestation is identical with the world. As a matter of fact the reality is one and the dual aspects of God and the world are only our ways of looking at it. We find that such a teaching on God is similar to the teaching of Shankara's advaitic philosophy, where he claims that it is maya (illusion) which blurs the Reality. Swami Vivekananda further elaborates this notion of God. According to him, when we see the world through the categories of space, time and causation the Absolute becomes the universe. The universe is the cause and the Absolute is the effect.

Islamic Philosophy of God

After having gone through the concept of God in Islam at various stages, let us now deal with the Islamic philosophy of God. The idea of pantheism was very common among the Muslims through the years. But there are Islamic and Sufi Philosophers who vehemently denounced the concept of pantheism. For example Shaikh Ahmad Sirhindi (1563 - 1624 AD), met Khwajah Baqi Billa, a Naqhbandi Sufi saint in Delhi, during one of his pilgrimages, and was introduced to Sufi way of life. He then came to the realization that unity with God is only experiential and not existential. God cannot be one with anything. God is God and the world is world. The world is only a mark of the existence of the Creator and it merely reflects the various attributes of God. However, followers of Ibn al'Arabi claim that pantheism is the final stage of Sufistic perfection, where reality is nothing but one of the states experienced by every believer. The pantheist acknowledges the presence of One God in everything and everything else is regarded as the incarnation of the One.

Al-Ghazzali, philosopher-Sufi denies the very idea of pantheism. It is a false and erroneous concept for him. At best one can claim nearness and proximity with God and nothing more. When we accept pantheism, we deny the special quality which only God possesses and none else can partake and it is the quality of self-subsistence. Only God is self-subsistent and everything else exists through him and not through its own essence. There are typical pantheistic utterances of Sufis of extreme type such as: I am the Truth, Glory be to me! How great is My Glory! .... For Al – Ghazzali, these are statements of passionate lovers in a state of ecstasy. Therefore they should be concealed and never to be spoken of. No doubt that these are emotive expressions indicative of deep inner experience. So they should not try to speak the unspeakable.

One of the rationalist schools of Islam was the Mutazilites. This school was founded by Wasil Ibn 'Ata (699-748 AD) in Basra, Iraq. It was a theological and rationalist school or movement in the classical period of early Islam which accepted reason as a primary criterion for establishing validity of the content of Islamic belief. Their fundamental theoretical position about God is summed up in the catch word: al-'adle wa'l-tauhid: Justice and Unity. They believe that God is just for he cannot reward evil and punish good. He does what is beneficial to people. Freedom of choice of man is very much part of their belief system. Again the divine omnipotence is opposed, for the all powerful mighty God could somehow predetermine the actions of people, which would go against the very nature of Just God. Another specific belief of the Mutazilites is that God is One. They deny all attributes of God and anthropomorphic view of God for it might lead to polytheism. For them the attributes are to be considered only as allegorical. One of the attributes of God is His speech, the Holy Quran. They are against the traditional belief of the

Muslims that the Holy Quran is uncreated. If it is uncreated then it must be eternal. But there cannot be two eternal realities, which is against the strict monotheism of Islam. So for the Mutazilites, Holy Quran is created in time so as not to suggest a division in God (Paul Jackson, 1988: 187).

Against the Mutazilites, Asharite school of thought emerged. This school was founded by a Muslim theologian, Abu al Hasan Ali Al-Ashari (873-935 AD), who was in fact a student of Mutalitie School. Later he denounced Mutazilites and founded the Asharite School. Reason is the basis of all their views. They did accept the attributes of God and held that anthropomorphic view of God is possible in the world to come. For the Asharites the Holy Quran was uncreated, as it is the speech of God which is one of His eternal attributes. They tried to keep absolutely pure the divine transcendence at the same time accepting the attributes of God.

According to Muhammad Iqbal (1875-1938) a contemporary prominent philosopher of Islam, man is understood properly as related to God, the greater Ego. He describes God as, 'Perfect Personality' which comprises everything and yet is not everything. The reality as a whole is eternal becoming and thus immortality is reached through love and prayer. He brings out the creative evolution of man. Through love and prayer we are drawn closer to God and derive some of his qualities. He believes in union of wills and not union of being, for man remains man even at the highest stage of his mystic path. Union with God is a never-ending quest and ever-ongoing process. The idea of creative evolution of man is found in the teaching of Iqbal, like Teilhad or Aurobindo.

Conclusion

The Islamic concept of God reveals the intimate relationship between people and God. A Muslim cannot think of his / her life without ones dependency on God. It is in humility and meekness that the Muslims find meaning in their life by faith in God. In the world of globalization, secularism and materialism Muslims have not turned away from their God-conscious life. They truly believe that God plays a vital role in every realm of their life.

Muslims take pride in their monotheism. Monotheism is the view that only one God exists, possessing necessary properties as: omniscience, omnipotence and omnibenevolence. Monotheism can be either inclusive monotheism or exclusive monotheism. Muslims believe in exclusive form of monotheism. Due to this concept, some of them even doubt if Christianity is a monotheistic religion in a strict sense, because of the concept of Trinity in Christianity.

The concept of God in Islam has gone through various stages of developments. But the core idea of God and the crux of their belief have always remained the same. We have gone through the concept of God during the Pre-Islamic and Islamic periods, the Quranic concept of God, Sufi understanding of God and Islamic philosophy of God. This distinction is only to view the Islamic concept of God through various perspectives and to have a wholistic and comprehensive idea of God in the Islamic tradition.

Allah whom Muslims reverently worship, constantly remember and adore is the God of Islam. It comes from the root word, 'a-ei-la' (alif, lam and ha are the three Arabic letters). The meaning of Allah reveals the very concept and constant God consciousness of Muslims all over the world. There are different meanings attributed to 'Allah.' Allah is the one to whom some one moves out of intense love. Love becomes the motivating force for a believer to move out to the Divine. Allah is the one who loves and the one who is loved. He is the only one who is worthy of worship and to be adored, as in the Quran, "There is no god but I; therefore worship and serve Me" (21: 25). Thus Allah becomes part and parcel of the life of a believer, whatever may be his state or rank.

Belief in God, who is the creator, designer, originator, sustainer and cherisher is the fundamental faith of every Muslim. The Islamic kalima (the creed or the succinct expression of Islamic faith) is very much part of the life of Muslims. When a child is born, kalima is whispered into the ears of the new-born child, when some one is dying once again kalima is recited by the individual or the members gathered around, recite the kalima on behalf of the dying person. So the recitation of kalima is a practice from cradle to the grave. Kalima becomes part of the formula of adhan (call to prayer), which resonates from innumerable minarets of the mosques through five times a day. A Muslim recites this formula any number of times in a day. Thus the formula of kalima runs through the veins of the Muslims. So they can never think of life without God as the essence of their life.

Muslims emphasize the omnipotence of God's will and His transcendence. It means that there is a purpose behind every intervention of the Divine. God is seen as involved in the destiny of man as commander, the Law-giver. It is through God everything comes into being and the Law (shari'a) is the end or purpose of life. Thus God is constantly active in the world through His Law and Will. The Islamic Law, shari'a means 'the clear path to be followed.' It brings forth the law of God and provides guidance for the regulation of life in the best interest of man/woman, to fulfill all his/her needs in the most successful, beneficial way. Today the Law that has come from God is a symbol of their cultural and religious identity. It contains both law and the very religion. So in following shari'a, Muslims find the Absolute God in every thread of life.

In conclusion, we can firmly affirm that God is the most powerful driving force, energy and agent of every believer in Islam. Islam is the embodiment of the 'code of life', which God has framed to serve as norm for humankind. Islam literally means 'to submit or surrender to God' and it also means 'peace'. Therefore Islam is a religion in which a believer totally submits oneself to God and by doing so, obtains real peace of mind and body. Today the world is in need of peace. There can be no peace without justice, respect and dignity of the other. It is only God who can instill these values in the individuals, provided one surrenders to God. No doubt, Islam is such a religion, having God as the hub of human life and they revolve around God constantly for all their needs and purposes and for their very existence.

Khuda Hafiz!

BIBLIOGRAPHY

1. AL-HUJWIRI, Ali B Uthman Al-Jullabi, *The Kash Al-Mahjub*, Reynold A Nicholson (Tr), Karachi: Darul – Shaat, 1990.
2. AL – QUSHAYRI, *Principles of Sufism*, Kuala Lumpur: Islamic Book Trust, 2004.
3. ARBERRY AJ., *Sufism*, Great Britain: George Allen & Unwin, 1950.
4. BURCKHARDT, Titus, *An Introduction to Sufism*, Great Britain: The Aquarian Press, 1976.
5. CRAGG, Kenneth, *Muhammad and the Christian*, New York: Orbis Books, 1984
6. __________, *The Call of the Minaret*, New York: Oxford University Press, 1956.
7. GIBB, Hamilton AR., *Studies on the Civilization of Islam*, New Jersey: Princeton University Press, 1962.
8. HITTI, Philip. K., *History of the Arabs*, Hong Kong: Macmillan Education Ltd., 1970.
9. HUGHES, Thomas Patrick, *Dictionary of Islam*, New Delhi: Oriental Books Reprint Corporation, 1976.
10. JACKSON, Paul, *The Muslims of India*, Bangalore: Theological Publications in India, 1988.
11. KHAN, Khaja, *The Philosophy of Islam*, New Delhi: Kitab Bhavan, 1981.
12. MIR, Valiuddin, *The Quranic Sufism*, Delhi: Motilal Banarsidass, 1977.
13. NASR, Seyyed Hossein, *Islamic Spirituality*, New York: SCM Press Ltd., 1989.
14. SEDGWICK, Mark, *Islam & Muslims*, Boston: Nicholas Brealey Publishing Company, 2006.
15. SHARIFF MM., *A History of Muslim Philosophy* (Volume I & II), Delhi: Low Price Publications, 1961.
16. STENT, David, *Religious Studies*, London: Made Simple Books, 1983.
17. TAKLE. John, *The Faith of Islam*, New Delhi: Deep & Deep Publications, 1988.
18. ULLAH, Mohammad Zia, *Islamic Concept of God*, London: Kegan Paul International Ltd., 1984.

8

Society and Religion – A Sociological Analysis

Surojit Sen Gupta*

Religion as a social force exerted influence in both the preliterate and literate societies. Religion is as old as human societies have been in some form or the other; and human beings have reflected on the nature and it's forces with effects on his pursuits both in the positive and negative dimensions have been a part of his ways of feeling, thinking and acting for centuries. Religion of one sort or the other appeared to be universal among human beings. Much evidence exists to prove this view of the universality of religion. Findings of both historians and anthropologists had supported the view of the universality of religion. However, the manifestations of religious behavior were so variable and so intricately interwoven with other aspects of human behavior that it was difficult to distinguish it from other aspects of human behavior, especially in pre-literate societies (Nottingham, 1971).

W. Lessa and E. Vogt observed that the universality of religion suggested that it corresponded to some deep and probably inescapable human need. Human life was necessarily a social life and to ensure conformity to some accepted

* Assistant Professor, Department of Sociology, Maharaja Bir Bikram College, Government of Tripura, Agartala – 799004.

standards of conduct, a minimum requirement for predictability of social behavior was required, which would provide some level of stability and continuity since humans were not governed automatically by biologically inherited instincts. It become all the more compelling to conform to these standards, when they were invested with divine authority and continually symbolized in rites and that appealed to the senses (Lessa and Vogt, 1965). However, the basis of religion in society was complex. The religious behavior of humans could not be traced to instincts and neither was it possible to trace religious behavior to any one distinctive human attribute, that is, intelligence, language or thought. The relationship between religion and society were fundamental to the nature of religion and according to some were basic to the nature of society.

Defining Religion

The word 'religion' came from the Latin 'religare', which meant 'to bind together' or from the word 'religere', which meant 'to rehearse, to execute painstakingly' suggesting both group identity and ritual (Yinger, 1957). Although most theorists accepted the statement that all known societies had been to some degree religious, not all theorists agreed as to just what constituted religious behavior. Discussions had continued for many years on how to define religion and in the early stages of scientism, how to distinguish it from magic, science and philosophy and from some kinds of political and social enthusiasms (Scharf, 1970). As James Frazer had pointed out, there was probably no subject in the world about which opinions differed so much, and to arrive at a definition that would satisfy everyone would be nearly impossible (Birnbaum and Lenzer, 1969).

Joachim Wach held that all religions, despite their wide variations, were characterized by three universal expressions: (a) theoretical, or a system of beliefs; (b) practical, or a system of worship, and (c) sociological, or a system of social relationships. Until all these were found, one may have religions elements or tendencies, but not a full religion (Yinger, 1975). Edward Tylor, in his pioneer study *Primitive Culture,* published in 1871, put forward what he called a 'minimum definition' of religion. He defined religion as 'a belief in spiritual beings' (Scharf, 1970). According to Radcliffe-Brown 'Religion is everywhere an expression in one form or another of a sense of dependence on a power outside ourselves, a power of which we may speak of as a spiritual or a moral power' (Scharf, 1970). For him, the crucial expression of this sense of dependence was ritual. Ritual and the social obligation to perform them was definite, in contrast to the beliefs concerning the objects of ritual, which were indefinite and variable. Thus, ritual and emotions of fear and awe were to Radcliffe-Brown the basic qualities of religion, regardless of the objects of the ritual (Scharf, 1970).

Sociologists, too, grappled with the effort to define religion. The approach of the early anthropologists to define religion was largely evolutionary and was based on the effort to explain the origin of religion in human society. They had sought to establish the earliest forms of religion. August Comte saw himself as the founder of the new religion of Humanity, but failed to provide a definition of religion. According to him, Humanity, the Positivist God, was the progressive realization of the idea that revealed itself in realization (Kremer-Mariette, 1987). Marx, in his economic deterministic approach, saw religion as nothing but the reflection of external forces that controlled the daily lives of humans. Religion was only a projection of the economic condition of depravity among the masses, the 'social opium' of the people (Marx and Engels, 1972). Emile Durkheim, like the earlier evolutionists, had also sought to find out the origins of religion, but he also offered an explanation of its function. He held that religion always existed in every society; there was always some group that was sacred to its members, and though religions changed and developed, no society was known to have existed without a religion.

Religion, according to Nottingham, was essentially a matter of how the religious realm, i.e., the supernatural, was experienced, although the experience could vary in the degree of intensity of experience and an individual's commitment and response to that experience. There was a general agreement among scholars that it was the supernatural that constituted the very core of religion. As Arthur Darby Nock, the Harvard historian of religion stated, 'Religion is what men do, say and think-in that order–concerning the supernatural' (Nottingham, 1971). To Yinger defined religion as 'a system of beliefs and practices by means of which, a group of people struggle with the ultimate problems of human life (Yinger, 1957).

Religion served an important integrative function in society. It both explained and expressed the ultimate values of a society and also maintained those values and managed tensions and anxieties that could possibly arise by providing defence mechanisms to individual members of a society. Beliefs and practices performed this basic function, although they varied infinitely from culture to culture (Lessa and Vogt, 1965). Robert Bellah saw religion primarily as a system of symbols and attempted an evolutionary interpretation of religion. He proposed a sequence of five typical ideal stages of development: primitive, archaic, historic, early modern and modern and examined each stage in terms of religious symbol systems, religious actions, religious organizations and social implications. Clifford Geertz, defined religion as, 'a system of symbols which acts to establish powerful, pervasive and long-lasting moods and motivations in men by formulating concepts of a general order of existence, and clothing these conceptions with such an aura of factuality that the moods and motivations seem uniquely realistic' (Banton, 1963). To Gerhard Lenski, religion is the system of beliefs about the nature of the force(s) ultimately shaping man's destiny, and the practices associated therewith, shared by the members of a group' (Lenski, 1961).

The basis of religion in human society was as complex as were human conditions themselves and the nature of religion could be understood only in relation to the total predicament of the human being (Nottingham, 1971). Religion was so encompassing a reality that no final definition of religion could be arrived at. As social conditions and circumstances changed, definitions would have to be reviewed and reformulated. Expressions and functions of religion were so buried in human societies that scholars recommended a description of religion could be more appropriate than attempts at its definition (Monahan, 2001).

Role of Religion in Society

Religion is a group phenomenon is significant both for what it says and for what it fails to say, for what it excludes. What it excludes is of course the individual aspect. Certainly religion is an individual matter in any number of ways: in that it involves personal emotions and thoughts; or insofar as one's religion is a matter of personal beliefs; or insofar as individuals are free to commit themselves to whichever religious system they prefer. Throughout history and in every corner of the world, people have engaged in religious behavior. Congregations, ceremonial gatherings, denominations, prayer meetings, family pilgrimages, ecumenical councils-all are examples of religious activity.

Elaborating the arbitrary division of religion into its personal and group dimensions, J. Paul Williams (1962) suggests that there are at least four types or levels of religiousness: (i) the secret level, which a person keeps to himself or herself and does not divulge or discuss; (ii) the private, which they divulges or discusses with only a few carefully chosen intimates; (iii) the denominational, which the individual shares with many others in a large group; and (iv) the societal, which the person shares with the members of society at large.

Whenever and wherever man has a sense of dependence on external powers which are conceived as mysterious and higher than man's own, there is religions, and the feelings of awe and self-abasement with which man is filled in the presence of such powers is essentially a religious emotion, the root of worship and prayer. The internal aspect of religion is the body of ideas, convictions, and emotions concerning man's relations to God, while its external aspect is the system of prayers, ceremonies and rites through which the religious feeling is manifested. The institution concerned with the regulation of these external practices is the religious institution.

Throughout the history of humanity the religious impulse has been always and everywhere present as one of the great permanent forces that make and alter man's destiny, and the deeper we delve in the past, the more evident it is how inseparable is the religious instinct from human life and society. The fact that men everywhere and always have developed religion—for there is no evidence that any tribe or race has existed without it—points to the truth that religion must have its roots in human nature. No accident of environment or tenacity of tradition can account for what is constant and persistent: that which is universal in experience must be a genuine expression of man's inner life (Galloway, 1909).

The historical origin of religion has hardly any sense, because it is as old as mankind. The only sensible course is to inquire into the subjective origin of religion. Concerning this, there are some who loosely speak about a religious instinct, but not even McDougall himself, the modern protagonist of the instinct theory, was inclined to accept this view. In his opinion the religious attitude consists in the emotion of reverence which is a composite of awe and gratitude. Of these, the former includes fear and admiration (which is composed of negative self-feeling and wonder) while the latter is made up of tender emotion and negative self-feeling-both of which are supported by such propensities as curiosity, self-abasement, flight, and the parental instinct.

Freud and his followers placed the root of religion in the unconscious. Thus the individual's idea of God is modeled after one's father; God, therefore, is nothing else but an exalted and sublimated father. William James also believed that the religious attitude of the individual originated in the unconscious, and manifested itself in the conscious side of the human mind, which he compared to an island of human consciousness floating upon the limitless ocean floor of the unconscious.

Religion, therefore, subjectively considered, cannot be placed exclusively on any special faculty-instinct, or particular trait-- but in the whole man. It resides in the whole of man's psychological powers orientated towards the Divine. Hence to speak of religion as an emotion or as a mere act of will or understanding is inadequate and misleading. The true religious attitude must include normally thought, will, and emotion; while, on the other hand, a purely intellectual religion that leaves unaffected the other potentialities of man is a long way unreal or abnormal. As Selbie remarks: It cannot be too often repeated that if religion is to hold men and work for their uplifting, it must appeal to the whole man, and satisfy his reason as well as his conscience and his heart (Selbie,1926). A healthy religious attitude, even when volitional or emotional elements prevail, implies a background of thought and knowledge acquired by tradition, experience, or personal effort on which the other elements including the more external like ceremony and ritual, develop.

The religious attitude may be considered as a negative and a positive phase, both of which are equally important. On the negative side man perceives his internal insufficiency and contingency in contrast with God's infinite power and perfection. This reality is most intensely felt by man in the great crises of life as when he considers the phenomena of life and death, or himself falls a prey to the ruthlessness of nature or to the interplay of forces that he cannot control or understand.

On the positive side man feels drawn towards the higher forms of life, and aspires to reach a place or state in which he will be perfectly happy with the enjoyment of permanent truth, justice, peace, beauty and everything that makes for supreme happiness. This intimate aspiration of the human heart is at basis of many social utopias and millennia and is typically present in the cosmic theory of indefinite progress towards a final consummation. There are many persons who do not actually have these aspirations because they believe them to be impossible; but the fact that man can conceive of them and in most cases can positively desire them, shows that man, unlike the animals, is capable of and made for that perfect happiness towards which religion tends to guide him. Here he gains an assurance that the present riddles of the universe have a solution; that his most sincere hopes are not unjustified; that there is a Supreme Power on whom the moral and cosmic orders depend; and that there is finally a perfect coherence and harmony behind the inconsistencies and chaos, shreds and patches of the present life.

Functional Interpretation of Religion in Society—An Analysis

Religion is ubiquitous and universal in its presence. Religion is one such central social institution that is found in all forms of society since the beginning of recorded human history although its form and content have been changing from time to time and from region to region. Religion, like the essence of culture, provides a blue print for the behavior of the individual member of society on the basis of principles sustained by divine, supernatural or transcendent order of morality. Religion is something that human beings follow as members of social groups.

In the *Elementary Forms of the Religious Life,* first published in 1912, Emile Durkheim presented what is probably the most influential interpretation of religion from a functionalist perspective. Durkheim argues that all societies divide the world into two categories, 'the sacred' and 'the profane', or more simply, the sacred and the non-sacred. Religion is based upon this division. It is 'a unified system of beliefs and practices related to sacred things, that is to say things set apart and forbidden'. To understand the role of religion in society, the relationship between sacred symbols and that which they represent must be established.

Durkheim argues that social life is impossible without the shared values and moral beliefs which form the 'collective conscience'. In their absence, there would be no social order, social control, social solidarity or cooperation. In short, there would be no society. Religion reinforces the collective conscience. The worship of society strengthens the values and moral beliefs which form the basis of social life. By defining them as sacred, religion provides them with greater power to direct human action. The attitude of respect towards the sacred is the same attitude applied to social duties and obligations. In worshipping society, men are, in effect, recognizing the importance of the social group and their dependence upon it. In this way religion strengthens the unit of the group, it promotes social solidarity. Durkheim emphasizes the importance of collective worship. The social group comes together in religious rituals infused with drama and reverence. Together, its members express their faith in common values and beliefs. In this highly charged atmosphere of collective worship, the integration of society is strengthened. Members of society express, communicate and comprehend the moral bonds which unite them.

Malinowski uses data from small-scale non-literate societies to develop his thesis on religion. Malinowski identifies specific areas of social life with which religion is concerned, to which it is addressed. These are situations of emotional stress which threaten social solidarity. Anxiety and tension tend to disrupt social life. Situations which produce these emotions include 'crises of life' such as birth, puberty, marriage and death. Malinowski notes that in all societies these life crises are surrounded with religious ritual. He sees death as the most disruptive of these events and argues that, "The existence of strong personal attachments and the fact of death, which of all human events is the most upsetting and disorganizing to man's calculations, are perhaps the main sources of religious beliefs'.

Talcott Parsons argues that human action is directed and controlled by norms provide by the social system. The cultural system provides more general guidelines for action in the form of beliefs, values and systems of meaning. The norms which direct action are not merely isolated standards for behavior; they are integrated and patterned by the values and beliefs provided by the cultural system. Religion is part of the cultural system. As such, religious beliefs provided guidelines for human action and standards against which man's conduct can be evaluated. Many of the norms of the social system are integrated by religious beliefs.

The norms which direct these areas of behavior prohibit manslaughter, murder and euthanasia. They are all based on the same religious commandment. In this way religion provides general guidelines for conduct which are expressed in a variety of norms. By establishing general principles and moral beliefs, religion helps to provide the consensus which Parsons believes is necessary for order and stability in society. As a part of the cultural system, religious beliefs give meaning to life, they answer 'man's questions about himself and the world he lives in'.

Social life is full of contradictions which threaten the meaning man places on life. Parsons argues that one of the major functions of religion is to 'make sense' of all experiences, no matter how meaningless or contradictory they appear. Parsons therefore sees a major function of religion as the provision of meaning to events that man does not expect or feels ought not to happen, events that are frustrating and contradictory. Religion 'makes sense' of these events in terms of an integrated and consistent pattern of meaning. This allows intellectual and emotional adjustment. On a more general level, this adjustment promotes order and stability in society.

In Marx's words, 'Religion is the sigh of the oppressed creature, the sentiment of a heartless world and the soul of soulless conditions. It is the opium of the people'. Religion acts as an opiate to dull the pain produced by oppression. It does nothing to solve the problem, it is simply a misguided attempt to make life more bearable. As such, religion merely stupefies its adherents rather than bringing them true happiness and fulfillment. From a Marxian viewpoint, religion does not simply cushion the effects of oppression, it is also an instrument of that oppression. It acts as a mechanism of social control, maintaining the existing system of exploitation and reinforcing class relationships.

Religion is not, however, solely the province of oppressed groups. From a Marxian perspective, ruling classes adopt religious beliefs to justify their position both to themselves and to others. The lines, 'God made them high and lowly and ordered their estate', show clearly how religion can be used to justify social inequality not simply to the poor, but also to the rich. Religion is often directly supported by ruling classes to further their interests. However, conflicting evidence suggests that Marxian views must be limited to the operation of religion at certain times and in certain places. Religion does not always legitimate power. It is not simply an expression of alienation or a justification of privilege. Marx stated that, 'Religion is only the illusory sun which revolves round man as long as he does not revolve round himself'. In a truly socialist society man revolves round himself and religion, along with all other illusions and distortions of reality, disappears.

A.R. Radcliffe-Brown focused on the role of religion in the maintenance of social solidarity in his sociological analysis of ritual. He was influenced by W. Robertson Smith in his emphasis upon rituals rather than beliefs in the study of religion. "An orderly social life amongst human beings depends upon the presence in the minds of the members of society of certain sentiments, which control the behavior of the individual in relation to others. Rites can therefore be shown to have specific social functions, when.... they have for their effects to regulate, maintain and transmit from one generation to another sentiment on which the constitution of society depends....." (1952).

E.E. Evans-Pritchard (1965) shows a shift in the explanation of supernatural phenomena from function to meaning. Witchcraft among the Azande was explained by him as a mode of causality for human misfortune. In his later work, 'Nuer Religion'(1956), the same shift from straightforward functionalism to the problem of meaning can be noticed, though he did not go into an explicit phenomenological analysis. He was close to Durkheim when he interpreted the Nuer religious thought and ritual in terms of social order.

The essence of Weber's sociology of religion lies in his emphasis on an 'interpretive understanding' of social reality, leading to causal explanation. From this perspective an understanding of 'religious behavior. can only be achieved from the viewpoint of the subjective experiences, ideas and purposes of the individuals concerned. Levi-Strauss subsumes the study of the 'sacred' under forms of thought, modes of classification, mythologies etc. He disagrees with the identification of 'totemism' with religious forms. He asserts that the sacred objects owe their significance neither to the narrow considerations of utility, nor to their social nor moral character, but to their availability as concrete manifestations or embodiments of abstract ideas. The primitives do not 'think' differently from the civilized but they symbolize differently. Religious systems, comprising myths and rites, are symbolic systems of signs, of communication, which establish through analogical reasoning continuities between nature and culture and between cosmic order and social life.

Clifford Geertz (1975), the American social anthropologist, has tried to resolve the problem of extremity in terms of emotion versus intellectual bias in the explanation of religion. Geertz presented a scheme that requires focus on both the rational and the emotional content of religion. The term ethos is used to denote the feelings or the personality aspects that are a part of religion. The concept of worldview is employed to account for human reason. According to him the 'ethos' is made intellectually reasonable by being shown to represent a way of life implied by the actual state of affairs, at least as perceived by a particular 'worldview'. In turn, one's worldview must be made emotionally acceptable by being presented as an image of actual state of affairs. In this way, Geertz proposes, harmony between the emotional and intellectual aspects of religion can be conceived.

Sir James Frazer argued that religion is an integrated substructure of the culture. His argument that religion evolved from magic with a projected evolution of religion to science is not accepted by other social scientists. His arguments have been persuasive for a wide audience though of lesser concern in sociology and anthropology. Another evolutionist Herbert Spencer approached the problem of determining the origin of religion through examination of Australian aborigines who were considered the most primitive of living cultures. Since these native paid much attention to their ancestors, Spencer reasoned that heroic ancestors were remembered and glorified by descendents. Over time, such grandparents assumed godlike qualities. In short long-dead ancestors became the realm of the sacred. These spirits began to govern the weather, health, education, family life and other vital areas of culture. Putting it succinctly, Spencer proposed that human beings intellectually created their religion, and that they progressed through rational, evolutionary stages. Incidentally, Spencer also noted a religious and political connection. He contended that while the fear of other living people was basic for political organization, a fear of the dead was foundation of religious control.

Religion in Present Day Context

If the large-scale social system operates with little regard to religion as an institution, it also ignores the religious orientations of individuals. The very fact that religion becomes an optional matter, the fact that there is freedom of religion, tolerance, and choice, is an indication that religion is apparently of little direct consequence to the functioning of the social order, at least as that order is understood by those who have helped to build it, modify it, and maintain it.

In the contemporary society there are an increasing proportion of people who are disturbed by the facelessness of modern bureaucracy, by the impersonality of relationships, and by the sense of boredom that is felt in the manning of the rational technical social system. The social problems of the modern society which is growing at an alarming rate vary from one society to another. The growth of crime, of vandalism, and of neurosis and mental breakdown, the growing disruption of marriage; the increase in various types of addiction, and the incidence of personal isolation, loneliness, and suicide, provide a commentary on the points at which the rational social organization apparently fails. Indeed, not only does the system fail to cope with these disruptions, it appears that they arise partly as a consequence of its normal operation.

The social system of advanced societies functions on rational premises. As large-scale, on-going, internally-structured systems, contemporary societies depend on the rational distribution of facilities and resources, and the pressure within such societies is for even greater rationalization. Anomalies, anachronisms, localisms, and individuality become implicit anathema to the system and those who, at every level, control it. Standardization and routinization become values almost in their own right because they facilitate the smooth operation of the system.

Traditional societies often had value systems that were not fully articulated, and which, indeed, often defied articulation. In the religious expressions of a people, these traditional orientations usually acquired elevated and rhetorical formulation, so that men were exhorted to live to do the will of God, or to fulfill the law, or to strive for perfection, or to overcome harmful desire, or to enhance the life of others. But a modern social system is increasingly conceived as operating without virtues; it becomes a neutral, detached, objective, rational co-ordination of role performances. The system induces those who actually man the roles—that is, human beings—to behave as if they had neither virtues nor vices. The pressure is towards the neutralization of human personality, so that roles might be performed with ever greater calculability.

Obviously, this pressure from the rational structure is not wholly successful. Nor can it be, since the system depends on human beings to perform roles, and human beings have to be socialized to cultivate dispositions that are molded for such performances. Modern man, in spite of the benefits of living in an efficient society, and despite his complaints when the system fails in one respect or another, is not wholly content with rational social organization.

Men busy themselves applying the procedural rules, doing this to achieve that, which in turn will become the means to something else, in an infinite linking of rational procedures and efficient techniques. But rationality alone supplies no specific substantive values, other than survival, either for the society or for individuals. And survival, taken just as such, may not be enough. Here, then, might be a place for religion. In itself, this suggests a somewhat private role religion functioning for individuals.

Modern society rejects religion on intellectual grounds, and fails to see what the cost might be in terms of the emotional sustenance that men need in order to live. The modern social system operates on implicit assumptions of secularity; in its narrowly conceived rationality, it leaves no room for super-empirical concerns because the relation of these concerns to human well-being is very imperfectly understood, and cannot in its nature, be subjected to precise rational calculation. The costs of this tension between religion and rationality in contemporary society already makes itself evident. There is a wide variety of signs of breakdown, which, however, manifest themselves in somewhat different ways in different societies.

In modern society the need of religion is no less paramount As long as suffering exists in this world, the value and essence of religion is necessary. There is much strain in modern life. The number of mentally deranged persons is on the increase. The cases of suicide, violence and crime are also increasing. Science cannot solve all the problems of modern life. If a population becomes too matter-of-fact in its attitudes, too calculating in its behavior, too sophisticated in its values, it is likely not to stick together sufficiently to maintain order and protection. It seems unlikely that science can entirely replace religion, any more than the latter can entirely replace the former. In order to make our lives more meaningful and purposeful, we will have to depend on some moral or spiritual truth. We will have to believe in some ultimate reality whether we call it God or a creature, life-giving force or vital energy. An integrated personality can be developed only out of the fusion of scientific temper, philosophical inquiry and faith in the unseen.

It is of course true that religion is sometimes too much associated with supernaturalism and dogmatism but the recent trends in religion have tended to place more emphasis on social values and less on dogmas. It has also tried to reconcile its doctrines with scientific knowledge. The religious leaders are now accepting more scientific data in the explanation of physical and social phenomena. They now encourage effective use of scientific knowledge to maintain health, reduce births, cure diseases, control sex and maintain economic activities. The humanists have attempted to construct a religion based entirely "upon the service of man rather than the worship of God". The modern trend is towards the socialization and secularization of religion. True religion is not found in temples but in mind. And once religion raises above all dogmas and super-naturalism, it will become a constructive societal force worth preserving. For future it should adjust itself to changes in life conditions. The more it is adapted to existing conditions and factual knowledge the greater the chance of its being effective as an institution. As Barnes (1964), said, religion worth preserving must seek to organize the masses of people and guide their activities for the benefit of society rather than for the purpose of pleasing God.

The functions and dysfunctions of religion with respect both to society and to individuals may be examined with reference to the most outstanding social and cultural development of the last several centuries: namely, the secularization of culture. In primitive and traditional societies, religion was all pervasive in the sense that religion ordained everything from birth to cremation or burial, including even mundane matters, such as occupational groupings. In short, religion determined the world-view of the believers. These characteristics are applicable to religious people in modern societies also. But a subtle difference has crept in and now people are gradually moving away from mythical interpretation to a more rational one. The rationalization of religious thought is part of a general process of the rationalization of thinking in general. Secularisation of culture involved not simply an increase in rationality in the thinking of men, but also a diminution of the sacred which is often characterized as desacralisation. Thus, the secularization of culture, combining both desacralisation and rationalization, means that a religious world-view is no longer the basic frame of reference for thought.

It is obvious that a rational world-view is opposed to religion because the latter is based on faith and as such is non-rational. People no longer interpret the world around them in religious terms. There has, therefore, developed what is called secularisation of consciousness. The separation between morality and religion is one prominent feature in the cultural changes of the past century, both in the sense that a clear distinction has been made between ritual and moral rules, and in the sense that, with the decline of religious belief, it has been necessary to find a new basis and content for the moral rules. Paradoxically, this separation between religion and morality brings the two closer on another level. As Bottomore (1972), points out "religion has become more an individual and private matter .... while morality has become more social, in that it is increasingly concerned with social justice rather than individual virtue. This change of emphasis is apparent even in the moral doctrines of religious organizations, which are much more concerned with social relations and social problems than ever in the past".

Conclusion

The history of mankind shows that religion is one of the deepest and most intimate urges of mankind which, in one way or another, is found everywhere. The tendency to reduce it to a particular instinct or drive, conscious or unconscious, is not substantiated by modern scholars who rather look upon religion as a spontaneous impulse of the whole man embracing thought, will, and emotion, whereby he perceives his internal limitation and contingency and aspires to achieve his perfection and happiness in permanent union with God. In this state the seeming inconsistencies in the physical and moral universe become integrated into a harmonious whole where the perennial problems of life find their solution and man realizes that his highest hopes are abundantly justified. But this perfect happiness cannot be attained in the present life because it is only a way to the eternal; the eternal in the making.

The role of religion in life manifests itself in the individual by giving him an integrated outlook on life which is conducive even to keep his mental balance. Religion is not only one of the most influential forces of society, it is also considered by many as the centre and origin of culture – 'the impulse that makes civilization'. It also supplies a great stimulus to moral progress and social reform. On the other hand, if the religious sentiment is addressed to undesirable objects, it may become very destructive.

REFERENCE

Bottomore, T.B., 1972. *Sociology: A Guide to Problems and Literature*, Bombay: George Allen and Unwin.

Barnes, H.Elmer, 1946. *Social Institutions*, New York: Prentice Hall.

Beckford, James A. (ed.), 2007. *The Sage Handbook of the Sociology of Religion*, New Delhi: Sage Publications.

Bellah, R., 1970. *Beyond Belief*, London: Harper Row.

Birnbaum, N. and G. Lenzer, 1969. *Sociology of Religion: A Book of Readings*, New Jersey: Prentice Hall Inc.

D' Souza, Leela, 2005. *The Sociology of Religion – A Historical Review*, New Delhi: Rawat Publications.

Davie, Grace, 2007. *The Sociology of Religion*, New Delhi: Sage Publications.

Durkheim, Emile, 1965 (1915) *Elementary Forms of Religious life*, Translated by J.W. Swaun, New York: Free Press.

Galloway,G, 1909. *The Principles of Religious Development*, London: Macmillan.

Geertz, Clifford, 1975. *Interpretation of Cultures*, New York: Basic Books.

Gisbert, Pascual, 1965. *Fundamentals of Sociology*, New Delhi: Orient Longmans.

Haralambos, M, 1980. *Sociology – Themes and Perspectives*, New Delhi: Oxford University Press.

Johnstone, Ronald .L, 1992. *Religion in Society—A Sociology of Religion*, New Jersey: Prentice Hall.

Kar, Parimal. B, 1985. *Sociology*, Calcutta: New Central Book Agency.

King, W.L. 1987. Religion in M. Eliade (ed), *Encyclopedia of Religion*, New York: Macmillan Publishing Co.Vol.12.

Kremer - Mariette, Angele, 1987. Positivism in M. Elade (ed) *Encyclopedia of Religion*, New York: Macmillan Publishing Co. Vol.-II.

Lenski, G. 1963. *The Religious Factor: A Sociologist's Enquiry*, New York: Anchor Books.

Lessa, W.H. and E.Z. Vogt., 1965. *Reader in Comparative Religion: An Anthropological Approach*, New York: Harper and Row.

Lundskow, George, 2008. *The Sociology of Religion – A Substantive and Transdisciplinary Approach*, London: Pine Forge Press.

Monahan, Susanne et.al (ed.) 2001. *Sociology of Religion: A Reader*, New Jersey: Prentice Hall Inc.

Nottingham, E.K., 1971. *Religion: A Sociological View*, New York: Random House.

Robinson, Rowena, 2004. *Sociology of Religion in India*, New Delhi: Sage Publication.

Scharf, B.R. 1970. *The Sociological Study of Religion*, London: Hutchinson University Library.

Selbic, W.B., 1926. *The Psychology of Religion*, Oxford: Clarendon Press.

Sociology in India, 2005. School of Social Sciences, New Delhi: Indira Gandhi National Open University.

Wach, J, 1947. *Sociology of Religion*, London. London: Keygan Paul Ltd.

Williams, Paul, J. 1962. The Nature of Religion, *Journal for the Scientific Study of Religion* 2, No.1.

Wilson, Brayan, 1982. *Religion in Sociological Perspective*, New York: Oxford University press.

Yinger, M.J.1957. *Religion, Society and the Individual: An Introduction to the Sociology of Religion*, New York: Macmillan Publishing.

9

Concept of God and Peaceful Coexistence

Tom Mangattuthazhe

Introduction

People do not live in isolation, but religions —in communities that are built on trust and in which are conducive to relationships – constitute a central element of the cultural conditions necessary for human life. Religious life is primarily life in community, and it is the adherents to a religion who themselves decide how to run their community, live their faith, and worship God.

The tradition of religion is ancient. Our ancient forefathers introduced and popularised the concept of religion to promote the feeling of love, brotherhood, cooperation and peaceful coexistence among humans.

Contemporary Faces of Violence

Identifying the different faces of violence will help us to discover relevant and effective ways of overcoming them. The following are some of the faces of violence that we identify.

1. *Physical Violence* – Warfare, the use of brute force such as battering and domestic abuse, terrorism by individuals state and non state actors.

2. *Political Violence* – When laws are enacted that militate against the recognition of each person's dignity, worth and equality with another.eg. AFSPA, state-sponsored Violence – Such as extra judicial killings, torture, and detention /incarceration without due legal process.
3. *Structural Violence* – Violence that is built into social, political, and economic structures such as ethnicity, caste etc.
4. *Ecological Violence* — The destruction of environment resulting from irresponsible use of natural resources.
5. *So called Lacerative Violence ?* – When individuals or groups – as a last resort – seek recourse to violence to respond to the above listed forms of violence and achieve liberation from oppression. Here we must realize that even in the face of real or perceived injustice, violence does not solve any problem. It only begets further violence. Lasting peace can only come about through peaceful means.

The Relation between Religion and Violence

The following are some of the ways in which we characterize the relationship between violence and religion:

Negative Forms of Engagement

- *Silence:* Religious communities often maintain silence in the face of violence. There are many reasons for such silence, including, the concern for the survival of their own communities and structures.
- *Sanctification:* Religious communities justify the use of violence by the state or extra state entities or by other agencies. Examples of this would be when a religious tradition attaches itself to the militaristic objectives of the state, e.g., violence against women.
- *Expansion:* Religious communities use violence for purposes of spreading themselves or of ensuring their own growth.

- *Images of God:* Some religious traditions have violent images of the Divine, which may have problematic implications for the self-understanding of their believers.
- *Images of Self:* Religious traditions promote violence by framing the worth of their adherents in terms of the 'lesser worth' of others.

Positive Forms of Engagement

- *Unmasking/Opposing:* Religious communities have played a role in opposing violence both within their own community and when others are injured.
- *Models of Non-Violence:* Each religious tradition has also had significant individuals and groups that have lived lives testifying to the peaceful impulses in religion.

Lessons from Christianity for Peaceful Coexistence

We have a mandate for mission

"Blessed are the peacemakers, for they will be called children of God." Mathew 5:9

Christian communities have received a mandate in the Word of God for Peace Making.

Pope John Paul II in his address to the UN General Assembly, October 5, 1995, said, In the context of the community of nations, the church's message is simple yet absolutely crucial for the survival of humanity and the world: The human person must be the true focus of all social, political and economic activity....This truth, when effectively put into practice, will point the way to healing the divisions between the rich and the poor, to overcoming the inequality between the strong and the weak, to reconciling man with himself and with God. For men and women are made in the image and likeness of God. So people may never be regarded as mere objects, nor may they be sacrificed for political, economic or social gain. We must never allow them to be manipulated or enslaved by ideologies or technology.

Pope John Paul II said with reference to the events of Sept. 11: "We must not let what has happened lead to a deepening of divisions. Religion must never be used as a reason for conflict." Religious believers must take the lead in building a world in which all peoples can live together in peace and brotherhood.

Pope Paul VI in his encyclical Ecclesiam Suam (1964) suggested that common ideals such as religious freedom, human brotherhood, sound culture, social welfare and civil order might be taken as themes of interreligious conversation.

Lessons from Islam for Peaceful Coexistence

The Qur'an suggests that the variety in humankind is one of the riches in God's world. The guiding verse is: O humankind, we have created you male and female, and appointed you races and tribes, that you may know one another. Surely the noblest among you in the sight of God is the most god fearing of you. God is All-knowing, All-Aware. (K. 49:14)

The Qur'an views human diversity as a basis for understanding and peaceful coexistence. Verse 49:13 states, "O people, We have created you from one male and female (Adam and Eve), We have created you in different communities and tribes so that you may know each other." Stated differently, human diversity should enhance the recognition of, rather than confrontation with, the other.

Thus the principle that God is the God of all creation and one who recognizes and embraces all his children is clearly established. Regardless of the contradictions, the preciousness of the individual and the embrace by God of all of his children is the dominant theme of the Koran. Indeed, it is the essence of monotheism.

Lessons from Judaism for Peaceful Coexistence

The compassion that Judaism commends is universal. It is extended, like God's, to all of His creatures. No race is excluded from the Law, because all human beings, according to

Judaism's teaching, are brothers, are children of the same Father, and are created in the image of God.

Lessons from Hinduism for Peaceful Coexistence

Swami Vivekananda's address at Parliament of Religions held at Chicago is worth recalling: "I am proud to belong to a religion which has taught the world both tolerance and universal acceptance. We believe not only in universal tolerance, but we accept all religions as true..." The religion referred to by Swami Vivekananda is the ancient religion of India which is also known as sanatana dharma which speaks of universal peace based on solidarity with the earth and all beings, nonviolence, humility and love in action i.e. compassionate service.

The author of the Mahabharata was once asked to summarize all the teachings in one or two verses. The author retorted: "Why one or two verses?" I shall finish in just half a verse: paropakarah punyaya, papaya parapidanam: help to others brings merit, violence or injury to others brings forth sin.

Inspiring Sacred Texts on Peaceful Coexistence from World Religions

This is the sum of duty; do naught unto others which would cause you pain if done to you. Mahabharata Hurt not others in ways that you Yourself would find hurtful - Buddhism

In happiness and suffering, in joy and grief, we should regard all creatures as we regard our own self. Jainism

That nature only is good when it shall not do unto another whatever is not good for its own self. —Zoroastrianism

Do not unto others what you would not have them do unto you. — Confucianism

No one of you is a believer until he desires for his brother that which he desires for himself. —Islam

All things whatsoever ye would that men do to you, do ye even so to them. —Christianity

What is hateful to you, do not to your fellow men, that is the law all the rest is commentary. —Judaism

The Common Basis of Religions: Human beings as Creatures of God

Whether from a Jewish, Christian, or Islamic understanding, every human being is a creature of God. As creatures of God, all people are fun-damentally equal and connected with one another.

Peace, freedom, and justice are concepts at the core of all the major world religions. The major religions indeed agree that peace, freedom, and justice cannot simply be declared, but are only real to the extent that they are actually upheld. These concepts are also demands that the religions place on the people and that need to be continually renewed and reimple-mented.

Common Principles for Peaceful Coexistence

- We all live in God's world. Muslims, Christians and Jews answer to the same God. The world is His, not ours, and His authority is not there to affirm our sectarian biases but for us to become attuned to the presence of God in all of life.
- The core values of most of the religions is the recognition that human beings are created in the image of God. "Human beings have been given sacred worth as their birthright and are therefore deserving of dignity and respect in all relationships." All of the world's great religions teach this truth, "and, yet, we often act as if we never knew it."
- Our own faith requires us to cross the boundary lines that normally divide us from each other.
- Justice is required for human flourishing and peace.
- Dialogue and Co-existence is Exemplified in Various Occasions. In every day life Christians and Muslims interact and live along side each other at various places of work, education, health, celebrations, support in funerals etc.

Lessons from Indian History

- The great Akbar married Jodhabai, Kalawati tied rakhi (wristband) on the wrist of Humayun,
- Maratha ruler Shivaji appointed Mullah Haider as his very personal secretary and Daulat Khan and Dariya Khan as his confidential naval commanders, thus promoting religious harmony.
- There are innumerable such examples which prove that many Hindu rulers provided land for Mosques, Mausoleums and cemeteries. Similarly many Muslim rulers provided land for the construction of temples, gurudwaras and other worshipping places.

Obstacles For Peaceful Coexistence

- The collapse of moral and family values. And this is a fertile ground for the nurturing of fundamentalist.
- The "Globalisation of bad news," by which atrocities committed in any remote part of the world are beamed through satelite for everyone else to see.
- The absence of a central (authoritative) interpretation of Sacred texts.
- Though, India is a melting pot of different religions and communities, but the petty politicians involved in vote bank politics, are continuously in an attempt to pollute and destroy the secular character of the country.

The Way Forward

- Multiple Identities. Amartya Sen wrote a book called "Identity and Violence: The illusion of destiny" in critique of Huntington's main concept of an inevitable clash along civilizational lines. In this book he argues that a root cause of violence is when people see each other as having a singular affiliation, i.e. Hindu or Muslim, as opposed to multiple affiliations: Hindu, woman, housewife, mother, artist, daughter, member of a particular socio-economic class...etc. all of which can be a source of a person's identity.

- The great Indian thought *sarve bhavantu sukhinah, vasudhev kutumbakam*. (The whole world is my family) should be our driving force.
- To protect the society from the misuse of religion, the children should get compulsory have peace education.
- Greater networking among civil society groups, including religious NGOs.
- Common meditation and action to respond to the challenge of corruption, misnamagement of resources, bad governance, collapsed infrastructure, widespread disease, especially the epidemic of HIV/AIDS, the fallen standard of education, the collapse of moral and family values, etc.
- We must all come to recognise that even in the face of real or perceived injustice, violence does not solve any problem. It only begets further violence. Lasting peace can only come about through peaceful means.

Conclusion

The concept of world peace is not new, it is as old as the history of human civilisation. Buddha preached non-violence and universal peace ; Christ got himself crucified for upholding the righteous cause of peace ; Gandhi was the great apostle of peace who dedicated his life to the spread of universal love and brotherhood The world seems to have not yet heeded their doctrines. Though we have failed more than once, yet we need not be disappointed. The nations of the world have started realising the value of peaceful, co-existence. The establishment of world peace does not seem- an impossibility now. Therefore, with heart within and God overhead, we should wish that our hopes for world peace come true.

Our own religious traditions give us ethical values and offer us a vision of peaceful co-existence. Only that we have to be conscious of it, promote it and go beyond narrow political, national, economic or military objectives.

Religious leaders have a special collective responsibility to sound the alarm quickly whenever any of God's children are threatened. The environment for doing the right thing in protecting the preciousness of human life is improving. But the instincts of political leaders to avoid brave or painful choices is a constant counterweight.

REFERENCES

1. Clash or Peaceful Existance? By Dr. Jaafar Sheikh Idris ISLAMIC FUTURE, SAFAR 1417 (JULY 1996) http://www.themodernreligion.com/world/clash.html
2. http://www.wcc-coe.org/wcc/what/interreligious/cd39-08.html
3. ZE06051207 - 2006-05-12 Permalink: http://www.zenit.org/article-15997?l=english
4. http://www.ittefaq.com/issues/2010/02/05/news0050.htm
5. The complete works of Swami Vivekananda, Vol. I, pp. 3-4.
6. http://www.gmu.edu/depts/crdc/docs/montville1.html
7. Abu-Nimer, Muhammad. "Conflict Resolution in an Islamic Context: Some Conceptual Questions," Peace and Change 21 (1) (January 1996):
8. Bernbaum John J. *Perspectives on Peacemaking,* Ventura, CA: Regal Books, 1984.
9. http://www.mscollege.ca/downloads/MSC_research-derksen2.pdf
10. http://www.mscollege.ca/downloads/MSC_research-derksen1.pdf
11. http://usip.forumone.com/files/resources/sr123.pdf

10

Indigenous Spirituality

Paul Pudussery, CSC*

Indigenous people have a deep and profound spirituality that is rooted in nature. That rootedness enables them to connect with the rest of the cosmos. Indigenous people in normal circumstances seek explicit permission from a tree, animal and other inanimate objects before they are put to use, for the benefit of the community or a member. Indigenous people's understanding of spirituality is very different from that of the other societies around them.

Spirituality Defined

How does one understand spirituality? The term 'spiritual' literally means that which inspires and gives breath to (Purpel, 1999). The challenge then in spirituality is to find the source of this energizing spirit and fathom that we are, where do we come from, where do we go to? Why things and events occur in a particular moment of history? Once certain answers are ascertained then what does one with them? A true spirituality enables one to use the imagination to give an access to truths, which otherwise are inaccessible to our experience, and an epistemological structure that connects truth and beauty.

* Dr. Paul Puthussery CSC, Agartala, is the Director of Holy Cross Higher Education Ministry in North East India.

According to scholars, spirituality is highly individualistic and intensely personal (Mitof & Denton, 1999; Giacalone & Jurkiewicz, 2003). It is the exploration of the inner territory and the search to know more about the meaning of life and our purpose in some grander scheme. It is the confronting of inner selves, wrestling with and resolving inner doubts, encountering their spiritual and transcendent beliefs, so that they could emerge with necessary courage and conviction to handle the conflicts and complexities of external hardships and challenges (Giacalone & Jurkiewicz, 2003). One needn't be religious in order to be spiritual. Some of the most spiritual people are not apparently religious.

The following are thoughts collected from different individuals about their understanding of the term spirituality. Spirituality is the basic belief that there is a supreme power, a being, a force, whatever you call it, that governs the entire universe. There is a purpose for everything and everyone. The universe is not meaningless or devoid of purpose. Spirituality is the feeling of interconnectedness and being in with it. Spirituality is also a feeling that no matter how bad things get, they will always work out somehow. There is a guiding plan that governs all lives. As long as a person has others, such as a family to fall back on, there is nothing to fear. There is as much, if not more, goodness in the world as there is evil. We are put here basically to do well. One must strive to produce products and services that serve all humanity. Spirituality is inextricably connected with caring, hope, kindness, love and optimism. It cannot be proved logically or scientifically that these things exist in the universe as a whole. There seems to be no universal agreement on a definition. The responses indicate that it is possible to be spiritual without believing in or affirming a higher power or God.

Faith, Religion and Spirituality

Many individuals, with whom the scholar interacted, explicitly included the notion of a higher power or God and concept of religion as an integral part of their definition of spirituality. Faith is an essential component of spirituality. The act of faith is double: the existential affirmation of a history as one's redemptive history and the existential appropriation of this redemptive history as one's personal background history, and therefore in a real sense, the foundation of one's existence (Herberg, 1976). Tillich describes faith as:

The state of being ultimately concerned: the dynamics of faith are the dynamics of man's ultimate concerns. Man...is concerned about manythings, above all about those which condition his existence, such as food and shelter. Man in contrast to other living beings, has spiritual concerns—cognitive, aesthetic, social, and political. Some of them are urgent, often extremely urgent, and each of them as well as the vital concerns can claim ultimacy for a human life or the life of a social group. If it claims ultimacy it demands the total surrender of him who accepts theclaim, and it promises total fulfillment even if all other claims have to be subjected to it or rejected in its name. (p.1)

There are numerous religious traditions, including Hinduism, Buddhism, Daoism, Confucianism, Judaism, Christianity, Islam, Jainism, Sikhism, Parsi, Chinese Popular religion, and primal religions. Each of them has a distinct way of addressing issues that relates to humanity (Kessler, 2008). Each answers questions which all human beings seem to be programmed to inquire about: Why am I here? What happens to me when I die? How shall I live my life? Each religion makes effort to answer these questions in a way that the ordinary people feel comfortable with.

Religion is human a priori, the essence of which is found in the human feeling or institution of the infinite or God. A community's religion represents its highest spiritual reach, its ideal of perfection (Livingstion et al. 2000). William P Alston (1967), a contemporary philosopher offers a cluster definition consisting of nine religion making characteristics. These include:- (a) belief in supernatural beings, (b) a distinction between sacred and profane objects, (c) ritual acts focused on scared objects, (d) a moral code believed to be sanctioned by the gods, (e) characteristically religious feelings, which tend to be aroused in the presence of sacared objects and during the practice of a ritual, and which are connected in idea with the gods, (f))prayer and other forms of communication with gods, (g) a worldview or a general picture of the world as the place of the individual therein. This picture contains some specification of an overall purpose or point of the world and the indication of how the individual fits into it, (h)a more or less total organization of one's life based on the world view, (i) a social group bound together by the above. Research indicates the following the orientations toward religion and spirituality (Mitroff & Denton, 1999).

1. A person can have a positive view of religion and spirituality. Spirituality and religion are understood to be the same. Spirituality can be experienced and developed only through religion.
2. A person can have positive view about religion and a negative understanding of spirituality. The religion dominates spirituality.
3. Spirituality dominates the religion and is the source of basic beliefs and universal values.
4. Neither religion nor spirituality is primary. Universal values can be defined and attained independently of religion and spirituality

Spirituality may be defined as a way a person lives his/her everyday life in view of his/her relationship to the gods/the 'spirit' world. It is "a mysterious inner force that animates a person's life of faith, and moves a person's faith to greater depths and perfection" (McGrath, 1997). Others define spirituality as the basic feeling of being connected with one's complete self, others and entire universe (Mitof & Denton, 1999; Giacalone & Jurkiewicz, 2003).

The following are the key elements found in spirituality

- Not formal, structured or organized
- Nondenominational,
- Broadly inclusive, embracing everyone
- Universal and timeless
- The ultimate source and provider of meaning and purpose in life
- The awe we feel in the presence of the transcendent

- The sacredness of everything, the ordinaries of everyday life
- The deep feeling of the interconnectedness of everything
- Inner peace and calm
- An inexhaustible source of faith and will power
- The ultimate end in itself.
- Is inextricably connected with caring, hope, and optimism.

The contemporary philosopher John Hick thinks of spirituality as a transformation from a selfish and egocentric state to an unselfish and caring state. One need not have exclusive religious practices to be spiritual. For indigenous people, spirituality is linked to the life force that flows through all creation.

Indigenous/Tribal Spirituality

Tribal understanding of spirituality is very different from that of the dominant societies around them. For tribals, spirituality is linked to the life force that flows through all creation. Tribals' very mode of life itself manifests a deep and profound spirituality regarding this force, devoid of wordy theological jargon (Kullu, 1996). The tribal community also upholds the dignity of every living being. Among them, there is a sense of equality among men, women, and children. For example, in a dispute resolution process, everyone has a voice and decisions are arrived at only after listening to different stakeholders.

Each indigenous group may have a unique spirituality, yet one thing is believed in common—the interconnectedness among all the animate and inanimate objects around them (Wilf, 1992). Tribal spirituality is strongly connected to habitat while societal values are adopted to bring harmony to all the living. The concept of power is understood in terms of service to the community. According to Wilf (1992), tribal spirituality is the summation and signifier of both concrete and non-material existence. Any significant rupture in this spiritual-concrete relation leads an individual to an alienation that is evident in him or her, often in the form of a maladaptive lifestyle. The respect for creation, gratitude towards the creator, non-transferability and nonpossessiveness of the earth are based on the belief that everything has its origin in and from god (Kullu 1996).

Each indigenous group has its own spirituality, depending on its habitat, history, and resources. An indigenous spirituality is an underlying force of life: language, social system, religious beliefs, and even the way they go about their daily life. Such an understanding may be defined as a set of concepts that relate individuals in any culture to the natural universe and to other humans who comprise their social reality (Christie, 1985).

In many groups, there is no concept of private ownership. The land is usually referred to as "mother," and any desire to buy or sell it is anathema. They use common assets only in so far as they enable them to meet their needs and in living the day to day reality of existence (Kullu, 1996). Many indigenous groups measure time as a function of the sacred circle of life (Cajete, 1994). A significant implication of such an understanding of life is the acknowledgment that life cannot be compartmentalized as a rational process that is detached from the natural and invisible world (Cajecte, 1999). In the indigenous worldview, learning is embedded in nature. According to Kawagley (1995):

Most indigenous peoples' worldviews seek harmony and integration with all life including the spiritual, natural, and human domains. These three realms permeate traditional worldviews and all aspects of indigenous peoples' lives. Their constructed technology was mediated by nature. Their traditional education processes were carefully constructed around mythology, history, the observation of natural processes and animals' and plants' styles of survival and obtaining food, and use of natural materials to make their tools and implements, all of which was made understandable through thoughtful stories and illustrative examples. This view of the world and approach to education has been brought into jeopardy with the onslaught of western social systems and institutionalized forms of cultural transmission....the western worldview with its aggressive educational practice and technoscience orientation has placed indigenous cultures in "harms way." These cultures, characterized as primitive and backward and therefore wanting, are subject to an endless stream of assimilative processes to bring their practitioners into the mainstream society. The indigenous people are forced to live in a constructed and psychic world not of their own making or choosing. Little is left in their lives to remind them of their indigenous culture; nor is there recognition of their indigenous consciousness and its application of intelligence, ingenuity, creativity and inventiveness in the making of their world (pp. 2-3).

In Australia, the indigenous people are referred to as aboriginal. A study found that aboriginal children learn best by personal trial and error, observation and imitation, and context-specific tasks (Batten et. al, 1998). The study further lists four main characteristics of learning, prevalent among the indigenous people: a) the group is more important than an individual; therefore, children are more comfortable with approaches that are cooperative rather than competitive; b) indigenous children are holistic learners and concentrate on understanding the overall concept or task before attending to details; c) indigenous children have a strong visual and spatial sense in their method of receiving and processing information; d) indigenous children have a reduced reliance on the role of language that predisposes them to perceive and think in ways that are unconstrained by the linear nature of verbal thinking. Western world view of life is controlled and influenced by the industrial-technocratic-political complex. In this process, we forget that indigenous knowledge is rooted in a local culture which flows from a spirit filled world and instead of imposing on them a different idea of the world one need to take into account their culture which has all the elements of the spiritulaity. Harris (1990) writes:

The hidden curriculum undermines Aboriginal values in a variety of ways.... The values held by non-Aboriginal teachers, and the values implied by school organization, such as being on time and keeping strictly to a program, can be unconsciously imparted.... Teachers may accuse students of cheating when they are actually cooperating with each other in ways praised in Aboriginal society. When European Australian teachers voice their concerns about the many days per year Aboriginal children spend at funerals and away from class, they are implying that funeral ceremonies are not as important as school.... When European Australians hold the most senior positions in the schools, a negative message is sent out to Aboriginal children about status or respectability of Aboriginal authority.

Indigenous knowledge is rooted in a local culture and is the source of community cohesion. This framework explains the origins and the happenings of the world (Orr, 1992). Indigenous knowledge is not really separated from the reality of day-to-day life. Such experiences will provide an opportunity for people to encounter something real and meaningful rather than merely the mastery of an abstraction (Kane, 1999).

Each indigenous group has its own worldview, depending on the habitat, history, and resources. An indigenous worldview underlies every aspect of life: language, social system, religious beliefs, and even the way it go about its daily life. Such a worldview may be defined as a set of concepts that relate individuals within any culture to the natural universe and to other humans who comprise their social reality (Christie, 1985). In many groups, there is no concept of private ownership. The land is usually referred to as "mother," and any desire to buy or sell it, is anathema. They use common assets as "tantum quantum" to meet their needs and in living the day to day reality of existence (Kullu, 1996). An indigenous community holds at high esteem the dignity of every living being. Research points out that there is a sense of equality among men, women, and children. During a dispute resolution process, everyone has a voice and decisions are arrived at, only after listening to different stakeholders.

Indigenous spirituality draws the individual to be in harmony with oneself and the universe. The connectedness that exists in the indigenous community may be the answer for solving many problems that our world is facing today. When one is spiritual, it is much easier to feel connected with, and have compassion for, and serve our families, companies, governments, and the environment.

REFERENCES

Alister E McGrath, 1999. Christian Spirituality: An Introduction. Adult Education and Formation. http://www.stjohnadulted.org/spir-1.htm.

Batten, M., Frigo, T., Hughes, P., & McNamara, N.1998. Enhancing English literacy skills in Aboriginal and Torres Strait Islander students. Melbourne, NSW, Australia: ACER.

Christie, M. 1985. Aboriginal perspectives on experience and learning: The role of language in Aboriginal education. Victoria, Australia: Deakin University Press.

Herberg, W. 1976. Faith in biblical theology. Philadelphia: Westminster Press.

Hewitt, D. 2000. A Clash of Worldviews: Experiences From Teaching Aboriginal Students. *Theory Into Practice,* 39(2), 111. Retrieved April 24, 2008.

Kane, J. 1999. Education, information, and transformation: Essays on learning and thinking. Upper Saddle River, NJ: Merrill.

Kapitzke, C., Bogitini, S., Chen, M., MacNeill, G., Mayer, D., Muirhead, B., et al. (2000, December). Weaving words with the Dreamweaver: Literacy, indigeneity, and technology. (Cover story). *Journal of Adolescent & Adult Literacy,* 44(4), 336. Retrieved April 24, 2008.

Kawagley, O. 1995. A Yupiaq worldview. Prospect Heights, IL: Waveland Press.

Kunnunkal, Thomas. 2003 A Catholic school becoming a Good News School. In Anikuzhikattil, Joseph et al., (Eds.).*Understanding Tribal Cultures for Effective Education.* (pp. 210-226). Commision for Education and Culture, CBCI Delhi.

Orr, D. 1992. *Ecological Literacy,* Albany: State University of New York Press.

Tillich, P., 1957. *Dynamics of Fath.* New York: Harper & Row

Wilf, Bean 1992. Reflections on a consultation on the development of tribals in Asia. *Convergence,* 00108146, 1992, Vol. 25, Issue 1

Willam Alston. 1967. Religion, in *The Encyclopidea of Philosophy,* ed. Paul Edwards, New York:Macmillan

11

Merging Religion with Politics in a Secular Age: Gandhiji's Interpretation of God, Religion and Politics

Nishikant Kolge & Roshani Rai

While conceiving of religion, for Gandhi problem was not 'religious pluralism' and task was not how to assess truthful claims of 'other' religions. For him, unlike many theologians, problem was also not to formulate an intellectual model wherein theology can somehow or the other be conceived of in universal form. Unlike many western secular scholars he did not believe in extracting a moral core from different religions, and injecting it in politic and other domain of life, will erase human problems. Indeed for Gandhi, in the field of religion, like any other field, fundamental problem was compartmentalization of human life. He found this 'compartmentalization of human life' at the centre of most of the human problems which also constitute core of our secular age. He proposed a holist way of life as an alternative to this where religious, political, economic and other aspects of life are seen as different aspect of one whole reality, and not different watertight compartments. It is known that his numerous public prayers were part of his political struggle

* Assistant Professor, Department of History, TU.

** Assistant Professor, Department of History, TU.

and for him his political struggle was part of his search of God. Arne Naess also observed 'the background of Gandhi's thinking is such that theology, metaphysics and politics cannot be separated- neither in life nor in semantics.'

He also discovered that politics, religion as well as other aspects of life in their present form are not comparable to each other and there is need to redefine them. He diagnosed that problem is not how to define religion or politics or economic but problem is that how one thing need to define equivalent to other. He had taken Himalayan task to redefine almost every aspect of life in relation to one and another but here in this paper we will look at how Gandhi had interpreted God, religion and politics where one cannot be conceived without other. Margaret Chatterjee, one of the prominent Gandhian scholars writes 'there is genuine sense in which Gandhi's life was an open book; another sense in which it is not at all easy to read the signs, to penetrate the mystery of this most complex personality.'

There are numerous reasons to appreciate Chatterjee's observation and it is equally applicable about Gandhi's views on different aspects of human life; at glance they may appear simpler than they actually are. But beneath the apparent surface of simple and open life and simple views, scholars often find surprising, complex, subtle enigmatic and contradictory aspects of Gandhi's life and his views on different aspect. Nevertheless, one can find so many places including his autobiography where Gandhi writes that those who say religion has nothing to do with politics, understood neither religion nor politics, it will be mistaken to take it as granted that Gandhi was against separating religion from politics. Available literature on this matter reveals that scholars have articulated Gandhi's views on religion and politics not only in different but also some time in a contradictory way. Scholars like Raghavan N. Iyer, Vimal Lal and Arnee Neass argue that major contribution of Gandhi in the field of politics as well as in religion is that he tried to combine both. Vimal Lal writes "nothing is more extraordinarily novel in Gandhi's idea of religion than his unshakeable conviction that it is no longer possible to divorce religion from politics." Or as observed by Joseph Prabhu that Gandhi weakens the traditional dualism between religion and politics and attempts to fashion a non-dual relation between the two.

But there are also many scholars like Amalendu Misra and Anthony J. Parel who argue with equal zeal that "Gandhi was a strong supporter of the secular state." And they also find justification from Gandhi's own writings. Misra argues that Gandhi advocated a policy of secularism for the state. Parel present two quotes of Gandhi in favor of his same argument. In first Gandhi says "religion is a personal matter. It ought not to affect the political field." And in second quote Gandhi says Religion and state would be separate. I swear by my religion. I will die for it, but it is my personal affair. The state has noting to do with it. The state would look after our secular welfare, health, communication, foreign relations, currency and so on, but not your, or my, religion. That is everybody's personal concern.

Now how to reconcile these seemingly different and diverse views is a question of immense importance to understand Gandhi's views on religion and politics and what can be the best way to enter in to the topic rather than just taking it for granted that Gandhi fought against compartmentalization of religion from politics. Surprisingly enough, in spite of that Gandhi made very clear contradictory sentences on several occasions, about so many things including religion and politics, most of the time he did not accept contradiction and inconsistency in his thought. Replying to a query asked about inconsistency in his idea, Gandhi said that though asked complain is justified from the standpoints of the complainants but it is unjustified from his point of view. He further explain that his aim in not to be consistent with his previous statements on a given question, but to be consistent with truth. And in this process he has grown from truth to truth. Following the same line of reasoning that though Gandhi made contradictory statements on several time, there is no contradiction in his ideas about religion and politics.

Now we will analyze the context and the sense in which Gandhi has used terms religion and politics, to resolve these seemingly inconsistency and contradiction in his views about religion and politics. When we understand the sense in which

Gandhi was saying that religion and politics should be separated, we find that he was referring to politics as a sovereign inappropriate and inadequate machinery of organizing human society—the state. We will call it 'science of organizing human life'. For Gandhi the state "represents violence in a concentrated and organized form. The individual has a soul, but the state is a soulless machine; it can never be weaned from violence to which it owes its very existences". Here by religion, he means, sectarian or organized religion like Hinduism, Christianity and Islam, which combine people on the basis of certain beliefs and rituals and he felt, it is a purely personal matter and has no place in politics. Raghavan N. Iyer argues that Gandhi was completely against state religion, even if a country had only one religion. He adds further that for Gandhi any society or group of people which depends partly or wholly on state aid for the existence of religion does not deserve or have any religion worth the name.

Here for Gandhi, separating religion with politics means any organized religion should not seek legal support from the state for its existence or flourishing and state should not legitimatize its existence with the help of religion. Gandhi agreed with the modern secular idea that state must be neutral towards every religion or must be equally distance itself from every religion, but not just because he believe that every religion is equal and every citizen irrespective to whatever religion they follow have equal right to actualize their potential. Gandhi takes it as granted, but he was primarily concerned about possible and inevitable corruption of both due to mixing them in these forms. He believe that if there will be any external agency like state for looking after or determine or protect people's religious beliefs than religion will become merely observation of certain rule and regulations and performance of certain duty and he was afraid that when already very powerful state will get legitimization from the religion it will become unmanageable. Therefore for Gandhi if politics is seen as science of organizing human society - the state, and religion is seen as group of people combined with certain belief—organized or sectarian religion like Hinduism, Christianity, or Islam, they must not be mixed with each other. When Gandhi was arguing that religion and politics should not be separated, he was referring to politics as a collective capacity of any people to live together in harmony we will call it "art of organizing human society'. Here he was referring religion as "a lifestyle and an open-ended system of universal ethics which could continuously integrate new inputs." Here for Gandhi religion was solely concerned with how one lives and not what one believes. And mixing religion with politics, on the one hand he means, religion as an open-ended system of universal ethics must provide moral basis on which people can nurture their capacity of living together in harmony. Or in other words religion should provide moral foundation for all political action.

On the other hand, politics must be seen as the arena for both realizations of truth as well as field where one can practice or test his or her religious values. As it is said above for Gandhi religion was way of life and it means that human being every act including minute acts like talking, eating, sleeping should be guided by some accepted moral values. As Gandhi says "I do not know of any religion apart from activity. It provides a moral basis to all other activities without which life would be of sound and fury signifying nothing." If religion is seen in this way it is impossible to exclude any aspect of human life not to speak about religion. Though, Gandhi believes that there are as many ways as human being in the world for realization of God. But he also believe that every YUGA has it own very specific way of realizing God and for Gandhi since in our YUGA politics has entered in every aspect of human life, it is best way for both realizing God and serving humanity. For this, Gandhi thought mixing religion with politics as mentioned, on the one hand, will spiritualize politics and on the other hand religious moral values will have concrete ground for their test. Therefore Gandhi in his whole life emphasized on practicing ethics and morality in politics as observing religious life.

In the preface to his autobiography, Gandhi declared that his devotion to truth had drawn him into politics. In 1938, he told to a group of missionaries that "I could not be leading a religious life unless I identified myself with the whole of mankind and that I could not do unless I took part in politics"

It means for Gandhi if religion is seen as a way of life and/ or system of ethics, and politics is seen as collective capacity of any people to live together in harmony, they must not be separated from each other. Now it is understandable that though Gandhi makes contradictory statements but there is no contradiction in his views about religion and politics because Gandhi uses religion and politics in multiple ways. He means religion and politics differently in both contexts when he was arguing religion should be separated and when he was arguing that they should not be separated. Till now, we have also tried to argue here that though Gandhi did not separate religion from politics, he did not find modern notion of a secular State very problematic, moreover he seems to agree with it because he believed if religion and politics are seen in particular way as they are often seen in modern time they must be separated from each other. What Gandhi had vigorously opposed was much more fundamental to modernity then the idea of secular state.

Gandhi was, however, far more interested in challenging modern way of defining things; where things are defined very exclusively and not in relation to other things. And he also believed most of today's problems are product of such exercise. Gandhi opposed modern way of defining religion as faiths in certain things and practices to be called it as very personal matter and argue that its association with state will corrupt neutrality of state. In this respect he strongly agrees with Veer van Der who said " "politicalization" and "depoliticalization" of something called "religion" are notions that belong to a discourse of modernity... developed in European Enlightment period, which assigns faith to the private domain as a matter of personal beliefs without political consequences" Gandhi knew the danger which lies in defining religion in this manner; it creates dichotomies of private and public space and divide human life into different watertight compartments. Gandhi had discovered same danger in the way politics is defined in modern time; a process of creating impartial and powerful state under which human society can be systematically organized and individual fundamental rights can be protected from everyone else. Gandhi knew that it also creates dichotomies of private and public spaces in life. But Gandhi was not working to destroy the dichotomies between private and public morals, religious values and political norms, ethical principles and political expediency as suggested by Raghavan N. Iyer and many other scholars, because he knew if things are defined in cubical from where they don't interact each other, they require different standards, values and norms.

Indeed, he was protesting the way things are defined in modern times and which create such dichotomies at first place. Gandhi presents us an alternative way of defining things and the world where life is seen as a whole therefore things cannot be defined exclusively because everything is not only interconnected but also interdependent. Here Gandhi largely depends upon the Advaita philosophy for his understanding of things and their place in the world in which the transcendental and metaphysical unity of every thing is assumed. He once told a visitor to his ashram, every act has its spiritual, economic and social implications. The spirit is not separate. It cannot be. Therefore, for Gandhi, problem is not how to create equal moral for public and private place or equivalent ethics for religion and politics. He did not believe like many theologians, that today there is urgent need of formulating an intellectual model wherein theology can somehow or the other be conceived in universal form. And on this basis practice of morality and ethics in every field of life can be argued. Unlike many western secular scholars he did not believe that, by extracting a moral core from different religions, and injecting it into politics and other domain of life, will solve the problem. Indeed for Gandhi it is an ontological problem; how to define things and the worldview and he believes if correct understanding of things and world can be created, then, ethical, moral and any other chaos will disappear from human life.

REFERENCES

Naess, Arne, 2005. Metaphysic of Sathyagraha in *The Selected works of Arne Naess,* Springer Netherlands. p 52.

Chaterjee, Margaret, 1982. *Gandhi's Religious Thoughts,* University of Notre Dame Press, Notre Dame Indiana, p. 94.

Ashis Nandy, 1985. An Anti-Secularist Manifesto, *Seminar*, No. 314. Otober p.14

Lal, Vinay, *Gandhi's Religion: A Few Thought*, p. 5.

Prabhu, Joseph, 2008. 'Gandhi's Religious Ethics' in The Philosophy of Mahatma Gandhi Allen, Douglas (ed.), *For The Twenty-First Century*, New Delhi: Oxford University Press, p. 163.

Parel, J. Anthony, 2007. *Gandhi's Philosophy of the Quest for Harmony*, New Delhi: Cambridge University press, p.60.

Misra, Amalendu, 2004. *Identity and Religion; Foundations of Anit-Isamism in India*, New Delhi: Sage Publication, p.66.

Parel, J., Anthony, 2007. *Gandhi's Philosophy of the Quest for Harmony*, New Delhi: Cambridge University press, p.61.

Gandhi M. K., *The Collected works of Mahatma Gandhi*, Vol-76.

Bose, N.K., 1957. *Selections From Gandhi*, Ahamedabad: Navajivan Press, p.41.

Iyer, N. Raghavan, 2000. *The Moral and Political Thought of Mahatma Gandhi*, New Delhi: Oxford University Press, p.43.

Nandy, Ashis, 2006. Final Encounter: The Politics of the assassination of Gandhi' in *Debating Gandhi*, ed. A. Raghuramaraju, New Delhi: Oxford University Press, p.57.

Cited in Iyer, N. Raghavan, 2000 *The Moral and Political Thought of Mahatma Gandhi*, New Delhi: Oxford University Press, p.41.

Ibid., p.41 (van der Veer 1995)

Iyer, N. Raghavan, 2000. *The Moral and Political Thought of Mahatma Gandhi*, New Delhi. Oxford University Press, p.40.

Ibid, p. 52.

12

Religion and Its Various Forms and Manifestations: A Few Case Studies

Samita Manna*

Religion provides the vital force for making up the foundation of a society through the history of mankind. It acts as a source of balance and stability which no other social institution can supply. It establishes moral codes and ethical principles by which norms are established and social control is recognized. It often provides strength to the individual in times of crisis. It is believed that there can not be any culture without religion. Religion manifests itself in the form of cults, shrines, deities or in the form of some objects. But from culture to culture this form varies.

Man and religion are inseparable in our everyday life. Religion ensures the identity of a person in a group. According to Mead (1934), Freud (cited in Adam and Sydie, 2001) and Cooley (1930), the process of identification of the member i.e. the formation of social self within the group starts through socialization. This identity of the self sometimes helps the individual to associate or dissociate from his group.

The English word religion comes from the word re-legare i.e. to gather or collect. On the other the Sanskrit word dharma

* Dr. Samita Manna is Professor, Department of Sociology, University of Kalyani, Nadia, West Bengal.

is derived from dhri means to hold, keep, maintain. From the meanings of these two words it is very clear that dharma like culture continues tradition after tradition.

Prof. Saraswati (2007) has written ten different contexts of dharma in his introductory note on religion in the book *Explorations in Anthropology*-P.K Bhowmick and his Collaborative Research Works. According to him "the basic form of religion may broadly be classified into 'simple' complex' and 'mixed'. Most anthropologists deal with the 'simple', form of religion whose characteristic features are: (a) belief in the divinity-given form of life, existing since the beginning of the world, (b) ahistorical, unfounded, unformulated, (c) beliefs and practices transmitted orally from one generation to the next, and (d) essentially descriptive, that is without explanation".

In his introduction he has critically analyzed the various research themes of Ph.D. dissertations produced by P.K. Bhowmick, an anthropologist who was active during 1955-1995 for his vigorous research works. He has mentioned "Among anthropologists, Prof. P.K. Bhowmick was concerned with social philosophy as well as social work, portraying the inner consistency of integral life and culture. His study of the Ramayana and the Mahabharata (1982) shows theoretical possibilities of constructing a form of cultural consciousness, imagining the integration of tribe and caste, through India's great epics, a stabilizing factor in the maturation of human psyche".

Religious benefits, rites, rituals and ceremonies constitute a crucial element of human culture. Religion constitutes a common platform of identity and shapes man's attitude to nature, environment and the supernatural power. It provides a cementing bond and establishes social solidarity in the midst of diversity. Religious values, beliefs and practices are deep rooted in the minds of people. It ensures cultural continuity and does not change as rapidly as it is not volatile. As a result, in spite of modernity, religious beliefs are till prevalent in every society-rural or urban, primitive or modern. All religious groups or ethnic groups have their own sacred world related to the beliefs in supernatural power, i.e., gods and goddesses. Beliefs in spirit are every where, as it is believed that life does not end with the death of physical body. In Hindu religion, for example, birth, rebirth, karma and dharma are inseparable from the idea of the soul. Al these belief patterns create heterogeneity of a complex network of religious world. Among the tribal people a simple from of religion is found whereas complex forms of religion are found among non-tribal population (Pramanick and Manna, 2007).

In this context, I would like to mention a few case studies of different ethnic groups who occupy different statuses in the line of tribe –caste continuum. Sometimes they are very rigid specially maintaining their primitive religion. But these ethnic groups with the passage of time and in course of survival strategies are forging themselves with the bigger social aggregates by following the rites and rituals of the existing dominant caste groups.

The origins of the history of these ethnic groups, who are now at the present inhabitants of the existing social structure of our village society, will portray different colorful emigrational histories to enlighten the scholars of that field. Considering the theme of the present research paper the author has considered four such ethnic groups who have settled in different villages of Paschim Medinipur in West Bengal. The criterion for selecting such groups is on the basis of simple to complex form of religion based on tribe- caste continuum.

Sample Villages

Community	*Police Station*	*Village*	*Total number of village*	*Total number of families*
Sukli or Solanki	Narayangarh	Birbira		9
	Do	Thatrachak		13
	Do	Mokrampur		15
	Do	Sandeula		16
	Do	Alamchak		47
Total			5	*100*
Bhogda or	Lalgarh	Kanchandanga	25	
Bhokta	Do	Daintikri		75
Total			2	*100*

Siyalgir or	Mohanpur	Singhas		6
Savara	Egra	Kasba Egra West		18
	Do	Kasba Egra		20
	Mohanpur	Panchkonia		21
	Egra	Dhaneswarpur		35
Total			*5*	*100*
Sahish or Hari	Lalgarh	Lalgarh		7
	Do	Ramgarh		11
	Midnapur Town Complex	Beherapara		82
Total			*3*	*100*

The first group is known as Siyalgir, a little known small community. People belonging to it live in the Bengal-Orissa border region, especially in the police station of Mohanpur. The popular belief, current about them, is that they are fond of consuming the flesh of jackals, which abound in rural settings. The earlier record about this group has been mentioned by Bose (1940) in his famous book, in Bengali, *Medinipurer Itihas*. He expresses the view that this obscure community has migrated from Gujarat and ultimately settled in this part of Midnapur, which was once full of thickets and jackals. Among the local people they still maintain some sort of isolation. The Siyalgirs in fact, speak in a dialect among themselves that is not understandable to others. After independence, specially during the Left rule in this state, their importance in respect of casting votes has been realised and through the Panchayat system the male folk has come nearer to the administration. And as a result drastic changes have been noticed among them in respect of participation in development work.

The Siyalgirs are a small community residing in the Mohanpur out post of the Dantan Thana. They speak a dialect of Gujarati and are supposed to have immigrated from the west some five or six generations ago, but nothing is known regarding the precise time of the settlement or the reasons which led to it. They are said to have thievish proclivities, and may possibly be the descendants of some wandering Bhil tribe which found its way to Midnapur and stayed there....

They profess the Hindu religion, but had no Brahmans to perform their ceremonies.... The dead is buried, not burnt (O'Malley (1911: 66).

However, in a compulsive situation, they began to stay here and became a part of the local socio-historical situation. Ultimately the Siyalgirs with their mystic background have been treated as local people in the present set-up and every wave of development programmes is about to touch them. It is to be noted here that they are now trying to be identified as Savara—who are scheduled and eligible to get constitutional benefits.

According to the regional social system they also have the privilege of the services of Brahmin (of course degraded), barber, washerman and others during the time of ceremonies. As per the local tradition they consider Vaisakh (April-May) as the first month of the year and the Chaitra (March-April) the last month of the year.

Familial rituals as well as village festivities scan the entire year. These are in tune with the local system. When it takes the shape of village festivals then the villagers distribute the activities to certain groups of people as per their socio-economic condition. Here, automatically the dominant Hindu rites, rituals and celebrations are observed. The groups sometimes forget their own identities and a new spirit dominates. It indicates that all these communities are in touch with rhythmic vibrations, indicating gradual incorporation of groups into the greater Hindu tradition i.e. they are under the process of Brahmanization rather Hinduization. Ultimately, with the slow process of Sanskritization (Srinivas, 1966) they have been assimilating with the greater Hindu society.

There are a few sacred spots in the village where some communal festivals take place when the elderly persons collect subscriptions and even now-a-days they participate in these with the other villagers. Thus we find Dasera puja, when Manasa, the Hindu snake goddess, is being worshipped at the time of summer months when the snakes move around the locality. This worship takes place in the familial level when a sacred basil plant is placed on the pyramidal shaped earthen mount and by its side a branch of Manasa (*Euphorbio nerifolia)* is planted. Milk, honey etc. are offered there on that day. A little quantity of milk is poured on the basil plant and also on the branch of the Manasa (a kind of plant). Some people say that they have seen the snakes to come and lick the milk poured on the plant at the time of celebration.

The communal worship of goddess Sitala is celebrated in the month of Jaistha (May-June) when all the villagers participate and everybody pays subscription and enjoys himself/herself for two days. The goddess Sitala is considered to be the goddess of small pox and epidemics and thus everyone is afraid of her. Worship is done by a Brahman priest.

During Ashar (June July) a formal Rathajatra, i.e., car festival takes place. It is believed that Lord Jagannath of Puri, during that period set out for his mother's sister's house on a chariot and this festival is in vogue in Bengal also in memory of the above. Naturally this festival takes place even in localities where the Siyalgirs live. After the festival, the people become busy with agricultural operations and thus the festive mood gradually becomes dull and the people have no time for rest.

Next comes some other rituals which are not in vogue among the members of Siyalgir community. But ultimately the Durgapuja festival is performed in the locality in which these people participate, as this festival is very common all over the state. Then Kalipuja is held in the month of Kartik (October-November). On that very day early in the morning cattle worship in cow-sheds is held in each an every house. This is known as Bandna festival (worshipping the cattle for agricultural purposes). At night the Sraddh ceremony (ceremonial food is offered to the spirits of the dead) takes place in each house. Gradually the last day of Poush (Dec-Jan.) comes and some festivals take place in each family.The paddy stalks are worshipped at the nightfall, after hearing the cry of the fox. It is known as khamar puja, but no Brhamin priest attends the ceremony. The important Charak festival is held on the last day of the Bengali calendar year when Lord Siva is worshipped.

It is to be noted in this connection that all the villagers worship the goddesses Sitala and Manasa. The Siyalgirs are now assert themselves as Savaras who are now getting the status of scheduled caste. The Todhas of that region also identify them as Savaras the Hinduised tribe who was once identified as criminal tribe.

The Bhogdas or Bhoktas constitute one of the little known communities in Midnapur, although even Risley (1969) does not mention the group in his memoir. However, they are found to live on both sides of the river Kangsabati that flows from Bihar through Jhargram sub division to Midnapur. This obscure tract of land is infested with snakes and occasionally subject to flood.

As usual, when the Bhogdas are asked about their identity they assert them as Bhagat Kshatriya, thus placing themselves in the bigger perspective of the Kshatriya group. It is very common at present that many people assume Kshatriya characteristics when their identity is questioned. For example, the Paundras assert them as Paundra Kshatriya, the Bagdis as Barga Kshatriya, and even the Mahatos—a tribal derivative living in the frontier tract—also assert them as Mahat Kshatriya.

It has been reported that these groups of people are not considered to be the people of this region. They came in the distant past and gradually acclimatised themselves to the setting when these places were not at all crowded. Whatever is their legendary or historical origin, the local people of this area look down upon them and think that they have criminal propensities and as such do not like to mix with them as neighbouring group of people. Gradually, they develop some attitudes of segregation from the bigger society.

But only the Bhogda still cling to their pristine beliefs in five more regional deities known as Garam, i.e., gram or village deity which are in vogue in other tribal or semi-tribal communities. This clearly indicates the survival of their original traits side by side the greater Hindu tradition

The Bhogda commuity divides the whole of the year into a number of festivals and worships. They claim to belong to one of the Hindu castes and as such they not only engage themselves in worships but also celebrate, individually or collectively, many festivals. The Bhogdas consider the Bengali month Magh (January-February), as the first month of the year. The first day of this month is known as Akshayan when they worship all the 'Garam' Debata (tutelary village deities). The 'Garam' Dabatas are again grouped into following categories: Daina Seni, Hadra Seni, Lata Seni, Daku Seni, Sannyas Baba, Manasa and Sitala. There are various dates when these deities are worshipped by a Bhogda community man. According to the local tradition, that particular man is blessed with the favour of all this these godes and goddesses. Before the worship, the villagers convene a meeting and fix up the rate of subscription for the villagers and this is collected accordingly and spent for worship purposes only.

On the fifth day of the month Magh (Janu-Feb) the Bhogda people worship goddess Saraswati. The Brahmin priest from the locality is invited for the purpose. They perform the Dol festival (the full moon day of the month of Magh) Sivaratri day in the month of Falgun (Feb-March) and the Charak festival on the last day of Chaitra (March-April) on the day of Chaitra Sankranti).

On ithe Ambubachi and Dasara days in the month of Ashar (June-July) the Bhogdas again worship the Garams when the priest of their own community starts the function of initiation. On Dasera or Dasahara day they all assemble and participate in merry-making. In the month of Sraban (July-August) they worship the god Dhanwantari to have sufficient rain and bumper production of crops. They also sacrifice one pegion to the goddess Kamaksha in the same month for the welfare of the community. Again on the Dak Sankranti day in the month of Aswin (Sep- Oct) they worship the god Kalapahar who is believed to protect the society from any sort of danger.In the month of Bhadra (August-Sep) they worship Bhadu and this continues through out the whole month through singing. On the last day of this month they prepare the idol Bhadu and worship her to overcome the curse of barrenness.

In the month of Aswin (Oct.-Nov.) They take part in the great Durga puja festival. Again on the new moon day they worship goddess Kali and perform Gobang Puja, i.e., they worship cattle in their respective cowsheds and on that very night they offer panda (ceremonial food) to their ancestral spirits after worshipping.

In the month of Agrahayan (Nov.-Dec.) before threshing the paddy in a Khamar they celebrate Khamar Puja. Through out the month they worship goddess Lakshmi. In the month of Poush (Dec.- Janu.). This month is considered to be the holiest month as they eat new crops and ceremonially they worship goddess Lakshmi. They also worship goddess Sitala on every Tuesday and Saturday of this month by their community priest. The female also worship the idol of Tusu through out the month and on the day of Sankranti (last day of this month) they float the idol into the river.

The third group, known as Sahish, comprises members who were basically the caretakers of the horses of the invading Marathas. The Marathas went back but the poor caretakers remained here; rather they harboured themselves in this blissful environment of mutual co-operation. They have been totally merged with the Hari (sweeper) community and have been still living near the bank of the river Kangsabati in west Midnapur and many other adjoining places of Midnapur and Bankura districts where they can afford a living as sweepers in nearby hospitals. The Sahish, being regarded untouchable do not participate in the worships performed in the Hindu community.

In course of the assimilation process with its strain and stress, slowly and gradually they were detached from their original setting. Thus, they lost their old social contacts and slowly began to forget their own language, but through ritual and religiosity, certain traits of their pristine culture still remain, though may be in a moribund form.

The Sahish (Hadi) community is considered to be one of the Hindu castes but due to their association with the filthy occupation they are considered unclean. No one takes water from their hands. They live more or less in isolation. The women folk of this community act as mid-wives and they help in the process of delivery at home. The different festivals associated with agriculture is totally absent in their community.

Occasionally they worship Manasa, the Hindu snake goddess, which resembles to a Manasa plant *(Euphorbia nerifolia)* and Sitala the goddess of contagious diseases.

The last group is known as Sukli who claim themselves as Solanki Rajput, a migrant group of people from Rajasthan. Risley (1981, 273-274) describes the group as follows: Sukli, a small cultivating caste peculiar to the district of Midnapur, claims to be descendants of a Solanki Rajput named Birsingh, who came to Midnapur about six hundred years ago and built himself a fort at Birsinghapur pargana...s

The Suklis worship many gods and goddesses. As one of the Hindu castes they propitiate different deities and believe in the Bhagwan, i.e., the Supreme Being. According to the caste group and Hindu tradition, the year starts from Vaisakh (April-May) and ends in Chaitra (March-April). The people of the community is busy through out the year by performing many rites, rituals,worships and festivals. Akshaya Tritia in the month of Vaisakh is an auspicious day when they start any good work. Then they perform Ratha Jatra festival and on that very day they usually initiate ploughing. After that gradually rain and storm come, the low land of the village is gradually field up by rain water and the agricultural people have no rest or time. They have to cultivate their land and as such their extremely busy. Gradually agricultural operation is over. A wind of rest slowly begins to blow and the occasion of Durga Puja arrives, which continues for four days at a stretch. A temporary committee for this purpose is constituted and all people as per their capacity begin to contribute to make the festival a success. A temporary fair is arranged by the local people and these people have to take part in it, wear new dresses and the relatives visit the respective houses. There are some other Hindu festivals like Kali Puja, Jagadhatri Puja etc. Different familial worships also take place at their houses in the month of Agrahayan and Poush (November, December and January). On every Thursday of these months, the maidens worship the goddess Lakshmi for prosperity and better life. The Astami tithi of the month of Agrahayan is called Porua Astami. On this day mainly the eldest son of the family is blessed by his mother for a bright and hurdle-free future.

They worship Manasa in Aswin (September-October) to avert snakebite and Sitala in Magh (January-February) to protect the community from the contagious diseases like cholera, Pox, Measles, etc. They believe that the goddess Sitala is tremendously malevolent in nature. These are communal worships. In a village some common places are there for the worship of the deities by the Brahman priests. Sometimes subscriptions are collected from the members of the community for the worship. Sometimes the worship takes place by the individual family.

Bandana or Cattle-caressing festival is generally held in the month of Kartika (October-November), on the day of worshipping the goddess Kali. The peasants express their gratitude through this festival to their cattle. They believe that by such worship they will be able to raise plenty of crops. On this day, various kinds of cakes and rich dishes are prepared by the female members of each family.

Ultimately paddy begins to ripen, days of leisure slowly come to an end and all the people become busy in harvesting activities. Again on the last day of Poush (December-January) a festival occasion sets in and it is expected that all activities related to harvest and threshing are to be over. On this particular day (Poush Sankranti) a worship takes places by the family members in the name of MakarPuja or Khamar Puja. They all rejoice and celebrate, prepare cakes and good dishes. Then we find some other festivals, which are dotted in their daily existence. Next, important festival is the Basanti Puja which continues for four days and ultimately comes the last day of the Bengali calendar year known as Chaitra Sankranti or Chhatu-Sankranti. The Gajan festival is held every year, during the end of Chaitra (March-April), the last month of the year. This festival is associated with the Siva-cult (Fata Siva). Siva is supposed to come out cracking the surface of the earth and he is the most powerful god, believed to be the god of destruction. On the last day of the Chaitra rice is powdered and cakes are prepared to have a sumptuous meal for all. Thus the festivities roll in and the people emotionally participate, without raising any questions (Manna 2003).

With all these events in the life of those communities in this particular frontier zone we find a gradual accommodation with the Hindu tradition being strictly followed by the caste groups. As they are migrant groups, in course of time they have got their placement in different hierarchical epochs. As a result they have to leave traditional occupation and as per situation accept caste bound professions. Naturally, all their activities are in tune with the caste groups: higher or lower as the case may be. These groups slowly coming to this tract and trying to follow many rites and rituals followed by the other castes in and around have been slowly consolidated into caste units through recurrent process of interaction. Ultimately these groups have developed their caste boundaries and caste organizations

Birth, marriage and death are important phenomena in the life of an individual. All these four groups respond in a same fashion more or less in these situations. In most of the cases the birth takes place in their respective houses. The mid-wife popularly known as Dhaima belonging to Hari community participates in the process of delivery and it is almost common in all cases. The placenta is buried in front of the house. Except in the Sukli community, the mother of the baby offers food and drink to that particular place during her pollution period for the welfare of her baby. But on the other hand, the Sukli burns that place daily to get rid of the bad smell.

The pollution period in each community is known as Narta or Chutuk Charano, which continues for nine days. For the Sukli, Napit (barber) and Dhoba (washerman) are essential but in earlier days the common Napit and Dhoba were not allowed to do the work in the houses of the other three castes. At that time the same functions were used to be performed by one elderly community member. Now-a-days the situation has changed; the service of the Napit (barber) and Dhoba (washerman) is requisitioned in imitation of the higher caste people. The mother of the baby in all communities worships the goddess Ganga. On the 21st day after the delivery a formal purification known as Ekusha is performed almost by all the communities, but nature of rituals varies from one community to another. All the communities also perform the rice-eating ceremony but the details vary. This indicates some sort of gradual accommodation into the system.

In respect of marriage there are some rituals and formalities. These vary from one group to another. It has also been observed that the services of the Brahman (Brahmin), Napit (barber) and Dhoba (washerman) have become visible especially in the lower groups, in the tune with the higher castes.

Similarly, after death, disposal of the dead is done by cremation. But formalities and minor rituals differ from community to community. It is to be noted in this connection that the Siyalgir in the past used to bury the dead body. Now they are imitating the customs of local castes and as such cremation has become a regular practice. But the mourning period varies from community to community – Sukli for 11 days, Bhogda for 29 days, Siyalgir for 10 days and Sahish for 9 days.

The Sraddh ceremony takes place with the help of the Brahman (Brahmin), higher or degraded. They all believe in the existence of Atma or spirit of the dead. During their mourning period the sons of the deceased, of all four communities, offer food and drink under a plant (Bena grass) which is planted by the side of the river or pond. After taking bath and before taking food they usually offer food and other articles to the spirit of the dead in the name of the departed soul.

Now it is clear that all these groups are trying to adjust themselves with the changing situation and gradually they are following the higher caste rituals in their day-to-day interactions. The operation of religious complex in different urban areas is also another important dimension of the study of religion. In these places, a complex network of sacred activities of the people is associated with performance of traditional rites of passage, visiting of temples, offering puja, observing manta (vow), worshipping of images and taking part in Barwari puja. In these ways they express their faith in Hindu philosophy, theology, and other spiritual aspects which show that a large section of people living in urban areas follow the traditional ethos of religious rituals through giving them new forms of expression.

Religion has its different perspectives and connotations. Religion gives the identity of the person within the family and gradually it becomes the part of the greater social understanding and reality which can be pointed out as a religion of humanity. The understanding of the man with love and sympathy is the ultimate motto of religion. In this way the people of the world come under one parlour. The microcosm and macrocosm of the religion meet with a common point of love, humanity and mankind. Bindu mese Sindhu te: Each drop of water ultimately ends with a big ocean – Sindhu. Man for its existence and survival bounded up with its culture i.e. religion. The integrity, security, group cohesion sand identities are essential for a man, family, group, village, nation and country. As a result religion originates from the core of culture of each and every group. Consequently its various forms and manifestations are interesting and unique. In this paper I have only tired to locate the existence of religion and its nature from simple to complex societies. Till today, tribal society is referred by simple society as the tribal means "a good number of so called tribal communities are found who are popularly known as Adivasis, i.e. the Bhumiputras, the early settlers or 'autochthonese'. These groups of people have simple technology. For conceptual purposes, they speak a common language or dialect, have a common culture, are more clan-based, i.e., kin oriented or ethnocentric in temperament with less hierarchy and less economic specialization, indicating 'mechanical solidarity' as propounded by Durkheim (Bhowmick 1994)".

In India more than five hundred tribal groups are found who have their own cultural traits. The clearest understanding of the group is that they have their own religion which separates them from the others. In this way their tribal religions in the form of bongaism, animism, spiritism etc. are in vogue. But gradually they become the part of larger society. The simple religion through social interaction and cultural assimilation gradually turns over into complex religion.

The origin of caste is understood through religion. As a result the Brahmin, the priestly class ascribes the highest position in the social structure. Particularly in Indian society till today we are stratified by our caste system which is ascribed in nature and always we are identified by our caste i.e. religion. The concept of 'sacred' and its application separates the world from the purity and pollution, pious and untouchables, vice and virtue, love and unlovable, acceptance and rejection and ultimately it comes to an end with war and peace. So the integrity of the society is only possible through the application of the religion.

REFERENCES

1. Adams, B.N. and R.A. Sydie, 200. *Sociological Theory*, New Delhi: Vistaar Publications.
2. Bhowmick, P.K., 1982. 'Ethnocultural Contacts, Conflicts and Co-operation in the Ramayan: A Sociological Overview'. *Journal of Social and Economic Studies*, 10 (1-2).
3. Bhowmick P.K., 1994. *Primitive Tribal Groups In Eastern India. Welfare and Evaluation*, New Delhi: Gyan Publishing House.
4. Bose, J.C. *Medinipur Itihas* (1st edition) in Bengali, Calcutta: Tapasi Press, 1346 B.S. 1940.
5. Cooley, C.H., 1930. *Sociological Theory and Social Research*, Robert Colley Angell, (Ed.) Henry Holt, New York.
6. Manna S., 2003. *Crystallisation of Caste in Frontier Bengal*, New Delhi: Classical Publishing Company.
7. Mead, G.H., 1934. *Mind, Self and Society*, Chicago: The University of Chicago Press.
8. O' Malley, L.S.S. 1911. *Bengal District Gazetteers*, Midnapur, Calcutta: The Bengal Secretariat Book Depot.
9. Pramanick, S.K. and Manna, S. (Eds.) 2007. Explorations in Anthropology – P.K. Bhowmick and His Collaborative Research Works. New Delhi: Serial Publications.
10. Risley, H.H., 1981. *Tribes and Castes of Bengal* (Vol. II), Calcutta: Firma Mukhopadhyay.
11. Saraswati, B. 2007. *Religion in Indian Perspective: Introduction. In Explorations in Anthropology* – P.K. Bhowmick and His Collaborative Research Works. Pramanik S.K. and Manna S. (Eds.) New Delhi: Serial Publications.
12. Srinavas, M.N. 1966. *Social Changes in Modern India*, Bombay; Allied Publishers.

13

Tribal Concept of God and Spirits

Francis Pereira SVD*

> *"Our first task in approaching another people, another culture, another religion is to take off our shoes, for the place we are approaching is holy. Else we may find ourselves treading on men's dreams. More serious still, we may forget that God was there before our arrival."* (Warren 1963:10)

There are about 5000 indigenous/tribal groups with a total population of 300 million living in more than 70 countries on five continents. Of these about 190 million tribals are in Asia. As per the Census 2001, the total population of the Scheduled Tribes in India was 84,326,240 which accounted for 8.2% of the total population of the country. In 2007, India had the highest number of tribals in the world, about 95 million tribals and the population was distributed into 645 tribes and sub-tribes (Puthenpurakal 2007:238 and http://en.wikipedia.org, 25 Nov. 2009).

The Concept of God: Creator and Supreme Being

Tribals believe in a supreme God who is the creator of all

* Professor, Comparative Religions, Regional Theological College, Sambalpur, Orissa.

that exists. He has created human beings and takes care of them. Different tribes use different names to indicate the Supreme Being. Uarons or the Kunrukhar call him Dharme or Dharmes, Mundas call him Singbonga, Santals call him Chando Baba or Thakur Jiu and the Kharias call him Ponomosor. Anthropologist Wilhelm Schmidt and others have observed that belief in a Supreme Being is universal among the tribals (Lakra, 2010:8-9). Tribals also believe in benevolent and malevolent spirits. But supreme God has control over all the spirits. According to the tribal understanding, God's work of creation does not end with the creation of heaven and earth and everything in it but continues, especially in making our crops grow and bear much fruit. After sowing paddy, while having a rice beer toast, the Mundas say, "This is our prayer: Haram (the Old One) has given us bullocks and buffaloes, ploughs and seeds, let him now grant us a good crop. By our own strength we can do nothing. However much we plough and manure, however good the seeds we sow, if Haram turns his back on us, not a single grain will grow" (Lakra, 2010:17). Tribals believe that the creator God is not only ruler and master of the universe but also of the various states of human beings. God is the master of all situations, good or bad, favourable or unfavourable. God is omnipotent, omniscient and omnipresent. God is holy and eternal (Lakra, 2010:19-24).

The Concept of God: Anthropomorphism

The Tribal concept of God is anthropomorphic. In the tribal religion anthropomorphism has been used especially in creation myths. The God of tribals is shown not only with man's physical and emotional traits but also with social traits. In a myth of the Uraons, God is depicted as a landlord or a king who has hobbies like hunting and he owns a royal horse called Hansraj-Pankraj (Lakra, 2010:34). According to some myths, God has also a female counterpart, a wife who plays the role of giving advice to him. Yet another aspect of anthropomorphism depicts God as making mistakes in his decision of destroying his creation and he feels sorry for his mistakes. In a Kharia myth, after destroying the human beings with rain of fire, God felt very lonely and very sorry for having destroyed them (Pereira, 2007:565). God takes advice and also seeks help from other beings in his work of creating the world. Some tribes speak of God creating the earth with the help of some creatures such as golden kingfisher, earthworm or tortoise. In the Uraon creation myth, the golden kingfisher (Kilkila) bird brings the seed of the earth from Patalpur in its nails and gives it to Dharmes who creates the earth by churning the mud in seven seas and sixteen currents (Pereira, 2007:434). In the Santal myth of creation, God levels the earth brought up by the earthworm who in turn was helped by the tortoise (Pereira 2007:556). In the Kharia myth of creation, it was the crab that formed the pillar of mud by bringing mud from the very bottom of the water and then extended this pillar into a huge island and God makes use of this earth to create human beings (Pereira 2007:564). In the Asur myth of Uraons and Mundas, God even uses trickery in order to punish the Asurs who had become a symbol of pride, arrogance and disobedience. He allured the Asurs to enter into the furnace so that they might collect plenty of gold and silver. Instead of collecting gold and silver, they were reduced to ashes (Lakra 2010:34). Sometimes God is seen as a grandfather figure or as the Old One. In the Genesis myth of the Uraons, the children who were saved from the rain of fire, the progenitors of human beings, address God as grandfather and God addresses them as grandchildren (Pereira, 2007:442). The creation myths of the Mundas speak of God as the "Old One" (Hoffmann, 1950:3981-3988).

Anthropomorphism is a tribal way of emphasizing certain aspects of God. Tribals do not mean that God is human as he is depicted. All the persons or characters associated with God are included in the story merely for the sake of convenience and smooth running of the story. The God of tribals, instead of having a soliloquy or a monologue, has dialogue with other persons or beings around him. Sometimes, God's own attributes like wisdom and righteousness are personified in the form of different characters of the story. In the Uraon myths of creation and destruction, the female counterpart seems to be nothing else but the Wisdom of God personified. In the living liturgy and worship these characters surrounding God never get a place of honour, they are never worshipped or remembered or even mentioned as helpers or consort of God. The use of anthropomorphism is mostly limited to creation myths alone. In their real life and liturgy, the tribals are quite clear about God's transcendence. They invoke God as all-powerful, all knowing and omnipresent. The human traits of God of creation myths are rarely found in their sacrifices and prayers to God (Lakra, 2010:34-35). African tribals believe that God the creator gives human beings the life force at conception. It is the part of the soul that animates human person's body. By means of this aspect of human soul, he/she is responsible to God and his/her ontological relationship with Him. It is the part of human person that does not perish with the body when life force is destroyed (Ahirika, 2000:62).

Tribal Concept of Spirits

Tribals believe in spirits but they do not worship them as they do the Supreme Being. Spirits are only creatures of the Supreme Being. Invisible spirits are the spirits of the dead human beings. Spirits can be benevolent or malevolent spirits. According to the Asur myth of Mundas and Uraons, all the nature spirits were formerly wives of the Asurs who were punished by Singbonga or Dharmes by burning them to ashes in the furnace because they were arrogant, disobedient and greedy. On the death of their husbands the Asur women demanded from him some means for their sustenance. Granting their request God changed them into nature spirits, as guardian of mountains, fields, rocks, rivers, ponds, tanks, and forests. They became tutelary spirits who are still in need of food. According to the tribal belief, spirits are more powerful spiritual beings than the human beings (Lakra, 2010:29). The benevolent spirits that the tribals believe could be ancestor spirits, clan spirits or household spirits. All of them need nourishment for their sustenance. Hence, even the benevolent spirits get angry if they are ignored and not offered any offerings or sacrifices. Tribals are afraid of the malevolent or evil spirits. Evil spirits cause pain, suffering, sickness and death. These spirits are treated with great awe and respect on account of the supernatural and uncanny powers they are supposed to possess. They believe that their life depends on these spirits to a large extent, and so they try to keep them in good humour by maintaining friendly relations with them. By keeping them on their side, they hope that these mysterious and supernatural powers would remain favourable to them to give good health, and protect their children, crops and cattle in times of need (Kujur, 2004:109). Hence, the rituals and sacrifices are more spirits-centred than God-centred. This is because God is good and harmless whereas the spirits need to be placated. If the spirits are not properly placated they would cause sickness, pain, suffering and death. However, when their prayers, offering and sacrifices do not yield the desired result, as a final recourse, they turn to their supreme God who has control over all the spirits. African tribals strongly believe that ancestral spirits and divinities are resident in spirit world. In addition to magical help from medicine men, ancestral spirits can also offer protection to their wards against the evil spirits and ghosts that may malevolently be employed to haunt them (Ahirika 2000:61)

Tribals also offer blood sacrifices to the spirits. Blood of animals and birds is offered to the benevolent and malevolent spirits. Blood contains life. By offering the blood of the victim, life is offered to God and spirits. The evil spirits are placated by black or coloured fowls. Different types of sacrifices are offered to different deities. For example, Pahan offers the sacrifice of a brown or red he-goat to Pat. On the annual sacrificial day of Darha-Deswali, the village priest of the Uraons first offers a white cock to Dharmes (supreme Creator God) and then offers the sacrifice of copper coloured cock for the departed souls of ancestors. Finally, he offers a red cock in honour of the Darha spirit (Kujur, 2004:113). Though human sacrifices were not common among the tribals, such a sacrifice was thought to be a perfect or a supreme sacrifice. A group of Kondhs of Odisha used to offer human sacrifice to Tari Penu, the earth goddess. When the British government prohibited human sacrifices and subsequently it was difficult to offer such a sacrifice, it was promptly replaced by the sacrifice of a buffalo. Uraoñs of Chotanagpur used to offer blood of human victim (Ondka) to Mahadania spirit to increase the fertility of the soil.

Priesthood and Magic

Priesthood is exercised by two categories of persons, i.e., by the head of the family and by a village priest. Sacrifices and prayers are offered to God and ancestor spirits by the head of the family. The presence of village priest is not needed to perform rituals during rites of passage. Anyone who knows how to conduct the ceremonies may officiate during the ceremonies. However, the village priest performs rituals during feasts and offers sacrifices to evil spirits. Village priest is known by various names such as Naigas, Pahan, Dehuri, Kalos or Baiga. Priesthood is not hereditary, but people may choose their priest from priestly household (Pereira 2007:541). Tribals also seek the help of tribal and non-tribal medicine-men, witch-doctors and exorcists known as Mati, Ojha, Sokha, Bhagat, Baiga or Deonra (Pereira, 2007:543). Tribals believe that some human beings are endowed with superhuman qualities (gun). With the help of evil spirits and special training, they become witches (dains) and wizards (bisaha) and are capable of harming others. They are credited with 'evil eye' and 'evil mouth.' The central ritual of the Uraons or Kunrukhar known by various names such as Palkhasna, Dandakatta, Bhakh Kattna, Bhelwaphari is meant to break 'evil teeth' and 'evil mouth.' The three colours used to draw cirlces, red (of burnt clay of hearth), white (of rice floor), and black (of coal dust) are believed to represent the rainbow – the largest and most powerful bow in heaven or earth and therefore most potent in warding off the evil eye and evil attentions of the malignant spirits (Pereira, 2007:537 and Roy 1985:126-128).

Life After Death

A general belief among the tribals of North East India is that the soul descends to the land or village of death where they believe they live a similar kind of life as they lived on earth. They do cultivation, rear animals, go hunting and do other activities. Hence, at the time of burial weapons, implements, pottery, clothes, etc are buried along with the dead bodies. Tribals of Chotanagpur such as Uraoñs, Mundas, Kharias, Santals and Hos believe that after death the shades of the dead reach the land of ancestor spirits where they have a lot of land for cultivation and where they can eat well and drink plenty of rice beer. Most of them do not think of such a place as "heaven" where God dwells. However some tribes like Ao Nagas believe that after the soul has reached the village of death, the soul faces God or the judge who judges soul according to the deeds of one's life on earth (Tirkey, 1998:201-202). Tribals believe that only those who die natural death go to the land of the ancestors or village of death. The souls of those who die unnatural death are not able to have communion with their dead ancestors but they become restless spirits or evil spirits and roam on earth and are causes of all sicknesses or misfortunes of human beings.

REFERENCES

1. Ahirika Edwin A. 2000. 'Contexualization of Ephesians 6:12: Liberation of African Christians from the Fear of Principalities: Spiritual Forces of Evil in the Heavenly Realms,' *Sevartham*, Vol. 25.
2. Hoffmann, John 1950. *Encyclopaedia Mundarica.* Patna: Superintendent, Government Printing, Bihar.
3. Kujur Scholastica 2004. 'Are Adivasis Hindus?,' *Sevartham*, Vol. 29.
4. Lakra John 2010. 'Tribal Theology,' *Sevartham*, Vol. 35.
5. Pereira Francis 2007. Faith Tradition of the Kuñrukhar (Uraoñs). Delhi: ISPCK.
6. Puthenpurakal J., 2007. 'Jesus the Tribal and Tribals of Jesus' in *Christ among the Tribals* edited by F. Hrangkhuma & Joy Thomas, Bangalore: Fellowship of Indian Missiologists.
7. Roy, Sarat Chandra 1985. *Oraon Religion and Customs*. Delhi: Gian Publishing House. (Reprint)
8. Tirkey Christopher Augustus Bixel 1998. *Religion/Primal Religion,* Delhi: ISPCK.
9. Warren M.A.C., in Introduction to John V. Taylor 1963. *The Primal Vision: Christian Presence Amid African Religion*. Philadelphia: Fortress Press.

SECTION-III

14

Islam and Muslims in Darjeeling Himalaya: Some Empirical Observations

Rajib Chatterjee*

Muslims constitute 12% of India's total population and are the largest religious minority group in India. In India we have a blend of all major religions of the world. Religion is certainly a factor of social diversification in India which shows a definite impact on the values and norms of the people. Historically, Himalayan region and its people have a great role in building a composite tradition of Indian culture where all religions contribute. Islam has a significant presence in the Indian Himalayan region and secures a special place in the Himalayan society. In fact their presence is historically not much old and they are numerically very low there. Muslims in Darjeeling hills are primarily a community migrated from the plains since British annexation to the tract. Though ideologically Islam does not make any kind of discrimination among the followers across the world, but the immense range of Himalayan culture, make Darjeeling Muslims different, which reflected in their daily life. The indigenous or local

* Senior Research Fellow, Centre for Himalayan Studies, University of North Bengal, Darjeeling – 734013, West Bengal, Email: rajibanth@gmail.com

influence on Muslims in Darjeeling hills are so strong that it is reflected in many aspects of their culture. The colonial history of Darjeeling reveals that, the rapid growth of the town attracted a large number of Muslims specialized in various occupations to serve the Europeans and their native companions, in the late thirties of nineteenth century. They came from various parts of the world and India and later domiciled permanently after marriage with native girls. Irrespective of their ethnic, regional and theological variations, they constitute a uniform cultural identity intermingled with the popular hill cultures by adopting them in their way of life.

However, the basic approach of this paper is to describe the Muslim behaviour according to their degree of religious devotion that the Muslim groups represent in Darjeeling. The primary objective of this paper is to analyze the cultural life and assimilation of the Muslims with the greater society of their habitat. The paper is based on empirical facts collected through intensive field investigation among the Muslims of Darjeeling hills.

History of the Muslims in Darjeeling Himalaya

It is very difficult to say the exact time of Muslim migration to this mountainous hill region, as there isn't any historical record available. But there are various popular myths among the Darjeeling Muslims regarding their migration to region, which are not validated by authentic evidences. However, these hill Muslims have a colonial history which reveals that the Europeans during the early part of 19th century encouraged a large number of Muslim groups to Darjeeling as the town was erected as a district head quarter and it was the centre of all type of administrative activities during the early British period. Dr. Campbell's supervision to the growth of trade and commerce added a new dimension to the importance of Darjeeling as a centre of 'trans-frontier' trade and an entry port for Central Asia. This encouraged a large number of Muslims to migrate and gradually some of these non familial male individuals later got married with the native Nepali girls and domiciled as a permanent resident (Mondal,

2004). These are the early Muslim families of Darjeeling hills. After that many other Muslim groups settled permanently with their families for the purpose of business. So one of the main reasons for the migration of Muslims to this region is trade and business.

Table 1: Muslim Population in Darjeeling Hills from 1941-1971 Census

Subdivision	*1941**	*1951*	*1961*	*1971*
Sadar Subdivision	1122			
Not Available	1259	1414		
Kalimpong Subdivision	332		1370	837
Kurseong Subdivision	350		402	740

(*Source:* * Dash A J, 1947 & Census Reports)

Table 1 shows the Muslim population of the three hill subdivisions based on census data. Darjeeling Himalayan region is composed of three out of four subdivisions of the district Darjeeling. Muslims are predominately an urban community in Darjeeling Himalaya and concentrated in the urban areas of Darjeeling, Kurseong and Kalimpong town.

Table 2: Muslims in Towns of Darjeeling Himalaya

Name of the Towns	*1941*	*1971*	*2001*
Darjeeling	1041	1117	4134
Kurseong	246	539	2124
Kalimpong	332	520	1473

(*Source:* Dash, 1947 & Census 1971)

In urban areas Muslim population was concentrated around the Mosqu, and the majority of the Muslims lived in Darjeeling town. The Darjeeling hills Muslims have diverse ethnic and regional variations. They come under four broad categories –

1. *Bihari Muslims* - Muslim groups migrated from various districts of Bihar and Uttar Pradesh
2. *Kashmiri Muslims* - Muslims migrated from Indian state of Jammu and Kashmir.

3. *Tibetan Muslims* - Bhutia/Bhote Muslims who took shelter from Tibet after 1962.
4. *Nepali Muslims* - descendents of early migrant Muslims who got married with native Nepali girls or embraced caste families of Nepali origin.

Numerically, Bihari Muslims rank first and then the Nepali Muslims. Kashmiri and Tibetan Muslims are very few in number. Except for the Tibetan and Kashmiri Muslims, majority of the Himalayan Muslims are backward in respect of economy and education. Their backwardness is ubiquitous as the general grievances of their socio-economic backwardness is identical with the other Muslim community elsewhere in India.

Table 3: Urdu Speaking People in Darjeeling Hills (Census 1971)

Police Station/Town	*Persons*	*Male*	*Female*
A. Sadar Sub-division	4718	2985	1733
Sukhiapokhri	1175	791	384
Pulbazar	35	34	01
Darjeeling (R+U)	1057	689	368
Darjeeling (M)	1019	666	353
Rangli Rangliot	21	18	03
Jore Bunglow	27	21	06
B. Kalimpong Sub-division	397	269	128
Kalimpong (R+U)	362	246	116
Kalimpong (M)	276	183	93
Garubathan	35	23	12
C. Kurseong Sub-division	632	428	204
Kurseong (R+U)	589	398	191
Kurseong (M)	481	313	168
Mirik	43	30	13

(*Source:* Darjeeling District Gazetteer, 1971)

Table 3 shows the population distribution of the Muslims in Darjeeling Himalayan region on the basis of their language

Urdu or Urdu speaking Muslims though a considerable number of them have their own mother tongue or dialect like Tibetan, Kashmiri, Nepali and Bhojpuri.

Organizational Structure of the Muslims

Islam in its orthodoxy does not recognize any form of discrimination based on castes or class. In theory all Muslims are brethren and can eat and pray together. They are all equal in the sight of Allah. There are two ways to understand Islam. One is by interpreting it theologically which is the ideal or 'textual Islam' and the other is 'contextual Islam', the way Muslims practice their faith. In this region people often speak about various types of Muslims, based on their popular religious practices. It only shows that heterogeneity is an established fact in the minds of the people, though theoretically Islam advocates an egalitarian social order. As we have already mentioned Muslims in Darjeeling Himalayan region are the descendents of the migrants from Bihar and UP and all the Muslims in the region come under four broad categories namely – Bihari Muslims, Kashmiri Muslims, Tibetan Muslims and Nepali Muslims. It is also interesting to note that there exists a social hierarchy among these groups. The members of these groups are always conscious about their family or ancestral tradition while selecting their life partners. They always prefer to marry within their own social group. Except some elite Bihari Muslims and Kashmiris, Muslims of Darjeeling Himalaya are deviated to some extent from the standard Islamic rules. One important deviation from the standard rules of Islam is the widespread worship of pirs (Sufi Masters) and saints. Irrespective of their sects and theological affiliations to Berelvi or Deobandi school, these Muslims are sympathetic and pay respect to all the members of Khanqah irrespective of any *silsila* (affiliation to pir). They often perform their Marriages in a standard dominant hill fashion and at the end call a maulavi or kazi who recites prayers as per Islamic rule and records the amount of the *denmohar* and settlement. Almost all the social functions are modified by the popular hill traditions like wearing *khada,* which is a most important practice among the Nepali castes and tribes. In the event of birth, marriage and death khada is used by the peoples which the hill Muslims accustomed during the course of time as a symbol of acculturation.

Religious Practices

The Muslim population in Darjeeling hills are Ahl-e-Sunnat-wal-jamat or Sunni in their faith and devoted to Hanafi School. Shias are almost invisible among the hill Muslim society. All the mosques at various places of Darjeeling hills are supervised by Sunni Imams. Muslims are free to observe their religious practices. The Sunni Muslims of Darjeeling (excluding the Tibetan Muslims) has two main sub-sects – the Berelvis and the Deobandis, which are two theological schools originated in India. But very interestingly, these two groups do not exhibit superiority or hostility to the other which is unique among the Muslim communities in India. Particularly the Nepali Muslims almost deny their affiliation to any of these two theological schools. Spiritualism is an important component of belief system among them. The spiritual specialist is known as "Sufis" or "pirs" and their disciplines are called as "mureeds". Belief in pirism is a typical feature of all the Darjeeling Muslims. Each pir has its own respective process of spiritual practices and teaching having their own hanquah and silsila order. Only the Berelvis believe in the pir-murid relations and the Deobandis always refused such affiliations. But in Darjeeling region the Deobandis never show disrespect to the Berelvis as of their spiritual affiliation towards pir. Very interestingly the Deobandis also follow the teachings of the Chisti order (one of the Sufi Orders) which is also unique among the Muslims in India.

Social Customs and Rituals

The most important widespread ritual among the hill Muslims is the worship of Pirs and saints which is considered to be an unIslamic practice by the Muslims. In Darjeeling, there is a *mazar* (tomb of a Muslim saint) where Muslims irrespective of their theological affiliation pay respect and worship by offering flowers, *khada, agarbati* or *dhup* and distribute sweets at the *mazhar*. They often take *mannat* at the *mazhar* for success in life and once they achieve their desire they come back to the *mazhar* and offer flowers and sweets. A huge number of Hindu Nepalis also frequent the *mazhar* and offer prayers along with the Muslims. Darjeeling Muslims celebrate all Muslim festivals like Id-Ul-Fitr, Bakrid or Id-Ul-Azha, Shabe-e-barat, etc.

Birth and death rituals are almost identical with the standard Islamic rule. But there are so many local traditions or influences in the marriage ceremony due to their contact with the locals in particular with the Nepali Muslims. But the *nikah* is performed according to the standard Islamic rule. The Bihari and Kashmiri Muslims strictly prefer to follow their traditional marriage customs and rituals. But the Nepali Muslims because of their intimate association with the Nepali culture often prefer to perform the marriage ceremony according to the Nepali Hindu custom. The Nepali Muslims have a very peculiar practice in their love marriage with a Nepali or Bhutia girl. The Muslim boy at the day of marriage goes to the bride's house along with his guardians and touches the feet of the parents of the bridegroom. After that some gifts are exchanged. *Khada,* a long silk towel, is wrapped around the groom by the bride grooms parents. Sweets are offered to each other and after that the girl is converted to Islam and a kazi or maulavi is invited to officially perform the nikah ceremony. This typical ritual is observed by the Nepali Muslims only in intercommunity marriages which is popularly called dhokbeth. All other Muslims observe the standard Islamic rule in their marriage ceremonies along with some local customs.

Assimilation and Integration

Culture is always wrongly interpreted as a static reality. We have a popular monolithic belief that the Muslims have less exposure to the world and other cultures and thus they are less tolerant to the alien traditions. But since last 200 years, Darjeeling Muslims are predominantly living among the dominant Hindu and Buddhist environment and thereby largely got integrated with them both socially and culturally.

The understanding of acculturation and diffusion thus allows us to better understand what is happening to the Muslim society of Darjeeling Himalaya. The indigenous or local influences on early migrant families are strong and is reflected in many aspects of their culture. Yet it was not unilateral and the influence of the particular experience, intensely affected the cultural development and political identities of the Muslims living in Darjeeling hills. Muslims are not much different from their ethnic Nepali and Tibetan or Bhutia neighbours in respect to language, food, dress pattern, occupation, culture, family organization, habits and customs. Their morphological similarities often made others confused in physical identification. Due to constant mixing and breeding with the ethnic Nepalis, these Paharia Muslims are almost identical with their non-Muslim neighbours. Any one can't distinguish the Tibetan Buddhists and Tibetan Muslims in respect to language, food, traditions, habits and customs. Even the Muslims often observe the major festivals of popular hill culture. Except some basic principles of Islam, the life cycle rituals have a great similarity with the Nepalis and Bhutias or Tibetans. Many Muslim families respect the local deities and pay their respect along with their next door Nepali neighbours. Due to this close association with the dominant hill culture, the Muslims in Darjeeling hills are gradually inclined towards the popular local traditions and thus assimilated with the greater hill society.

On the question of assimilation, a plurality of Darjeeling Muslims believe that Muslims should adopt the customs and ways of life of the hills, though a significant minority Muslims think that they should try to remain distinct. Muslim population in Darjeeling Himalaya is ethnically and linguistically diverse. There are various groups within them. Some came much earlier in comparison to other groups and their inclination towards the wider integration is much more noticed in their way of life. Those Muslims who came to the hills much later always struggle to find a balance between the two different cultural traditions.

Concluding Remarks

Muslims are considered as the 'ornaments' of Darjeeling Himalaya. Since the beginning of their arrival in the area Muslims have actively interacted with other segments of the greater hill society rather than keeping themselves aloof as a minority. Their existence is noticed at various levels in the society though their percentage is very low. Their peculiarities in cultural tradition never make barrier in relationship and thus remain an integral part of the greater society, which has become a cultural mosaic. Since colonial past, Muslims were considered as the most important group in an urban life because of their specialized services in the society. Even today they are considered to be part and parcel of the social life of Darjeeling Himalaya.

Due to close association with the hill society and culture, the Muslims share many cultural traits of their neighbours. The Muslim society and culture of Darjeeling hills has been shaped by the interacting forces of several set of traditions viz. Islamic, Nepali caste and tribe, Tibetan and so on which led to propagate a meaningful coexistence of Muslims and non Muslims in the large range of Himalayas. But communal harmony has always been preserved in the area. This harmonious coexistence thus enriched the secular environment which helped the Muslims in adapting to the social environment of their habitat. The rich cultural traditions of the Muslims are well integrated with the people of the area and thus the Muslims have become a dynamic and efficient minority of the hills.

REFERENCES

Ahmad, Aziz, 1964. *Studies in Islamic Culture in the Indian Environment*, Oxford, Clarendon Press.

Ahmed, Imtiaz (ed.). 1973. *Caste and Social Stratification among Muslims in India*. New Delhi, Manohar.

Ali, Meer Hassan. 1832. *Observations on the Mussulmanaus of India*. London, Oxford. (republished in 1916).

Ansari, Ghaus. 1960. *Muslim Caste in Uttar Pradesh: A Study of Culture Contact*. Lucknow, The Ethnographic and Folk Culture Society.

Chatterjee, Rajib. 2007. *Socuio-Economic Profile of the Dhunias of Sub-Himalayan Darjeeling. in Islam and Muslim Societies,* Vol. 3, No. 1, 2007

Dastider, Mollica. 1995. *Religious Minorities in Nepal*. New Delhi, Nirala Publication.

Hunter, W.W. 1871. *The Indian Musalmans*, London

Imam, Zafar (ed.). 1975. *Muslims in India*. New Delhi, Orient Longman.

Mondal, Sekh.Rahim. 1983. *For a Sociological Understanding of Indian Muslims*. in NBU Review, Vol. 6, No. 2. pp. 95-108

________. 1994. *Dynamics of Muslim Society*. New Delhi, Inter-India Publications.

________. 1997. *Muslims of Siliguri: Aspects of Their Society, Culture and Relationship with the Metropolis*. New Delhi, Institute of Objective Studies.

________. 1997. *Muslims of Nepal: Aspects of their Economy, Society and Culture in Relation to Habitat. in Islam and the Modern Age*, Vol. XXVIII No. 3. New Delhi: Jamia Millia Islamia, pp. 198-217.

________. 2000. *Muslims of Sikkim in Islam and the Modern Age*, Vol. XXXI No.1. New Delhi. Jamia Millia Islamia. pp-101-116.

________. 2001. *Tibetan Muslim Refugees in India: The Problem and the Prospects*. in S.C.Roy (ed.) *Refugees and Human Rights*. Jaipur, Rawat Publications, pp. 236-255.

________. 2001. *The Muslim Minority in the Buddhist Kingdom of Bhutan: A Socio-cultural Perspective. in Islam and the Modern Age*, Vol. XXXII No. 2, Jamia Millia Islamia, New Delhi. pp- 113-125.

O'Malley, L.S.S. 1907. *Bengal District Gazetteer: Darjeeling*. New Delhi, Logos Press.

Sharif, Jafar. 1832. *Qanun-I-Islam (The custom of the Mussalmans of India: comprising a full and exact account of their various rites and ceremonies from the moment of birth to the hour of death)*, translated by G. A. Herklots, 1921. London. Curzon Press Ltd.

Siddiqa, Shamima. 1993. *Muslims of Nepal. Kathmandu*. Gazla Siddika NPR.

Titus, Murray T. 1930. *Islam in India: A Religious History of Islam in India and Pakistan*. Calcutta, YMCA Publishing House.

15

Bathou Religion and Its Transition

Luke Daimary*

Bathou religion is the traditional religion of the Bodos. Bodos have their own concept of creation. According to their concept, before the creation of the universe there was a great void in which the Supreme Being-Anan Gosai or Obonglaori existed formlessly. The Supreme God was tired of living in a formless nature and desired to live in flesh and blood. He, therefore, descended on this void with all human characteristics and created the universe. Anan Gosai – the supreme God in his first appearance in the form of a man called himself Siw Bwrai or Jiu Bwrai. He then created his consort Siw Burwi. He also created Dari Muba and Singri Coba a couple for the propagation of the human race on the earth. Siw Bwrai or Jiu Bwrai is also known as the Bwrai Bathou. In Bodo Siw or Jiu means life or soul. Bathou is also represented by Sijou (Euphorbia Splendor) tree. Si here stands for soul and Jou for great or high. Hence Sijou means great soul. This relates to the first great human soul. Bathou philosophy is based on the concept of 5 (five) Ba connotes five and thou suggests profound or deep. While worshipping Bathou the Bodos recite the following verse:

* Senior Lecturer, Department of History, Nehru College, Pailapool, North Cachar Hills, Assam. lumsram@yahoo.co.in.

Thaigirni khongna khongba (Dillences indica fruit has five rinds)

Sijouni siria siriba (Euphorbia splenden has five ridges)

Siphungni gudunga gudungba (A Bodo flute has five holes)

Bathouni bandwa bandwba (A bamboo fence around the altar has five knots)

Boro Bwraini raoabw phongba (Bodo Oldman's words are five).

Around this verse the beliefs, rites, social customs and economic institutions of the Bodos are interwihed. The Bodos worship five gods including Sibrai who is the most Supreme of all. They adhere to five moral preaching. They have five laws to control the society and the individuals. They celebrate five festivals and have five kinds of marriages.

Bathou religion is based on five moral and spiritual messages.

1. Five Holy Realizations
   i) Realization of the Sijou the Supreme soul.
   ii) Linking up the Jiwma (human soul) with Sijou, the Supreme Being.
   iii) Realization of Mainao – the goddess of property.
   iv) Realization of the five great elements – earth (Hailong) water (Agrang), Air (khwila), light or fire (Sanja Bwrlee) and Rajkumbri (Sky).
   v) Realization of the worldly affairs.
2. The Five Holy Sermons of the Bathou – i) Meditative prayer to God; ii) Conversing religious and spiritual subjects; iii) Making charitable gifts to the poor; iv)Loving fellow – beings; v) Doing things unitedly.
3. Five Senses of Love – i) Love to Anan Gosai (Eternal God); ii) Love to fellow beings; iii) Love to wife and children; iv) Love to other lower beings and objects of nature; v) Love to one's mother land and the world.

4. Hatred for the Five Sinners :- i) Hatred for the murders; ii) Hatred for the thieves; iii) Hatred for the liars; iv) Hatred for the ones indulging in illicit and unnatural relationships and iv) Hatred for associating with men guilty of offences.
5. Five principles for Leading an Upright Life - i) Peace of mind (Saithi) ii) Control of mind (laothi); iii) Co-operation of mind and body (Nalathi); iv) Activeness (Maothi) and v) Love (Sonathi)

Bathou religion thus has much relevance with the numerical five. It has a philosophy which defines the basis of a religion.[1]

Preparation of the Altar

The altar of the Bathou is divided into three parts. The first part is fenced by bamboo strips and it is the principal altar. Here the supreme God Bathou is worshipped. The second part of the altar is an extension from the principal altar to the northern direction. Here Noni Modai i.e the subordinate deities of Bathou are worshipped. The third part of the altar is an extension to the southern direction. Here the Hagrani Mwdai i.e. the deities not belonging to the Bathou family are worshipped.

In the first part of the altar a white piece of cloth is hung above the ground which indicates the formless existence of the almighty. In the middle of the principal altar, a branch of the Sijou tree is planted. Before planting an egg of a hen and a stone are burried. The egg stands for reproduction and the stone for truth and longevity. In the upper region of the branch five curls are made by a white fresh thread. This stands for worldly illusion and attraction.

The Sijou tree is surrounded by a round fence of small bamboo strips woven by five bits symbolizing the religious and spiritual principles of Bathou. The fence is erected by eighteen pairs of bamboo strips which are planted in vertical direction. Three pairs of these strips in the front are twisted in traditional style called Daothu Bikha Hebnai which symbolizes three fold power of Bathou, viz. creation, nutrition and dissolution. A banana leaf is also laid on which a pair of betel nut and betel leaf, a bunch of banana fruits, resin, incense and a lamp wick are placed. While the preparation of the alter is on the worshippers keep singing accompanied by the traditional instruments such as Kham (Bodo drum), Sifung (Bodo flute) and Jotha (cymbal).[2]

The Worship

Before the worship begins the propitious articles are placed on the alter. Holy men like Douri and Ojha are important in the ritual. The Douri (priest) leads the worship from the beginning till the end. The Ojha is responsible to recite the holy hymns and hypnotizes the Daudini. When the Daudini is hypnotized she can neither speak nor understand other languages. She expresses only by signs. It is only the Ojha who understands her signs. The act of worship continues for three days and nights. Through out these three days and nights kherai dances are performed to please Bwrai Bathou or Sibrai. Traditionally a pig or goat is sacrificed as oblation to Sibrai. Daudini sucks the blood on behalf of Sibrai. When the Daudini completes the act of sucking she becomes unconscious while the drums, flutes and cymbals continue to be played. After she regains her sense she begins to dance turning around the altar five times. The process continues for several times. The Daudini is the key dancer in the Bathou worship. It is a role to be played by a women or a girl only. Her role bears great importance as she receives divine power to predict and tell about the past. It is during this worship ritual the faithful ask her to foretell their health conditions, their dangers in the times to come. They also ask forgiveness for all the wrongs committed as individuals or as a community in the village and promise not to repeat the same. During the Bathou worship she becomes the medium of Sibrai the almighty.[3]

Transition

The original beliefs and rituals of the Bodos have undergone changes in the course of time. According to a theory, the Aryans migrated to India and gradually expanded in different directions. With the Aryans came the religion of Hinduism.

Their expansion in the east led to the cultural contact with the aboriginal tribes. In course of time they got absorbed in the Hindu-system. This cultural contact led even to systematic conversion of the Bodos which can be traced back to the 7th century A.D. under the patronage of the Varmans and Salastamba line of rulers. With Hinduism penetrating into the royal families the names of the royal families were changed and places and rivers were given Sanskrit names.[4] But for centuries together Hinduism was confined to the royal families. In this connection A.D. Nath writes "......it was not until the time of Sankardeva (1448-1569) the great 16th century reformist that attempts had been made to Hinduise the masses......".[5]

Several aboriginal tribes of the Brahmaputra Valley came under the fold of the Vaishnavism preached by the great Sankardeva Ek Sharan Nam Dharam. The major tribes who accepted the Neo-Vaishnavism were the Bodos, Rabhas, Sonowal Cacharis, Chutias, and the Morans. They abandoned their old religion, custom and even languages and adopted caste Assamese Hindu culture. This continued upto the first quarter of the 20th century. It was at this critical juncture that Kalicharan Mech later known as Kalicharan Brahma appeared with new vision and mission to rescue the Bodo society. Thus from 1906 onwards a new religious movement preached by Kalicharan Brahma began to take shape among the Bodos. Brahma Dharam is a Vedic religion. With the coming of this religion among the Bodos the cultural assimilation with the Hindus became inevitable. In other words it was another wave of Sanskritisation of the Bodo culture.

Another cult of Hinduism the Satsang of Anukul Thakur also made its inroad among the Bodos of Assam. A large scale conversion of the Bodos into this sect was due to the influence of the Hindu philosophy. A small number of Bodos have also embraced Sai Baba Bhakti cult of Hinduism. The Bhakti cult of Chaitanya has also made its entry in the Bodo society. But their impact is quite insignificant. Thus the influence of Hinduism has been so forceful that the traditional Bathou religion could not remain intact. A new sect has emerged out of the traditional Bathou religion initiated by Guru Rupamani Devi. This sect has brought about a major change in the concept and practice of the traditional religion.

The fundamental change in this new sect is that it has discarded the sacrifice of birds and animals and use of liquor for propitiating God. It has become more ritualistic and goes to the extent of claiming it as pure Hindu religion. This sect claims that the Bodos are of Aryan descent. It does not use Kherai for worship purposes. Rituals are performed by the Brahmins. Above the Brahmins there are the Rishis and above the Rishis the Maharishis and finally the Moni.

There is yet another sect of Bathou religion preached by Swami Nabin Brahmari. It has drawn its philosophy from the Hindu scriptures such as Upanishad, Puranas and the Vedas. It believes that Siva has founded the Bathou religion solely for the Bodos. It advocates that the spiritual urge of the Bodos can be culminated only through the Bathou religion.[6] For this a true knowledge of Siva need to be accomplished which will lead to the fulfillment of the religion.

In the realm of the deities also several non-Hindu deities have been abandoned and some got identified with those of the Hindus. For instance the Supreme God Sibrai has been identified with the Hindu God Siva. The chief female deity Burwi Bathou has been identified with Parvati. Mainao the guardian of wealth and protectress of the paddy field is regarded as Lakhsmi. Bullibari, the Goddess of learning has been drawn parallel with Saraswati. The traditional Bodo trinity has been identified with the Hindu trinity - Brahma, Vishnu and Maheshwara. The new Bathou sect of Guru Rupamoni Devi has accepted all the Hindu Gods and Goddesses such as Siva, Bhagabati, Indra, Lakshmi, Swaraswati, Brahma, Vishnu Karma, Gandeswar, Durga, Ganga, Kali, Kamakhya and so on.[7]

The traditional religious rites, rituals, customs and manners of the Bodos have fused with those of non-mongoloids. Such practices even began to be looked down upon and equated with those of the low castes Hindus. The concept of caste hierarchy also entered the psyche of some followers. All such changes have taken the Bodo society much closer to the main stream Hinduism. In fact, the Bodos other than the Christians call them selves Hindus while many of them claim to follow a religion with a separate philosophy.

Conclusion

The Bodo society is an egalitarian society. It does not give any special position or status to any group on any ground. It concedes equal social standing to all religions that the Bodos follow. Therefore for progress and integrity of the Bodos egalitarian values should be upheld. Since recent time some followers of the Bathou religion have been making concerted effort to revive the originality of their religion under an umbrella organization called - All Bathou Religious Union. The organization is trying to cleanse Bathou religion of its sanskritic influences and engages itself in researches and holds seminars and symposiums at intervals with a sole objective to make the Bathou religion a unique and independent religion like any major religion in the world.

REFERENCES

1. Liladhar, Brahma, 2003. *Religion and Dances of the Bodos,* Onsumwi Library, Kokrajhar. pp. 2-7, 11-14.
2. *Ibid.*
3. *Ibid.*
4. R.N Musahary, 1989. *Aryanisation and Hinduisation of the Bodos,* in the Proceedings of NEIHA, tenth session, Shillong,, p.166.
5. A.D. Nath, *'Early Hinduisation of the Ruling Tribes of North East India'*, in the Proceeding of the NEIHA, Pasighat, p. 256.
6. Thaneswar Brahmari, *Guru Mohima* – Ultapani, P. 49.
7. Sekhar Brahma, 2006, *Religion of the Bodos and their Socio-Cultural Transition – A Historical Perspective,* Guwahati. p. 84.

16

Syncretic Religious Cults of Sundarban Delta

Binita Basu*

Introduction

Sundarban is a part of the world's largest delta formed by the mighty rivers Ganges, Brahmaputra and Meghna. It is also the world's largest estuarine forest. Geographically, it is positioned at the lower end of the Gangetic West Bengal. The Sundarban delta region covers altogether 9630 sq. kms. area (recognised as Sundarban Biosphere Reserve) in the districts of North 24 Parganas and South 24 Parganas of West Bengal in India. It includes 4263 sq. kms. (Sundarban Tiger Reserve) of forest area and 5367 sq. kms. (non-forest area) comprising 103 islands out of which only 54 islands are inhabited by human population. Sundarban is formerly known as Sunderbunds, comprises of vast tract of forest and saltwater swamp forming the lower part of the Gangetic delta. Literally Sundarban means 'beautiful forest' (Raha & Bhui, 2006). The name was perhaps derived from the meaning 'forest of sundari trees', a reference to the large mangrove tree that provides valuable fuel. Hunter (1998, Reprint) explains that the Chanda Vanda, an old tribe, might be related with the name of the area. Sundarban is the corrupted version of Chanda Vanda or Chandraban or Chandradwipvan (Chattopadhyay, 1999:3).

Almost 62% of the Sundarban area is situated in Bangladesh, while the remaining 38% lies within India. The area is bounded by the river Hooghly to the west, the Bay of Bengal to the south, the Raimangal, Ichamati, Kalindi, Haribhanga rivers in the eastern part of the Dampier-Hodges line to the north. It is located between 21°32′ and 22°40′ north latitude and between 88°05′ and 89° east longitude. A number of estuaries, rivulets and creeks are the other features which can be found in this area.

Historical Background

The history of reclamation of land in Sundarban dates back to 1770 when the then Collector General Claude Russell planned to make use of forest land for the purpose of agriculture. In 1785, the Commissioner of Jessore, Tilman Henckell with the permission of Warren Hastings, Governor General of Bengal, distributed the land among cultivators. It took 40 years for the ijaradars (who held plots of land) to reclaim the land in areas such as Sagar islands in south and Canning in the east. In 1814, the East India Company decided to distribute the land directly to the cultivators and for this purpose the post of Commissioner was created in Sundarban during 1816. Scott, the first Commissioner observed that the company has not received the revenue from the ijaradars and zamindars for a long time. In consequence thereupon the land of Sundarban was declared as Government property in 1817.

From historical records it is apparent that a large number of labourers were engaged to clear the forest and to reclaim the marshy lands for making it habitable. These labourers were tribesmen drawn mostly from Chhotonagpur plateau of Jharkhand, West Bengal and Bangladesh. These early settlers gradually increased in later decades and they migrated to this area in varied strength and successive waves in quest of livelihood. After the Independence of India in 1947 the influx of migrants at this place was further added from East Pakistan. In course of time, they also settled at Sundarban making it a place of cultural mosaic.

Ethnic Composition

Most of the people of this area are of multi-ethnic background having different occupational pursuits with pluralistic religious beliefs. Previously Sundarban was a no man's land and later Hindus, Muslims, and tribal communities inhabited the area. Among Hindus there were Brahmin, Bauri, Goala, Tanti, Kayastha, Mahisya, Poundra Kshatriya, Bagdi, Bedia, Chamar, Jele Kaibarta, Malo, Namasudra, Rajbanshi and Napit communities. Among the Muslims the section of Fargis is dominant. The tribal groups who have migrated from Chhotonagpur plateau to this region are the Bhumij, Munda, Oraon and the Santal. The Hindus and the Muslims have migrated and settled from Medinipur and the former group has also come here from erstwhile East Pakistan, now Bangladesh.

Economy

Man is compelled in this particular environment to depend as a receiver mainly on the forest products and river products for their livelihood from remote past. So, from this point of view 'ecology' of Sundarban as a donor at the macro level remains unchanged or static for its inhabitants both in case of collecting forest products and agriculture, which is full of uncertainty, unpredictability, harshness with high life risk. Only the change can be seen at the micro level.

To meet one of his basic needs - hungriness, man has to earn their livelihood. So their mere sustenance forced them to visit the forest which is the abode of man- eater, ferocious Royal Bengal Tiger, poisonous snakes and other wild animals. On the other hand the rivers of this area are full of crocodile, kamot (shark), etc. Having no other alternate way, the islanders frequently visit the forest to collect forest products knowing every danger, uncertainty of their life there. In addition to this, the river system in this area is also unique since the river is divided into several tributaries giving rise to creeks criss- crossing the forest. So, in order to collect river products also, people have to interact with the forest indirectly. They catch fishes, crabs, tiger prawn (*jele* or fishermen) from the river whereas from forest they collect honey and wax (*mauley* or honey collectors), fuel wood and medicinal plants (*bauley* or woodcutters), etc. While doing so, they often face confrontation with the ferocious Royal Bengal Tiger, crocodile, etc. In these situations, out of their helplessness, anxiety, they seek courage through the religion in the form of various gods and goddesses. But with the progressive motion of time gradually this forest based economy was replaced by settled agriculture, wage labour and meen dhara (collection of tiger prawn). Sundarban is a monocrop type of zone where saline water gradually engulfs the land and makes it unsuitable for producing crops for the next few years. This is a threat to the economic life of the inhabitants. At present the inhabitants of this area, therefore depend on agriculture along with pursuance of forest based economy to a minimal extent. The pattern of seasonal mono cropping has forced the people to engage in other forms of employment like prawn seed collection, honey collection, timbering, rearing of domestic animals and deep sea fishing. But still they are forced to depend on the forest and forest based resources primarily because agriculture does not fulfill their needs due to salinity of the water and secondly due to lack of modern amenities and less scope of other jobs. Having no other alternate way, people depend on nearby forest and river resources. This in turn makes the inhabitants harnessing the same environment for their mere subsistence into a conflict situation between man and animal (tiger, crocodile, snake, shark, etc) and also between man and authority. Hence, the economy of man of this area is dynamic in nature.

Role of Religion

Man can exist in a variety of ecosystems and is able to adapt himself in different external conditions. Together with a capacity to subsist on a wide range of diets, this quality has enabled man to spread over the largest part of the globe. Nature plays an important role in shaping the culture, society and also the subsistence pattern of the inhabitants of the Sundarban delta region. This adaptation to environment takes different forms and involves reactions and various strategies. The economic profile of Sundarban region has its own unique characteristics. It is one of the largest mangrove ecosystems in the World. It is a riverine area comprising hundred and three islands with a labyrinth of innumerable rivers, rivulets and creeks. From the very beginning religion plays an important role in the daily life of the inhabitants in this harsh, inimical ecology. It has a great impact in the life of every individual. Though, in general, the concept of religion varies from society to society, individual to individual. In Sundarban delta, religion has been adopted as a survival strategy centering through various gods and goddesses, pirs and darbeshes of both little and great traditions, in order to reduce the fear and anxiety of the islanders because this region is very much unpredictable, harsh, inimical and with full of uncertainty of life. Among various folk deities of this region, some significant and dominating deities are – Bonbibi, Ali Madat, Badar Pir, Kalu Rai, Chandi, Bara Khan Gazi, Manik Pir, Manasa, Sitala, Kasto Devi, Noybibi and so on. Among all the great traditional religious faiths, the entire religion of the area revolves around little tradition, territorial saviour goddess Bonbibi who is the predominant cult figure in this Sundarban delta region among all. They worship all these deities mainly because of two reasons-for their survival and safety, and to get rid of various diseases (as cure deities).

It is hardly a surprise that the oral tradition of Sundarban is rich with myths and stories. These myths and stories are common throughout the expanse of Sundarban, and various rituals and events take place to keep this tradition alive. The myths are an encapsulated form of their past. Their interaction and relation with the forest are explained in the light of these various myths. It is the crises of survival that brings together people under a common canopy of belief.

The Saviour Goddess Bonbibi

In Sundarban, 'Bonbibi' is the predominating cult who is also considered as the saviour goddess by all the islanders. As the name implies, Bonbibi has an impact of Muslim community where Bibi is a Urdu term means dignified, aristocrat lady and Bon [actually according to dictionary, Muslims used to call their sister as Bun or Baheen] means sister. Again in Bengali terminology Bon means forest or it can be said that Bonbibi is the noble, dignified, respectable lady of the forest. The Bonbibi cult does not represent any religious affiliation of a particular group. It celebrates the intimate bond that nature shares with man in the Sundarban. Bonbibi is represented by an icon seating on the back of a tiger with Dukhe (a small child, literally means sadness) in her lap or standing beside her feet in the left side. Bonbibi is also represented by a stone slab or by a pot vessel. The face and dress-ornaments of Bonbibi are quite similar to that of Hindu goddess Lakshmi or Saraswati wearing a sari and traditional ornaments with her feet decorated by red colour 'alta' as it is commonly seen among Hindu women folk from remote past. All the idols are shoeless which indicates the impact of Hinduization, as most of the idol makers of this region belong to Hindu background, whereas her brother Shahjangali stands beside Bonbibi with a club (gada) in his hand with which he drives away the tiger and his attire suggests Muslim influence. In most of the places the idol of Bonbibi is accompanied by her brother Shahjangali, Gazi Saheb, Dakshin Rai in the form of a tiger. In some places, instead of seating on a tiger, she seats on a deer or fowl. It states that Bonbibi was nourished by the milk of deer during her infancy. The parallel cult of Bonbibi is Dakshin Rai, the male figurine of non-forest area standing against Bonbibi. Both of them have formed a mythical background which is embedded in the belief system of the local inhabitants as is reflected in their symbolized rituals.

All the inhabitants of Sundarban area propitiate Bonbibi in three different dates in a year according to their traditions – in Poush Sankranti (January), on the very next day of Poush Sankranti or on the first day of Magh (January) and in Basanta Panchami (February on the day of Saraswati Puja). All these three dates are maintained through Bengali calendar. On the day of Bonbibi worship Bonbibibir Johurnama (The Bengali chronicle depicting the life of Bonbibi scribed by Muslim scholar) is read out as panchali from back to front as is done in case of Muslim scriptures, justifying that scribing the episode of Bonbibi was positively patronized by Muslim thinkers. Previously, Muslim persons depending on the forest and riverine products were there to read this panchali seating in front of the idol. But in course of time, some of them have passed away; some became too aged to read it out. Now a day, along with few Muslim souls, Hindu people from lower caste group and mostly from medium age read this panchali at various places including household level. Mainly, the local people preferred to call those persons who have good tonal quality, good pronunciation and read the panchali with full faith, feel and emotion. In this area caste doesn't play any role to become a priest or in other words, any person from any caste or community background can act as a priest.

Myth of Bonbibi

The story of Bonbibi is elucidated in Bonbibir Johurnama, Dukhe Kahini and Dhana Manar Pala. It runs as follows-

Once upon a time there used to live a fakir, named Berahim (literally means cruel, heartless) and his wife Fulbibi in Macca city. As they were childless, one day they went to Madina and prayed their heart's desire. Going there, Berahim came to know from Hajarat Nabiji that if he could marry for the second time, he would be blessed with two children of either sex. Knowing this Fulbibibi put one condition that is after the impregnancy of his second wife Berahim would have to desert her into the forest to live in exile. Thereafter, Berahim got married with Shah Jalil's daughter Gulalbibi in Mecca. At the time of Gulalbibi's ten months of impregnancy, Berahim took her on the way to her father's home through a deep forest where Berahim deserted her there to keep his commitment to his first wife Fulbibi. On the way Gulalbibi became weak and ill and she slept under a tree. Taking that chance Berahim left her wife Gulalbibi alone into that forest and set out for home. Awaking from sleep Gulalbibi could not see anybody and she started crying, lamenting and got fainted. After spending ten days into the forest Gulalbibi begot twin children of either sex - Bonbibi and Shahjangali. Thereafter leaving Bonbibi alone into the forest, Gulalbibi went elsewhere into the forest taking her son in her lap. Bonbibi was brought up by four fairies with motherly affection and survived with the milk of wild deer. On the other hand Shahjangali started growing up with his mother and they had their food from the forest. After spending seven years in this way Berahim could not bear with the guilty conscience any more and started searching for his wife Gulalbibi into the forest to take them at home. But by the order of God (Khuda), Bonbibi and Shahjangali refused to go with their parents and they decided to stay together and to set out for badabon. With the passage of time the siblings grow up in the forest enjoying all the resources (food and drink) available there.

In their adulthood both of them along with Gazi Baba (a Muslim saint) fought a war with Dakshin Rai, a tyrant son of a demon, Dandarakshasa and mother Narayani who claim themselves as the owner of Sundarban and its wealth. But lastly Dakshin Rai and his mother were defeated in the battle. Gazi Saheb negotiated the whole matter with Bonbibi and divided the atarobhati (land of eighteen low tides) where Dakshin Rai got his share between Kendokhali and sea shore and Bonbibi established her rule over the remaining.

During the month of Chaitra (March-April), the forested area of Sundarban stuff with honey and people go to collect this honey during mahal. Like the other people of this region, Dhonai and Monai mauley, two brothers who belonged to Barijhati, were planning to go in search of honey. Thinking this Dhonai told Monai to prepare a seven sailing ship (sapta dinga) for the said purpose. Monai tried to make Dhonai understand not to go for collecting honey citing many reasons as – fear of tiger into the forest, their monetary abundance, etc., but it was a vain endeavour. After arranging sapta dinga and man power, they noticed that one more person was required. Dhonai therefore went to his poor, fatherless cousin Dukhe's home. Dhonai made him understand that only he would be there in the boat and in return he would get a lot of money also. Hearing about the plan Dukhe's mother forbade him to go there and told him about the danger of tiger and many more things into the forest. But Dukhe (literally means sadness) was not interested to his mother's speeches. He was determined to go with his uncle-Dhonai. When Dukhe was leaving his home, his mother told him that mother Bonbibi is one kind hearted mother who resides into the forest and only she can save his life in any danger. They all set out in search of honey and wax but roaming about all the forest they didn't get any trace of honey and wax. On the other hand, Dakshin Rai became very angry finding that nobody gave him any offerings, human sacrifice and hence he disappeared all the honey and wax from the forest. Feeling a long for honey, Dhonai and his companions roamed about from here to there into the forest but they didn't get any trace of honey and wax. Feeling very sad they remained foodless and they assumed that it was surely the pretence of any God. At that very night when Dhonai was sleeping, Dakshin Rai appeared into his dream and informed him that he was the son of great demon Dandarakshasa and Narayani. He is the creator of all the honey and wax of the forest. If Dhonai can give a human sacrifice as votive offering, Dakshin Rai will give him honey and wax full of seven canoes. Dakshin Rai also gave a condition that if Dhonai can not give Dukhe as an offer in sacrifice; he will feed all Dhonai's companions to crocodiles. Finally, Dakshin Rai informed him to offer Dukhe to Kendokhali Island so that they can take plenty of honey and wax and he dispersed.

When Dukhe awoke he came to know everything about the conspiracy and he remembered his mother's instruction and immediately he prayed thrice in the name of Bonbibi, the rescuer of danger in the midst of forest. On the other hand, kind hearted mother Bonbibi came to see every thing and she told her brother Shahjangali that she is the mother of atharobhati and hence, if anybody prays to her immediately she will be there to rescue him or her. After few minutes, taking a deceptive figure mother Bonbibi appeared to Dukhe and she asked him to tell what the reason was behind his pray. Knowing everything mother Bonbibi with compassion and affection took him in her lap and also informed him to utter her name when Dhonai would offer Dukhe to Dakshin Rai in Kendokhali. Just at that time mother Bonbibi would reach to Dukhe and she would rescue him from the paw of Raimoni. Telling Dukhe these entirely mother Bonbibi disappeared.

After that night, taking the sapta dinga Dhonai set out for Kendokhali. There he collected plenty of honey and wax and at last leaving Dukhe alone to the beach of Kendokhali,

Dhonai again set out for his country. Then Dukhe seeing Raimoni in the form of tiger started uttering the name of maa Bonbibi and got fainted. Listening Dukhe's call maa Bonbibi who was in Bhurkunda then, reached there to save Dukhe with her brother Shahjangali immediately. Here, seeing Dukhe alone to the beach of Kendokhali, Raimoni in the form of tiger rushed to Dukhe. Seeing Dukhe to the beach of Kendokhali in that situation mother Bonbibi took him in her arms and ordered her brother Shahjangali to give Raimoni and his companions a big punishment. Raimoni couldn't manage to bring that war under his control against Shahjangali even though his all companions—crocodiles, demons, etc., were with him. Lastly to save his own life he reached to Gazi Saheb to whom he informed all incidents happened with him. Listening everything Gazi Saheb told Raimoni that his actual collision was with the bhati's God maa Bonbibi with whom his mother Narayani had established a friendship when her mother was defeated in war by mother Bonbibi. By that time during their discussion Shahjangali reached there chasing Raimoni. Being afraid of Shahjangali, Raimoni requested Gazi Saheb to do something and then Gazibaba mediated between Raimoni and Shahjangali. All of them went to Bonbibi where Gazi Saheb reconciled Bonbibi with great effort. According to the order of Bonbibi, Dakshin Rai by making friendship with Dukhe compensated him with wealth.

Meanwhile, Dhonai mauley after returning from forest informed Dukhe's mother that her only son has fallen prey under tiger's paw. With this news Dukhe's mother became blind and deaf out of extreme shock. This in turn reeled the seat of kind hearted mother Bonbibi into the forest and she immediately sent Dukhe back to his mother within a very short time with her pet crocodile Seko. Again with the grace of mother Bonbibi Dukhe's mother got her eyesight back and got cured of deafness. After recovery, Dukhe's mother advised him to give hajot to Bonbibi by begging alms from seven villages and also to propagate the name and fame of Bonbibi. Dukhe did so. Later with the blessings of Bonbibi Dukhe became a rich man and Chaudhury (local landlord) of that area. Seeing all these and remembering the past incidences Dhonai got afraid and begged mercy to mother

Bonbibi. Then according to the order of Bonbibi Dhonai gave his daughter to Dukhe. On the day of their wedding Dukhe remembered the name of Bonbibi and Bonbibi appeared in disguise of a white mosquito and blessed the couple. Thereafter, Dukhe lived happily.

Discussion

If one looks into the core issues associated with the legend, one finds that the legend is essentially a story of class struggle where a woman, deserted daughter of a commoner, frees the society from a tyrannical ruler (Bera et al. 2006). These parallel stories of colonial struggle and the identification of class are necessary. The woman is in a position of multiple marginalization; she is marginalized in the society because of her class, her position in her family and also because of her sex. Bonbibi stands as a typical post colonial feminist figure. Her elevation to the status of a goddess is a sort of emancipation. This myth of Bonbibi is very much popular among the people of Sundarban delta region. Along with Bonbibi, the name of Shahjangali, Gazi Saheb, Dakshin Rai and Dukhe get popularity and an identity also. They together with Bonbibi are worshipped and appeased.

Since this area demonstrates nature based economy, the ritual practices interweave these concerns into their structure. Bonbibi is the most powerful, undisputed, predominating saviour goddess of this region. Everybody living in the forested area of Sundarban worships Bonbibi considering her as the 'Sylvan Goddess of the Forest'. She is the sole protector of all the inhabitants who depend on the forest for their mere sustenance. Irrespective of caste and creed people (mainly the jele, mauley and bauley) worship this deity with their full faith and reverence. Before starting the journey into the deep, dense forest, creeks of Sundarban, all the bauley, mauley and jele belonging to Hindu, Muslim, Christian and Tribals devote themselves, pay offerings and propitiate Bonbibi for her blessings to overcome all sorts of danger. Crossing the boundary of the forest now she has taken place in villagers household also and now she is also worshipped for family welfare, for getting issues, to get rid of serious diseases, etc.

Sylvan goddess and the sole protector Bonbibi and her myth lie at the cognitive dimension of the people. The cult of Bonbibi has been manifested here in manifold manner. This gives an understanding that Bonbibi has been transformed here as the tutelary deity of Sundarban where she not only protects the inhabitants from the attack of tiger, but also heals and cures and blesses with desires. So, if empirically observed her tutelage gives a protecting shadow over the inhabitants of the forest.

The dependency on the forest of the islanders and their fear of tiger attack were also present in past as is evident from the story of 'Dhonai mauley and Dukhe Kahini' in Bonbibir Johurnama, where it says-

chaitra masete hae modhur srijan

(during the month of Chaitra, honey is created)

mahal korite gea pouchhe lokjon

(for honey collection people reach there)

dhonai monai name chhilo dui bhai

(there were two brothers- Dhonai and Monai)

bonbada kore khae hamesa aechhai

(often used to go to badabon for the same.)

It means, during the Bengali month of Chaitra, the forest becomes flourished with honey and wax and the people from various parts of this area reach the forest to collect honey. Likewise, two brothers of this area Dhonai and Monai subsist on the same. Once Dhonai decided to set out for forest in search of honey and found one person was needed in his team. Soon he reached to poor lad Dukhe (one of his fatherless cousin) to convince him to go with them. At the time of their journey, Dukhe's mother instructed and informed him about mother Bonbibi—the saviour goddess and guardian of the forest saying-

dayar maa bonobibi boner majhare

(kind mother Bonbibi in the midst of the forest)

muskile porile deke ma bolea tare

(in case of any problem remember her saying 'mother')

maa bole dakile tare dayaban hoeya

(if anybody calls her mother, being so kind hearted)

bipade kandari hoa loibe uddharea

(she will help you to overcome all adversities)

supinu tomar tare bonobibi mae

(devoting you to mother Bonbibi)

boner ma bonobibi twarabe tomae.

(The Goddess of the forest Bonbibi will make you able to cross all adversities.)

Dukhe's mother told Dukhe to remember and call mother Bonbibi in any kind of problem, hazard in the midst of the forest and she devoted her son's life in the name of Bonbibi believing that Bonbibi would save her son from every misfortune. After a long search of honey, they did not get any trace and became sad. On the other hand Dakshin Rai became angry seeing that and told Dhonai maule-

dakho bhai dhona maule mahale aelo

(see Dhonai maule came for honey collection)

puja bolidan more kichhu nahi dea

(without offering me any worship and sarifice)

phanki dea amare se jabe modhu lea

(by deceptioning/ cheating me he will return

with the honey)

....

....

....

yabat na daya more narabali puja

(so long human sacrifice is offered to me)

nahi diba mom- madu- dekhaibo maja

(will not give honey and wax rather I will show you)

jodi tumi narabali puja paro dite

(if you can offer me human sacrifice)

sat- dinga- mom- diba tomar dalite

(will give you seven boat with loaded wax).

Later Dakshin Rai asked Dhonai in his dream to sacrifice Dukhe only in Kendokhali Island. Dukhe came to know this and remembering his mother's instruction, he started praying to Bonbibi that very night. Later, maa Bonbibi saved Dukhe's life taking Dukhe in her lap from the mouth of Dakshin Rai, who was in disguise of a tiger and was about to attack Dukhe in Kendokhali. Bonbibi ordered her brother Shaihjangali to catch and punish Dakshin Rai by saying-

hoea rakkhas beta bagher akar

(taking the shape of a tiger, the son of demon)

cholilo dukher tare korite ahar

(started towards Dukhe to eat him)

....

....

....

dakhoho rakkhos beta ache danraiya

(see the son of demon is standing there)

dhorea bohut sajai karoho uhae

(catch him and punish heavily)

khaite esechhe jaechha amar betae

(as if he has come to eat my son)

jaechha kam taechha saja deho namakule

(according to his work punish him seriously).

Even, mother of atarobhati says about herself that-

atharobhatir modhye ami sabar ma

(I am the mother of all in this land of eighteen tides)

ma bole je dake tar dukhho thakena.

(who ever calls me mother, he or she gets alleviation).

The Process of Syncretism

The emergence of Bonbibi can also be seen as a part of syncretism as Bera (2005. 2008) has attempted to establish it. He stated that the interesting part of the legend of Bonbibi is that today Bonbibi is 'worshipped' as a Hindu deity by a Muslim priest wearing a long loincloth (lungi). During the worship the priest seats towards the west and the idol towards the east and offers the deity hajot instead of prasad. Moreover, the very term 'worship' of an idol does not fit in the normative pattern of Islamic mode of religious sacrament. The acceptance of a Muslim girl, daughter of a Muslim parenthood, as a Hindu deity comes under the purview of the process of syncretism that took birth under the canopies of acculturation and assimilation. Again the *Bonbibir Johurnama* (a Bengali chronicle, depicting the life of Bonbibi) which is read out from back to front as is done in case of Muslim scriptures, justifying that scribing the episode of Bonbibi was positively patronized by Muslim thinkers. It should be mentioned here that during this study it has been noticed that a very few idols of Bonbibi wear shoe of typical Muslim type. But now all the idols are shoeless which indicates the impact of Hinduization, as most of the idol makers of this region belong to Hindu background; whereas her brother Shahjangali stands beside Bonbibi with a club (gada) in his hand with which he drives away the tiger and his attire suggests an Islamic influence. Gazibaba, by his attire, name and beard seems to be a Muslim saint standing in the set beside Dakshin Rai (Niyogi, 1987). May be the concept of Bonbibi came in to existence in this lower part of Sundarban by the hands of those pirs, fakirs, and darbeshes of Bangladesh who migrated to this part of Sundarban for reclamation of land. All these features, faith on Bonbibi suggest a living example of syncretism, where the concept has been borrowed from the twin faiths of Islam and Hinduism.

The Cult of Ali Madat

Another predominating cult is Ali Madat, who is confined to occupy only one seat in Sundarban. Before going to start the discussion on Ali Madat let us know something about Gazi, Pir or Fakir. Gazis, Pirs, Fakirs were found everywhere in Sundarban. They were intimated with daily life of the people of Sundarban. They have been most influenced figures to the people of Sundarban. Gazi, Pir, Fakir are different from view of nature. Gazi fights with the religious view. Pir is a Muslim having all the powers of performing the miracles. Fakir is also a Muslim but lesser in power. He is having easy access to any house in the village. He sings the songs referring to both Hindu God and Muslim saint in any house irrespective of their religious affiliations. Allah the almighty is adorable to them. They are very experienced and have the knowledge about all the problems which the people face in their daily life. With this experience and knowledge they help the people in various ways. People are also very dependant on them.

Ali Madat is a Muslim saint with an obscure origin playing important role specially in agricultural families. Previously, Ali Madat got a very high importance to the jungle goers. At the present day he has lost his relation with the economic life of community and now he is adored as the deity of diseases by the people of Sundarban. But who is Ali Madat in reality? As the name implies 'Ali' are those persons who follow an austere ascetic life engaging themselves in glorification of God and 'Madat' means help. Thus Ali Madat is considered as a blessed soul of God who helps the people seeking his cooperation in some problem (Basu, 2010a). The idol looks like a Muslim saint with his uplifted right hand in the form of giving blessings. A section of people used to call Ali Madat as Ali Madhav or Ali Madan where 'Madhav' or 'Madan' stands for Lord Krishna. It is probably a later cult in its origin which has come into an existence after Bonbibi. No written document is there about Ali Madat as in case of Bonbibi (c.f. Bonbibir Johurnama).

Biharilal Raptan's son Gobindo Raptan lives in Pakhiralay at Gosaba. Biharalal Raptan's ancestors first came here from Bangladesh. They belong to the Poundra Kshatriya community. Gobindo Raptan's grandmother first got Ali Madat in her dream and thereafter he has been accepted in their tradition. In any kind of problem people use the soil of the "than" and the Kabach of Ali Madat with their full faith and reverence as because the family is credited with mantras. Only one Poundra Kshatriya (Raptan's) family has acquired the right to worship this God both at community and family level, which they got through a divine dream of Ali Madat. Both Hindu and Muslim communities of this area actively participate in this communal worship. The priest (now Gobindo Raptan) got the sole right to give a Kabach to a person who is seeking God's blessings. They take the 'mantras' of Ali Madat while starting anything. The worship of Ali Madat takes place annually on the last day of Aghrahayan (middle of December) which is one month ahead of the annual worship of Bonbibi (Makar Sankranti). This is the time when the harvesting is over and the people are ready to go to the forest. But the preparation of worshiping of Ali Madat starts from the very first day of the same month, Aghrahayan (middle of November) and continues throughout the month. At the time of offering hajot (a typical way of offering prayer as per Islamic norm) the priest faces towards the west and the idol faces the east, resembling the norm of Muslim prayer. For adoration of than milk, coconut water, water of Ganga, incense, dhuno are all required. Before adoring the than priest removes the previous year's idol of Ali Madat and places the new idol there. The priest, Gobinda Raptan, the elder son of Bihari Lal Raptan learnt the art of worshiping Ali Madat. On that particular day the priest abstains from food.

People who have serious problems make a promise to offer a particular sacrifice to Ali Madat on fulfillment of a prayer (manat). Votive offerings include malsha (a small earthen pot with fried rice, parched paddy, parched rice, fruits, etc.), idol of Ali Madat, only batasa (a sweet cake made of flour and molasses), etc. Traditionally by norm, Raptan's family offers five malshas to Ali Madat during worship. The villagers from different castes and religions also offer malsha. Those, who offer malsha must have to pay one rupee, otherwise the offering remains incomplete. People, who had made a votive offering, also abstain from taking food. The adoration of than is held in the evening. People, who make the votive offering, carry the idol of Ali Madat on the top of their head to the priest.

People, who make votive offering, take incense in two hand and dance in front of the idol of Ali Madat if their desire is fulfilled. Before the adoration of Ali Madat the priest cleans the whole room. The priest places five old round earthen pots made of soil on the floor in front of the idol and puts one batasa into each of the round earthen pots and offers to Ali-Baba.

At the end of the worship of Ali Madat the priest followed by the present people utter this mantra:

"baba alir name ekbar allah allah balo
lokkho kalar name ekbar allah allah balo
eklakh asi hajar pirer name ekbar allah allah balo
tettiris koti debotar name ekbar hari hari balo"

Here also in the above mantras the existence of syncretism is very much clear. During this worship, the islanders in addition to worshipping thirty three crores of Hindu gods and goddesses including Hari or Narayan worship Allah, the almighty God of Islamic religion. People suffering from any distress, disease, like stomach pain, accident case or in an auspicious work, can put on a *kabach* (talisman) if they trust in Ali Madat. They can wear it on any day but it is better to wear it in the morning or in the evening. But there are some prohibitions written in the prescription of that *kabach*. Like, the persons who wear this kabach and the priest, Gobinda Raptan who gives this *kabach* to the people, cannot eat *kankra* (crab), *kachhap* (tortoise) and *kunchemach* (a kind of small fish) and if they transgress this then there is high possibility of being *kala* (deaf) in their generation and the same is also applicable to themselves. It can be noted that all these seven terms i.e., *kabach, kankra, kachhap, kunchemach, kumir, kaikhali* and *kala* begin with the particular word "Ka". This is known as "Ka"-Syndrome which has been scattered in all directions of Sundarban. Almost all the people of Sundarban have a venerable image to it (Sarkar et al, 2003). Ali Madat is considered as a cult of this area who is worshipped annually due to various problems mainly related to disease.

Other Deities

Other than Bonbibi and Ali Madat, Dakshin Roy is another presiding deity, known as the "Lord of South" (non-forested area). He is considered as a malevolent deity in this area. He is a male figure either sitting on a tiger or often in the forum of a tiger. In lower part of Bengal there exists some deities related to water till date, like Kalu Rai, became the presiding deity of the Crocodiles which infest numerous creeks and rivers of Sundarban. Due to this he is appeased for safe fishing in such creeks and rivers of Sundarban.

The local people of Sundarban especially the Muslims propitiate 'Badar Saheb'- a saint of river. The rivers of this part of Bengal become turbulent and pose a danger while crossing on a boat. During crossing those rivers at rough weather, the people of the boat need the help of Badar Saheb.

Then they utter his name thrice, i.e. badar badar badar for their safe journey through the river and safe return.

Among the Hindu deities Chandi is another known Goddess of this region. In each and every boat the head of the boat is known as Chandi, which is red in color and paste of vermillion is there. At the outset of any journey on boat to the deep sea, the head of the boat is worshipped with incense, flower and coconut and Chandi of the boat is bathed with coconut water. Later this coconut is used as prasad and distributed among the members of the boat.

It has been observed that Narayani deity has a dominating position in rural area of the South Bengal. This deity is known as the mother of Dakshin Rai. The people, who enter into the forest, ask her countenance for their safe journey and safe return from the forest and also to cure from the diseases.

Among the other welfare deities Ateswar, Basanta Ray and others occupy a very prestigious position in this area. Ateswar wears sacred thread on his body like Brahmin God. He is known as the protector of the village. His presence protects the villagers from the attack of tiger, robber, etc., whereas Basanta Ray is just an iconic representation and he is regarded as equal to God. Among the other welfare deities Sitala, Noybibi, Gopal or Krishna, Kali, Panchananda, Panchanan, Manasa, and few others are the most popular deities in Sundarban.

Conclusion

In this new ecological area, people with different religions, castes and creeds are influenced by the twin faiths of Islam and Hinduism. The cult like Bonbibi, Ali Madat, which are prevalent in this area seem to have been developed as a process of continuum of communal beliefs against a common opponent, the legendry Dakshin Rai (in the form of ferocious Tiger). So, people irrespective of caste and creed propitiate these two cults which are more dominant than any other gods and goddesses of their respective faiths. Some of them are worshipped for survival strategy, while the others are appeased to ward-off evil spirits and diseases like pox, cholera, etc., since this tropical area is endemic to these diseases. This new ecological settings of Sundarban have forced the inhabitants to live under a common canopy of syncretism. This setting again is responsible for the survival of the society and its people.

In this context, Bera (2009, 2010) opines that "the amalgamation of people's belief system and the encroaching ideas probably formed a system that was different from either of the two original cultures. This probably laid the stage for the process of formation of syncretism in this part of lower Bengal".

He again stated that there was also "a tendency or effort to reconcile and unite various systems of philosophy or religious opinion on the basis of tenets common to all and against a common opponent. This fusion of two or more inflectional forms, which were originally different, has emerged in such a fashion that it can be understood under occupational pursuits and from the pattern of immigration to this soil".

An important point which is mooted here is that Bonbibi in Sundarban has assumed a new dimension with a new social meaning in the changed socio-political environment. Hence, the cult of Bonbibi has been understood here "as an integral part of the whole process of social evolution rather than as self congruent, self contained domains that generate non-assimilative meaning. It is the phase of a cultural understanding in this part of poly-ethnic mosaic where one finds as essence of assimilation, secularization, syncretism and universalization of culture while delineating the cults as a cultural process".

REFERENCES

1. Basu, Binita. 2010a. 'Sundarbaner Loukik Devata - Ali Madat'. (in Bengali)) in *Loukik* (A registered journal on Folklore & Cultural Studies),2009, No.3, Vol.-I & II.
2. Bera, Gautam K. 2005. 'Syncretic Folk Deities of Sundarbans Delta'. *Sacred Science Review.* Vol 6. Special Number on God and His Kindreds. pp. 53-62.
3. Bera, Gautam K. 2008. 'Syncretic Folk Deities of Sundarbans Delta', in Baidyanath Sarasati eds. *Voice of God: Traditonal*

Thought and Modern Science, New Delhi: D.K Printworld (Pvt.) Ltd. pp. 191-200.

4. Bera, Gautam Kumar. 2009. Tutelary Cults of the Sovereigns: Understanding Secularization and Universalization in Tripura. Agartala: Tripura Bani Prakashani.
5. Bera, Gautam Kumar, Asok Kumar Mukhopadhyay & Amitabha Sarkar. 2006. 'Syncretism at Sundarbans: Anthropological and Linguistic Dimensions'. The Oriental Anthropologist. New Delhi: Serials Publications. 6(1). pp. 5-25.
6. Bera, Gautam Kumar & Vijoy S. Sahay. 2010. In *The Lagoons of The Gangetic Delta,* Delhi: Mittal Publications.
7. Chattopadhyay, Haraprasad. 1999. *The Mystery of Sunderbans,* Calcutta: A. Mukherjee & Pvt. Ltd.
8. Hunter, W.W. 1998 (Ori 1875). *A Statistical Account of* 24 *Parganas,* West Bengal District Gazetteers, Govt. of India.
9. Niyogi, Tushar Kanti. 1987. *Tiger Cult of Sundarbans,* Calcutta: Anthropological Survey of India.
10. Raha, M.K & Sudip Bhui. 2006. 'Tribal Situation in Sunderban', *The Oriental Anthropologist*. New Delhi: Serials Publications. 6 (1). pp. 27-43.

17

Religious Beliefs and Rituals Among Riang

Jannet Tellis

Introduction

Riang of Tripura is the second largest tribal community in the state and is enlisted as Primitive Tribal Group. (PTG). According to 2001 Census, Riangs are about 1, 65,103 persons which is about 16.62 % of the total tribal population of Tripura. It is evident from the legends of Riangs that they migrated from Burma to Tripura through the forest-clad regions of Chittagong hill tract (Bera, 2009). After settling down in Tripura, the Riangs got the patronage from the ruling Tripuri kings of Tripura as defense personnel in the State army (Chaudhuri, 1983). But the Riangs are primarily shifting hill cultivators. They have their own dialect, and have still retained their individual identity by clinging to their traditional core cultural markers. Riangs have carved out for themselves a special position in the state of Tripura. The Riang dance is a commonly seen item in any cultural programs of Tripura. At present Riangs are sporadically distributed in all the four districts of the state, the largest concentration has been found in North Tripura district followed by the South, Dhalai and West Tripura districts.

The Riangs are also known as Bru. The term Riang usually denotes the tribe. There are many stories about their ancestry and origin and some of these are even contradictory (Chaudhuri, 1983 & Bera, 2008). Scholars suggest that Riangs migrated from Burma (Barooah, 2008). "Rajmala" seems to suggest that the Riangs were settlers of Maynai hills. They are also found in Mizoram, Bangladesh and Assam, besides Tripura. Riangs consists of thirteen sub clans known as: Meska, Molsoi, Choraki, Apeto, Raichak, Warem, Msha, Chongpreng, Toimoi, Nouhkham, Yakchow, Riang, Yakstam (Barooah, 2008; Chaudhuri, 1983).

Riangs are identified as one of the one of the seventy five primitive tribes of India during the sixth plan period by the Ministry of Home affairs, Government of India on the basis of their pre-agricultural level of technology, extremely low level of literacy, declining or stagnant population as recommended by the state Government (Bera, 2010). This categorization is mainly due to the impact of colonization throughout the world particularly, that of the British, who have reflected in simplistic images of indigenous people as either primitive or dangerous. In this context, the term primitive is a result of different types of ethnocentrism derived from narrow enlightenment philosophies (Lauderdale, 2008).

Origin of Riangs

The Riangs of Tripura have a story which tells us about their beginning in Tripura. They had a king, Kachak, who was particularly cruel and tyrannical. Being unable to bear his rule, the people dispatched six emissaries to the court of Govind Manikya. These emissaries got lost in the valleys and forested peaks of Devtamura and so were forced to take the water route along the river Gumti. As fate would have it, this route had been closed by Govind Manikya as he was performing Ganga puja near his capital at Udaipur. The emissaries were arrested and were about to be sacrificed when the king gave them reprieve. After hearing their fate he dispatched a huge force with them to destroy Kachak. But the troops did not return; some were killed by the Riangs and the others married Riang damsels and settled down there.

Many expeditions sent later similarly failed to return. The Raja got worried and sent seven of his most faithful warriors to unravel the mystery. These people were accosted by Kachak's minister as they entered the Riang country. He was armed with a dao. The seven wise men got him engaged in a conversation on bravery telling him that only the person who can cut seven bamboos with a dao could be considered brave. Then they cleverly stuffed the bamboos with stones and handed them over to the minister whose dao became blunt by the time he had cut four. He was easily overpowered and killed. The king of Riangs, acting without his wise minister's counsel, was easily overpowered and arrested. The Tripura army then entered the land of the Riangs, arrested everybody and condemned them to death. The Tripura Maharani, being commanded in her dream, interceded on their behalf and got them a reprieve. When she visited the jail, the Riangs thought her to be a goddess. She told the Riangs that she had no children and would like to adopt them. She made them drink milk from her breasts and take a vow of fidelity to the state. From that day the Riangs started living in Tripura (Samanta, 1980).

World View

There are many historical and primal religions and each of them have a distinct way of addressing issues that relates to humanity. Each answers questions which all human beings seem to be programmed to inquire about: Why am I here? What happens to me when I die? How shall I live my life? Each religion makes effort to answer these questions in a way that the ordinary people feel comfortable with. According to Kawagley (1995), most indigenous peoples' worldviews seek harmony and integration with all life including the spiritual, natural, and human domains. These three realms permeate traditional worldviews and all aspects of indigenous peoples' lives. Each indigenous group has its own worldview, depending on its habitat, history, and resources. So also the Riangs of Tripura has a worldview underlying every aspect of life: language, social system, religious beliefs, and even the way they go about their daily life. Such a worldview may be defined as a set of concepts that relate individuals within their culture to the natural universe and to other humans who comprise their social reality.

Religion Defined

According to a definition "Religion is the recognition on the part of man of some higher unseen power as having control of his destiny and as being entitled to obedience, reverence and worship". In brief, Religion is human belief in some super natural power as well as the worship of this power (Bhowmik, 2003). There are Sociologists who have defined religion in different terms. E.B. Tylor (1832-1917) introduced the term in 1871 to characterize the religions of so called primitive societies. Tylor located the origin of all religion in animistic belief. Animism refers to religious practices and beliefs centering on the notion that spirits or souls inhabit and animate most, if not all, natural phenomena. According to (Durkheim, 1915) Religion is a unified system of beliefs and practices relative to sacred things, that is to say, things set apart and forbidden—beliefs and practices which unite into a single moral community. According to him, early humans associated such feelings not only with one another, but with objects in their environment. This led to the ascription of human sentiments and superhuman powers to these objects, in turn leading to totemism. The essence of religion, is the concept of the sacred, that being the only phenomenon which unites all religions. Religion acts to pull people together (mentally and physically, in the form of religious services or assemblies). By doing so, religion is able to reaffirm collective morals and beliefs in the minds of all members of society. Karl Marx differs when he states on religion as the opium of the people, the sigh of the oppressed creature, the heart of a heartless world, just as it is the spirit of a spiritless condition.

Religion: An Appraisal

Religion is a universal tool for explaining realities that exists in and beyond a world that envelops humanity and often remains as a mystery. The earliest known evidence indicate that religions emerged in to an organized form some thousand years ago. To this present day religion continues to exercise a very influential role in human society. Religion appears to help individuals and communities to cope up with negative experiences resulting out of natural disasters and human tragedies. Religion seems to serve as a platform for people to unload their worries and anxieties. It provides meaningful answers to many questions to which science fails to provide a convincing scientific answer.

The absence of a sharp division between religion and science can be easily found in the primal world. For a primal world there is one single cosmos that sustains every living creature. Primal people are concerned with maintaining personal, social and cosmic harmony and with attaining specific good rain, harvest, children, and health. The concept of salvation seems to be virtually absent among the Riangs. For them life after death tends to be a shadowy semi -existence in the vaguely designated place in their single domicile. Primal people are different but not backward.

Riangs: Concept of God

Religion of the Riang is connected to the world of Gods and spirits. Riangs believe in a spirit world that pervades their physical world; for them God manifests in various ways and his presence is seen in anything and everything around them. As in most societies people believe that the process of nature and the success of human endeavor are under the control of entities outside the range of everyday human experience, and whose intervention can change the course of events. Riangs of Tripura is no exception. Riangs are deeply rooted, associated and influenced by the environment that they live in. Their religious practices are centered on the rites of passage.

God is present in every culture and every culture has a capability to express some truth about God to its own people. So also in the life of Riang. Traditional Riangs see their culture as their basis and foundation of their understanding of how God interacts with them. Yet religion of the Riangs often present and absent at the same time in their society but differently across time. Composition of the socio-cultural fabric created by circumstances that existed among the Riangs, led them to particular ethos beyond their religious beliefs. Besides the rites of passage the religious practices are present at the time of Jhum cultivation. They have meticulously elaborate rituals to divine the success or the failure of the Jhum, as the cultivation is gamble with the nature.

Riangs are the worshippers of supernatural powers and are very much religious minded. They believe that they should always worship and propitiate all those who possess supernatural powers or else if the spirits are annoyed with them, then their wrath may befall on the entire family. They propitiate evil spirits in order to appease and keep them satisfied and fulfilled. In case of diseases and natural calamities these spirits are worshipped and appeased so that they might withdraw the evil influences from the victims and their family or the village concerned. Therefore even opening up a new Jhum site, the evil spirits are worshipped properly with a view to escape from the wraths of the evil spirits by way of scanty rainfall, pest infection etc.

Concept of Soul and Heaven

The permanent place of the soul in a body is between the chest and the navel and it leaves the body for ever after death. An honest and virtuous soul will have place in heaven. The soul of the dead is received by Tui Buma after the performance of post funeral rituals and offering of ashes and bones of specific parts of the river. To identify the reincarnate child, a mother marks the body of her child with ink spots. If a married woman dies her husband plants plantain tree on her cremation ground. As there is a belief if not done she may not have child in next birth.

Concept of Evil Spirits

Riangs believe in the evil spirits. Buraha is the major evil spirit in Riangs religious thought and they try to satisfy by worshipping and sacrificing pig, cock, eggs and fruit. Besides Buraha there are other spirits which are feared. There are rituals in the name of Buraha for the satisfaction of the evil spirits or ghosts. The Riangs feel that there is close relation between their traditional deities and the Hindu Gods and

Goddesses. Riangs believe that the Hindu Gods can be pleased more quickly. So there is a tendency among some Riangs to move towards Hindu Gods and Goddesses. Sickness and ill health are either involvement or wrath of a spirit. Some magico- religious rites are observed to get cure from a disease.

Traditional Beliefs and Practices

Riangs believe that there is a Supreme Being, a Creator, a Great Spirit, and God. Many lesser spirits wander the earth, some control weather, some interact with humans, some inhabit the underworld. Plants and animals, as well as humans, are part of a spirit world. This spirit-world exists side-by-side with the physical world and often intermingles with this physical world. Before one is conceived, before one is born, one has a spirit. When one dies, his/her spirit will live on. Riang community is guided by the different old traditional socio-cultural norms, values, beliefs, and so on.

The Riangs believe that once Achu Sibrai, the Supreme Being, was engaged in deep meditation on two sacred stones for the creation of the Riangs. Nearby his wife, symbolized by a bird, while hatching two eggs, felt hungry and picked up these two stones, taking them to be fruit. She carried them to her nest but not being able to eat them, she hatched them. After 12 years, Debtarani and Deblakshmi were born from these stones. They became the ancestors of the Riang people. Sammlimland and Tampuima, born of the two eggs, became the ancestors of the Riang deities. Achu Sibrai woke up and blessed Debtarani and Deblakshmi and instructed the deities to keep a watch on them. Since then the deities live in this world, threatening the human beings with death and disease when the world becomes sinful. Of the deities, Achu Sibrai, when he becomes dead drunk, is reincarnated as Buraha, the dreaded God of destruction, who can be loosely equated with Shiva. Achu Sibrai blessed the ancestors of the Riangs, and gave them His Law, Law of truth and righteousness. He instructed Sammliland and Tampuima to keep watch on the ancestors of Reang in order to make sure that they lived by His Law. Then He departed from them. From that time on, their ancestral Gods and the subordinate deities lived with them here on this earth. The ancestral Gods in turn were assisted by their deities.

Major Deities

Tuima	:	The goddess of the River.
Garai Sangrama	:	Deity of the Hills.
Burcha	:	Lord of the Forest.
Khulangma	:	Goddess of Cotton.
Lampa	:	God of the sky and the Ocean.
Mailong Ma	:	Goddess of wealth.
Buruirao	:	Deities of evil spirits
Lampra	:	God of the sky and the ocean.

The Riangs believe in a very close relationship between them and the deities who can do them much good or harm. If Riangs do not abide by the laws of Achu Sibrai, these deities will punish them with drought, pestilence and famine. Rituals have to be regularly performed to appease these deities. The evil spirits, or Buruirao, have to be worshipped near their homesteads or the boundaries of their villages. The visible form of the ghosts is believed to be a forest fire. Ghosts are also believed to be the cause of the thumping sound heard in a bamboo forest. The Riangs believe that good and evil pervade the world. Goodness comes out of the happiness that emanates from truth and righteousness, and evil from the lack of them. The idea of rahau (sacredness) and haia (profanation) are also well developed in them. Sacredness comes out of performance of prescribed rituals, cleanliness and sanctification. Cotton is also considered sacred and is used in almost all rituals. Eating without taking a bath is considered profane. It is believed that diseases are caused by some specified deities and evil spirits who have to be regularly appeased. For any disease, medicine is prescribed by the vaidya (medical man), but it cannot be warded off by medicine alone; rituals have to be performed by the akchai. Rituals can be classified as those performed by the individual family, by the members of the clan and community and by the chief. They aim at achieving economic, social and personal security for the person who performs it.

Spirits

They have a belief on the benevolent (Buraha, Longdrai,etc.) and the malevolent (Songrongma, Mainokma, Khunokma,etc.) spirits, Animatism (Attribution of life to physical objects), Animism (Belief on the natural objects), Totemism (Transmigration of soul), beliefs in Dreams/Divinations, Magic/Witchcrafts, Omen, etc. The belief of animism is probably one of man's oldest beliefs. From its earliest beginning it was a belief that a soul or spirit existed in every object. In fact, this religious practice has been the core of the indigenous way of life to the Riangs. Traditionally, the tribal religions are historically evolved. The Riang can be loosely described as animists, having their own belief of local spirits. In general, they see their world filled with various invisible spirits (often called Phola). They associate spirits with rice, soil, water, fire, stones, forests, etc. Priest Akchai in each village contact these spirits and prescribe ways to appease them. In times of crisis or change, animal sacrifices may be made to placate the anger of the spirits. Illness is often believed to be caused by evil spirits. In addition to belief in spirits, villagers believe in taboos on many objects or practices. The worship of the supernatural beings is supposed to protect them from all evils and calamities.

Religion serves to engender and strengthen group consciousness and solidarity. The Riang priest Akchai performs all worship individually and also on behalf of the whole village. Major pujas / rituals of the Riang is performed by the priest which includes the entire rituals starting from birth to death viz., Gbeing Bumo, Aabu Sumo, etc. before and after the birth of a Child. Mai Khlungmo, Mtai Ktor, etc. to get relief from diseases. Nohsuh Mtai, Maibaohmo, Ha Splehmo, etc. held after the death of a person. The priest is regarded as physician possessing knowledge of medicinal herbs and capable of curing the sick by using herbs and magical chantations. The Riangs believe that Gods are to be worshipped to get relief from different uncertainties of life. Priest is respected by the villagers and enjoys manifold privileges. He plays a prominent role in the life of Riangs.

Rituals

The rituals act as intermediaries between the Riang and his deities. Nokhungswami aims at keeping the house sanctified, Khangmi is for recovery from illness and Khangkachang Khangmi for keeping the individual sanctified from birth until marriage. These rituals comprise oral invocation, offerings, divination and sacrifice. Rituals are performed before cutting the jhum (shifting cultivation), for the prevention and cure of disease, for the protection of newly-built house, for protection against snake-bite, for rains, for wealth, for the welfare of a clansman, and for various other individual and clan needs. In addition, they offer worship to all the rivers, including the Gumti, Karnafuli, Mahuri and Feny. They also perform Lakshmi puja, Ker puja, Matungi puja, Tripura Sundari puja and Chitragupta puja every year. Every family participates in one or more such pujas every year. The occasion of the rituals gives an opportunity to Riangs from all parts of the state to meet and demonstrate their unity. This occasion is utilized for a meeting of all the chiefs and all disputes are solved and misunderstandings removed. These pujas, once a powerful integrating force, are now dying out mainly as a result of the decay of the power and influence of the Katardaga. Over the years people have embraced different faith that makes them not to be part of some of their traditional dance festivals as well.

The Riangs believe in a very close relationship between them and these deities. Drought, pestilence, and famine for them are not natural calamities but the result of divine wrath and punishment for their disobedience to the Law of Achu Sibrai. They have a simple theological notion that Godliness is the cause of true happiness. Therefore, for them, a truly happy person is a godly person. This idea has been changing over the years.Their goodness harmony and integration with God depends not on their faithfulness to the Law of the Supreme Being but on the performance of the rituals. Thus Ritual has become a valuable means to obtain this harmony and integration with Gods. The rituals give them the capacity to please and appease the deities. Thus with the coming of the rituals there is a shift from personal sanctity to institutionalized sanctity.

They perform rituals

- to appease the deities who caused their diseases.
- to protect them from snake bite.
- to protect their new houses.
- to recover from their illnesses,
- to acquire wealth, rains.
- to obtain favors for individuals and for their clansmen.
- to keep the house sanctified and also the individual from birth until marriage.

Major Rituals

At every major step in their lives they have rituals to propitiate God, to help them live through the time of misery and disease. The Riangs quest to find answers for natural calamities, sickness and death which leads them to believe in a power that is beyond their control. In order to appease such a power they come up with various types of rituals. Some of these rituals involved sacrifices, offering of food and drink. The religious life of the Riang revolves around the process of human life cycle in relation to cultural events and Jhum cultivation. All the ceremonies and festivals are linked to invoke a blessing from different Gods and Goddesses in order to obtain greater happiness and prosperity. Such numerous deities are commonly worshipped through various rituals to safeguard and cure them from different evils and illness.

Imshih Tainmo	- For health and family welfare
Soinai Rao	- For family welfare
Boni Rao	- To get rid of illness
Mai Khlum Mo	- For sanctification of agricultural outputs
Homa Pha Khami	- For women health and welfare
Norah Khemi	- For household peace and prosperity
thu nai rao/Imtai Raja	- For health
Hathai Kchu Ri Mi	- For Longdrai God-In a haunted place
Haa Spleh Mi	- Protection against ground related illness

Hata Malai Mi	- During the new season of Jhuming/Jhum Cultivation
Tui Kto taola ri mi	- Ending an oath taken in parents' name
Tui Chao Mi	- During Illness
Para Ker Mi/Para Puja	- For village welfare
Tao Chro Ri Mi	- During high fever
Mai Nok Ma/Boisu	- To appease the Goddesses of Grains
Khao Ruh Mi	- Before beginning a journey
Toi Kha Mi	- For Barren Women
Bah La	- For Village welfare
Asari Kamo	- Thanks Giving.

Mahadev Arag Bao Mo - Earlier during a death ceremony, usually the people belonging to the Reang/Bru community would be mourning day and night without eating or indulging in any constructive works, so Mahadev, a deity after seeing such chaos in the village wanted to make the people realized that instead of wasting valuable time in mourning, they should do some constructive works that will be helpful during the death ceremony as well as for the village. So, he taught the Riang people to prepare a local wine that really helped the people, because they could enjoy the local wine during the ceremony and after that they could go for their daily works. But the condition was that during any such ceremony the first drops of drink must be offered to the deity, i.e. Mahadev.

Some of the Rites de Passage

Before/After Birth of a Child

1. Tui Chao-This puja was performed for the smooth birth of the child and also the health of the child is determined by examining the intestine of the fowl that was sacrificed.
2. Gbeing Bumo-In this puja one pig and four fouls are sacrificed for the good health of the child and the mother.
3. Aabu Sumo-By sacrificing five fouls and placing five local wine bottles, this puja indicates the purification and naming of the child.

4. Bachak Kamo- After 4-5 months, for the good health of the child this puja was performed by sacrificing five fouls and placing five to six bottles of local wine.
5. Khong Khok Kamo-For the proper growth of the child' brain and his long life, this puja was performed. The woman will have to wear a new cloth and sacrifice one fowl and one cock. She will also have to offer 60-70 local wine to the priest.
6. Saja Thunairao/Saroi Thunairao- By sacrificing two fouls and one pig, this puja was performed for the well-being of the child.

During Marriage

According to riang customs and traditions there is no fixed age of marriage, generally the marriage is after the attainment of puberty. Monogamy is generally in practice. Betrothal is known as chhoikhemo is arranged immediately before the marriage. Initiating marriage proposal is done by the father of the bridegroom to the parents of the bride through a match maker. On a fixed day matchmaker with parents of the bridegroom and some relatives go to the bride's house with two bottles of country liquor. If the proposal is accepted then the groom's party offers some pig and country liquor to all who are present there. Then the day is fixed for a formal betrothal. After the betrothal meal the date of marriage is fixed and other various matters. Like items to be given by the bridegroom's party at the marriage, the years of service to be rendered by the groom to the house of brides parents. If service of the bridegroom can be in kind or cash is also finalized. At marriage there is no particular ceremony, but a great deal of drinking and dancing. The marriage ceremony is performed in the house of the bride. A quantity of oil, cotton, chilly, salt, ginger, onion, rice, one Dao, a piece of iron, stone, and two bottles of liquor kept on a winnowing fan in front of the bridegroom. Earlier days only a rnai cloth representing bride was kept left of the bride groom symbolically to represent bride. The akchai chants hymns while the articles are kept in front of the groom.

1. Songrongma Puja-The main ceremony that deals during the marriage where one fowl and one cock along with two pure local wine/brew are offered.
2. Kati Chamo- This puja is performed after the bride is brought to the bridegroom house. It was usually performed both on the land and in water by sacrificing two fowls or in some case one goat. This puja is basically for a new couple after marriage.

The principles of marriage in the riang society are undergoing changes and there are cases of cousin marriage of all types taking place. Interview with the youth who move to cities for education, job opportunities seems to be very far from knowing the traditional rituals. Slowly the traditional practices are diminishing in the life of the Riangs.

Related to Death

The Riangs believe in the re incarnation of the soul. Those who follow the path of righteousness in their lifetime will be reborn as human being. A sinful man is reborn as animal. The dead may also be reborn in same family in new birth. That is why mother marks the body of the dead child with black ink to have him in the family in rebirth. Ideally the mourning goes on for three days. And no one goes to forest those days. Wife and children of the diseased refrain from drinking and dancing during this time. Widow abstains from worshipping deities.

The Riangs cremate their dead. The dead body is cremated near a river except those of infectious diseases. Children below one year are also buried. There are some pre-funeral and post funeral rites to be observed. The bones of the dead are kept in a shed for few months or a whole year. This shed is called Simangnok. After a period of feasting and dancing, the bones are immersed in the river on a bamboo raft. Belief in the immorality of the soul and its reincarnation is very strong. They belief that life is divided into two parts, the soul blending with the wind and the body seeking refuge in the water. Thus the soul returns to Achu Sibrai from whence it came.

1. Yaphaik ow, Tao Buthaik ow-for lao tao (God i.e. Owner of the Death) and for the Death person.
2. Sampli Bahcha ow-The Whole night people would be drinking and dancing by taking the dress of a Biang goma (A typical type of huge bird). The dead body would also be dressed up.
3. Thereafter, a small hut (Smang Nok) would be built where the bone of the death person will be kept for at least 3-4 months. Another small hut will be built called (Kaa Nok) exclusively for the older women for crying. But for the rich people like the Chowdhry of the village their bones will be kept in a special hut called Chrai Nok.

Other Rituals

Relating to Individual/Personal (General Welfare)

1. Nokkhok Puja- Here, Basically Four Types of Puja was Performed Namely;

Sani Puja during the month of August-September with only the samogri (Ingredients).

Baroi Tainnai in the month of September-October with a sacrifice of two male-goats.

Soi nai rao tainnai in the month of February-March with a sacrifice of two male-goats.

Hata Malai Mi in the month of April-June with a sacrifice of two male-goats.

Nokkhok Puja as a whole is performed by sacrificing a Buffalo. This four system of Puja revolves whole year round. After this puja comes another puja called Bar Yachak mo Puja. Here there will be a procession of the village people with the owner of the house at the front followed by five priests. During the course of the puja nobody could cross the road that was taken by the procession.

2. Samung Maimo (Knowing Works)

Two Pigs are usually sacrificed, one at night and the other on the next morning. But the body of the pig is kept on a small hut that will be guarded by two priests and one of their followers. Near the Pig a Ink Cham (Rope), seven Khuchloi (seed of a cotton) and seven Rice grains will be placed. The Puja will end the next day, which then is followed by a puja called Sema nai mo (Observation), If there is any increase in the number of the cotton seed and the rice grains say up to 8-9 with a teeth mark on the Pig then the puja is a success and there will be a community feast. Thereafter another puja is performed called Khum bai li where all the people will drink local wine from the two wine pitchers that will be placed in front of everyone. Here, the owner of the house i.e., the one who is performing the puja would have to imitate the priest wearing a new cloth. The priest would be dancing in an intoxicant manner on the tune of a godly drumbeat. The priest would shiver and throw the burnt wheat seed. The owner of the house usually receives the seeds before it falls on the ground by spreading a new cloth. This festival takes place for two days and nights.

Jhum Cultivation

Men and women participate in the Jhum cultivation. The Riangs themselves divide the forested areas among themselves by mutual adjustment. Then they start the work of clearing the forst.Once the trees are cut, fallen and dried before the fire is set the priest akchai performs rituals and offer a pig or a fowl in anticipation of a good crop. They have site for Jhum cultivation is located outside the village having no stable boundary as the Jhum fields shift every year leaving behind the cultivated site. The singing and dancing with the drums takes place when the weeding starts. As the crops grow and gets ripened merry making still increases till the stage of harvesting. Before harvesting the paddy the priest akchai performs rituals by way of sacrificing a pig and or a fowl in the field. Harvesting is done as it is matured. Both men and women join in the activities of the Jhum.

Tribes in Transition

Among the above 68 million citizens of India, who belong to different tribal groups, the religious concepts, terminologies, and practices are as diverse as number of tribes, but majority if not all of these groups have one thing in common: under constant pressure from the major organized religions. Most of the pressure comes from the process of integration within a national political and economic system that brings tribes into increasing contact with other groups and different, prestigious belief systems. In general, tribes those remain geographically isolated in desert, hills, and forest regions or on islands are able to retain their traditional cultures and religions longer. Those tribes that make the transition away from hunting and gathering and toward sedentary agriculture, usually as low-status laborers, find their ancient religious forms in decay and their place filled by practices of Hinduism, Islam, Christianity, or Buddhism.

Changing Face of the Riangs

The religion is so much interwoven into the life of the Riangs and we are often confronted with relative absence of compartmentalization in the life of the Riangs. Due to absence of compartmentalization it becomes a challenge to identify and to ascertain the features of religious practices as per the western world view and norms. A hunter does not set out simply to the forest to find means to satisfy his tribesmen. He launches on a sequence of meditative acts some of which preparatory prayer, purification ceremonies and again the sacramental manner by which the animal is slain and subsequently treated in the sacred manner.

The Riangs today practice a religion which is a blend of their old animistic faith and Hindu beliefs and practices. As per the scholars of their original 66 rituals only 28 are now regularly performed. Their mythology now includes the names of many Hindu deities like Ram, Sita and Shiva. A number of Shiva and Krishna temples have been set up where worship is done by Riang priests. They are also taking to kirtan (community singing of devotional songs) after the example of their Bengali neighbors. Most of the Riangs, except those who have embraced Christianity, now call themselves Hindus of the Shakha cult. The few have adopted Vaishnavism, abjure fish and meat and have given up animal sacrifice.

Riangs initially had very little contact with the other religions. They later adopted certain rituals from Hinduism as they came in contact with the Bengali community. Over the years Riangs have changed their pattern of belief, customs and so on. The main reason for this is their close interaction with Hindu Bengalis, socio-cultural relationship with Hindus, impact of modern economy, Globalization, urbanization, developed agricultural technology and modern education. The Riangs are influenced and molded mostly by Hindu Bengalis in every sphere of their life. Over the years the spread of Christianity through the missionaries of different Churches and denominations succeeded to bring about a marked change in the sacred, social, educational and economic status of the Riang. The census of India 1991 enumerates 91.28 percent of the riang as Hindu, 8.50 percent as Christians, 0.14 percent professing Buddhism, 0.06 percent Islam, and 0.02 percent other religion. (Bera, 2010). Today the many Riangs keep pictures of Lord Shiva, Goddess Lakshmi and worship them, even though they are firm non believers of Idol worship. There is also influence from Hindu neighbors and they adopt some of the Hindu rituals from them.

Conclusion

Riangs have many myths, which seek to reveal truth concerning mysteries of life, understanding of god, and rituals. They revisit their myths of creation on special occasions, and what breathes and animates the "spirit" of the spirit life of the Riangs. In traditional Riang societies grandparents and parents have the primary responsibility of feeding the children, nurturing them to being, feeling, knowing and doing the Riangs way of life. Riangs were careful not to break any known taboos of their God.

Now a days the old superstitious beliefs are mostly given up and Riangs go for modern medicine however the role of akchai in the interior villages and his ritual skills carry way. As a result of close contact with the neighboring Hindu communities, different Hindu deities and the cult of Vaishanavism have found place in their religious life. The young Riangs today who are moving across different states for education, job opportunities and other provisions of life get chance to interact with the people of other faith, with the contact and influence many of these youth are converting themselves to different religions mostly Christianity, Hinduism and discarding their traditional practice of animism, animatisms, dream, divination, magic, totemism and witch craft. I end with what John Collier, one time United States commissioner of Indian affairs, said of his charges. "They had what the world has lost: the ancient, lost reverence and passion for human personality joined with the ancient, lost reverence and passion for the earth and its web of life. Since before the Stone Age they have tended that passion as a central, sacred fire. It should be our long hope to renew it in us all."

BIBLIOGRAPHY

Acharya R.K., (1999). *Insight into the Riang*. Tribal Research Institute, Govt. of Tripura, Agartala.

Bera, Gautam Kumar, (2009). *Marriage customs of the Tribes of Tripura,* Agartala: Tripura, Bani Prakashani.

Bera Gautam Kumar, (2009). *Echoes from the Hillocks: A compendium on the Tribes of Tripura*. Agartala, Tripura Bani Prakashani.

Bera, Gautam Kumar, (2010). *Social Unrest and Peace Initiatives: Perspectives from North east India*. (Edited). (jointly with B. K. Medhi, R.P. Athparia and K. Jose SVD).Guwahati. Eastern publications.

Bera, Gautam Kumar, (2010). *The Land of Fourteen Gods: Ethno Cultural Profile of Tripura*. New Delhi: Mittal Publications.

Bhowmik Dwijendra Lal, (2003). *Tribal Religion of Tripura,* Tribal research Institute, Govt. of Tripura, Agartala.

Chaudhari, J. Gan, (1983). *The Riangs of Tripura*. Tripura. Directorate of Tribal Research.

Chaudhari, J. Gan, (2006). *A Cultural History of Tripura,* first edition: January. Published by Basudeb Pal.

Coogan, Michael D., (1998), *World religions* (edited) New York Oxford University Press.

Kilikdar, Bibhas Kanti, (1998). *Customary laws and practices: Riangs of Tripura*. Tribal research Institute, Govt. of Tripura, Agartala.

Samantha, R.K., The Riangs of Tripura: Socio-Cultural and Agro-Economic Changes.

18

Aspects of Death and Disposal Among the Tengapania Deoris of Assam

Arifur Zaman*

(I)

Death means the termination of life of an individual along with it's biological functions. It is one of the indispesable aspect of many traditions and organizations and is an important feature of every culture and civilization of the world. In common parlance death refers to the moment at which life ends and one of the difficult task of defining death is to distinguish it from life of an individual. When death occurs an individual it requires drawing precise conceptual boundaries between life and death. Life of an individual is defined on the basis of consciousness and when consciousness cease, a person is said to have died. Death describes a situation where something has ceased, in human society it is life. This is followed by care of the dead as well as afterlife and disposal of it upon the onset of death. Disposal of human corpse is often defined as the practise of dealing with the dead and practises regarding corpse disposal, is integrally a religious

* Assistant Professor, Department of Anthropology, Dibrugarh University, Dibrugarh-786004. Email : arifurz1@yahoo.com, Mobile : 94351 45920

part of every culture and civilization. There are many intangible aspects of culture associated with the death and disposal of corpses, which have intricate relation with the religion of that culture. It is often followed by observance of some customs, rites and rituals, as well as ceremonies. 'Ceremonies may be performed for the dying. The ritual treatment of the dead usually includes far more than the actual funeral ceremony, usually begining at death and continuing at intervals for many years' (Notes and Queries on Anthropology; 1954 : 129).

Death is considered as one of the important rites of passage in human society. Rites of passage are connected with the critical but usually expectable events of the life cycle of an individual like birth, sexual maturity, marriage, death, etc. Arnold Van Gennep (1960) defined the rites of passage which ushar individuals through the crucial crisis of their lives, such as birth, puberty, marriage, parenthood, advancement to a higher class, occupational specialization, and death. Among all the crisis rite death is considered as the end phase of the life cycle of an individual and it involves elaborate funeral rites. After the death of a person, a community generally observes different rituals, and different taboos and customs are followed by the family members of the deceased. In this paper an attempt has been made to evaluate the disposal of death as well as integral rites, cutoms, etc., among the Tengapania Deoris of Sanapur Deori Goan, Philobari, District Tinsukia, Assam. Data has been collected during the month of April-May of 2010 at Sonapur Deori Gaon, a homogenious village, inhabited by the Tengapania Deoris.

Death and disposal are integral element of each culture and it has an indispensable relation with religious belief system of the society. Elaborate ethnographic study of a particular community regarding the customs, rituals, taboos, etc., related with death and disposal were carried out by different scholars like Medhi (1980), Mills (1980), Bordoloi (1984), Bordoloi, Sharma Thakur and Saikia (1987), Playfair (1998), Gurdon (2002), Endle (2007), et al. and they also focus on the corelation of religious beliefs and practices regarding death with social life.

(II)

The Deoris are one of the important scheduled tribe of Assam. The word 'Deori' is originated from the Sanskrit word deva grhika meaning in charge of the temple or the priest. Deori (2002 : 33) mentioned that 'the word 'Deori' literally means priest. The persons who has a better knowledge about gods and goddesses and can appease them are known as Deoris'. The original habitats of the Deoris were on the banks of the river Dibong, Tengapani and Patorsal which was within the jurisdiction of Lohit district of Arunachal Pradesh and Dibrugarh district of Assam. Racially the Deoris are Mongoloid and Mongolian characteristics are still visible among them even today. Sarma Thakur (2007 : 173-174) has described that the Deoris are one of the four divisions of the chutiyas like Hindu Chutiya, Ahom Chutiya, Borahi and Deori. The last division has been able to retain its pristine religious beliefs and practices intact inspite of socio-cultural and political ups and downs through the decades. Dalton (1872) writes about the Deoris that 'An isolated colony on the river Dikrang in Lakhimpur calling themselves Deori chutiya were found who had a peculiar language which they called Chutiya and they were styled Deoris'. At present main concentration of the Deoris is found in the district of Lakhimpur, Sonitpur, Jorhat, Sibsagar, Dibrugarh, Dhemaji and in the Sadia region of Tinsukia district.

On the basis of places of origin, there are four divisions *(khel)* among the Deoris and each division is composed of number of lineages *(bamgsa)*. The Deoris who were believed to reside near the bank of the river Dibang are known as Dibangia, those near Tengapani and Borpani or Borgang are known as *Tengapania* and *Borgoya* respectively. Again the people who inhabited in Pat Sadia were named as Patargonya. The people of Sonapur Deori Gaon where the present study is carried on belongs to Tengapania khel who have seven sub-divisions or lineages *(tikas)* among themselves. These are—Machiotika, Bikarmiyatika, Phagimegeratika, Khutiotiks, Senabariatika, Phapariatika and Sakusarutika.

The Tengapania Deoris are Hindu by religion, more specifically the follower of Sakta cult, the worshipper of Sakti.

They still retain their traditional religious belief system and practices. Balia Baba is their supreme God who is believed to be the parochial version of Lord Siva or son of Siva. Other than Balia Baba they also have other indigenous gods and goddesses like Na-Konwar and Sat-Konwar who are considered as eldest and youngest son of Balia Baba, Lohit Devata also known as Bhaba Raja or Jala-Narayana, and goddesses like Durga Mai, Ai deo, etc. Than Ghar is their worshipping place which consists of three parts- the Balia Baba than is centrally located, towards left of it stands the Indra-ghar and another structure known as Sat-Konwar mandir is located towards the right side of central structure. Among the Tengapania Deoris, the religious rituals are performed by four priests—chief among them is known as Bar Deori who is invariably selected from Machiotika lineage. He is assisted by other three—these Soru Deori, Bor-Bharali, Saru-Bharali who belongs to Bikarmiatika, Phagimageratika and Khutiotika respectively. Apart from these four, there are Bora, Barik and three Parias, who also assist the priest in the performance of religious duties.

(III)

Religion plays an important role in the social structure of the Deoris of Sonapur Deori Gaon. They observe elaborate rituals for birth, initiation, puberty, marriage, death, harvest, etc., which bind and control the society with the intervantion of the sacred. Frazer (1870) in his networthy book Golden Bough says that by religion it is meant that a propitiation or conciliation of powers superior to man who are believed to bind and control the course of nature and of human life. Thus defined, religion consists of two elements, a theoretical and a practical, namely a belief in power higher than man, and an attempt to propitiate or please them. Karsten (1935) stated that, primitive rituals must be essentially an expression of mans instinct of self-preservation, in other words, of his desire to make existence as tolerable as possible. The relation between man and the supernatural powers, which he tries to influence by his invocations, prayers, and offerings is not originally an ethical relations. Various practices and beliefs serve a variety of psychological and social functions of religion in society. The people of the said village also observe elaborate customs, rites and rituals for the death of an individual as well as for the salvation of the disposed corpse.

Soon after the death of an individual, the family members inform it to the neighbours, fellow villagers, as well as near and distant relatives. When the villagers and relatives assemble in the house of the dead, an egg is broken on the forehead of the deceased. It is believed that the egg has a life inside it, which is released when it is broken so the soul of the departed person is also free from that day onwards. Then the corpse is carefully washed by the nearest relatives, the arms and legs straightened out, the head anointed with oil, and the hair reverently combed. The dead person's body is then clothed with new white colour garments. After that the corpse is covered with big white coloured cheleng chadar, a big wrapper, generally used by the males. Then they observe another custom which is known as *lakhimi suwa*, i.e., a kind of divination to verify good or evil for a particular household due to the death of a person. A small portion of the cheleng chadar which covered the corpse is torn out from one corner by a person who was involved in washing the corpse; five small elongated pieces are made from it. Then a bunch of paddy is brought, five grains are plucked out from it and tied into the finger encircling the nails, in case of male the right hand and female the left hand respectively. After sometime the paddy grains are taken out and kept on a *kula* (winnowing fan). Then the winnowing fan is covered with a white piece of cloth and kept it in a safe place for seven days; nobody should touch it during that period. After seven days, the winnowing fan is taken out. The cloth is removed from it and the condition of paddy grains are checked. If the number has decreased from five, it is considered as a bad omen for the family and if the opposite happened then it means the number has increased by one or if some hairs have come out from the grains, it reflected a good sign and long life of the family and believed that the departed soul has blessed the household. During the period of these seven days one cheleng chadar is hung infront of the granary so that goddess Lakhmi may not leave her abode because in their belief system as well as in Hindu pantheon granaries are considered as Her abode. The whole period is considered as period of mourning and pollution and everyone in the household debar themselves from access to the granary. They also observe some custom regarding food, consumption of meat, fish, eggs, curries of an alkaline condiment (khar), etc., are tabooed during these days.

There are two recognised ways of disposal of the corpse among the people of the village- cremation and burial. Cremation of the dead is the rule but in case of children pregnant woman and sucide victims the corpses are generally buried. The dead body is taken out from the house and placed it on a *perangani* (a bier made of split bamboo). If the deceased is an elderly person or the head of the household then the fellow family members and consanguinal kins present bow down before it offering betel nut and betel vine leaf on a *sarai* (disc on stand). Before the starting of funeral procession, some of the elderly members of the village go to a nearly jungle and choose a dry tree for firewood meant for making the *chita* (pyre). Before cutting down the tree they convey their respect and regards towards the local deity kneel down before the tree and cut it down in the name of god and make the pieces of wood from it according to the requirement.

The funeral procession starts from the house of the dead with an assembly of people of all ages and both sexes but females generally proceed from the behind with small pieces of firewood made of mango tree in the hand for placing it on the pyre. The dead body is carried to the cremation ground by four male members of either uterine sons or blood relatives of the deceased. The eldest or youngest son of the deceased lit the pyre and in the procession he is dressed in a white colour *dhoti* (an unsewn cloth worn from waist) and with a *chadar* (a wrapper), veiling his head and holding a burning firewood *(jumuthi)* taken from the deceased home. Cremation initiated by the eldest son is the rule, and in his absence the youngest is permitted to perform the same. If there is no son in the household then son of the nearest blood relative of the deceased is allowed to do the funeral rite. One member of the funeral procession taken an *ugha* (a bamboo made bobbin), winding with white colour yarn for the purpose that if they had to pass a river or an irrigation canal on the way, yarn from the bobbin is stretched from bank to bank at the crossing place, either above or below the water. It is believed that with the help of the yarn the soul of the deceased could cross the river or the canal.

Soon after ariving at the cremation ground which is located near the Doomdooma river running adjacent to the village, the bier is laid on the ground. A suitable place is selected for preparing the pyre and four wooden posts are erected by four elderly members of the village. Then they imitate to communicate with the soul of the dead and tell 'him' that the pyre will be his resting abode from that moment onwards. After that two wooden logs are horizontally placed inside the posts and layers of woods are placed above them for making the pyre.

If the deceased belongs to Khutiotika or Senabariatika lineages, then seven layers of woods are required for the pyre and for the rest of the lineages it is made of five layers.

The reason behind is that people belonging to both these lineages consider themselves as brothers and sisters and are descendent of one of their local god Lohit Devata or Bhaba Raja, who was a king and so deserve the honour. Then the deceased's sons, relatives and fellow villagers pass round it in procession in anticlockwise direction, seven times in case of Khatiatika/Senabariatika and five times for the rest of the lineages. While encircling, they also pass the yarn which they bring in bobbin around the each corner where the four posts that are erected, in order to prevent the spirits of other men from interfering with the repose of the deceased. Thereafter the body is placed over the pyre. The head of the corpse is placed towards the northern direction, feet towards south and the face upward. A coin is inserted into the mouth of the corpse for the reason that during his journey towards the world of the dead he has to cross a river, for which a small tax is required. They believe that with the help of that coin he can overcome the situation. Then above the body, pieces of woods are placed both by men and women folk with their left hand and the funeral pile is set on fire by the eldest son on the face, seven times if the deceased belongs to the Senabariatika/Khatiatika lineage and five times for the rest of the lineages.

The eldest son or any person who lit the pyre, take some ashes and bone remains *(asthi)* of the disposed, tie it in a piece of cloth torn out from one corner of the covering of the dead body. Then he proceeds towards the nearby river, takes dip for seven times and five times for Khatiotika / Senabariatika and for the other's, respectively. White plunging in river water with asthi in hand, one of the members who erect the post for the deceased, as well as a near relative like maternal uncle of the person in river ask him what he is doing. Then the person in water replies that he is immersing the asthi into the river water so that it can intermingle with the holy water of the river. Ganga. This custom is known as asthi bisarjana.

Death in the family of someone is considered as unholy and hence some purificatory rituals are always observed by the Deoris. Haviland (1978 : 333, 342) said ritual is religion in action, and prayer is a common form of ritual. Religious ritual is the means through which persons relate to the sacred; it is religion in action. Not only is ritual the means by which the social bonds of a group are reinforced and tensions relieved, it is also one way that many important events are celebrated and crises, such as death, are made less socially disruptive and less difficult for the individual to bear. So, among them soon after the dead body is taken out from the house towards the cremation ground, the rest of the family members as well as the relatives and co-villagers wash the floor and plinth of the house and sprinkle *santi jal* (holy water) taken from Than ghar on all corners of the household to make it pollution free. The members who return home after attending the funeral ceremony have to purify themselves by observing a ritual. A girl or woman from the village who belongs to a different lineage than that of the deceased sprinkle holy water on them with sweet basil leaves ; after that in a bowl she brings a copper coin dipped in mustard oil. All the persons touch the oil with the little finger of the left hand five or seven times according to their lineage. After this observance, the person who lit the pyre sacrifice a red colour cock and it's meat is preserved for seven days for giving *pinda* (oblation) to the soul of the deceased. During these days, at dawn the sacrificed cock meat along with cooked rice and suze (rice beer) is offered as pinda to the deceased in the backside of the house near the *mudha khuta* (the main post of the house) just below the kitchen of the household.

After seven days they observe another ritual named sasori tana. On that day, the bhakats (elderly members of the village) from three different lineages are invited to bless the deceased and his family. Rice is prepared along with pulses, leafy vegetables and also a fowl is sacrificed. The invited guests are offered the prepared meal along with rice beer. On this day the *Lakhimi suwa* custom is observed, which has already been discussed in the previous paragraphs. The three invited elderly persons *(bhakats)* are allowed to sit in the Bor kuthali, a spacious room located just near the *mojihali* (kitchen) of Deori household, where male members of the house sits and eats together. In front of the bhakats in three plantain leaves the prepared meal is offered by the daughter-in –law of the household, which is actually meant for the salvation of the soul of the deceased. Then the bhakats bless the departed soul by uttering some spells so that the soul may rest in peace. Afterwards the daughter-in-law takes away the offered meal in plantain leaf with a new broom stick in her left hand which is meant for clearing the place from Bor kuthali towards the kitchen. She sweeps and drag the broom stick with the offered meal to kitchen and throw it down from the pile dwelling just near the *mudha khuta* (main post) of the kitchen by making a hole in it. While throwing the things she utters from her mouth 'bare heto khero' which means from that day onwards they bid farewell to the departed soul and the soul should leave the household and enter into the world of the dead. Other than this they have another ritual known as kaz or daha a ritual which is observed on the seventh to tenth day from the death. It is a community feast where the fellow villagers including the persons involved in funeral procession are invited where pig, fowl, etc., are sacrificed and served it to the invited guests. There is no fixed time for observing the ritual and it depends on facilities and economic conditions of the family.

(IV)

The above mentioned customs are observed by the Deoris in the study village in case of a normal death. If a person dies in an accident outside the household, they observe another practice for his or her cremation. Here six elderly members belonging to different lineages than the deceased are invited. Three of them enter inside the house of the deceased and three stand outside. There is a belief among them that a person should die inside it's home. So, for the matter of entering the soul of the dead inside it's home, three persons who stands inside soon after taking the corpse in it question the outside three whether the soul of the dead has come inside the house or not. The persons inside the house reply that the soul has entered and it implies the completion of the custom. Thereafter they cremate the dead like the cremation of a normal person. The Deoris of the village also follow the practice of burial of the dead, in case of suicide, pregnant woman and children. They bring the corpse by observing the already mentioned customs to the cremation ground which is located near the bank of the river of the village. After selecting a suitable place they dug a grave in the north-south direction. The corpse is placed inside the grave, a coin is inserted into the mouth and the head is placed towards the north. Earth is then laid over it, on the top of which the dead man's mat and bier are laid and covered with small branches, leaves, bamboo splits, etc. After returning from the cremation ground they follow the same pristine rules as in case of the others. Death by suicide is considered as inauspicious among them.

From the above discussion it becomes evident that the Tengapania Deoris of Sanapur Deori Gaon have elaborate rituals integral to death and the disposal. The socio-economic tradition is immensely guided by their own parochial pristine traditions. But at contemporary time due to the close contact with caste Hindu population of Assam, many impinging religious factors of the latter have been percolated to the Deori society. The rituals like *Asthi bisarjana,* belief on the holy water of river Ganga, use of leaves of sweet basil, etc., are Hindu concepts, which have been diffused into the Tengapania Deori society from the neighbouring Assamese

Hindu society. Sacrifices of goat, chicken, etc., are made in most of the Deori observances and consumption of country liquor is on integral part of their rituals. They propitiated a good number of traditional deities with a few Hindu gods and goddesses. Though lots of impinging factors like urbanization, westernization as well as advancement in English education have percolated into their socio-religious life yet the Tengapania Deoris have maintained lot of traditional elements in their day to day life.

REFERENCES

A committee of the royal anthropological Institute of Great Britain and Ireland, 1954, *Notes and Queries on Anthropology* (6th Edition), London, Routledge and Kegan Paul Ltd.

Bordoli, B.N., 1984, *The Dimasa Kacharis of Assam,* Guwahati, Director, Tribal Research Institute.

Bordoloi, B.N., G.C. Sharma Thakur and M.C. Saikia, 1987, *Tribes of Assam : Part – I,* Guwahati, Director, Tribal Research Institute.

Dalton, E.T., 1872, *Descriptive Ethnology of Bengal,* Calcutta, Superintendent, Government Printing Press.

Deori, Heramba, 2002, 'Deori Janagosthir Chamu Katha' in Sonali Saurabh, Tinsukia.

Endle, Rev. Sidney, 2007, *The Kacharis,* Guwahati, Bina Library.

Frazer, J.G., 1870, *Golden Bough,* New York, Doubladay, Anchor Books.

Gurdon, Major P.R.T., 2002, *The Khasis,* Delhi, Low Price Publication.

Haviland, William A., 1978, *Cultural Anthropology,* New York, Holt, Rinehart and Winston.

Karstern, R., 1935, *Origin of Religion,* London, Kegam Poul.

Medhi, Birinchi K., 1980, 'Beliefs, Rituals and Ceremonies Connected with Principal Events of the life of the Pati Rabhas of Assam', in *The Bulletin of Anthropology,* Dibrugarh University, Vol. I : 40-53.

Mills, J.P., 1980, *The Rengma Nagas*, Gauhati, Spectrum Publications.

Playfair, A., 1998, *The Garos*, Guwahati, Spectrum Publications.

Van Gennep, Arnold, 1960, *The Rites of Passage*, Chicago, University of Chicago Press.

19

Religious Pluralism Among the Kinnaurese

Sumitabha Chakraborty*

'Religion' has been marked as the dominant concern of mankind because it is something, which can only be realized, conceptualized and even feel the essence. Due to dynamic and elemental characteristics, the religion is very hard to define in a very appropriate and concise manner. It comes from the Latin word 'religio' meaning 'to bind' and literally, religion is a principle of unification and harmonization. In a lucid way, any discipline, which binds us, altogether in a wholesome way, is religion. It is not mere belief but behaviour; nor mere conviction but conduct; not mere faith but functioning. In religion, the whole of human being's personality is involved.

William James conceptualized 'religion' as 'the feeling, acts and experiences of individual men in their solitude so far as they apprehend themselves to stand in relation to whatever they may consider the divine' (James, 1902: 32, c.f. Mohapatra, 1984; 3). In Patrick's word 'religion is the consciousness of our practical relation to an invisible spiritual order (Patrick, 1968: 367). Religion is viewed as 'the hunger

* Research Associate, Anthropological Survey of India, Eastern Regional Centre Kolkata

of the soul for the impossible, the unattainable, and the inconceivable' (Stace, 1952: 3). In his work Durkheim opined that 'religion' is a system of ideas by means of which individuals represent to themselves the society of which they are members and the obscure, but intimate relations they have with it' (Durkheim, 1965: 479) and that's why the religious faith has its origin in society, then upon psychology. Being a member of the human society, men follow religion, when they are not capable to answer against those external supernatural forces, which control their life. Clifford Greetz critically opined that 'religion is a system of symbols which acts to establish powerful, persuasive and long-lasting moods and motivation in men by formulating conceptions of a general order of existence...' (Greetz, 2005: 33).

There is hardly any human society which does not follow the religious conviction. In India, religious practices influence the social and political life of the people. Religion gives the keynote to most of the great changes that have occurred in the history of the races inhabiting this country from the earliest ages to the present day. The religious system of the Kinnaurese is not an exception of that. In one hand, the people believe in worshipping the devi-deota (kimsu) of the Hindu religious fold; believe in appeasing of spirits, demons and omens by following the Bon religion of Tibet and on the other hand follow the practice of Tibetan Buddhism.

According to the concept of religion, 'original Bon' refers to the animistic (believing that nature is pervaded by good and evil spirits) and shamanistic religion, indigenous in Tibet. The word 'Bon' means invocation. Bön doctrine was a dualistic theism, teaching that the creation of the world was brought about by coexistent good and evil principles. The Tibetan Buddhism is a form of 'modern Bon', began in the 14th century when some Bon teachers adopted Buddhist practices related to Padmasambhava. The philosophy of modern Bön is generally in accord with Buddhist non-theistic tenets. Bön ritual includes worship, iconography, and meditation on peaceful and wrathful deities divided into tantras. In Tibetan Buddhism, meditation on the wrathful deities is a means of understanding reality and attaining enlightenment. In this fold Bon shares with the Nyingma schools of Buddhism the structure of the nine yanas (ways of vehicle, which climax in the meditation of 'the great perfection' (excerpts of an interview to a Lama). In the belief of devi-deota (kimsu), the supernatural power – God is manifested with the other subordinate powers. Here the conception corroborates about the presence of two types of deity – (a) principal deity, (b) subordinate deity, whose pleasure and displeasure may cause harm to them. The devi-deota of Kinnaur is the ruling deities like as the Raja.

Locale & People

Geographically, the district Kinnaur lies between 31°05′55″ and 32°05′20″ north latitude and between 77°45′0″ and 79°00′50″ east longitude. Kinnaur is spread over the Himalayan mountainous terrain, stretching over about 80 kms. in length and 64 kms. in breadth. It is the northeastern district of Himachal Pradesh covering 11.7 per cent of the total state area. The high altitude inhabited area is ranging from 2500 meters to 4000 meters. Physiographically, the district is bounded in the north by Spiti; on the east by Tibet; on the west by Simla and on the South by Tehri Garhwal and Uttarkashi of Uttarakhand, covering both the sides of Sutlej River (*Source:* District Hand Book, 1981).

Map of Himachal Pradesh: Showing the Kinnaur District

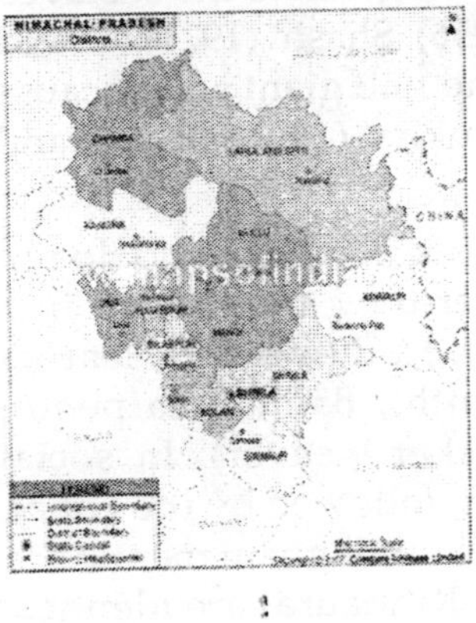

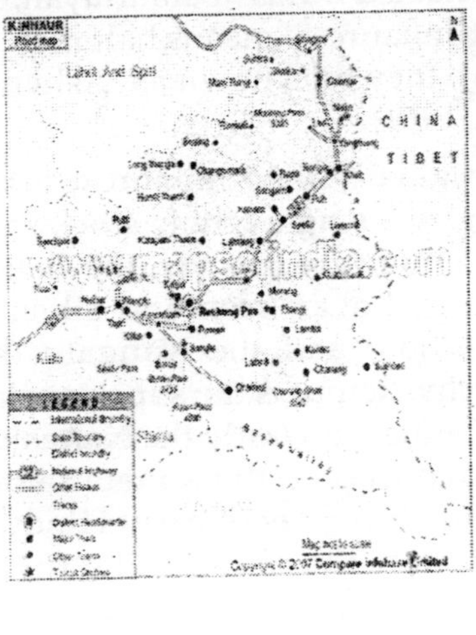

From time immemorial, Kinnaur had been referred to as Kunawar, Koonawar, Kinner, Kanawar or even Kanaur, which was an integral part of Rampur Bushahir state until the formation of new district in the year 1960. There are many legends about the origin of the district. In spite of all, this place first rose to power as the head of a confederacy of petty chiefs or Thakurs (Thakaras). Rahul Sankirtayan revealed that 'Kunawar' were divided into seven such Thakaras, which were later known as khunds or pargana, like, (a) khund do-shan (b) pandrah-bis (c) atharah-bis (d) banpo (e) pagramang (f) shuwang and (g) tukpa, on which the total Kinnaur district is spread up.

Many of ancient Indian literatures cited the name 'Kinnaurese' (super beings) who are different and higher than the common man and are nearer to the god along with Gandharva, Yaksa, Kirata, etc. In *Raj Tarangini,* the Kinnaurese are said to be born from the shadow of Lord Brahma (Sen, 1969). In *Matsya Purana* they were introduced as the descendents of Arishta and Kashyapa *(Matsya Purana)*. Vyas in his India in the Ramayana Age recorded this way – 'the Kinnaurese were an effeminate race always represented as indulging in amorous sports' (David Neel, 1967). In Meghdootam, Kalidasa mentioned the name of Kinnaurese who have the quality of melodious voice and beauty. Apart from mythology, few scholars revealed their identity as – 'Kinnaurese is a corruption of the name given to the enslaved and defeated Dasas' (Sankirtayan, 1956). Shashi (1971) viewed that 'Kinnaurese' means half men and half giant and because of that, they are known as 'Ashvamukha' (c.f. District Hand Book, 1961).

Originally, the Kinnaurese is a generic name who do not belong to a single ethnic stock rather they are divided into many ethnic groups, viz, the Rajput, Koli (weavers, leather workers); Lohar (iron and silversmith); Badhai (carpenter and mason) and the Nangalu (basket weaver). In social hierarchy, Rajput is the superior class, followed by the Lohar, Koli, Badhai and lastly the Nangalu. Cunningham mentioned in his report that 'the Kanet (Rajput Kinnaura) are identical with the Kunindas of early Hindu History, are a mixed race sprang from the Khasas, who first entered to the Himalayas at about two thousand years B.C. from eastern Central Asia (Cunningham, 1884). Ibbetson (1881) expressed that the Kanet have descended by the intercourse between Aryan immigrants and the woman of the hills. Atkinson (1882) reported that the Kanet are the m embers of the Himalayas and mixed up with the tribes. The Khasas claim to be Hindus and have been recently fast adopting Hindu surnames and trying to establish connection with the Rajputs and Brahmans of the plains (Majumder, 1944).

Since earliest known times, the Kinnaurese have primarily been identified as agro-pastoral group following crop farming in one hand and pastoralism on the other. After Chinese aggression (1962), when the exchange of commodities with Tibet had been stopped they shifted their subsistence towards horticulture with a little bit agriculture and animal herding. The horticultural pursuit gradually raises high their economic strength. In an enumeration Chib (1984) mentioned that the area under fruit trees has increased from 290 hectares in 1960-61 to 1515 hectares by the end of 1975-76 and the total production of fruit has also arisen from 300 to 6208 tonnes during the period of fifteen years. Nowadays, the quality of apple of Kinnaur is identified as the best in India.

Social Structure

The social structure of the Kinnaurese is categorized in two groups—the Khosia, which includes the Rajput or Kanet; while the other group is the Beru, which includes the other caste group (Koli, Lohar, Badhi, Nangalu) who have occupational specialization and further sub-grouped as (a) Domang (Lohar and Badhi/Orech); (b) Chamang (Koli) and (c) Chanala (Nangalu). The Khosia is grouped into three statuses, known as khel, like, Orang; Maorang/Orangmech and Waza (Raha, 1995) and arranged hierarchically in social structure. In regard to hierarchy among the different social groupings Majumder held the view, 'for cis-Himalayan region, the Simla, the Doon valley, Kullu and Kangra valleys there exists a hierarchy, a social status though the rigidity of the caste system does not exist here. The upper class consists of Rajput and Brahmin...the lower status is composed of numerous artisan groups' khandans, which are different for different khel. It is observed during the field work that rigid sense of hierarchical social structure of the Kinnaurese has been relaxed today. Inter-marriage between the Khosia (high caste) and Beru (low caste) has been reported. This is also observed that when a member settled in the village after migrated to this place will get immigrant khandan. The khandan is associated with the affiliation to the temple or monastery like, lamapang, charas, mathas, pujaras etc. It is quiet natural that among the types of khandan (original and immigrant) the original khandan is always superior to others in position and status. The khandan system is only prevalent among the Kanet and by its rule a wife would accept her husband's khandan.

The smallest operational unit in the Kinnaurese social system is the household locally known as perang, based on individual house – 'kim'. A household in Kinnaur is virilocal in residence, patrilineal in descent, patronymic in nature and patriarchal in inheritance. It is their belief that the people who prepare and eat food from the same melling (hearth) are the family members. The kimperang acts ideally as the basic, residential, economic, social and religious unit of the Kinnaurese.

Kinnaurese Social Structure

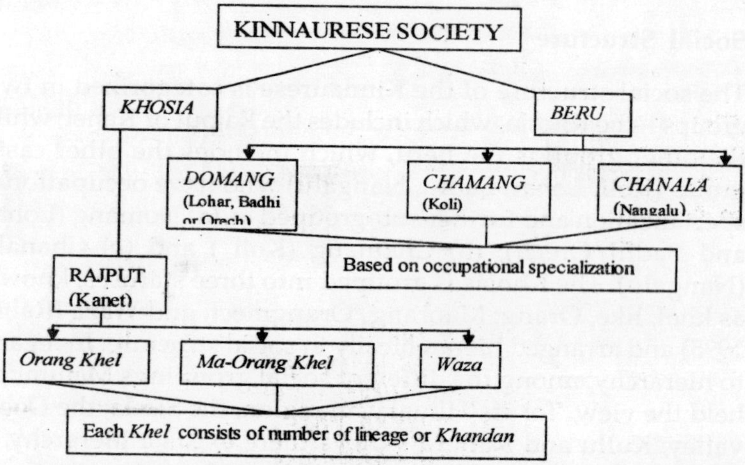

The kimperang when consists of husband, wife and the unmarried children and termed as monandry and when it consists of man, his wives, brothers, sons, their wives and children and unmarried daughters and sisters is termed as polyandry. The household is headed by the senior male member and the eldest son takes over the household authority and responsibility. Khandan system among the Kinnaurese is a societal norm about the unilineally traceable kinship system. Patrilocal household is the unit for the structure of lineage, which is traced to a unilineal descent. In a kim or house, the members trace their relationship with different kin groups either through father or through mother or through father's mother or through wife. The people recognize their lineage affiliation with the known khandan only.

The Religion of Kinnaurese: Reflection on Belief and Faiths

Religion is conceived of as an essential institution of the Kinnaurese life. It is a social phenomenon set in cultural matrix of their societies. It is deeply associated with the concept of supernatural and is an outcome of illogical mind of them. Atkinson opined that 'mans' life centers round religious faith and practices right from his birth to his death, when one seek salvation. He also pointed out that 'the truth is that the popular religion in these hills is a worship of fear' (Atkinson, 1882; 839). The people always seek safety and a sense of security, which comes when they fail to get the desired results or apprehends some undesirable events. Durkheim differentiated beliefs and practices related to supernatural into sacred and profane in which the former is the religion and the later merely magic. The concept of Durkheim has much relevance in the beliefs and practices of the Kinnaurese.

Propitiation of Spirits, Demons & Omens

The concept of supernatural remains in their faith and appears from 'fear' against the malevolent spirits believed to exist in the mountain ranges and in the surrounding nature. Since they dwell in an arduous, rugged mountainous terrain they are always confronted with uncongenial environment and awe-inspiring manifestation of nature and the people are compelled to seek refuge in blind acceptance to belief in supernatural powers. Faith in spirits evolved due to defenselessness and incompetence towards the natural forces like, storm, rain, earthquake, avalanche, etc. According to them, belief and faith in the spirits are their age-old tradition by undertaking propitiation and appeasement. The Greek word 'demon' implied to their society as the possession of superior knowledge and applied to the elements of nature. The demon acquired an evil meaning, actively associated with malignant evil spirits which have also regarded as spiritual power. These powers do not have any particular shrines nor have any visible symbols. But in their belief, every mountain peak and mountain pass is the abode of demons, which have the power to control the winds, storms, falling rocks and the avalanches believed to be the weapons of their wrath. While passing a snow clad mountain pass, the people generally keep quite and try to maintain silence till they reach the top, lest they offend the spirit. A cairn with flags representing the deity of the pass is found at the summit of every pass.

According to their faith, many of the forest trees, especially the deodar and kail (regarded as most precious tree in Kinnaur) are the abode of Bansir, a ghost. It has numerous forms, viz. a giant, a monkey, a fox; usually appear at night and do harm to those, who do not appease it. Bakr-Suna, another ghost inhabiting in the dense forest and mostly come across at the deserted place as a bleating goat very often is believed to assume some other form or shape. It is supposed to horrify its victims with hail of pebbles and stones. Chan is a highway ghost and portends illness and met with at odd hours of the night. Ruksas is the ghost of an evil person usually residing at the confluences of two streams, on a high boulder or in a cave or on a tree. Khunch, an evil spirit residing in certain inhabited houses, is credited to migrate with the bride or the cattle to the house of the new master. According to them, these malevolent spirits always have some association with every distress and therefore, they have a tendency to appease those spirits by undertaking propitiation of the deities (gods/goddesses).

Hinduism in Kinnaur

The religious element of the Hindu doctrine is predominantly followed by the people of Kinnaur. It was observed during the field work in Kothi, Duni, Brelinge, Khwangi, Roghi,

Pangi, Rarang, Kashme and Kalpa (Chini) that the practice of Hinduism in these villages neither adhere to the classic Hinduism by enchanting Sanskrit mantras and slokas, nor does it follow the Brahmanic way of life. More to say that the Sanskrit way of four fold varna system (Brahman at the top; Sudra, the untouchable) prevalent in the plains is absent in Kinnaur. In the religious doctrine the Hinduism followed by them abides by the worship and appeasement of spirits, demons, ghosts and ancestors as a shield. So, their belief in Hinduism is justifiably identified as 'local Hinduism' (Chandra, 1992; 211). In one way, they follow the element of sacrifice as an important mode of offering, structure and pattern of deity worship, similar to other Hindu paharias of the Himalayas and on the other hand they have belief in supernatural, fate, karma, ethics, etc. as like the norms of great tradition of Hinduism (Srinivas, 1965: 214). They believe in the existence of Yama, who determines the form, to which an individual soul should pass into. They also have belief and faith in classic Hindu scripture - Bhagavad Gita; epics like Mahabharata and Ramayana.

In Kinnaurese religion, it is 'devi-deotas' (God) – the Hindu pantheon which controls every suffering, misery; regulates thoughts and ideas of the inhabitants of the valley. All the manifestations like, good harvest, prosperity, failure of crops, loss of property, outbreak of epidemics, pestilence, incidence of natural calamity etc. are believed to be guided by the pleasure and displeasure of the principle deity and its subordinate powers. The 'devi-deota' is a personified image covering the household deity (kimsu), village deity (ghori deota), pargana deity (khunt deota), whose control over the action of themselves is being decided by his/her 'karma'. The philosophy behind it is that whatever performances a person does in his present life will be the resultant of blessings of the deities.

Every devi-deota (God) has personified image, enthroned in a palanquin and have control over an area, exerting authority and power by maintaining a hierarchy. A principal deity is a supreme religious power coincides with the administrative and political authority of a territory. He/She is supported by a number of subordinate deities. Devi Chandika, the mother goddess is such a principal deity of Shuwang pargana (khunt) under which various village deities (gaon-deota), like Markaring (Khwangi village), Pathoro (Rarang village), Vishnu-Naranas (Kalpa village), Sheshering (Pangi village), Naranas (Rogi village) perform their duties as subordinate powers. This is peoples' belief that every village deity conveys the problems of the villager to the Principal deity when She or He makes the yearly visit to the jurisdictional village under His/Her control. Often the subordinate village deities paid frequent visit to the Principal deity for His or Her consent. In both the cases, the deities are carried away by the people of that particular village in a procession. When the village deities assembled in the court of the Principal deity, He or She is taken out from the temple and sit on higher platform to convey his/her opinion.

Besides, every house has one household deity, kimsu, and worship secretly in the individual house without employing any religious functionaries. It is noticed that any kind of household objects viz., iron tools, iron boxes, utensils, copper water vessel (cro) etc can be identified as sacred with having supernatural power and worship preferably by an aged person at the time of childbirth, marriage, illness, crop failure, which is a household affairs.

Kinnaurese Religion (Faith and Belief)

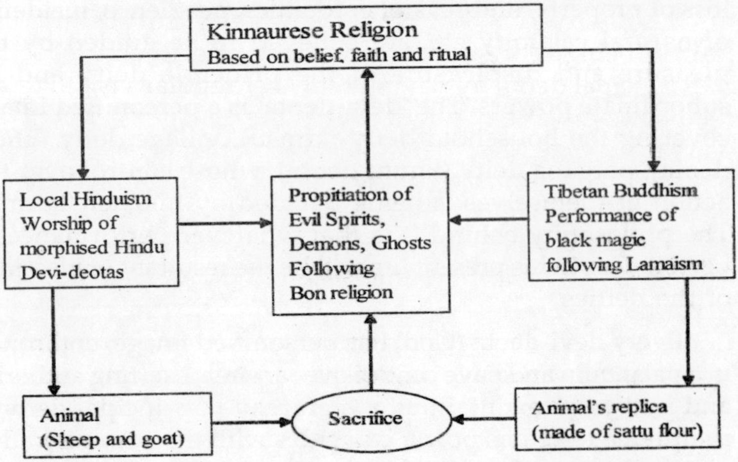

Morphism of Devi-Deota:

All the deities of Kinnauri pantheon irrespective of principal and subordinate have the structure alike. The deities do not possess any anthropomorphic figure with limbs; rather a number of faces, made of gold and silver are fixed on a central wooden pole in a circular manner and adorned with colourful clothes. A bunch of long, black fur is put on the top of the central pole to depict the hair of the devi-deotas. Moustache, ear ring, nose pin are the main depicting feature, clearly shown on the mukhang to differentiate the gods and goddesses. The central wooden pole then rests on a square wooden structure having four legs which is comparable to the palanquin. The free ends of both sides are held by two persons and they give a jerk motion to swing the body of devi-deotas, when they are interrogated and worshipped. This is very interesting to notice that the whole adornment differ in the case of principal deity and subordinate deity. For example, the principal deity of Shua Pargana, Devi Chandika has as many as nine gold made faces (reported by pujari) and her clothe are brocade; wooden poles are covered with silver coverings. On the other hand, the subordinate village gods have silver made mukhang (face) furnished with ordinary clothing. This kind of differentiation perhaps means to maintain the different status among the devi-deotas.

It is observed that in Kinnaur the devi-deota behave like human being. The subordinate deota offer their respect to the principal deota by paying him/her regular visit. During fieldwork, it was often noticed that the visit of a subordinate deity to their superior was almost regular whereas there were only occasional visits of the superior to their subordinates. When a principal deity made a visit to the subordinate deity either on invitation or on his/her own accord at regular intervals, known as bonning system (Raha & Mahato, 1985; Chandra, 1992). In this system, the programme of the visit of that principal deity is planned and fixed according to the wish of that particular deity. The principal deity positively paid his/her visit to each of village deity as per schedule once in a year. When the deity gives his/her consent, the preparations are made by the host village. All the functionaries – groksh (the oracle of deota), mathas (the spokesperson of the people to the deota), kardars (members of the administration of the deota), baijantries (musicians belonging to lower caste) and the villagers accompanies the deity in a procession. The motto of this type of visit is that the principal deity usually wanted to converse with the subordinate village deities and confirms the welfare of the people. During Her stay at the host village, a number of goats and sheep (khadu) are being sacrificed in his/her honour and plenty of ghanti (country liquor) have been consumed by both the parties as a gesture of mutual love and affection. Ghanti is also offered to the deity and after that it is consumed as 'mahaprasad' by the functionaries and the general mass. On return journey, the deity sometimes paid his/her visit to other villages' enroute before reaching to his/her own village.

Systems of Visits of the Deities:

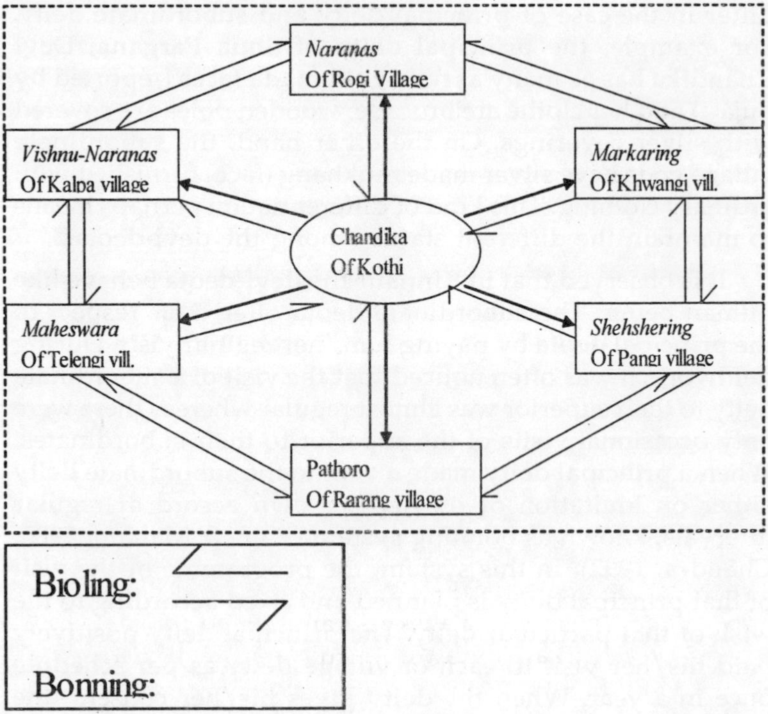

Source: The Kinnaurese of the Himalayas (Raha & Mahato, 1985)

On the other hand, when a subordinate village deity pays his or her visit to the principal deity, the system is called boiling system (Raha & Mahato, 1985; Chandra, 1992). In this system, the subordinate deity first expresses His/Her wish and purpose of visit to the principal deity. Moreover, if the principal deity gives His/Her consent, then only the village deity can move. The village deity has to seek the permission of principal deity for his/her visit. On such occasion, the village deity is accompanied by His/Her functionaries – groksch, mathas, kardars, baijantries. Besides religious importance, the bonning and bioling system have implication on the people to get fearlessness from any kind of fear and harm caused by the evil forces. It is believed that inter and intra visit within the deities is performed for maintaining a nexus of relation among the devi-deotas.

Based on the nexus, the deities are classified in the following manner –

Mahesur Deota – Chandika, Usha, Chitra, Rekha, Virasan and Pirasan residing in the villages like Kothi, Sungra, Bhaba, Poari and Mehbar respectively.

Nag Deota - All the Nag (serpentine) gods live in the villages namely Brua, Sangla, Sapni, Barang, Yula, Urni and Natpa.

Narayan or kul Deota – The Vishnu-Narayan god live in the villages like Sunmgra, Bhaba, Chagaon, Kamru, Chini (Kalpa), Urni, Panwi, Gharsu, Asrang and Roghi.

Domestic Gods and Goddesses – They are worshipped all over the district. The deities are Mahesa, Veer, Lakhoot, Mating, Chhanga, Nagas, Dedum, Kali and Nenge.

Two types of worships – (a) daily worship, (b) occasional worship; followed by the conversation of the Devi with Her people. The worship pattern is neither exactly similar nor perfectly performed in accordance with the Brahmanic way worship by enchanting Sanskrit mantras and hymns. In daily worship, the pujari follows the rule of Hindu pantheon of worshipping the deities in four times (char prahar) with playing of various musical instruments. Every temple functionaries have to present during worship. A silver pot (cro) filled up with country liquor (ghanti) is placed in front of the mukhang and worship as a representative of the deities. Sacrifice of animal is an essential feature in Kinnaurese religion for propitiation of supernatural power and appeasement of evil spirits. The interesting feature of Kinnaurese religion is absence of Brahmans because they always felt that the deities are as authoritative as religious head to govern their societies. This type of religious system is restricted within the deities and the functionaries.

Mode of Functions:

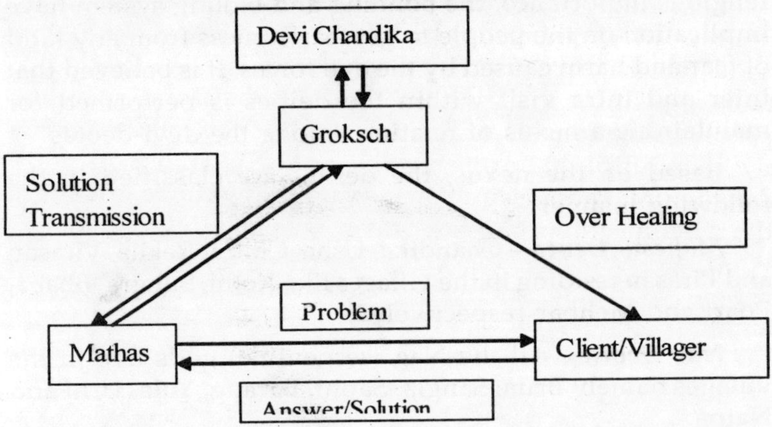

Source: Highlanders of North-Western Himalayas (Chandra, 1992).

Buddhism

Buddhism emerged as a religious faith with Gautama, the Buddha, had flourished in India during the reign of King Ashoka and spread in neighbouring countries of Tibet, Burma and Nepal. In the Himalayan areas the element of Buddhist philosophy mixed with the native 'Bon' religion prevalent in Tibet and gave rise to 'Lamaic Buddhism' (Chandra, 1992; 25) which is predominantly prevalent among the Kinnaurese. Location point of view, Kinnaur district is adjacent to Tibet and before the Chinese aggression in 1962 the district had close contact through trade. Thus it felt reasonable that the traditional religious element of Tibet (Bon religion mixed Buddhism) came and imbibed into the faith of Buddhist Kinnaurese. In fact, Buddhist Kinnaur looked for spiritual guidance from Tibet for its religious superiority and harsh physical proximity. Earlier scholars opined that when Buddhism had entered in Tibet around 4th century A.D. a traditional form of animist-shamanist religion (Bon religion) was practiced (Bell, 1931; 33). Later, this was accumulated with Buddhism and formed "Tibetan Buddhism", popularly known as 'lamaism' (Hoffman, 1956; 28) because of the influence of lama (the priest). The Kinnaur Lama are under Nyingma-Pa, Druk-Pa and Gellug-Pa sects of Tibetan Buddhism.

Lamaism or Tibetan Buddhism is the offshoot of Buddhism; believe to be borrowed from Tibet, adhered to nine texts or 'nyadharmah' of Mahayana sutras, which is referred as 'great faith', 'great value'. In the faith of Tibetan Buddhism, the people follow some of the religious tradition of core Buddhism by worshipping Lord Buddha and His incarnations – Sakyamuni, Padmasambhava, Avalokiteswara; maintaining the religious importance of prayer wheel, lotus, the lion etc. which are made available in the form of emblems and murals. People having faith in Tibetan Buddhism in one hand profess eight different worlds signifying the whole of nature and on the other believe in 'karma' during one's life time. "Karma" defined as 'chetana', means consciousness of good and bad; merit and demerit. One's excellent 'karma' helps him to salvation and gets a high place in the world during his future life.

Tibetan Buddhism is realistically emphasized by tantric rituals and practices perform to appease the demons, ghosts, corpses and other malevolent spirits. Stein (1972; 170) pointed out that the tantric element moves round the concept of 'absolute' involves two characteristics – the bliss and the compassion. "Absolute" has regarded as two planes – (i) mother (yum), the female principle; (ii) method, the male principle. Padmasambhava, one of the incarnation of Lord Buddha, propounded Lamaism has a vision as 'unreformed religion'. It has taken formation by the agglomeration of various sects of tantric element (Mantrayana, Vajrayana, Sahayana, Kalachakrayana) with shamanistic faith of 'Bon' religious concept. 'Om Ma Ne Pad Me Hum', the single syllable formula have six different stages to follow the mystic path as a medium of salvation, because these six mystic paths satisfies the different yoni (world) of the Universe. Om stands for Dev yoni (world of Gods); Ma stands of Asur/Daitya yoni (demon's world); Ni stands for Nar yoni (human's world); Pad stands for Jeev yoni (animal's world); Me stands for unworthy yoni (world of unworthy place); Hum stands for Narak yoni (dark world). It is a common belief that recitation of such mystic syllable enable to carry a philosophical merit and a seat in Heaven. The separate mystic path have separate colour significance – white, blue, yellow, green, red and black respectively, which have merit wise preference of good and bad.

Observation

- In Kinnaur, people cohesively practiced worship of devi-deotas following Hindu religious fold and propitiate deities, spirits following Buddhist religious path and this fact makes the Kinnaurese conspicuous.
- They have tremendous faith on malevolent spirits that reside in the nature and create harm to them if once dissatisfied. To make Him satisfied they propitiate Hindu devi-deotas, side by side perform magico-religious performance following Buddhist doctrine.
- In one hand they believe in 'karma' of one's previous life that escorted him/her to the punar janma (rebirth) of next life. If one performed better karma (deeds), in his previous life obviously take rebirth as human being unless as any form of animal and birds. On the other hand, they have the belief in sradh, pinda-dan to the deceased soul. For these rituals, they practice Hindu and Buddhist forms of initiation.
- In both cases of worship or propitiation, the people follow 'local tradition'. There are no Sanskrit mantras and slokas are enchanted during the worship of devi-deotas and there is no greater tradition of Buddhism.
- The people believe 'reincarnation of soul'; 'transmigration of soul', following the Buddhist philosophy and in the same way have the belief in deceased soul following the Hindu element.

- For the appeasement of malevolent spirit, Tibetan animist-shamanist religious element came into fold of Buddhism as a mystic path.

At the end it may be inferred that a type of religious pluralism exist among the Kinnaures as a cohesive amalgamation of Hindu-Buddhist elements. In one hand people worship the devi-deotas for their good and prosperity and profess black magic, go to monastery (gompha), worship awe-inspiring deities and spirits. The amalgamation of these two religious strain have got a stronghold in the people's mind and it is implemented at the right time to seek remedies to the problems posed from the external forces and urge to seek moksha.

BIBLIOGRAPHY

Atkinson, E.T., 1882. *The Himalayan Gazetteer*, vol. II, part-I & II, Delhi, Cosmo Publication (reprint, 1973)

Bell, Charles, 1931. *The Religion of Tibet*, London (reprint, 1968)

Census of India, 1961. *District Census Handbook*, Kinnaur district.

Census of India, 1981. *District Handbook*, Kinnaur district.

Chandra, Ramesh, 1992, *Highlander of North Western Himalayas*, New Delhi, Inter-India Publications.

Chib, S.S., 1984. *Kanauras of the Trans-Himalaya*, New Delhi, Ess Ess Publications.

Cunningham, J.D. 1984 Notes on Moorcraft's Travels in Ladakh, *Journal of Asiatic Society of Bengal*, vol. XIII, Part-I..

David-Neel, A. 1967. *Magic and Mystry in Tibet*, London.

Durkheim, Emile, 1965. *Elementary Forms of the Religious life*, trans. J.W. Ward, New York; The Free Press (reprint).

Fraser, J.B., 1820. *Journal of a Tour through part of Snowy Ranges of the Himalayan Mountains*, London

Fraser, J.B. 1820. *Journal of a Tour through Part of Snowy Ranges of the Himalayan Mountains*, London.

Greetz, Clifford, 2005. 'Islam Observed Again' in *Islam Obscured* edited by Daniel Martin Varisco, New York, Palgrave Macmillan.

Hoffmann, H. 1956, *The Religion of Tibet* (Translation), London, George Allen & Unwin Ltd, (reprint, 1961).

Ibbetson, 1881, *Punjab Census Report,* Lahore.

James William, 1902, *The Varieties of Religious Experience,* London, David McKay Co.,

Majumder, D.N. 1944, *Fortunes of Primitive Tribes,* Lucknow.

Matsya Purana - Vol. II.

Raha, M.K. & S.N.

Mahato, 1985, *The Kinnaurese of the Himalayas,* Calcutta, Anthropological Survey of India,

Raha, M.K. 1995 *Society and Religion in Kinnaur in The People of the Himalayas* (eds.), Calcutta, Anthropological Survey of India.

Sankirtayana, Rahul, 1956, *Kinnaur Desh Mein* (Hindi), Allahabad.

——, 1956, *Himalaya Parichaya* (Hindi), Part-I, Allahabad.

Sen, Biswajit, 1969, Caste, class and leadership in a Himalayan village in *Proceedings of Seminar of Indian Institute of Advanced Studies,* Simla.

Snell D. & H. Richardson, 1968, *A Cultural History of Tibet,* London.

Stace, W.T. 1952, *Religion and the Modern Mind,* Philadelphia, J.B. Lippincott Co.

Tambiah, S.J., 1970, *Buddhism and Spirit Cults in North-East Thiland,* Cambridge University Press, London.

Tylor, E.B., 1954, *Anthropology*. London.

Verma, V., 2002, *Kanauras of Kinnaur: A Scheduled tribe in Himachal Pradesh*. Delhi, B.R. Publishing Corporation.

Photographs:

Kalpa Village in Kinnaur District,

Kinnaurese of the Kinnaur valley

Kalpa Naranas Temple Spirits,

Demons reside in Kinnaur hills

Bhimakali Temple : Sarahan,

Kinnaur Devi Chandika Temple, Kothi

20

Neo-Vaishnavism and Social Harmony in Assam

Ravi Khangai*

Bhakti, i.e. devotion to God is inherent in the growth of every religion, though we may call it by different names, like Sufis in Islam calls it 'Tassawuf'. When human mind fails to solve the intricacies of life, we turn to God, either to help us in our mundane affairs or to find solace. Like any other religion, the feeling of devotion is prevalent in Indian religious tradition since antiquity. But 'Bhakti' or devotion as a means of salvation had assumed special significance in the medieval period of the Indian History. It had brought many changes in the socio-religious life of the Indian people and so it is termed as Bhakti Movement.

When we use the term Bhakti movement in general, we should be also conscious that it was neither a homogeneous or unified movement having same philosophy and practices all over the country, but there were many variations in it and even at a time contradictions. Yet, by and large they had contributed towards reducing the discrimination towards the lower caste, improved the position of women and encouraged literary and creative activities.

* Asst. Professor and HOD, Department of History, Ambedkar College, Fatikroy, Dt. North Tripura – 799 290. E Mail: ravikhangai@gmail.com

The Bhakti movement had engulfed the almost whole of India during the medieval period and also reached Assam with Sankardeva in the 15th century. It gradually gathered the strength and became an important factor in the process of socio-cultural change in Assam. The main focus of the Bhakti was religion, but one aspect of human life has a spill-over effect on the other aspect, so we cannot entirely separate religious and social life. By trying to create relatively harmonious individuals, the Bhakti saints had contributed towards creating a relatively harmonious society. Having a perfectly harmonious society is probably a utopian dream. But after all it is a dreamer who dares to challenge the stereotype, established norms and initiate reforms. Without the dream of Martin Luther, the condition of the Blacks probably would have not been as good as it is today and without Mahatma Gandhi, there would have been more bloodshed in the world. The Bhakti saints were also such dreamer-visionary, who profoundly influenced the socio-religious practices of the medieval India including Assam. This paper is an attempt to understand the contribution of one such dreamer-visionary, Sankardeva towards Assamese society as it stands today.

Sankardeva and Neo-Vaishnavism

Sankardeva was born in the middle of the 15th century and his father was a landlord called Bhuyas. Some of them were Brahmins and others were of lower castes. The family of Sankardeva belonged to the lower caste.

Sankardeva showed the qualities of genius since beginning. But it was a demise of his wife that made him introspective and he became more inclined towards God. It is an irony that a man turns to God when he goes through the suffering in his personal life. It may be that when God selects someone to shower his bounty, he himself snatches away those things from his devotees that are likely to create attachments with the material world. Tukaram, the 17th century Maharashtrain saint says, 'Bail meli mukt zali/deve maya sodvili' (Marathi)[1]

{My wife had died and got liberation and God had made me also free from 'Maya' (illusion).} (Translation mine). So when material possession and the people who create bound with the world had gone we feel increasingly drawn towards God.

Sankardeva's first wife had died and after that he went for a long pilgrimage. According to Katha Guru Carita[2], he visited important places of pilgrimage spread across the country. During his tour he was influenced by the ongoing wave of the Bhakti movement throughout the length and breadth of the country. After coming back he started preaching worship of Narayana (Vishnu) and established 'Satras' (places of prayer) at different places. His disciple, Madhavadeva also played an important role in the spread of Vaishnavism in Assam.

Vaishnavism forms the major part of 'Bhakti' movement of the mediaeval period. The worship of Vishnu was prevalent in Assam earlier also, but Vaishnavism that was introduced by Sankardeva brought in the wake, lot of churning in the society and affected almost all aspect of life in Assam, social, cultural and political. So, this came to be known as Neo-Vaishnavism.

Practices of Neo-Viashnavism

The rituals of Neo-Viashnavism are centered around 'Satra', the prayer house. The word had originated from the Sanskrit word 'Sattra', which means a sacrifice lasting from a few days to a year or more.[3]

The Satra is a complex, which is the centre of religious activity of Neo-Vaishnavism. It consists of main prayer hall in which a religious scripture is kept. This is called Kirtan Ghar. Kirtan Ghar does not have an idol. Only religious scripture like Dasama4 of Sankardeva is kept in the Kirtan Ghar.

There are four important scriptures of Neo-Vaishnavism. The Dasama (a commentary on the tenth chapter of Bhagavata) and Kirtana-ghosa'of Sankardeva and Nama-ghosa and Bhakti-ratnavali of Madhavadeva.

Some of the Satras have idols, which are kept in a separate room adjutants to the Kirtan Ghar. Surrounding to this Kirtan

Ghar is row of rooms in which the people who had devoted themselves to the service of the 'Satra' stays. These are celibate and called Kavyalaya. Women are allowed in the Satra during daytime only. They are not allowed to become Kavyalaya i.e. monk. Sankardeva preached Dasya-Bhakti in Assam. In Dasya-Bhakti, the relation between God and the devotee is like master and the servant.

Neo-Viashnavism and Caste System

Caste system is one of the most discriminatory practices and had done a lot of harm to the Indian society. One bold act that Sankardeva had initiated was that he appointed some non-Brahmins also as head of the some of the Satras and he do not seem to have encountered cpposition to this.

Assam, being on the border of the Aryavarta, the influence and rigidity of the caste system is relatively on the lesser side. Compared to Sankardeva, the Bhakti saints in many other parts of the country had not shown similar courage. Even many of them showered undue praise on the Brahmins, almost bordering on the servility. Gyneshwara, the 13th century Maharashtrian saint and Tulsidasa, the 16th century Bhakti saint from Northern India had a very high opinion about the Brahmins. Gyneshwara says,

> *"Varnamaji Chatrachamar,*
>
> *Swarga Jayache agarhar,"* (Marathi) (Gyneshwari Ch.IX)
>
> (The Brahmins are at the pinnacle of the Varna system,
>
> Heaven is their natural dwelling place,) (Translation mine)
>
> Tulsidasa takes this further and says that,
>
> *"Pujiya Bipra Shil Guna Hina,*
>
> *Shudra na Guna Gyan Pravina"* (Hindi)
>
> (*Ramcharitmanas,* Aranyakand)

(A Brahmin without character and qualities should be worshipped, but not a Shudra with all the good qualities and knowledge) (Translation mine).

This attitude of giving equality to the lower caste in Bhakti and treating them as inferior in social practices do not go down well with the rational mind. This undue importance given to the person born as a Brahmin and discrimination against the lower castes is one of the important causes of the lower castes walking away from the fold of Hinduism and embracing Buddhism, Islam and Christianity throughout the Indian history.

With due respect to the genius of the many Bhakti saints, It is felt that many of them were a half-hearted or confused reformers. They were pained at the discrimination but they could not rise above the prevailing social practices and assert equality of all. For the genius like Gyneshwara also it becomes difficult to rise above the contemporary influence. It is also difficult for the privileged section of the society to introduce the radical changes which may challenge their privileged position. Gyneshwara and Tulsidasa both were born in the Brahmin family and could not imagine a society without a regulating mechanism of Chaturvarna system. Being themselves Brahmins, they were probably also reluctant to let the privileges go from the hands of the Brahmins. In comparison, Buddha appears to be more courageous, who out rightly rejected the caste system. Similar courageous spirit we also find in Kabir.

Sankardeva, being born in the low caste Kayastha and working away from the centers of orthodox Brahmanism like Kashi was relatively bolder than his counterpart in other parts of the country. He did not show servility towards the Brahmins like Tulsidasa and Gyneshwara, on the other hand as already referred; he appointed non-Brahmins also as head of the Satras. But at the same time it may also be mentioned that he did not initiated any radical reforms in the Hindu society. That was not his basic motive. His main focus was to preach the Bhakti of Narayana. Other things came as a complimentary. Unusual domination of the Brahmins, their superiority based on the birth irrespective of the wisdom and humiliation of the lower caste continued as before. In Satras higher and lower castes mingled together, but once they stepped out, the old way of life continued. This duality of practicing semblance of equality during prayer and continuation of the discrimination after it is one of the glaring lacunae in the Bhakti movement. This is true of the Bhakti movement not only in Assam but in other parts of the country as well. Rather it was more glaring in the other parts of the country.

The caste system had taken such a hold of Hindu psyche for centuries together that the attempts of reformers starting from Buddha to B.R. Ambedkar had made a very little dent in it. The Bhakti saints in general had also refrained from any attempt of demolishing it. Yet they must be given credit that they contributed towards reducing the intensity of discrimination towards lower castes. Gyaneshwara, who had a very high opinion about the Brahmins as quoted above also, says that, *'Bhakti ga ath sare, Jati aprman'* --- (Marathi)(*Gyneshwari* Ch.IX)

(Devotion is everything and castes are irreverent) (Translation mine.) Sankardeva is bold enough to say in his *Dasama* "A Chandala who remembers God with heart and soul is superior to a Brahmin observing religious vow"

It is also possible that even though the Bhakti saints wanted to eradicate the discrimination based on the birth, they were cautious that they should not make the powerful Brahmin lobby hostile. We see in case of Sankardeva, he encountered the hostility of the Brahmins and the Brahmins taking advantage of their proximity to the kings instigated the royalty and Sankardeva and his disciples had to suffer. He was compelled to leave the Ahom kingdom and seek shelter in Koch kingdom.

The network of the Satras'and Namghar spread in the Brahmaputra valley. The Namghar is a place of worship in village similar to 'Satra' but on a smaller scale. The population of belonging to different tribes and communities found a common place to come together and satisfy their spiritual thrust. Out of these gatherings the common identity as

Vaishnavas began to develop. Religious practices are one of the important unifying factors.

The Neo-Vaishanvism had also given freedom to the people from the tyranny of the Brahmin priest and complicated, costly rituals. They could also escape from the heinous practices of the prevailing 'Shakta' cult.

Coming to Satra or Namnghar and singing the praise of God Narayana became new rituals in Assam. These rituals were simpler and were accessible to everyone in comparisons to the complicated and costly rituals of the 'Shakta' and orthodox Brahmins.

Neo-Vaishnavism and Women

There cannot be social harmony in a society where half of the population is discriminated against. The women had been always at the receiving end in the male dominated society. Men thought about their own emancipation and looked upon women as distraction from the spiritual path. It is always easy to externalize the problem and blame someone. One who is not strong enough to protest generally becomes scapegoat. Sankardeva like many other Bhakti saints also discriminated against the women. In the Neo-Viashnavism women are not allowed to enter in the main prayer hall, i.e., Kirtan Ghar. They cannot become kaivalya i.e. monk. Sankardeva says,

"The dire illusions created by women—the most hideous of all illusions".[5]

Bhakti Movement and Hinduism in general do not treat women equally. Probably they overemphasized the sexual aspect of women, which possibly distract the men and strengthens the bonds with this world. Religion generally tries to break us away from the world.

In comparison to Bhakti saints, Buddha was more liberal towards women. Though he initially hesitated, but later accepted women as Buddhist Bhikuni (women monk) in the Buddhist Sangha. However this proved disastrous. Young unmarried boys and girls staying together in the Sangha (monastery) led to moral degradation and subsequent decline of Buddhism. But purely from the humanistic perspective, barring half of the population for the sake of the other half is not justified. But probably this experiment of Buddha and tantric practices of Shaktas involving women had also contributed towards shaping this attitude of the Bhakti saints towards women. They thought it is better for the men to maintain safe distance from the women. Nevertheless, the fact remains that no alternative method like having a separate dwelling quarters for the women monks or allowing them to enter in the Kirtan Ghar during a specific period exclusively kept for the women was not thought about.

However, the women did come to the Satras during day time. Allowing the women to become monk is also fraught with the danger. As monks had to travel, there was always fear of violence against the women. One can also imagine the condition nearly 500 years before, when the life was relatively unsafe. The number of women coming forward to participate in the rituals of Satra must be considerably on the lower side.

In spite of this discrimination, Kanaklata, the grand daughter in law of Sankardeva played an important role in managing the 'Satras'. Women in other parts of the country also got avenues through the medium of the 'Bhakti Movement' to give vent to their creativity and satisfy their spiritual thirst. But in my reading so far, I have not come across the name of any women Bhakti poetess of Assam.

Neo-Vaishnavism did not advocate the life of celibacy Shankardeva himself married twice. Though his disciple, Madhavadeva, who played an important role in the spread of Neo-Vaishnavism was a celibate. But he also did not encourage others to remain unmarried.

Limitations of the Neo-Viashnavism

Hinduism is not based on one particular scripture and do not subscribe to any rigid ideology and practices. There are many variations. The process of assimilation of the different ideas and practices is a continuous process. This is having advantage and disadvantages both. Advantage is that in this process of assimilation and churning whatever is best will survive with the progress of civilization. It can also satisfy the people who had diverse orientations. When we all are so different than each others, how one ideology can satisfy everybody? At the same time many times many undesirable practices gets assimilated and the degeneration sets in.

This degeneration was obvious in the growth of Vedic religion. The simple Vedic religion of the early Aryans became more complicated, violent and ritualistic during later Vedic period. To make it more appealing to the masses, many superstitious and unrefined practices were assimilated into it.

As a protest against this complication, Buddhism had come into existence, but the similar process was repeated again. After the demise of Buddha, the simplicity of Buddhism had given way to complications and rituals, and degeneration had started again.

Probably it was the prevailing heinous practices and superstitious of the Tantrism'and Shakta that prevailed in Assam before the spread of Vaishnavism that Sankardeva had taken extra care to keep his newly founded creed pure and away from the degraded practices. That is the reason that he gave supreme place to only one God, Narayana and looked down upon the worship of any other God. His disciple Madhavdeva even expelled one of his disciples for worshiping Kali.

Giving place to only one God and expulsion of others went contrary to the ancient wisdom of the Vedas,

'Ekam satyam Vipra Bahuda Vadanti'

(Truth, i.e., God is only one but the learned call it by the different names)

Sankardeva's standpoint seems to be rigid as he rejects the worship of any Gods other than Narayana. But due to this rigidity the appeals of Neo-Viashnavism had remained confined to the plain people of Brahmaputra Valley and could not spread in the hilly areas of the North East India. The geographical factors and other racial and socio-cultural differences further resisted the attempt of unification and assimilation.

Sankardeva did have some disciples among the tribal and there was a Muslim disciple as well. Though these are the good examples and can be quoted in support of the exercise of the nation building. The fact nevertheless remains that Neo-Vaishnavism have failed to bring any fundamental changes in the socio-cultural and religious practices of the Hill people in the North East. It remained mainly confined to the plains of Brahmaputra valley. Tribes by and large continued to practice their animism with some influence of superstitious Tantrik practices. In the plains also, the tribal and non tribal differences continued as usual.

During the British period of the Indian History the gulf between the Hill and plain people in the North East of India has widened further as British restricted the movement between plains and hills of the North East. It suited them that the hill people should not be influenced by the ongoing anti-British movement for independence. Conversation of the tribes to Christianity further increased the gulf between the hill and plain people.

In post Independence period, political and economic dimensions were further added to the socio-cultural differences. Now we see the tribes of the North-East of India underlining their separate identify vis-à-vis that of the non tribals. Whatever the influence of the Hinduism they might have had in the past; there is a tendency to reject that. They try to either go back to their pre-Neo-Vaishnavism, pre-Hinduism practices or try to become westernized in their manners and dress, to assert their separate identity.

This gulf between tribals and non-tribals many times culminates into the violent conflicts as we see Bodos, Dimasas,Karbis and other tribes of Assam taking up arms against the domination of the non-tribal and also fighting among themselves. Different religious practices and beliefs by itself do not give rise to the violence but it does help in the process of polarization.

The Bhakti literature in general is dominated by the fatalist and escapist tendencies. It proclaims that everything happens according to the will of the God and human endeavour are futile. These tendencies are having advantage and disadvantage both. Advantage is that it helps us to cope up with the drudgery of the life. But the meek submission also adversely affects the industrious spirit. The Bhakti movement had not attempted to create rational thinking and the religion of the masses continued to be the religion of superstitious beliefs, only the rituals had become more simple and less violent.

How Far the Message is Relevant Today?

The Bhakti movement of Assam and in other parts of the country as well tried to reduce discrimination and injustice done to lower castes in the name of religion. Yet the injustice and discrimination continues even today. They tried to purify religion, yet the superstitious and degenerating practices still continues. Shall we conclude that their efforts had been all wasted?

Probably there cannot be a simple answer 'Yes' or 'No' to this question. The progress of civilization and development of philosophy and socio-cultural changes are very slow process. It takes centuries for the mindset to change. But the beginning has to made, as a Chinese proverb goes, "A journey of thousand miles begins with one small step"

Our predecessors like Shankardeva, Gyneshwara, Kabir, Vivekananda and Mahtma Gandhi had taken couple of steps towards building up of a civilization and this seminar is also a small step towards it. This is small step as we progress from material civilization to intellectual civilization, from intellectual civilization to spiritual civilization.

The socio-cultural situation in Assam and in India would have been worse than today without the efforts of the Bhakti saints of making religion relatively simple. The division and conflict that we see around us would have been probably sharper without them.

By reducing the complications, the Bhakti saints had tried to create harmonious individuals. Harmonious individuals makes Harmonious and peaceful society. The disharmony and conflict that we witness around us are but extensions of the disharmony and conflict that we carry within us. If the inside is purged, the outside will become pure as well.

In a pluralist society like India, the policymakers in education are afraid to include religion in the curriculum. They usually find a safeguard under the cover of Secularism. But we are creating the generations whose spiritual aspect remains underdeveloped. The crises of values and rampant corruption are probably fall out of this. What qualities the Bhakti saints had tried to inculcate among the devotees is obvious from the following verse of 'Uddhava Gita' which is a part of the Bhagavata.

"Pure, genial by nature, sweet and a source of imparting holiness to men, the sage-resembling water-purifies all, being seen, touched and praised by them" (Uddhava Gita, Ch.II) Instead of bringing out any radical social reforms the practicing ethical behaviour and moral values were more important to the Bhakti Saints. In a pluralist society and in the time of the rapid globalization, one particular creed may not satisfy the spiritual need of the humanity. Any attempt of doing that is bound to fail and give rise to the conflict. But through interfaith dialogue we should try to reach what Dalai Lama calls the 'core' of the religious tradition, i.e., love and compassion.

SPECIFIC REFERENCES

1. Vinoba Bhave 'Tukaramchi Bajane' (Marathi), ('Devotional songs of Tukaram') (Devotional songs are known as 'Bhajan' in Marathi and Hindi as well.)
2. An 18th century important work about the Neo-Vaishnavism in Assam.
3. Dr. Sarma S.N. *The Neo-Vaisnavite Movement and the Satra Institution of Assam,* Lawyer's Book Stall, Panbazar, Guwahati, 1999, P.143.
4. Commentary of Sankardeva on the 10th Chapter of the 'Bhagvata'.
5. Devgoswami, Ranjit Kumar (Ed.), *Essays on Sankardeva,* LBS publication, Guwahati, 2005, p. 50.

GENERAL REFERENCES

1. Vinoba Bhave 'Gyandevachi Bajane' (Marathi), ('Devotional songs of Gyandeva')

2. Tulsidasa 'Ramcharitmanas' (Hindi), Gita Press, Gorakhpur.
3. Swami Madhavananda, *Uddhava Gita*, Advaita Ashrama, Kolkata, 003.
4. A.N. Deshpande, 'Prachin Marathi Wangmayacha Itihas' (Marathi) (History of ancient Marathi literature)
5. Maheswar Neog, *Sankardeva and His Times*, LBS publication, Guwahati, 2008. Sir Edward Gait, 'A History of Assam' Bina Library, Guwahati, 2008.
6. S.L. Baruah, *A Comprehensive History of Assam*, Munshiram Manoharlal, 2007.
7. The Dalai Lama, *The Power of Compassion*, HarperCollins, 2001.

21

Concept of God and Religion Among the Tribes of Tripura

Bikash Bhargab Sarma*

Religion is the recognition on the part of man of same higher unseen power as having control of his destiny and as being entitled to obedience, reverence and worship. It is the human belief in some supernatural power as well as the worship of this power. The religious beliefs in different times and places widely differ, and every people claims that they belong to a good religion. The power worshipped by different peoples is of diverse nature-small Gods and Goddesses, fetishes, trees, animals, stones and an almighty God of the great religions of the world. The majority of the world's population believe in some short of religion with a God under different names and affiliations.

Spiriticism and Tribes of Tripura

Each and every religion has a set of moral principles of its own. The more ethical a religion is, the more reliable it is as a form of religion. In fact, Ethics is the basis of all essential forms of religion. Generally tribal ethics agrees with that of others.

* Asst. Professor and Head, Dept. of philosophy, Ambedkar College, Tripura(N) bbhargab@rediffmail.com

Tribal religion is one of the many aboriginal forms of religion. The tribal religion could not go beyond spiritism at the initial stage. In course of time, it could not develop by adopting ideas and practices from other sources. Living an isolated life they have retained their primitive tribalism almost intact, however the tribal's of Tripura in close contact with the non-tribal population. As a result the tribals here are a step ahead of other tribals in respect of assimilation with the main religious stream of the country. The tribal religion of Tripura is an instance. It was all spiritism-in its earlier stage, and with the passage of time it has developed, to a material extent, by deriving much from the neighbouring Hindu sects. Though some of them have abandoned their original religion and adopted other religions like Buddhism and Christianity.

Here we are mainly concerned with the tribes of Tripura, and these tribes have imbibed the religious concepts of surrounding peoples besides their own. The worship of the peculiar tribal deities is a part of the tribel religion and we should like to call it their tribalism. This is practised side by side with their Hinduism. It may be called as a sectarian peculiarity of the tribals. The religious practices of the Tripuris are derived from Hindu mythology also indicates the early adoption of Hinduism or Aryan religion by Tripuri and other tribes of Tripura.

The tribals of Tripura of the present day are not without traces of the early forms of religion like any other tribal people of the world. In addition to the so-called animism, spiritism and totemism, the tribals of Tripura worship a number of deities of their own. The tribals of Tripura say that the supernatural beings of their belief are mostly deities or Gods and Goddess, not spirits as some think. Inspite of this original spiritism-beleif in an worship of various spirits of undefined character, the tribals may have the conception of a great God.

Idea of God

In Tripura, the idea of a Great God has evolved among some tribals, mainly the Tripuries, who call the great being Matai Katar. But they also admit a consort to this God, who is called Matai Katar Ma (The great Mother God). Matai means

'God' and Katar means 'Great', so that Matai Katar means the Great God of Hindu Mahadeva. So Matai Katar Ma is Durga or Kali. This puja is performed outside the house like that of Kal-Bhairav. Some animal sacrifice is made in it. This obviously due to the influence of Hindu mythology where divine couples Siva-Sakti, Laksmi-Narayan, Radha–Krisna and so on are admitted.

The idea of one God, however, is not noted in any tribe other than the Tripuris, for none except the Tripuris have a name for the Supreme God in their own tribal pantheon. It is a curious finding that though Matai Katar and His consort are admitted as supreme God and Goddess, scarcely any one is found to give any special importance or honour to them- so that they also remain like other smaller spirits. We may say that Matai Katar as a name of the Supreme Being has not made any impression on the people and it is destined to go. So it is not wonder that the Tripuri Matai Katar has not succeeded as a name of one God. The important thing to note here is that they have at least a name of God.

The Tripuri tribe is mentioned in the Mahabharata by the term Traipur, and this shows the great antiquity of this tribe here. Their religion therefore dates from that age, if not earlier. The tripur or tripuri tribe is the largest single community and is supposed to be descended from the ancient royal family of Tripura. The traditional Tripuri deities are Matai Katar, Matai Katar Ma, Akhatra, Bikhitra, Tooima, Saugram, Mailooma, Thoomnairok, Banirok, Chhakabjook, Burasa, Haichukma, Siri Jamdu, Siri Judu and so on.

Pujas and Festivals of Tripuri Tribes

The tribals of Tripura give preference to the nature of deities, spirits, and ancestors to carry on struggle for existence. Tribal religion of Tripura is essentially polytheistic and is expressed in Pujas and Festivals both at the family and communal levels. Pujas and festivals constitute the major part of the tribal religious life. The aim behind majority of the puja is to evert an impending danger or calamity which might fall upon them or for food production or crops and also to achieve punya.

Besides, some Pujas are arranged to drive out the evil spirits from a body of diseased person.

The Akhatra and Bikhitra are the sons of Matai Katar and his consort Matai Katar Ma. This worship is held at the beginning of all religious and social ceremonies. It resembles the worship of Ganesa, the bestower of all success, in Hinduism.. The religious activities of the Tipra bigin with the Lampra puja. The worship of Akhatra and Bikhitra jointly called as Lampra puja. Sangram is worshipped by the Tripuris for prosperity and recovery from illness. This deity is regardedas a male deity who is the husband of the Goddess of water. Tooima is a family deity regarded as Goddess of water and consort of the deity Sangram. A buffalo and a hegoat is to sacrifices to her. Thoomunairok and Banirok are Gods of death like Yama of Hindu pantheon. Haichukma is a family deity, regarded a consort of Burasa. She is worshipped by those who have lost some animals in the jungle. Burasa is a male deity causing disease. The Burasa puja is rendered so that the patient may be cured by blessings of the supernatural spirit. Naksu Matai, a female deity, is regarded to be the guardian of homestead by the Tripuris. The Tripuris perform her Puja for the purpose of recovery from some illness. Garia is the natural benevolent spirit of the house hold who looks after the increase of production. In case of the Garia Puja, we find that the basic form of the Tipras religion consists of belief in a hierarchy of supernatural with a co-related body of rituals, performed towards fulfilment of some great or small motive.

It is observed that in some of the cases, some of the deities are reflections of well known Hindu deities. This similarities between Hindu and tribal deities arise, as because both people being neighbours for long centuries. The religious beliefs and practices of the Tripuris of Tripura depend almost entirely on the Hindu mythology. But peculiarity of the tribal conception of Gods is that it is almost wholesale male in character. Only a few of them are said to be female. It is seen that both Hindu and tribal Gods have got mixed in the tribal pantheon. In modern times, many tribal people have received initiation from various Bengalee Hindu religious preachers of West Bengal, Ramkrisna, Ramthakur, Swarupananda, and others.

Thus the tribal people are gradually being assimilated to the Bengalee race in respect of religion and culture. Majority of the tribal people have accepted the deferent sects of the Brahmanism which may be found in their religious practices. The involvement of tribal woman in the various religious activities are, no doubt, important pointer of the Brahmanical influence. An example of Laksmi puja is may be cited where the tribal woman take active role and they perform the ritual themselve. Instead of engaging the Brahmin prist. Besides, the Sani Puja, and Satya-Narayan puja are also performed by the tribal people reciting the glory of the respective deities from Pachali. It is equally interesting to note that the Kharchi Puja, Goria Puja and the Ker Puja of the tribal people have influenced the non-tribal people in developing their religious faiths and a large number of non-tribals are visiting the Chaturdasha Devata temple and offering the ingredients to the deities.

The Belief in Spirit

The philosophically important fact here is that the Tripuris believe in a world of spirits which is a metaphysical or spiritual world. The Tripuri spirits are not given any names, and are regarded as causing disease and other harms to man. The tripuris, like the Hindus believe in the existence of a soul or Atman in human body. The soul is called Fala in their language. The Tripuris believe that the soul during sleep temporarily goes out of the body and later on returns to the body. The belief in spirit is an important aspect of the religious life of Tripuris.

The Tripuri tribals have no sense of dearth of a religion. They are surrounded by the Hindus and most of them are Hindus themselves. So the Hindu ideas of religion and philosophy are usually put forward in support of the tribal religion. As yet, the traditional religious life of the Tripuris differs with caste Hindu in case of some religious pujas and forms of worship. They worship the supernatural powers, nature deities, ancestors and spirits who are associated with the ceremonial worship in their day to day life. The pantheon of the tribal deities in the tripuri community is innumeral.

The tribals of Tripura have given their religion a philosophy, an universal connotation in respect of the occultism. The religion in fact, is an order of their lives which prepares them for incessant struggle. The tribal religion along with Pujas and Festivals constitute the basis of development in the society. As to the future prospect of the tribal religion of Tripura, it may be said that there is a strong tendency towards assimilation with the general Hindu stream. What will remain of their original tribalism will be looked upon in future. The tribal scholars may bring about this regeneration of Hinduism here by their writings in newspapers, periodicals and book form. It is they who can supply further information on tribal religion and Philosophy from every nook and corner of the tribal habituations. This will help further thinking of the subject and pave the way to tribal renaissance of a greater multilingual religion in Tripura. With this, let us hope that the tribal religion of Tripura will gradually develop the idea of the spiritual brotherhood of the religious society and will try to transform itself into a form of universal religion in future.

BIBLIOGRAPHY

1. D. L. Bhaumik, *Tribal Religion of Tripura,* Agartala, Tribal Research Institute.
2. D. Debbarman. Treatise on Traditional Social Instituation of the 'Tripuri' Community.
3. D. M. Edwards, *The Philosophy of Religion,* Calcutta, Progressive Publishers.
4. J. Gonchoudhuri, (ed.) *Tripura the Land and Its People.*
4. *The Tribes of Tripura : A Dissertation.*
5. J.H. Hick, *Philosophy of Religion.*

22

A Conceptual Analysis on the Tribal Religion of Tripura

Lincoln Reang

Introduction

Religion has been an important aspect in the course of development of culture, heritage and social solidarity of any community. Infact, there has been a strong emphasis that religion and culture are inseparable. Religion is the system of worship of God as a means of code for the growth of spiritual and social behaviour of men. Man always believes in the supernatural as the cause, continuity and end of his existence. Infact, religion permeates all aspects of life. An important characteristic of tribal religion is that it doesn't have any sacred scripture. The religious ethos is contained in the people's hearts, minds, oral history and rituals. The paper intends to highlight the traditional religious ways of life and its transition with the change in modernity among the Tribals of Tripura. This paper also highlights a special focus with detailed analysis on the Reang (Bru) religion and rituals.

Tribal Religion in Tripura

The tribal communities in Tripura comprise 19 (Nineteen) tribes as per the Government of India Notification of 1956, (vide *Tripura District Gazetteers*, p. 143 edited by K.D. Menon, Agartala, 1975). The tribals in Tripura include Tripuri, Reang (Bru), Jamatia, Chakma, Halam, Mog, Noatia, Kuki, Garo, Munda, Lushai, Orang, Santal, Lepcha, Khasi, Uchai, Bhil, Bhutia and Chaimal. The tribals in Tripura enjoy a special status with regard to religious diversity. The tribal religious forms like animism bears a rich legacy from the past. In due course of time there was a culturalism of tribal religious rites and rituals with that of the Hinduism, the main religious practices of the majority of the people in India. They also profess different religions like Hinduism, Islam, Christianity, Buddhism, etc. (Appendix-I). Nevertheless, the tribals of Tripura profess their traditional methods of worshipping their deities which have their own local names like Tuima (Water Goddess), Haichukma, Garia, Lampra (Akhitra and Bikhitra), Mailuhma (Goddess of Paddy), Khuluhma (Goddess of Cotton), and so on. The Supreme God is often called as 'Mtai Ktor'. Another notable peculiarity of tribal religion in Tripura is that the gods or deities do not have any particular image or a place of worship but are represented by means of decorated bamboo poles, or in some cases a stone or piece of rocks. The sacrifice of fowls, pigs (swine), goats, etc. are a common sight in tribal rituals in Tripura.

The tribals concept of Spirits and Gods are of utmost important in terms of their belief in religion. They have a belief on the spirit (Phola) who has a tremendous influence on a person's life. The spirit (Phola) of a person may reside in any object or material. They may reside in a person, animal, fish, tree, river, etc. The spirit (Phola) may either be good or bad, depending on the life when he/she was alive and having done good works or the causes of his/her death being a suicide or some other unnatural death.

The Reang (Bru) Religion

The Reang (Bru) are one of the tribes residing in the states of Tripura, Mizoram, and Assam. The Reang (Bru) in terms of appearance basically belonged to the Mongoloid groups and speaks the Tibeto-Burman language. The total population of Tripura according to 2001 Census Report is 31,99,203. The total Scheduled tribes constituted 9,93,426 and out of them the Reangs (Bru) constituted 1,65,103 i.e., around 16.6 per cent of the total scheduled tribe population in Tripura. Among the Reang (Bru) community, with regards to the religious population (2001 Census) those who are adherents to Traditional Belief or Animists consist of 84 per cent, Christianity accounts for about 9.98 per cent (See Appendix-II).

The Reang (Bru) follow their religious practices and usages for ages. They have a belief on the benevolent (Buraha, Longdrai, etc.) and the malevolent (Songrongma, Mainokma,Khunokma, etc.) spirits (Phola); Animatism (Attribution of life to physical objects); Animism (belief on the natural objects), beliefs in Dreams/Divinations; Magic/Witchcrafts; Omen, etc. But the faith and belief that the majority professes is animism. The belief of animism is probably one of man's oldest beliefs. From its earliest beginning it was a belief that a soul or spirit existed in every object. Infact, this religious practice has been the core of the indigenous way of life. Traditionally, the tribal religions are historically evolved. The Reang (Bru) have been loosely described as animists, having their own belief of local spirits. In general, they see their world filled with various invisible spirits (often called Phola). They associate spirits with rice, soil, water, fire, stones, forests, etc. In times of crisis or calamities, animal sacrifices may be made to placate the anger of the spirits. Illness is often believed to be caused by evil spirits. In addition to belief in spirits, villagers believe in taboos on many objects or practices. The worship of the supernatural beings is supposed to protect them from all evils and calamities. Religion also serves to engender and strengthen group consciousness and solidarity.

The Reang (Bru) village has a community priest known as Akchai. It is he who performs all worship individually and also on behalf of the whole village. The priest (Akchai) in each village contacts the spirits and prescribe ways to appease them. Major pujas/rituals of the Reang (Bru) performed by the priest include the entire rituals starting from birth to death viz., Gbeing Bumo, Aabu Sumo, etc before and after the birth of a child, Mai Khlungmo, Mtai Ktor, etc.

to get relief from diseases. Nohsuh Mtai, Maibaohmo, Ha Splehmo, etc. are held after the death of a person. The priest is also regarded as physicians possessing knowledge of medicinal herbs and capable of curing the diseased by means of herbs as well as magical inchantations. He is held in high esteem by the villagers and enjoys manifold privileges. Infact, the religious life of the Reang (Bru) tribes revolves around the process of human life cycle in relation to cultural events and cultivation (Jhum). All the ceremonies and festivals are linked to invoke a blessing from different gods and goddesses in order to obtain greater happiness and prosperity. Such numerous deities are commonly worshipped through various rituals to safeguard and cure them from different evils and illness.

Major Rituals of the Reang (Bru)

Imshih Tainmo, (for health and family welfare) Soinai Rao (for family welfare), Boni Rao (to get rid of illness), Mai Khlum Mo (for sanctification of agricultural outputs), Homa Pha Khami (for women health and welfare), Norah Khemi (for household peace and prosperity), Khroak Phang ow thu nai rao/Imtai Raja (for health), Hathai Kchu Ri Mi (For Longdrai God-In a haunted place), Haa Spleh Mi (for Protection against ground related illness), Hata Malai Mi (during the new season of Jhuming/Jhum Cultivation), Tui Kto taola ri mi (ending an oath taken in parents' name), Tui Chao Mi (during Illness), Para Ker Mi/Para Puja (for village welfare), Mahadev Arag Bao Mo (earlier during a death ceremony, usually the people belonging to the Reang/Bru community mourn day and night without eating or indulging in any constructive works, so Mahadev, a deity after seeing such chaos in the village wanted to make the people realized that instead of wasting valuable time in mourning, they should do some constructive works that will be helpful during the death ceremony as well as for the village. So, he taught the Reang/Bru community in preparing a local wine that really helped the people, because they could enjoy the local wine during the ceremony and also after that they could go for their daily basis of works. But the condition was that during any such ceremony the first drops of drink must be offered to the deity, i.e. Mahadev),

Tao Chro Ri Mi (during high fever), Mai Nok Ma/Boisu (to appease the Goddessess of Grains), Tao Toi Taing Khao Ruh Mi (before beginning a journey), Toi Kha Mi (For Barren Women), Bah La (for Village welfare), Asari Kamo (thanks giving).

Before/After Birth of a Child

1. Tui Chao - This rituals performed for the smooth birth of the child and also the health of the child is determined by examining the intestine of the fowl that was sacrificed.
2. Gbeing Bumo - In this rituals one pig and four fowls are sacrificed for the good health of the child and the mother.
3. Aabu Sumo-By sacrificing five fowls and placing five local wine bottles, this rituals indicates the purification and naming of the child.
4. Bachak Kamo- After 4-5 months, for the good health of the child this rituals was performed by sacrificing five fowls and placing five to six bottles of local made wine.
5. Khong Khok Kamo-For the proper growth of the child' brain and his long life, this rituals is performed. The women wear new clothes and sacrifice one fowl and one cock. She also offers 60-70 local wine to the priest.
6. Saja Thunairao/ Saroi Thunairao- By sacrificing two fowls and one pig, this ritual is performed for the well being of the child.

During Marriage

1. Songrongma rituals-The main ceremony that deals during the marriage where one fowl and one cock along with two pure local wine/brew are offered.
2. Kati Chamo- This rituals is performed after the bride was brought to the bridegroom house. It was usually performed both on the land and in water by sacrificing

two fowls or in some case one goat. This rituals is basically for a new couple after marriage.

Rituals relating to Individual/Personal (General Welfare)

1. *Nokkhok Puja-* Here, basically four types of rituals was performed namely,
   i) Sani rituals during the month of August-September with only the samogri (Ingredients).
   ii) Baroi Tainnai in the month of September-October with a sacrifice of two male-goats.
   iii) Soi nai rao tainnai in the month of February-March with a sacrifice of two male-goats.
   iv) Hata Malai Mi in the month of April-June with a sacrifice of two male-goats.

Nokkhok rituals as a whole is performed by sacrificing a Buffalo. This four system of rituals revolves whole year round. After this rituals comes another rituals called Bar Yachak mo rituals. Here there will be a procession of the village people with the owner of the house at the front followed by five priests. During the course of the rituals nobody could cross the road that was taken by the procession.

2. *Samung Maimo (Knowing Works)-* Two Pigs are usually sacrificed, one at night and the other on the next morning. But the body of the pig is kept on a small hut that is guarded by two priests and one of their followers. Near the Pig a Inkcham (rope), seven Khuchloi (seed of a cotton) and seven Rice grains will be placed. The puja ends on the next day, which then will be followed by a rituals called Sema nai mo(Observation), If there is any an increase in the number of the cotton seed and the rice grains say upto 8-9 with a teeth mark on the pig then the puja is a success and there will be a community feast. Thereafter another puja is performed called Khum bai li where all the people drink local wine from the two wine pitcher that are placed infront of everyone. Here, the owner of the house i.e., the one who is performing the rituals have to imitate the priest

wearing new clothes. The priest dances in an intoxicant manner on the tune of a godly drumbeat. The priest shivers and throws the burnt wheat seed. The owner of the house usually receives the seeds before it falls on the ground by spreading a new cloth. This festival takes place for two days and nights.

Rituals Relating to Death

1. Yaphaik ow, Tao Buthaik ow-for lao tao (God i.e. owner of the Death) and for the Dead person.
2. Sampli Bahcha ow-The Whole night people drinks and dances by taking the dress of a Biang goma (a typical type of huge bird). The dead body would also be dressed up.
3. Thereafter, a small hut (Smang Nok) is built where the bone of the death person will be kept for atleast 3-4 months. Another small hut will be built called (Kaa Nok) exclusively for the older women for crying. But for the rich people like the Chowdhry of the village their bones are kept in a special hut called Chrai Nok.

Culturalism in Tribal Religious Belief

There are many tribal traditional deities identified with the Hindu concept of gods and goddess, for example among the Reang (Bru) Mailuhma, the goddess of rice and Khuluhma the goddess of cotton are identified with Hindu Goddess Laxmi. While Tuibuma, the goddess of water is linked with Ganga. The influence of Vaishnavism and Hinduism on the traditional religious practices have infact brought a tremendous change in the system of worship among the tribal community. There is also a feeling that there is a close relation between their age-old religious system with that of the Hindu gods and goddess. The Reang (Bru) perform rituals to Buraha (Sibrai) and Lampra who is recognized, as being overall powerful is equivalent to Mahadev or Shiva of Hindu religion. With the passage of time some of the tribals have received initiation from various Hindu religious preachers like Ramakrishna, Swarupananda and others and gradually assimilated into their religious and cultural way of life. The worship of major Hindu deity like Vishnu, Kali, Krishna, Shiva, and so on has more or less become a prominent form of religion in Tripura.

The wave of Christianity entered Tripura during the reign of Amar Manikya (1577 A.D. to 1585 A.D.) whereby Jesuit Missionaries were invited to work in Tripura. Later, different denominations of Christianity like British Baptist Missionary Society (1879), New Zealand Baptist Missionary Society (1890), etc. reached to the different sections of the people of Tripura. Infact, there are different denominations of Christianity like the Catholic, Baptist, Evangelical Free Church of India, Seventh Day Adventist, Presbyterian, United Pentecostal Church, Salvation Army, etc. who undertook their evangelistic works among the tribes of Tripura. Christianity reached the Reang (Bru) community after Khu Rai was baptized in 1922. Thereafter more evangelistic works took place from 1926 onwards. The advent of Christianity among the tribals in Tripura has infact been a new era which ushered into the tribal society. Christianity provided an ideology that helped the people to maintain their identity during the course of serious defects in the traditional sphere of life, socio-cultural and political institutions. Many evils, superstitions, burden of animal sacrifice, etc. were transformed by the teaching of Christian ideology.

The influence of Christian and Hindu religions has been a dominating force in eliminating most of the traditional religious beliefs and practices. The essence of religion among the tribals of Tripura is their belief in the law of Karma and rebirth, where both Hinduism and Christianity have a special effect on their traditional belief and practices. But, their influence among the tribal community in Tripura has been revitalization for the search of a new ideology, which aims at securing an efflorescence of a new identity. The worship of different deities is a system to get relief from different illness or diseases. The Akchai (priest) or the medicine man has a prominent role in curing the diseases by performing various rituals with regards to the illness by sacrificing domestic animals like fowl, pig, goats, etc. Infact, the Akchai is highly respected in tribal society for his role in conducting various religious rituals. Even women can also become an Akchai in the Reang (Bru) society.

Indigenous religion and Christianity are fundamentally incompatible. The former is essentially tribal and animistic. It shares with other primal religions and a belief in ever-present spirits that use natural objects as instruments to bring about good or evil. The spirit world is at work in human beings and nature alike. Particular geographical features, plants and animals are thought to have special powers to help or harm the tribe. Rituals are designed to express adoration or achieve propitiation of such mysterious and dangerous entities. In tribal religion, there is no sharp distinction between the spirits and the essential unity of nature and humanity. The world is filled with spirit beings, which can be approached and revered through the material objects to which they have attached themselves. Ritual actions that celebrate the significance of these signs are acts of faith through which each generation binds itself. In contrast to deep indigenous curiosity about the beginning of things, Christianity believes that creation is the unparallel act of divine love that cannot be explained by any scientific concepts of causation. But the tribals of Tripura recognize that their ancestral religion is incapable of reshaping any appeal to its apparently simple virtues and beliefs.

Conclusion

Religion is a powerful force that influences how people think and act. One of the biggest changes is that a century ago, people were born with their parents' religion. They tended to stay with that religion for their entire lives. Now people choose their religion. They switch; they go back and forth. Human existence and history have also given a relative value. Because the transcendent God confers their ultimate purpose and destiny, human beings are free to engage in historical, sociological and psychological studies without calling upon gods for support. The influence of Christian and Hindu religion is seen in the celebration of Christian festivals like Easter, Good Friday and Christmas and Hindu festivals like Durga Puja, Laxmi Puja, etc. The tribal communities in Tripura are therefore now mostly motivated towards other religions viz., Vaishnavism, Hinduism, Christianity, etc. Such conversion has significantly affected the socio-cultural life of the tribal communities in Tripura and in this process most of the traditional religion belief and practices are either lost or intermingled with the process in the worship of the different sects of others religion.

Appendix I: Tripura: Scheduled Tribe Religious Population, 2001

Religion	*Total*		
	P	*M*	*F*
All religions	993,426	504,320	489,106
1. Hindus	796,020	403,334	392,686
2. Muslims	2,356	1,294	1,062
3. Christians	98,971	50,643	48,328
4. Sikhs	43	28	15
5. Buddhists	94,980	48,476	46,504
6. Jains	112	55	57
7. Other religions and persuasions	713	368	345
8. Religion not stated	231	122	109

Appendix II: Reang (Bru) Religious Population, 2001

Religion	*Total*		
	P	*M*	*F*
All religions	165,103	84,155	80,948
1. Traditional Belief (Animism)	135,041	68,690	66,351
2. Muslims	818	446	372
3. Christians	27,894	14,303	13,591
4. Sikhs	6	3	3
5. Budhists	1,255	664	591
6. Jains	14	8	6
7. Other religions and persuasions	21	11	10
8. Religion not stated	54	30	24

REFERENCES:

1. An interview with Shri. Dontoirai Reang (82), a Village Priest (Akchai), S/o.Munghamya Reang, Vill.Longkajoy Para, Bokafa on 04/12/2009.
2. An interview with Smt. Moiloti Reang (89), a Village Priest (Akchai) from Choronpai Para, Birchandra Manu, Santirbazar, South Tripura on 23.01.2010.
3. An interview with Shri. Rambahadur Reang (68), a Village Priest (Akchai), Chowdry (Village Headman) and a village Chairman from Rambahadur Para, Tuisama, North Tripura on 01.02.2010.
4. Bera, Gautam Kumar, 2010. *The Land of Fourteen Gods,* New Delhi: Mittal Publication.
5. Bhattacharyya, N.N., 1995. *Religious Culture of North-Eastern India,* New Delhi: Manohar Publishers.
6. Bhowmik, Dwijendra Lal, 2003. *Tribal Religion of Tripura: A Social-Religious Analysis,* Agartala: Tribal Research Institute, Government of Tripura.
7. Rao, Narayan Singh, 2006. *Tribal Culture, Faith, History and Literature,* New Delhi: Mittal Publications.

23

Ultapani: A New Religious Belief of the Mech

Paulami Chattopadhyay*

The Mech are an Indo-Mongoloid tribe of West Bengal. In West Bengal they are mainly concentrated in Jalpaiguri, Koch Bihar and Darjeeling districts. They are the eleventh largest scheduled tribe of West Bengal. Actually they are one of the Bodo-Kachari (Cachari) tribes who live in West Bengal. According to the Census of India 2001, the population of the Mech in West Bengal is 35,996. They speak the Bodo language, which has no written text until the nineteenth century. At present they use Bengali, Roman and Devnagari scripts. Their language, Bodo, belongs to the Tibeto-Burman family of languages. The Bengali Language is used for inter-group communication (Singh, 1981). Hodgson (1880) describes that the Mech have entered to India from Morong (Nepal) and country of Kichoks in Nepal. According to Sunder (1895) the Mech and the Kachari are the same people. In the Duars they call themselves Bodo. They have distinct Mongolian features. When the western part of Duars was under the Bhutan dynasty, the Mech migrated there. Gierson (1928) opines that Bodo or Bada are Meches or Kacharis. The word Mech is a Corruption of Mleccha. The inhabitants of north Kachar are called Dimasa and Assamese call them Kacharis.

* Paulami Chattopadhyay, chatterjeepaulami26@rediffmail.com.

The Bara people were known as Koch in North East Bengal. Vasu (1922) states the Meches and the Kiratas belong to the Asura dynasty. They were Mlechchas and so abbreviated into Mech.

According to Sanyal (1973) in the Vedic age those among the Asuras who offered their worship in vulgar expressions of dubious meaning were known as Mlechchas. From several literatures we find that their possessions extended from Asia Minor to the Caucasus Mountain. It is known that one branch of the Asuarians marched off westward till they reached Asia Minor and succeeded in establishing their influence and culture, under the name of Mlechi-Zedak and the other branch under the name of Mlecha, crossed the Kailasa mountain and reached Kamrupa via Tibet. Kamrupa was a beautiful strip of land, situated in eastern part of India. It was bounded on the north by the Himalayas, on the south by Mandachala generally known as the Garo hills, on the east by Dikkara-Vasini and on the west by the river Karatoya.

Sanyal (1973) opines that Bodo migrated into India through Patkoi hills lying between India and Burma. Gradually they spread into the whole of modern Assam, North Bengal and parts of East Bengal and probably they marched into three directions. One part went up to Kachar and was called Kacharis. The second part went along the river Brahmaputra and settled down in the whole of modern Assam up to Goalpara and some parts of Jalpaiguri and Cooch-Behar under the name Bodo or Bara. They were further divided into four classes, namely, Mech, Koch, Rabha and Garo. The Mech moved towards the west along the foot of the Himalayas up to the river Mechi between India and Nepal and established themselves on the north bank of the Mechi river as Mech or Mechia. Then they crossed the river and settled in dense forests of Darjeeling Terai and Baikanthopur of Jalpaiguri. Again they moved towards east and crossed the Tista and established themselves in the Duars of Jalpaiguri district. After that they marched towards further east, crossed Sankosh river and moved towards Goalpara in Assam.

During the fieldwork the researcher met with some old and elite persons of the Mech community. They have given their idea about the origin of their community and they have also portrayed their historical background. They opine that the original land of the Bodo was the Bod, a land strip located at the westwards of present China and north-eastern side of the Himalaya. There they worshipped five spirits like earth, water, fire, wind and sky and they recognised themselves as Saba Madauni Fisa (Badasa) means we are the children of the five deities. The word Badasa originated from the word 'Bodasa'. In short it was Bod. Later on this Bodo was divided into sub groups like Koch, Garo, Mech, Dimasa, Bodo, Rabha and Kok Borok. They think that one Indo-Mongoloid group who belong to Tibeto-Burman language group entered into India from three different directions-(i) through Patkoi hills lying between India and Burma (ii) through Nathula Pass lying between Sikkim and Tibet and (iii) through North-Eastern part of India i.e. they came along the bank of river Indus. Those people came through Patkoi hills they spread themselves in whole of Assam, North Bengal and different parts of East Bengal. Again they moved into different directions. One group who reached up to Kachar they became Kachari (Dimasa). Another group went along the river Brahmaputra and established themselves in whole of Assam, Jalpaiguri and different parts of Cooch-Behar. They were known as Bodo. Again they are divided into different groups like Mech, Koch, Rabha and Garo. The Mech people marched towards the river Mechi between India and Nepal and settled there. The leader of this group was known as 'Meche' and the name of his group 'Mech' was derived from his name. After that they entered to the Terai of Darjeeling and Baikunthopur forest of Jalpaiguri district. Again they crossed Tista and settled down in Duars. Later they moved to Goalpara district of Assam.

They are undoubtedly found well outside the limits of modern (political) Assam, i.e. in North-East Bengal, Koch-Behar, and also in Hill Tippera, where the language of the people gives decisive evidence that they are of the Bada Stock. These may perhaps be conveniently divided into a (1) Northern and (2) a Southern group, the Brahmaputra being taken roughly as the dividing line, thus North Group includes Bara (Kachari), Rabha (Totala), Mech (Mes), Dhimal, Koch, Solanimiyas, Mahatiyas, Phulgariyas and Saraniyas. And the

Southern Group includes Dimasa, Hojais, Lalungs, Garos, Hajongs and Hill Tippera (Tripura) people. To these may be added one or two smaller communities, e.g., the Morans and the Chutiya in Upper Assam, whose language, not altogether extinct as yet though apparently dying out rapidly, would seem to prove them to be closely akin to the Kachari (Bada) race (Endel, 1911, pp. 5). The fact is that the Bodo people, divided into several tribal segments as above came to be dispersed and widely distributed. While these segments came to be identified by outsiders by different names, and people recognise themselves by their self name Bada (i.e. Bodo). They also retained their linguistic tradition and religious practices intact.

Bathou: The Traditional Religion of the Mech

The traditional religion of the Mech is Bathou and they worship nature.The great god of the Mech is also known as Bathou. He is worshipped in the Siju *(Euphoria nirifolia)* plant and he is addressed as Siva. He is household God.

Bathou is originated from the principle of five. Ba means five. The earth, water, fire, wind and sky are these five virtues of Bathou. If we explain the word Siju then we can get Si, which means supreme spirit. This spirit is immortal and pure. Thus, Siju is the symbol of supreme God. And Euphoria nirifolia plant has five rows of thorns. Thus, the Mech believe it is the symbol of their five deities, i.e. Ailoung Burai (the deity of earth), Agrang Burai (the deity of water), Swanjabrali Burai (the deity of fire), Khaila Burai (the deity of wind) and Rajkhandra Burai (the deity of sky). They worship the Siju plant as their supreme deity.

The womenfolk of every households worship Bathou everyday except during the menstruation period. At that time of annual worship of household deities (Baisagu) they call Roja (Priest) to worship the Bathou. At that time they replace the old Siju plant. They plant a branch of old Siju plant in place of old plant. Ripe plantains, milk, sun-dried rice and flattened rice are offered. Hens, cocks, pigeons and pigs are sacrificed as offerings. Blood and cooked meat are offered to the Gods. The neighbours except Muslims and Christians are invited to participate in this puja. As the expenditure of Baisagu is quite high so they organise the Baisagu and annual worship of Bathou according to their suitability. Now they organise the Baisgu and worship of Bathou at an interval two to four years. Some families already stopped the scarification of games due to the high price of them.

The Religious Practices of the Meches

At present the Mech call themselves Hindu though their traditional religion is Bathou. They practice rituals with Vedic mantra and without scarifice and liquor. They are known as followers of Ultapani religious belief. They are trying to initiate a religious reformation among the Mech. They are disciples of Swami Nabin Brahmaritritha. The name of their organisation is Signerjar Ultapani Sanstha and their head quarter is located at Kokrajar of Assam. They are mainly Roja, Mahakalgiri of their Samaj.

Ultapani: The New Religious Belief

Swami Nabin Brahmaritritha is the founder of Ultapani religious belief. He is an ascetic man and he has achieved divine grace through his austere religious practice on the bank of river Uttarsorta in the jungle of Chiknajhar. According to him Lord Shiva is the creator of the whole world and its all creatures. Thus, he opines Lord Shiva disapproves the scarification of his any creation in the name of worship of God. They start every puja with worshipping of Lord Shiva. Fire worship and chanting of Vedic mantra are also must at the time of any puja. Lord Shiva is the supreme deity of them.

In their opinion Goddess Mahamaya created a man who slept on water and from his navel a lotus bloomed. From that lotus the Lord Brahma appeared. Then a tomb of light was created on water and from that tomb the Lord Bishnu appeared. After that a conflict was started regarding the creation of creatures. At that time lord Shiva came on that spot and told he is the creator of Lord Brahma and Lord Bishnu. He ordered Lord Brahma to go to sky to create creatures of it and Lord Bishnu to go to earth for the creation of creatures. For creation of creatures a woman is required so he gave Goddess Swaraswati to Lord Brahma and Goddess Laxmi to Lord Bishnu. Lord Shiva also expressed his desire of creation to Goddess Parbati and he created the Mech. So they recognise themselves as Shivagotriya or descendants of Lord Shiva.

As other Mech people they worship Siju plant as Bathou and they also believe Bathou is the symbol of Lord Shiva and rows of thorns of Siju plant is the symbol of five virtues i.e earth, water, fire, wind and sky. The lines of a pair of thorns are found in each and every row of thorns of Siju plant. A pair of thorn is the symbol of Lord Shiva and Goddess Parbati and the leaf of the Siju plant is the sign of tongue of Goddess Parbati. They think Man and woman are created from same place and that is nature. So they imagine Lord Shiva and Goddess Parbati together in Siju plant. The pulpit of Bathou is thought as symbol of whole world and it is shaped as Linga. According to their belief Lord Shiva lives in Himalaya which is situated at north. Therefore, the Linga is made facing towards north. The Lord Ganesha is found at south of the pulpit.

Religious Observances

The Mech perform different pujas in different time of the year. They worship various Gods and Goddess and perform various religious rites. Their main deites are Bathou, Maino, Tista Budhi, Dak Lakhi, Manasa, Mahakal, Durga, Kojagari Laxmi, Kali and Biswakarma. The observance of religion generally centres round the priest. In all system of religion, individuals are required to perform or assist at the performance of certain activities by means of which super natural power are propitiated. The terms priest in its widest sense, refers to a man who serves a society as a religious practitioner. The Mech call their priest as Roja but in time of idol or image worship the Brahmin priest gets importance. Now a days they have curtailed some of the religious practices from their life. In the opinion of the old people high cost of the pujas, tendency towards Hindu rituals, want of proper organisers are the main causes to curtail their some traditional religious practices. The religious rites consist of sacrifice of animals and birds. They generally sacrifice goat, fowl, duck and pigeon. Blood and cooked meat are offered to the God. Their usual offerings are milk, fruits, flowers, flattened rice, egg, honey, liquor etc. In every puja priest performs prayers through enchanting mantras before god for the protection of the villagers, the domestic animals and the crops. Their main pujas are Baisagu, Gram Puja, Meceni Khela, Gotsi Punna, Dak Lakhi Puja, Manasa Puja, Dhan Kata Puja, Chorok Puja, Mahakal, Durga Puja, Kojagari Laxmi Puja, Kali Puja, Biswakarma Puja.

Like other Mech the followers of Ultapani religious belief observe different pujas through out the year and they worship Bathou, Maino, Shiva, Laxmi, Durga, Saraswati, Manasa and so on. But difference is found in terms of offerings. They do not offer liquor and sacrifice any animal. They offer fruits, flowers, milk, flattened rice, sun dried rice, batasa (one type of sweet) and water. The idol worship is the rule amongst them. Instead of Roja their worship is performed by their own priest and he is called Purohit. Their important pujas are Baisagu, Shivaratri, Manasa Puja, Durga Puja, Kojagari Laxmi Puja, Kali puja, Saraswati Puja, etc. Agriculture is their main economy and for agriculture, they depend upon the nature where human being has no control over circumstances. Therefore they perform various religious practices to reduce their internal anxieties and tensions. Before starting agricultural practices the land owners perform Gosthipunna puja. It is the worship of Goddess Laxmi. In this puja they offer flowers and fruits. Before cutting of paddy the womenfolk cut the flowers of paddy and offer these to Goddess Laxmi and then they start cutting of paddy. As the scarification of animal is compulsory in the puja of Dak Laxmi so they do not perform it. They always fix the date of any worship according to almanac.

Purohit

The Purohit is thought to be able to relate to Gods who are beyond the ordinary person's control. In their system the people who will get the power of priesthood has to be undergone more or less intensive training. He generally enjoys high status. The post of priest is not hereditary. A man can achieve this status through some process. First of all a willing person has to fill up an application form and submit it to the organization with recommendation of some members of Signerjar Ultapani Sanstha. Then the Guru trains them various spiritual practices. After completion of training a test is conducted and only qualified person gets the status of Purohit.

Life Cycle Rituals

A ritual may be defined as repetitive behaviours that communicate sacred symbols to member of the society i.e. between the kin and non-kin. The life cycle rituals, otherwise called rites de passage, are those rituals, which are associated with different stages of life of an individual. All people in all cultures go through such stages (birth, childhood, puberty, adulthood, marriage, old age, death) and they suppose that these critical phases of life are replete with danger both for the individual and the society. Thus, they perform various rituals at these moments of life-crisis for their sacredness and insecurity and also to restore their confidence and hope. The religion and rituals are very much interrelated. The rituals generate views and ways of living of a community. Thus, here an attempt has been made to describe the life cycle rituals of the Mech who are the followers of Ultapani religious belief.

Birth

The Birth is regarded as an outcome of intermixing of an adult male and an adult female. They opine the pregnancy is the natural result of a married life. The main ritual related to birth is Annaprasan (First rice feeding Ceremony). Annaprasan of a baby is organized at the age of his or her seven months or nine months. After consulting the almanac the date of Annaprasan is fixed. On that day the household deities and ancestors are worshiped. Then the maternal uncle feeds the baby. As the baby starts his/her rice eating from that day so the day is known as Annaprasan. After feeding of the baby one custom is performed. In this custom, pen, book, coin, earth, vermilion, paddy and Durba grass are kept on a dish and this dish is placed in front of the baby. A divinatory study as to the future career of the child is made from the article on which he places his or her hands at first. Their priest conducts all the rituals.

Sacred Thread Ceremony

There is no fixed time for sacred thread ceremony. After initiation all male members are rained in rules of Ultapani religious belief. Then purification of body is performed. After that sacred thread ceremony is observed. On the day of sacred thread ceremony first of all their priest takes permission of Lord Shiva through worship and then fire worship is performed. Finally sacred thread is put on the body of initiated person. The number of thread differs according to the status of the person. The numbers of thread of the Guru, the Purohit and disciple are seven, five and three respectively.

They opine scared thread is the part of their life from time of their jungle life. At that time they had no Guru but they worshipped the deities. And to control their mind and body they tied their body by Kush (a type of grass).

Marriage

They take the help of Panjika (Almanac) to fix the date of marriage. The marriage is held in bride's residence. The rituals of marriage start with Odhibas. A day before the marriage Brahmin priest or their priest performs the Haro – Gauri puja (the puja of Mahadev and Parvati). In the early morning of the wedding day generally before the sunrise the groom and the bride take curd and flattened rice and then they keep fasting up to Dharma Puja. In the morning the ancestor worship or Tirsiri is done. Then turmeric-anointing ceremony is performed. In the evening, groom and his party come to the bride's house. The bride's mother and bairaties welcome the groom. Then blessing-giving ceremony of groom and bride is done by the elders. Before beginning of the actual rituals of marriage the son in law who is married earlier is welcomed by giving some offerings. Generally father of the bride performs this ritual. Then the groom is welcomed in a similar way. It is originally Hindu custom then the Narayan Puja is held. Exchange of views of the bride and groom, fire worship, Kanyadan are performed. The bride covers her face with betel leaves and the bride and groom exchange garlands at time of exchanging views. They take permission of Lord Shiva for exchanging views of the groom and the bride. The Sindoor dan (Smearing vermillion) is done at time of fire worship. The Dharma Puja is also performed. On the next day the newly married couple go back to the groom's residence and Bhoubhat is arranged in the same evening.

All the rituals are performed under the guidance of Brahmin priest or their priest because only these people follow Vedic rule to conduct the marriage rituals.

Death

Rituals associated with death are the last of the series of life cycle rituals, which sometimes prolong for a few days after occurrence of death. The Mech consider that death is the natural outcome of life.

After death the corpse is placed in the room and the head is always placed towards south and feet to the north. The followers of Ultapani religion observe the death rituals differently. They do not perform any traditional Mech rituals. They follow Vedic rules to cremate the dead. They observe mourning period for ten days. On the fourth day married daughters offer pinda in the name of their father or mother. Their mourning period lasts for three days. On the tenth day Dasha is performed. All the mourners take purificatory bath and before taking bath they cut their nails and hairs. The son(s) performs tonsure rite and after that they take purificatory bath to ward of pollution. With the help of Brahmin priest or their priest the son(s) offers pinda in the name of his father or mother. On the thirteenth day Sradh is performed and they call it Mathau. The Brahmin priest or their priest conducts this ritual by chanting Vedic incantations. Various offerings are offered in the name of dead persons. Offering pinda in Gaya is another important ritual for them.

The View of Ultapani Followers and Other Tribesmen

The followers of Ultapani religious belief think the scarification of animal is quite barbaric and uncivilized act and this custom gets down their position to the eyes of other people. Their view is that though they are scheduled tribe but they are civilized Hindu people. Thus, scarification of animals cannot be part of their religious life. By fire worship and chanting of Vedic mantra worship can be done purely and properly. And this purity can only stop the tendency of conversion to other religion. All people are allowed to observe their festivals. But they are not welcomed in the festivals organized by their other tribesmen.

The older generation of their non Ultapani counter part still avoid accepting water and cooked food from their hand. They also avoid taking the offerings of Ultapani religious festivals. If they enter into the house of followers of Ultapani then after returning to their house they purify their body in front of Bathou. Now the younger generation not agree to observe this rule. In their opinion they have to come to their contact daily for the purpose of their education and economy. In the eyes of the traditional Mech people they are degraded persons because they break the rule and tradition of their society.

Findings

The main focus of the present paper is on the Ultapani, a new religious belief of the Mech. On the basis of the present data collected from the field a scenario of Ultapani religious belief is sketched. The descriptions which have been written in the proceeding pages are precise statements, opinions and explanations given by the Mech of the Jalpaiguri district in West Bengal along with researcher's personal observation.

We can say a section of Mech people have started a reform process in the name of Ultapani. They are against of animal sacrifice at the time of any religious occasion. They think animal sacrifice bears the uncivilized identity. Their intention is to uplift their social position and they think the Ultapani way of life can raise their social position. Thus, they observe some of their traditional religious practices in modified ways. Observing their own traditional religious practices help them to retain their identity as Mech. They have already moulded their life cycle rituals in the form of Hindu upper caste. It is clear this new religious belief has brought change in their ideology, faith and religious practices. They have consciously organized an attempt of social reform within the fold of their tribal identity.

REFERENCES

Endle, S., 1911. *The Kacharis*. London: Macmillan & Co.

Gierson, George Abrsham.1928. Linguistic Survey of India. Calcutta: Central Publication Branch.

Hodgson, Brian Houghton.1880. *Miscellaneous Essays Relating to India Subjects*. London: Truner & Co.

Sanyal, Charu Chandra. 1973. *The Meches and The Totos: Two Sub Himalayan Tribes of North Bengal*. Darjeeling: The University of North Bengal.

Singh, K.S., 1994. *People of India: The Scheduled Tribes, National Series,* Vol. iii. Delhi: Oxford University Press.

Sunder. 1895. *Survey and Settlement of Western Duars*.

Vasu, Nagendranath.1922.*The Social History of Kamrupa*. Delhi: Low Price Publication (Reprinted in 1990).

24

God, Demons and Spirits: Wisdom of Lepcha Munism

Sumitabha Chakraborty*

Introduction

What is God? Or what is the meaning of the word God? Most philosophers want to know the essence of the word by discussing the concept of divinity. Indeed, before attempting a definition, it is essential to know what sense of the term is used for; because there are a number of widely different senses of the word 'God'. In the essence of 'philosophy of religion', God is believed to be a supernatural being having monotheism (believing in one God) and polytheism (believing in more than one God). In Western thought, God is traditionally described as a being that possesses at least three necessary properties—omniscience (all-knowing), omnipotence (all-powerful) and omnipresence (present everywhere). In other words, God knows everything, has the power to do anything, and is present where He wishes. Many other properties (e.g., omnibenevolence) have been alleged to be necessary properties of a God; however, these are the three most uncontroversial and dominant in Christian tradition. In polytheistic belief

* Research Associate, Anthropological Survey of India, Eastern Regional Centre, Kolkata, EN- 79, Sector- V, Salt Lake City, Kolkata – 700 091. chakru4_su@yahoo.com.

existence of many Gods is accepted but differ in their responses to that belief, worship only one of the many Gods, either because it is held to be more powerful or worthy of worship than the others, or because it is associated with their own group, culture, state, etc. In pantheism, God is asserted as the natural world and holds that the physical universe is part of God, but that God is more than this. By expressing pantheism in this way and including such elements, rather than limiting it to this particular planet, and specifically limiting it to human experience. Moreover, concept of God is linked with religion having some recognizable attributes. God is more powerful than spirits and can effectively alter all of nature and human fortunes. God is commonly worshipped and requests are made of them to help in times of need (Speziale, 1987).

In religion, a demon is a supernatural being that is generally described as a malevolent spirit. However, the original meaning of the word demon does not carry any negative connotation. The term first acquired its evil connotations in the Septuagint translation of the Hebrew Bible, informed by the mythology of the ancient Semantic Religion. The existence of demons is an important concept in many modern religion and occultist traditions. Demons are still feared in popular superstitions, largely due to their alleged power to posses living creatures. Sigmund Freud (1950) developed on this idea and claimed that the concept of demons was derived from the important relation of the living to the dead. 'Demons are always regarded as the spirits of those who have died recently and shows better than anything the influence of mourning on the origin of the belief in demons'(ibid.) Demon has a number of meanings, all related to the idea of a spirit that inhabited a place, or that accompanied a person. According to most Christian demonology, demons will be eternally punished and never reconciled with God. Other theories postulate a universal reconciliation, in which satan, the fallen Angels, and the souls of the dead that were condemned to Hell are reconciled with God. In Hindu mythology, numerous varieties of anthropomorphic beings that might have been classified as demons, including rukshasas, asuras, etc.

Spirit is a transcendent reality, might reflect and intent to interpret through faith and belief. Renowned historical theologian Eric Mascall remarked that behind and beyond the physical Universe, there is a realm of purely spiritual beings, in whose affairs we have become implicated. Many of the famous theologians having the idea that the nature can be perforated by spiritual powers, available in a three-storied Universe consisting of heaven, earth and hell. Robust belief in spirits are now expressed as the primary concern of religion because religion is allowed to attend practical matters, like, marking important moments in a person's life, propounding an ethic and providing psychological council for people in times of grief, distress and misery. The existence of spirits experienced with both good and evil beings transcend the known world. According to occultist and spiritual philosophy, evil spirits do exist in the lower spheres from which they may reach the medium. Their appearance may be accidental, and attempt to oust the control. On the other hand, if an evil spirit has already taken possession of the medium, it is considered imperative to maintain the circle unbroken until the invader can be ousted.

In spite of all, residing on the lap of nature the Lepcha have faith and belief on God, demons and spirit as part of their religion. They believe that all the highest peaks, mountain caves, mountain trails, avalanches are the abode of supernatural beings, which they revere and offer sacrifice, unless the people suffer anxiety, misfortune and ill-health. They perform many ritualistic performances and prayers to appease those supernatural beings. They have the belief that prayer is an unfailing means to achieve the purity of heart. On keeping this view in mind, an attempt has been made to highlight those aspects of traditional religious system of the Lepcha trying to establish their concept of God in the theological parlance.

Area and People

Living on the western flank of the Eastern Himalaya, Sikkim, one of the smallest states in India is flavoured with floral bounty and land-locked terrain. It is located between 27°05′ - 28°09′ N latitude and 87°57′ – 88°56′ E longitude, having an area of around 7096 sq.kms., and is known as the paradise for nature lovers. The state is bounded by Nepal in the West, Bhutan in the east, Tibet in the north and north-east and the State of West Bengal in the south. The Chola range separates the state from Tibet and Bhutan, while Singalila range separates it from Nepal (Gazetteer, 1931). Historical information reveals that before 1641 the area was ruled by the Lepcha kings and between 1641 and prior to 1975 Sikkim was ruled by the Bhutia Kingdom. In 1975 Sikkim became an independent sovereign state. A number of mountain passes, like Nather La (4392 m.), Gelep La (4388 m.), Donkia La (5520 m.), Kongra La (4809 m.) along the ranges have sustained a two way traffic of traders, pilgrims and adventurers from Tibet and central Asia. About 36.3 per cent (2656 sq. kms.) of the total area of the state is under forest coverage.

The topography of Sikkim is quite varied. The elevation ranges from 1250 meters to 8558 meters, with almost no flat piece of land anywhere. The snow-clad mountains, the lower hills covered with dense evergreen forests, many rivers and rivulets cascading down from the rocky heights and rippling through the green expanse of the valleys constitute a magnificent and eye inspiring panorama. Mt. Khangchendzonga (8598 meters), the world's third highest mountain is treated as 'sacred mountain' to the Sikkimese as their guardian deity and is considered as the holiest of the holy. The present study had been undertaken in the hamlets of west and north districts of Sikkim, as Dzongu is one and only isolated dominating habitation of the Lepchas situated in the north district.

Once the ruling tribe, the Lepcha are the earliest settlers of Sikkim profoundly proclaimed as 'Rong' (the son of the snowy peak) 'motanchi' (term for intra-community identity) nowadays concentrated on the lap of Kangchendzonga ('mayel lyang'—the land of hidden delightful paradise). The derogatory word 'Lepcha' is derived from the Nepalese term Lepchey, which means scurrilous speakers. Originally, the term Lepchey was anglicized by the British people and was coined as 'Lepcha', who proclaimed themselves as Rong, meaning 'snowy peak'. The history of the state reveals that the Lepcha are the oldest inhabitants of Sikkim. They had kings and kingdom. They had their own script (Rongring). It was believed that at one time the Lepcha dominantly ruled out the whole of north-eastern states including Sikkim. During the reign of Gaeboo Achok, the area of his kingdom extended in the highest unit. But the reign of whole Lepcha kingdom was ruined within a very short period and the condition of the Lepcha was gradually fallen poor.

The Lepchas were living mostly through hunting and gathering from the forests and since the later part of the last century they took initiative in terrace farming and subsequently adopted the system of cash crop plantation, like cardamom and ginger. The Lepcha raise maize, paddy, buckwheat, barley and millet in their terraced agricultural field. Maize is the most important staple food and millet is commonly used for making local beer 'chi'. Fish is taken occasionally but meat – both fresh and dried are taken regularly. They do not have any inhibition in consuming beef, pork, rabbit, porcupine, monkey, deer, etc.

The Lepcha are kin based community and are sub-divided into a number of patrilineal clans, which are locally known as pu-tso or termed as moo. According to their belief they have ten such pu-tso or moo, which have been originated from the ten snowy peaks of Khangchendzonga mountain. Each pu-tso is considered to have a common supernatural or legendary ancestor. The chief function of pu-tso is the regulation of marriage alliance and the prevention of incest. The Lepcha do not have any centralized authority. In older times, during the reign of kingdom, there were two divisions or social classes namely: (i) Rongboo (patricians), (ii) Mangboo (plebeians). According to them, the Rangboo Lepcha belonged to the mobility classes, who were appointed by the king as priests; while the Mangboo class of Lepcha consists of farmers, potters, carpenters, blacksmiths, weavers, etc. At the time of marriage alliance, Lepcha has to enquire about the clan of the bride and the groom, because they strictly follow the rule of pu-tso or moo (clan). It is observed that the settlement pattern of the Lepcha is also usually clan centered. For this the clan—Sandyanmoo, Lutsomoo and Hee-moo are prevalent in Sikkim. It is in their belief that these clans are conferred from the 108 main snowy peaks of Sikkim Himalayas. It is to be mentioned here that a kind of social order was embodied where both the father and the mother are the heads of the family at a time and therefore, the male children or sons belongs to the father's clan and the female children or daughters belong to the mother's clan. The girls or daughters inherit her mother's clan from generation to generation, and as such a daughter has no right whatsoever over her father's any moveable or immoveable properties.

In Lepcha society, extended family is an operative group, which renders possible identification with the community. It is their opinion that the extended family imparts positive training to the child and teaches a strong control over behaviour. While describing the society, the Lepcha men often state that they have no class, creed and ranking among themselves. No one is big, no one is small, and there is no gradation as such. It was evident that among the Lepcha of Dzongu, a system of self-rule still functions in the form of an informal council of the elders, which they term as 'Lyang-ganbu'. In spite of the existence of the Panchayat, it is very important to settle-up various disputes regarding marriage alliance, fixing up of bride-price, cultivation of crops, land holding disputes, crimes, disputes within the family members, difficulties of the member within the community etc. are settled by this self-rule system. According to their belief, any kind of quarrel is the result of the evil action of three spirits or devils, i.e.—Soo-moong (enmity of speech), Ge-moong (enmity of thought), and Jhor-moong (enmity of action).

The Lepcha certainly had evolved a strong cultural base. Their folklores, mores, myths and legends, dance, songs have been cherished and transmitted to the younger generation. The Lepcha have their own ancient religion, named Boongthing-ism and Mun-ism. They believe in the existence of God called 'Rum' and to Him they offer their prayers and thanks giving. They also have strong belief in evil spirits, who cause illness and misfortune. Many of the earlier scholars had mentioned that the Lepcha did not have any religion, rather they believed in atheism. But in reality, for the God fearing Lepcha prayers, supplication and worship through the medium of Boongthing and Mun are no superstition. They believe prayers and chanting spring out from the core of their hearts. They also believe that prayer is an unfailing means to achieve the purity of heart. The Boongthing and the Mun plays the role of mediator between God and the people.

Other than the ancient religion during recent time, the majority of the Lepcha are converted into Buddhism and a few of them are converted into Christianity. It was informed that the people have accepted the ritual, the validating mythology, and the organization of Lamaism. Like other 'high religious' Lamaism is individualistic; it holds that a person's chief concern should be with his own spiritual welfare. Thus, the key-concept of Lamaism, is an alien attitude to disapproval of social acts, and not individuals. It is the society and not the evil-doer, which bears the burnt of wicked acts (Gorer, 2005. 135). The Lepcha language as dubbed by many scholars as a 'mystery' language, because it is not related to any other language, prevalent in this region. Some have a belief that the language belongs to the Tibeto – Burman family, while others have found its root in the Austro-Asiatic family. Dr. Suniti Kumar Chatterjee had mentioned that the Lepcha language belongs to the Himalayan group of the Tibeto-Burman sub-family (Thakur, 1988).

Being a man of the forests and having a perfect harmony with nature, the Lepcha have developed an intuitive relationship with surrounding environment. They have extremely rich knowledge for variety of plants, beasts, insects and flowers and some of them who, even today, live in the mountainous forest patches have the capacity to identify the species which are beneficial for them.

Concept of God: Lepcha Theology

The first fruit of the season are always offered to God. But question arise—what is God? In the philosophy of religion God is traditionally described as a being that possesses at least three necessary properties: omniscence (all knowing), omnipotence (all powerful) and omnipresence (present everywhere). God knows everything, has the power to do anything and is present where He wishes. According to the theological concept the religion in general have categories—

monotheism (belief in one God), polytheism (belief in more than one god or goddess) and pantheism (belief as God is itself the natural universe). The Lepcha religion falls under the third category. To them, 'God, locally termed as Rum is the world and the world is God'. By uttering this they want to mean the vastness of the Universe, where God resides. On the other hand, the existence of malevolent spirits, demon, generically termed as moong is prevalent in the nature; whose displeasure may cause misery, unhappiness, fatal injuries, illness and sometimes even death.

According to their religion, it is a system of beliefs and faiths usually involving the worship of supernatural forces and beings by the performances of rites and rituals. Religious beliefs provide shape and meaning to one's perception of the Universe. Religion also provides understanding and meaning for inexplicable events such as a loved one being killed in an earthquake or some other unpredictable forces of nature. The purity of their belief towards nature is diverted with Tibetan Lamaism, which was introduced into Sikkim three centuries ago and is regarded now as the official religion. It is difficult to determine the extent of Buddhist influence has had on Lepcha psychology, but it is clear that the pre-Buddhist religion is not entirely dead.

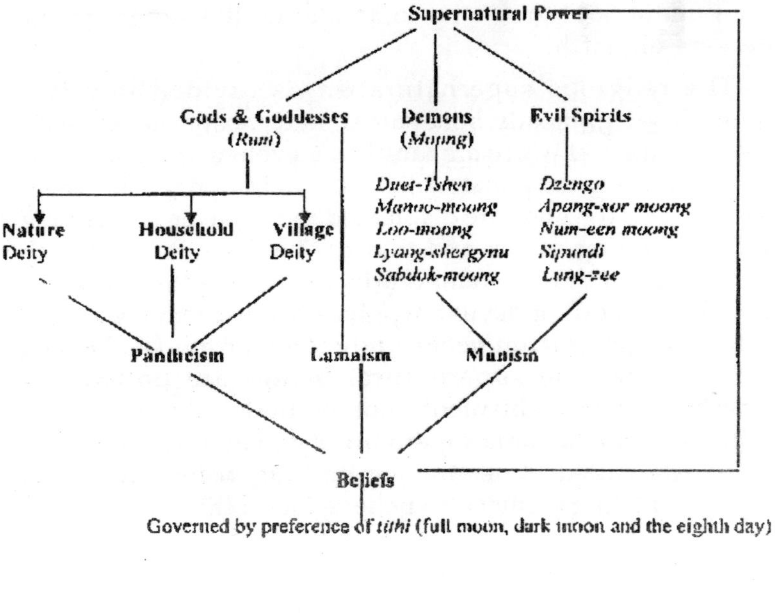

Lepcha Religion: A Belief in Supernatural

The discussion of the Lepcha religion is rendered extremely complicated by the fact that they practise simultaneously and without any feeling of theoretical discomfort. The older Lepcha religion is contradictory and nameless, but on the analogy of Lamaism, it is better termed as 'Mun' religion (after the title of the priests); the worship of the people of Mayel, which was possibly originally separate, forms nowadays a part of the Mun religion; and this religion is in all its major beliefs opposed to Lamaism. The 'Mun' religion principally supports the manifestation of a supernatural spirit which is attached to a family line, so that there can never be more than one simultaneously in each group (there may be two in one biological family, one spirit descending from the father's group and one from the mother's). The chief function of the Mun is to ward off the misfortunes and illness caused by devils, which is done, partly by sacrifices, especially animal sacrifices, and partly by direct communication with the supernatural. On certain occasions the Mun become possessed by their guardian spirit and prophecy; at death ceremonies they summon the soul of the dead man to speak his last wishes through their mouth, and then conduct it into the rum lyang—the place of the Gods, where the God is reborn as an infant, and grows up to an eternal life similar to the life here on earth.

The religious supernaturalism is divided into two categories, e.g. mostly benevolent, and mostly malevolent. The supernatural which are mostly benevolent are called gods (Rum), those mostly malevolent devils (moong). The agent agrees that if the gods are displeased they take on a terrifying and threatening aspect and that the best way to deal with devils is to flatter them temporarily by treating them as gods; and whether gods or devils are prayed to the ceremony always ends by begging them vehemently to go away. The Lepcha believed that the supernatural beings are potentially dangerous. The ambivalent supernaturals—thyak-dum or Hlamen Djeme (a Lama supernatural equated with the Mun spirit), are called either moong or Rum according to the personal dealings. They also believe that if the supernatural being is displeased by any action, He may then show his activities through the dream.

The Mun agreed the meaningful and prophetic characters of the dreams, which are significant to those who have the knowledge to interpret them. The Lepcha can understand few incidents by seeing the certain objects which have some symbolical significance. The causation and interpretation of dreams is however different in the two religions. As Mun depicts that the dreams are sent by the supernatural, while the Lamas outlook about the dreams are the experienced of the soul released from the body by sleep; unbound by space or time the soul has experiences with the souls of other people, supernatural and objects, and, on its return, informs the body it inhabits. When the Lamas give importance to the soul, the Mun said it as a vague concept, practically only having an independent existence after the death of the body.

The Mun Religion

It is a kind of shamanic religion based on traditional belief systems whose emerging manifestation is being observed. It is a living tradition consisting of a collection of simple techniques for assessing energy, power, vision, healing and creativity. Theory reveals that the shamanic journey helps the people forge powerful relationships with the world around us, rediscover our links with ancestral energies and helping spirits. Owing to pre-religious, pre-political and pre-philosophical in nature, shamanism is a way of life, or living in harmony, respect and oneness with all life forms. According to Basilov (1999) shamanism has three views—(a) 'psychological view'—arguing as phase of trance (or ecstasy); (b) 'religious view'—regards the trance as originating from a phenomenon of possession by the sacred contact with the spirit; (c) 'trance-possession view'—regarding the possession of spiritual power to communicate with supernatural beings, including spirits. It is one of the earliest and farthest-reaching magical and religious traditions, vestiges of which still underlie the major religious faiths of the modern world. The function of the shaman is to show his or her people the unseen powers behind the mere appearances of nature, as experienced through intuition, in trance states or during ecstatic mystical visions. The manifestation of trends of shamanic elements could be observed through the performances of Mun in Lepcha society. In their society shamanism is practised when the Lepcha economy was supporting by means of hunting and gathering. In the idealistic character of the Lepcha shamanic world view the most important are the beliefs towards— (i) all the surrounding world is animated, inhabited by the spirits who can influence man's life; (ii) there are general and reciprocal interconnections in nature (human beings included); (iii) human beings are not superior but equal to other forms of life; (iv) human society is closely connected with the cosmos; (v) it is possible for a human being to acquire some qualities of a spirit and visit the other worlds; (vi) the aim of religious activity is to defend and make prosperous a small group of kinsmen.

The Mun religion has a good impact on the Lepcha theology; the Mun and their parallel priests are simply individuals who, through their possession by a spirit, have certain gifts and duties. Other than Mun three other types of priesthood by possession are recognized, like— (i) the Padem, (ii) the Yaba and (iii) the Pau. The Mun spirit is a female spirit, while the other three are male spirits. They are attached to family lines and are roughly hereditary; they often descend from grandfather to grandson or from grandmother to granddaughter. But there is no regularity about this and a man may inherit a possessing spirit from a woman, and vice versa. The manifestation of the spirit (like immortal beyond Khangchendzonga) may choose anybody for its effect, with one exception; none of the spirits will enter a lama or his own children, though they may enter his family. Both men and women can be Mun, but only men can be Padem (or Bum-thing as they are called outside Dzongu); these are also the Lepcha spirits and are less powerful, capable of exorcising far fewer devils; they cannot go for prophcsy nor perform the death ceremony. A Mun has to gather three year course of instruction. The other two categories—the Yaba and the Pau are different from Mun and Padem as they neither can do not make sacrifices nor perform exorcism, but can merely get possessed by supernatural. Both wear special clothes for their performances: the Yaba wear bandoliers of tinkling bells and have their clothes fringed with bells; they hold a metal plate and beat it as they dance. Pau wears elaborate wool head-dresses and dance with a skull-drum in one hand and a bell in the other. Both Yaba and Pau are rare because the possessing spirits are not Lepcha but have been introduced through inter-marriage with foreign women, the Yaba spirit comes from Limbu women and the Pau from Sikkimese-Tibetans.

In the Lepcha tradition the Mun is hierarchically classified as per their status –

- Pilden Mun – considered to be the most superior as they can communicate with the soul of the dead, (b) Mun-mook-Mun – this type of Muns are thought to be evil doers who cause hardship to the people, (c) Mun-jyum-mun – they are quite like as Pilden mun but they cannot communicate with the souls of the departed. They can cure the sick with the help of herbal medicine, (d) Tang-li-Mun – considered to be the specialist physician who has very good knowledge about herbal medicine and considered to be the custodian of Lepcha cultural tradition by reciting folklore, legends, myths etc. Amongst them it is believed that Tang-li Mun is a good group owing the benevolent spirit and a bad group called Mun-mook Mun owes the malevolent spirit, like the white and black magicians. Mun-mook Mun are like thieves: they think and do evil and are possessed by devils which they employ for their own selfish ends; they alone can send devils (the term used for sorcery). They are believed to have an influence like the evil eye. The Lepcha have a belief that the Tang-li-Mun sacrifices with benevolence towards them and their houses, which they are summoned. They depend on the type of Mun as his or her teacher and not on the possessing spirit. One Mun, Gnadok, described his spiritual life. According to him the whole invocation is extremely rapid but falls into the sing-song rhythm, often saying the same thing twice or four times in different words. The Mun generally uses onomatopoeic words, many of his own invention and from his prodigious memory; once started goes continuously. If it breaks down in the mid-way he cannot recall the sequence for elaboration. Gnadok Mun has a great demand in the village; officiating nearly all the ceremonies except the household rituals. When sacrificing him falls into what is almost a very light trance; his eyes become glazed and unfocussed as he intones his rhythmic chants. Gnadok Mun has nervousness and suffers from giddiness, experienced with frequent unpleasant dreams of falling down or flying down. According to the Lepcha Mun usually have such a type of nervousness, giddiness and instability of mind.

When a person intend to being a Mun, he or she has to learn minimum three years of complete rigorous training of meditation and become a loong. During that period the trainee is capable of knowing the history of every evil doer, the process of exorcism as well as the story of creation and the birth of Tak-bo-thing and many things more. During training period the trainee abstains from eating pork or goat or chicken or hen's egg. At the end of training, when one trainee gets his or her degree of loong, the Mun boils all the forbidden foods and puts in a basket and then she is given chi and butter to drink and a ceremonial scarf. From that day the trainee acquire the power over all the devils. When a trainee is given a loong degree a second ox is being sacrificed. In such a traditional religion there is no quarrel between the Padem rum and Mun rum; as the Lepcha believes that they are husband and wife respectively and are pleased to inhabit the same body. The Mun only takes full possession twice a year, once in the hot season and other in the wet season. A Mun must on no account touch a human corpse; should he do so the god will depart and he will be very ill for two months and Lamas have to perform ceremonies to cure him. This is the only occasion on which the spirit will leave a Mun. After his death, the soul of the Mun has to be conducted to the rum-lyang (place of the gods) in the normal course. A Mun admits that at the time of her trance if she orders to sacrifice many animals; this sin is not borne by them but to appease the devils that make the sacrifice necessary.

It is noteworthy to mention that except for the bi-annual prophecies the Mun do not possess supernatural powers as the Lepcha understand them, and they differ in degree rather than in kind from the laymen; they can always see devils, whereas only some laymen can see them and that only on some occasions; they can always communicate with the supernatural.

The Mun religion has a very copious validating mythology and theology. The origin of everything in the world, visible and invisible, animate and inanimate and the changes they have undergone to bring them to their present state are told in a great number of stories of varying emotional importance. The most important stories are about 'creation', which is only known in its full details by the Mun. The world is an ocean; under that ocean there is an earth of twelve super-imposed stories, and under that there lives Itpomu, the Creative Mother, and her husband Debu. Their first children were Tak-seu and Tak-from, who are also called Nar-zong-nyou and Komsithing. Afterwards there were Mlum Mukyam, Sakyeun-faat-it, Saba-faat-chaum, Suk-dum-lung-ming and Chi-lel, all of whom are the present earth; Palyou and Pakyam who are gladness and joy; then Ta-lyang, Ta-kook and Ta-kok who are the blue sky without ornament: then Bru-nong and Jil-vong, Long-mu and Tso-kor who are the forest in the sky where the stars live: then Tak-bru-num and Jit-it who are the stars. The ocean between the two worlds is called Lyang-tak-yoor oong, Tagum-lyang-shin-mu oong and is the home of Tal-i-nau and her husband San-go. Under the second earth there are two huge copper vessels beside Itpomu, full of water, and under them is a fire; this is the reason why the earth becomes warm and wet. Then was born Panjer-roong and Pantsong-roong, which is actually the Rangit River. The origin of hot streams, Kum-zer roong may cure all ills while Num-ri and Num-ra begat the thunder bird sadher-moo.

The Cherim: Performance of Mun

In the Cherim ceremony, which is held twice in a year – once at the beginning of the rains and second at the beginning of winter respectively to ward off epidemic diseases like malaria. Three separate rituals are performed for this; two by Mun and the one by the Lamas. In such communal sacrifice at least one individual from each household has to be present and each household contributes a little amount of grain and Mun's participation is necessary. The first part of the ceremony consists of offering to the devil spirits. This ceremony is called rum after the name given to the chief article of sacrifice. In a large basket filled with earth and covered with a banana leaf into which are kept a number of eight pieces of each article manifesting 'demon's walking stick' consisting of decorated bamboos with flowers inserted in holes, water in a container, milk, tea and chi (country liquor); pieces of mica; stems of warm wood decorated with threads, fresh eggs, heaps of grain and dried bird, dried fish and ginger. The offering articles also includes two ta-ming which consists of long sticks to which are attached and wrapped in leaves samples of every sort of food and drink. When the offerings have to be made, the Mun, sitting opposite to the people, intones a long chant to invoke the gods (rum) and then takes the eggs and touches them to his forehead while keeping his eyes shut; the line which he envisages inside the eggs foretells the future health of the community.

The second ceremony – 'Tsandong' is also performed by Mun, consists of offerings to the Gods of Khangchendzonga and the plains. The offerings consist of rice, butter, chimi (a variety of wild fruit), a rupee and eight eggs. The offering is made in two parts; first grain and strained chi (traditional liquor) are thrown out by the Mun and her assistant and later a goat is dedicated and then sacrificed. These two ceremonies together take about four hours time. At least one member from each household has to attend this ceremony. Usually the male members attend the ceremony. In this ceremony prayers are also attributed to the God of mountains (SungmuI) from the protection from snow, hailstorm and blizzard. The people present in this ceremony are busy in cooking, eating, gossiping and watching the preparation.

The third ceremony is performed by the Lamas with the preparation of a very elaborate ceremonial object. The chief of these are the 'deu', the 'nine – storied palace', consisting of elaborate regular polyhedral in different coloured threads supported on bamboo splinters through a central bamboo. This 'palace', which took over four hours to complete is made to mollify the demons or ghost of an old king of Tibet called Dayom. In his lifetime this palace and monasteries were destroyed so that he had nowhere to live. In revenge his spirit roams about harming people. The palace is offered to beg his pardon and to persuade him to return home without hurting the people in the neighbourhood. The foreground of the structure was occupied by an elaborate representation of the female demon Mamoo Moong, portrayed as a snake-haired female riding on a tiger and surrounded by hundreds of lesser objects. The demon was principally made out of buckwheat powder and it was impressed on the onlookers. According to the sacred books, when the whole object has been made, the invocation and readings from the Holy Scriptures begin with the accompaniment of musical instrument. An offering of boiled rice and fresh buckwheat bread is cleared and cherkem is offered to the demons. The Mamoo Moong herself is summoned and gratified with the offerings of copper pots and clothes. When the demon Mamoo Moong is presumed to be in a good mood or temper, her image is taken off the temporarily erected altar and handed over to all present during the observance to wave out the malevolent action. Lastly the image is carried out with a procession and immersed into the junction of three streams. It is a perception that if any animal has not devoured within three days, it is a sign that there will be serious sickness in the coming season. Before taking out the image a Mun sang a song alone for thanking the god for coming and blessing them and now to go back. On these occasions, Mun always sang more or less sacred songs.

The services of the Mun are continuously necessary in the every sphere of Lepcha life. During the time of every passages of life (birth, marriage and death) the Mun must always be present as essential priests, while at the death their role is of more emotional importance than the lama. The Mun are necessary for cleansing from supernatural danger, for blessing and solemnizing different undertakings and, above all for expelling devils. At the time of ceremonial cleansing the Mun waved certain objects from the actual or potential sufferer. In Lepcha cognition both the parents are pek in the fifth month of pregnancy with a bunch of elephant grass to insure an easy delivery – if the labour time is difficult the mother in child birth is pek with a live chicken, and, if she or her husband have neglected a pre-natal precaution, with the object which has been wrongly handled or finished. In the same way, after an abortion or still born the child has been thrown into the river, a Mun will pek the carriers with a bunch of stinging and thorny plants and the parents will be pek with a live animal which will later be sacrificed, in order to prevent the devil which has caused one death causing more. Pek-ing is the nearest approach in Lepcha life to ritual cleansing and is employed in number of circumstances, sometimes alone and sometimes as part of exorcism. Though it is not essential but Mun's blessings are invoked and solemnized by a ritual, sakyou faat, where the pouring or drinking of strained chi with butter is necessary. This ritual is performed to solemnize a marriage, to set up the ing-zong relationship, to mark the formal swearing of an oath or before starting any unusual undertaking, sometimes alone or sometimes with the lafet sacrifice. This ritual is always made privately by the member of each household after the sowing of a field. It is recognized as the most solemn sacrament in Lepcha life.

It is their opinion that when a Mun is called to exorcise a specific devil that he has been divined, the Mun spends a night in his own home— munthen-ing for summoning and communing with the possessing spirit. The question of causation is bound up with the conception of tamtoom – the necessary consequence of an earlier act; often this act was not committed by the sufferer, but by fairly remote ancestors. The Mun worships two supernaturals, Hit-rum and De-rum, who are considered to be ancestral gods who look after all dead Lepchas. When a Mun has discovered as much as possible about the supernatural and immediate causes of the illness he indicates the necessary objects of sacrifice. These are almost always animals, but on occasion other objects are needed as well or instead. Sometimes these objects are valuables, which are just displayed to gratify the supernatural; sometimes other edibles—crops, chi, dried bird, dried fish, and ginger. According to the ceremony these are either abandoned to be eaten by wild animals, or consumed, as part of the ritual, by all present except the Mun himself.

When animals are sacrificed they are first offered alive to all the supernaturals; then they are slaughtered and divided up. Parts of intestines—the lungs, liver and heart—called sha-fot are cooked with rice and chopped up and thrown for the devils; the head, one fore-leg, and one hind-leg (these portions are called gazook) are laid out and dedicated to the devil specially involved. After the dedication the meat is eaten up by the members. It is often the Mun's fee but he does not always take it all. The Mun intones prayers both before and after the animal is killed; the praying may take four hours, and is usually not attended to by the other people present. In daylight ceremonies, when the weather is fine, the Mun often withdraws a little distance from the house in order to pray without disturbing or disturbance. This relatively simple sacrifice is usually performed when there is a parallel exorcism being performed at the same time by Lamas; for some other devils, particularly those with which lamas cannot deal in any way, much more elaborate ceremonies are necessary. It is impossible to generalize about these exorcisms as one can about the lamaist ones, for they have no apparent common principle. I have therefore selected three 'prescriptions' out of the considerable number I have witnessed or heard about, as samples; in their different aspects they embody the greater number of motives in elaborate Mun ritual.

Mun Regulated Rituals

1. *Sor moong (violent death) or Apang moong (genitor-urinary diseases)* – To get rid of urinary disease or violent death, a goat is put in a snare having three knots tied in its length, first of all, all the members of the afflicted household must touch the knots and then the Mun would call on all the devils to be contended with the blood of the sacrifice and not to take the patient, after which he throws the rope into the air. If the rope falls end outwards (i.e. the end away from the goat

falls towards the door), it means that the devil is satisfied and if it falls towards the house the prognosis is bad. After this the animal is killed and the gazook and sha-fot offered to the devil/demon with a plate and a pot filled with rice, a rupee and a ceremonial scarf (chada), together with some of the invalid's ornaments and clothing and also a cup of chi with different grains in it. Then the Mun constructs a phallus out of wood, which is called in its guardian function moong long tik. This phallus is set up between two stones leaning slightly forward, somewhere in the forest, and anointed with the blood of the slain animal and chi, which will keep the devil/demon away from the area and household.

2. *The ghost of a dead child, called Num-een moong* – The young children death caused by infantile diarrhea, which is believed to be caused by a demon named Num-een moong. To drive away that demon (moong) the Lepcha people sacrifice a goat or a sheep. Even after the sacrifice of an animal if the person continues to be troubled by the moong. Then the troubled person stands on the right side of the stream and the Mun on the left of it. Then a 'gateway' is made over the stream of two bundles of elephant grass and brambles, while the Mun holds in each hand a bundle made out of wild raspberries, nettles and some other thorny and prickly plants. These bundles are dipped in water and peek over the sufferer several times. A bamboo chi (beer) holder filled with blood and chi and shut up at both ends and a leaf filled with fried rice, meat and blood are peek over the patient and thrown through the gateway for the demon. The branches of thorny plants are thrown through the gateway and finally the gateway is filled up with thorny plants, so that it looks like a tree. The Mun does this at two other places; one is some way apart on the streams and the other is either above or below the first one. After completing the Mun must return straight to his own house without meeting anybody. If he meets people Num-een moong will start haunting him.

It was told that Num-een moong is the demon released by the death of young children. Older people who die do not let loose a devil/demon. The Num-een moong persists for about three years after the child's death.

3. *Chyom moong or Rot moong* – This ceremony is called Moong Sot, killing the devil, and should be performed by the surviving members of the family in which one member has either died violently or committed suicide. It should be performed every three years, but it is sufficient if the ceremony is done after the violent death and at the birth of each new member of the household. If the ceremony is not performed the devil will return and claim another victim. A dead goat is skinned except for its legs below the joint and is laid on its back with its hind quarters towards the bowman. Beside it is a hole already dug and above it is made a small shelter of bamboos thatched with reeds. Beyond that is set up a red head of banana flower stuck into the ground and against it a post on top of which is attached the goat's heart, in such a manner that the blood drips on the banana flower. In a line with this stands a bowman with an arrow in his bow ready to shoot. The Mun is at one side not looking at the post. The other men who are present are all armed with knives.

After a time, the Mun starts shivering uncontrollably and summons the devil in a loud voice. As he calls some insect or other will climb up the pole towards the heart, and the bowman must shoot it with his arrow before it reaches it. As son as he has shot he must call to the Mun to say whether he has hit or missed the insect; if he has missed the Mun must recall it. When the insect is killed it and the goat are chopped to pieces by the bystanders with their knives and buried in the prepared hole; stones and earth are rammed on top of the sacrifice to fill up the hole, and then a second time to make a little mound.

The local religion is also governed by the Mun and very much connected with harvesting and hunting with having a number of rituals. The worship of the people of Mayel is categorized as Pong rum, the god of hunters and Sakyou rum, the god of harvesting crops. Though, unfortunately very little is known about the both religion but the people believed that there is a close nexus between both. According to the oldest Lepcha custom men are preferably perform the sacrifice but if he is absent then a women, especially a virgin girl may perform the sacrifice; but if they do so the ceremony is curtailed and fewer objects are employed. The chief offerings to the people of Mayel are the lafet sacrifice and sakyou faat. The small bird for the lafet must be killed by a virgin boy, and the strained chi (country liquor) poured into the cup with full of butter by a virgin girl. It is the common belief and also traditional custom that if a special bird were not killed and if the killer and the chi-pourer were not virgins the gods would be angry and the harvest spoiled.

Munism and Supernatural Power

The Lepcha religion, Munism is animist in nature. While defining the old religion Tylor (1871) first used the term 'animism' to denote belief in supernatural beings. D.N. Majumder held it to be a 'crude form of religion' involving belief in the continuation of soul even after to the death of the body. It acknowledges the soul of even trees, rocks, rivers, mountains and animals.

The animist Lepcha believe that there are two types of spirits—one type is benevolent spirit which looks after the well-being of an individual, a household, the cattle, the husbandry and crops, etc. But the most numerous are those which cause enmity, jealousy, diseases, illness, death, epidemics, loss of property, failure of crops and other hazards. Whenever any misfortune befalls, the Lepchas attribute it to the spirits they called 'moong', to the good they pay no heed. 'The good spirits do us no harm; the evil spirits, which dwell in every rock, grove or mountain, are constantly at mischief, and to them we must pray, for they hurt us'. They acknowledge the existence of one supreme God and other gods and goddesses. But do not make regular offerings to these benevolent spirits and gods. Even to the dreaded evil spirits they pay attention only when something goes wrong. Some spritis play dual roles. Good spirit—Sakyo-rum and evil spirit—Aami-moong are but the same spirit so long as it is pleased and looks after the prosperity and richness of an individual it is Sakyo-fum, but it will take the form of Aami-moong if it is displeased by someone's' especially trespassers—unauthorized use of the garden or orchard. In extreme cases the victim suffers from paralysis. In Lepcha society the tradition of Mun and Boongthing, the female priestess and male priest, has great significance in religious matters although this tradition is gradually on decline. The coming of Buddhism gave a fatal blow to the tradition of Munism, yet the tradition of Mun survives and holds sway over the Lepcha society.

Malevolent Power of the God (rum):-

Position	*Local Name*
Village God	Lyang-rum
Household deity	Tong-thing
Household deity	Lee-rum
Common deity	Tsandong- rum
Common deity	Lung-no rum, Ajo Gyantho
Seasonal deity	Shukbu-rum

Malevolent Power of the Demon/Devil/Ghost (Moong)

Position	*Local Name*
Place of dense forest, rock and cave	Duet-Tshen moong
Places of flowing streams, rivers	Manoo moong (female ghost)
places of flowing streams, rivers	Loo-moong (female demon)
Places inside the bustee	Gey-bo-moong
Places of a village boundary	Lyang shergynu (female ghost)
Places of outcrops of a rock	Sabdok moong
Places of roadside area	Arof moong

Malevolent Power of the Evil Spirit

Position	*Local name*
Reside in the nature as a whole	Dzengo
Reside in the tree trunk	Apang moong sor moong
Reside in the dead child's soul	Num-een moong
Reside in the open barren field	Sipundi
Reside in the fruits, vegetables	Amee

and grains	
Reside in a huge tree, a crag, a tarn, a cave, a cluster of trees, a hillock	Lung-zee
Reside in the huge stone situated at the entry point of the bustee	Sandong Long-chuk
Reside in the open air just outside the house	Maknyam
Reside in the dense forest	Sor

Mythology and Religion: Reflection through Rong-Folk

The most difficult task is to separate the pure Lepcha beliefs from the 'loan-myths'. With the dissemination of Tibetan-Buddhist ideas probably the motives of Tibetan folk-lore have spread to the Lepcha theological world. It was the natural borrowings of tales of the Bhutias and Nepalis with whom the Lepchas have mixed over the years. But Rong-folk is the original folk tales of the Lepcha primarily based on the beliefs on supernatural being (god, demon/devil, and spirits) as they exhaustively spread over in the nature in and around of the foothills of the Himalayas. In these tales, one can trace two distinct phases of Lepcha mentality. What probably belongs to an earlier period, or to some species of more primitive culture absorbed by the Lepcha, is the atmosphere of animistic beliefs. According to them, humans occupy only a secondary position, and the animals, insects and plants receive the whole attention of the narrator. The second phase belongs to a culture of a much more advanced group, and deals chiefly with heroes and demons. Both elements are prominent, and it would be unfair to treat the more primitive ideas as being merely the incidental survivals of an earlier state of Lepcha mentality. However, the mythology of the Lepcha ultimately develops on the basis of belief to natural objects and the supernatural exist in the nature.

Mythology of 'Origin of Devils'

While recollecting the origin of devil, the Gnadok Mun narrated a mythological story of same kind—the first children of Itpomu and Debu were Komsithing and Narzong-nyou. Although they were brother and sister they married and as a consequence all their children were devils, snakes and lizard. As soon as they were born their mother cast them aside without giving them milk. Finally she produced a normal child called Rilbu Shingbu whom she nursed; but when the devils saw this child getting the milk that had been denied them they were jealous and they took counsel and killed the child. Their incest was betrayed by the dog that guarded the door. When the parents were shamed and the child was killed they buried the child in the black rock on the right of the Talung valley, which can be seen to this day, and thereafter in disgust they divided their property and separated. Komsi-thing went to Tibet and he took with him all the riches and jewels and animals which the Tibetans have till this day. Nazong-nyou turned towards our country but she was careless and that is why our country is so poor. After that Komsithing summoned all the devils to him and all came except Doam moong who is the devil of leprosy, and he counseled the devils and said to them that 'all the devils must act according to their nature by taking an oath that when men were born they accept them and if those men offered pig, oxen and rice them to eat, the men must go away, must obey the Mun and Pandem.' Henceforward, Itpomu had placed all the devils in the big plain area, Azum Patham; but there they had nothing to eat. Then Itpomu created the Mun spirit and sent her to feed them. All the devils sword three great oaths – first, they cut their finger nails and swore on them, secondly, they spat on the Kashou tree and the tree withered, finally, they spat in the sea and the sea dried up. Since then the Mun must find out what sacrifices are needed and give them to the devils and the devils will always obey them.

According to the Lepcha the two feminine deities Itpomu and Narzong-nyou are the chief supernatural of Mun. Itpomu herself is never directly invoked; it is always her creations that are sacrificed and prayed to. Narzong-nyou is really the chief Lepcha goddess as well as the local God of Sikkim, of the Lepchas' country, where she lived and responsible for its geography, flora and especially fauna. Her elder brother and husband Komsithing is also responsible for a number of habits and institutions, but he is in a way a foreigner; after he and his wife separated he took himself to Tibet. Except in the harvest rites the two of them are always mentioned in prayers and sacrifices, together with all the other supernatural involved. It is a common practice that for all their manifestations all the relevant gods with their wives and children are worshipped by invocating their name. On the other hand the people also worship the personal and ptso gods by sacrificing the animals. It is observed that nearly all the Lepchas follow the lung-then, a word applied for the traditional custom by applying stories, giving of feasts.

Lung-then, as opined by the Lepcha can be categorized in to two groups—those dealing with supernatural and human beings; those dealing with the animals. In this context, Gorer's (2005) anecdote is worth mentioning where he mentions that the feature of lung-then is dealing with anthropomorphic characters that played a preponderating role by the genitalia, endowed with independent life. Peculiar formation and characteristics, and the adventures of these organs together with the bodies to which they are attached are told in a number of tales. One such tales is 'origin of menstruation', unparallel to the mythology of the Lepcha. The story would appear to be capable of two interpretations, both of them congruent with the Lepcha attitude to the similarity and difference between men and women. One hand it indicates the conception of equality of men and women but at the same time on the other hand it interpreted as male envy of women and their more conspicuous physiological functions, a deeply hidden envy which can be supported by the Lepcha belief that male intervention is necessary to start the physical signs of female puberty (Gorer, 2005; p.226).

REFERENCES

Basilov, V.N., 1999. Cosmos as Everyday Reality in Shamanism in Romano Mastromattei and Antonio Rigopoulos (eds.) *Shamanic Cosmos: From India to the North Pole Star*, New Delhi, D.K. Printworld, pp. 17-39.

Freud, Sigmund, 1950. *Totem and Taboo*, London, Routledge & Kegan Paul *Gazetteer of Sikkim*, 1931. *Gazetteer of Bengal and Sikkim* by A.E. Porter, vol.V, Part-I & II, Delhi. Usha Publication.

Gorer, Geoffrey, 2005. *Himalayan Village: An Account of the Lepchas of Sikkim*, London. M.Joseph Ltd.

Mazumder, D.N., 1944. *Fortunes of Primitive Tribes*, Lucknow. Allied Publishers.

Speziale, Arturo, 1987. *The Ethical and Religious Values of Ancient India*, Calcutta, Sujan Publications.

Thakur, R.N., 1988. *Himalayan Lepchas*. New Delhi. Archives Publisher and Distributors.

Tylor, E.B., 1871. *Primitive Culture: Researches into the Development of Mythology, Philosophy, Religion, Art and Customs*, Vol. 1 & 2. Gloucester. Mass Smith.

SECTION-IV

25

The Ramakrishna Mission Movement in the Khasi Hills during the Pre-Independence Period

Prof. Satyadeo Poddar & Nirmalya Karmakar

The Khasi's began to be drawn into the wider life of India from 1833 when the Khasi Hills became a Political Agency of the East India Company, which had acquired the Diwani of Bengal in 1765. Modern education was introduced in 1842, when Thomas Jones, a Welsh Calvinistic Methodist missionary opened a school at Mawsmai, near Cherrapunji, and by 1874 there were 73 such schools with an average of 22 pupils per school. There was, however, by the end of the nineteenth century, a growing apprehension among the Khasis that their culture, religion, and traditions were being threatened by alien forces. This is seen from the setting up in 1899 of an Organisation called Seng Khasi, which was formally registered in the name of all the 'sub-tribes'. Its aim was the preservation and promotion of the Khasi cultural heritage and the all round development and welfare of the Khasi population. Other movements of a similar nature followed. In the early 1920's there were still many among the Khasis who were anxious to have some society starts schools in their hills to which they could safely send their children without any danger of their being exposed to the propaganda of the existing schools.

Thus it was that in September 1924, a young man of 22 arrived at Shella, in the southern part of Khasi Hills. Swami Prabhananda or Ketaki Maharaj was sent there by Ramakrishna Mission in 1927 to work among the tribal people. He had come from the Ramakrishna Mission branch in Dhaka. In his earlier life his name was Ketaki, to be known later as Swami Prabhananda. He was involved in building a centre of educational and welfare works among the Khasis till the end of his life. Since his death the work had continued to grow in Shillong and Cherrapunjee. There are now more than forty schools in the Khasi Hills with a high school at Cherrapunji which has a high reputation throughout Meghalaya. Books in the Khasi language are published from Cherrapunji, and weekly classes in Khasi religion and culture are held in Khasi at the Ashram. Various rural industries are organized in conjuction with the Khadi and Village Industries Commission.

The Ramakrishna Mission is made their beginning by opening a high school for adults. It is interesting to see that from the very begenning Swami Prabhananda decides that the village elders hold the supreme power in decision making. He said that, "it won't be possible for Ramakrishna Mission to open school without the help of local people with their moral and financial support." Though the Khasis were so poor, they were ready to take the financial responsibilities. Khasis offered food to Swami Prabhananda in their houses. Though first the Khasi peaple were in a doubt that whether a Bengali will take food from other places. But Swami Prabhananda had no problem with it. This marked for Swami Prabhananda the relationship of love, goodwill & trust, which grew stronger & stronger. The school was a success. When the school had gone for some months, the elders of the village decided to open a school for children at day time. After this school started, Swami Prabhananda was only the sole teacher in this school. He visited each & every members of the family of the village to send their children into the school.

Swami Prabhananda arrived at Khasi hills without any motive to hinduise the Khasi people. He was very upset to see the conversion because the people were poor and uneducated. He was in a fear that the people will never trust the plain people because of this conversion. The Khasi people were very simple & ignorant, that's why very hard for Swami Prabhananda to convince them that he had come not for any material gain, but to serve them the selfless service of the Ramakrishna Mission. Swami Prabhananda had realized this hard reality that unless or until he has capable of speaking Khasi, he will never entered into the hearts of them. Swami Prabhananda had mastered himself in the Khasi language in an unbelievable time with a fluency. Not only that, he discourses on Khasi on subjects of wide interest. Some of the Khasi people were shocked and amazed to see Swami Prabhananda that how he delivered all his lectures in the Khasi language. The local Khasis were very happy to have a man like Swami Prabhananda.

Though Swami Prabhananda had mastered himself in Khasi language, but never tried to influence the Khasi people in any particular direction. He always gave importance to their own traditions that they inherited from the past. He tried to motivate the Khasi people also by saying that they have to overcome themselves from the mental closureness of being deprived as a nice and simple people. They should think in a progressive mind. He expressed these views for the betterment and welfare of the Khasi people. It becomes the fresh air from the new world for them. He was quite different from the other plain people. Even today, people have remembered him because of his great enthusiasm, racial pride, his talks, and a great smile which had earned so many friends. Even of his last days, when he was suffering he still got that smile.

After the arrival of Swami Prabhananda, the news soon spread to other villages that a young man had arrived at Shella who was running schools without any attempt to convert the pupils into his religion. Moreover he was anxious and worried for the Khasis people themselves. The leaders of the other villages soon approached as well as requested him to open schools in their villages, because at that point of time they needed it badly. Soon there had so many schools established and Shella became the headquarter of them. The school at Shella had been raised to the status of M.E.School. Rs. 500/- has sanctioned as an annual grant by the village elders who was elected through the adult franchise.

But the school faced few problems also as Swami Prabhananda was the sole teacher in it and that's why it was impossible for him to carry on the work. He was then looking for assistance, who would not work for money but for the local people. Satish, his friend from Dacca, was first to join him in the Khasi hills. Though Satish was a great boost for him, but he need more people to expand his work. But it has not an easy job. Finally he managed to find some young men. They came here not for love, but for the adventure. Though everybody was not suitable for the work, but some are good. In the meantime a brother monk was also arrived there. He was fond of music and also had a good hand in Homeopathy. So many other monks also came, but not all of them were able to stay for long.

The Khasi students who used the text books were based on Christian theology. According to Swami Prabhananda, liberal education wouldn't be possible unless appropriate text books here in use not only in his schools, but everywhere. Then he decided to write text books himself and was able to publish some books in a span of very short time. Some of the books are still in use. A brother monk also wrote few books based on songs. These songs were a great hit at that time among the Khasis because of the time sentiment expressed in charming notes. Some of the songs were sung over the radio even today.

Swami Prabhananda felt that his efforts would be fruitless unless he had a high school over there. He noticed that the children who went to the high school in Shillong often came back with such exotic habits and tastes that they became complete misfit in their rural society. Moreover the people of Shella begged him to taste a high school in village, where their children & children of the neighboring villages to receive education in a congenial environment. He felt that Cherrapunji was the best place to start a school as it was easily accessible from different parts of Khasi Hills and it was also the seat of ancient Khasi culture. But the people of Shella were disappointed as Swami Prabhananda did not select their village for the proposed school.

Swami Prabhananda soon visited Cherrapunjee to explore what help and co-operations he might get from the local people to start a high school over there. But the Christians opposed the idea of a Hindu organization starting of any school there. That's why when he has almost given up hope of being able to start a high school there, one Khasi gentleman came up with a piece of land saying at any time he start a school. The proposed site was distant plains of syllet (Now in Bangladesh) was judged best possible site for a school. Swami Prabhananda, hasting no time formed a committee consisting prominent men of the village, belonging to all religions.* But there has some problem regarding the land as some one spread the news that Swami Prabhananda had given land gift in an allmost free condition. The local Raja called Syiem was then probably under pressure of some parties and he had a notice served on both Swami Prabhananda and donor of the land by saying that they were not to proceed further.

Though this land problem had solved after that and the major problem that arised was the fund to construct School building. Swami Prabhananda also managed to engage few educated Bengali youths who would work in various schools, though later he find that few of them were not suited for the work in rural areas. From now onwards Swami Prabhananda spent more time in Cherrapunjee to boost the work. Moreover, the gurdians of the students were also present there to motivate him. His main problem was men and money. He was though handicapped by these circumstances, but never lost faith in himself.

It was the in year 1934, from when the condition of health of Swami Prabhananda became weaker and weaker. Ever since his arrival at the Khasi Hills, he had never enough nutrition and proper food. He had great faith in his physique and he could not bring himself to believe that there was anything wrong with him. But his health gradually worsens day after day. He was sent to Dr. B.C. Roy Hospital in Calcutta for better treatment. He was suffering from some kind of virus attack. The symptom of the disease was muscular atrophy. He was taken back to Shillong where he wanted to spend the rest of his days. He quietly sleeped into death on a cold morning in 1938.

In this way we can see that how Ramakrishna Mission under the dynamic leadership of Swami Prabhananda expand their works and activities in the Khasi Hills. Through these educational institutions set up by the Ramakrishna Mission, the Khasi people's pride in their own tribal culture started growing once again. Now there are more than forty Schools located in different places over the Khasi Hills. Cherrapunjee become the head-quarter. The School at Cherrapunjee considered as one of the best in the Meghalaya. This helped the Khasi's to some extent to being swept off their feet by the onslaught of the western culture. The liberal concept of respect for all the religions practiced by the Ramakrishna Mission has also attracted many students of the other sects, which were engaged in conversion. With this attitude towards the people and society, it's became a movement among the Khasi's in the region.

NOTES AND REFERENCES

1. Atmapriyananda, Swami, (Compiled and edited) "*Ramakrishna Mission: A Saga of Service, for a hundred years and more...*" Foundation Day Commemoration Volume – 1 May 2010.
2. Bandyopadhyay, Amalasankar, "*Brahmos outside Calcutta, Case studies in East and North-East India: 1828-1900*", Progressive Publishers.
3. Banerjee, Dipankar, "*Brahmo Samaj and North-East India*", Anamika Publishers and Distributors (P) Limited, 2006.
4. Collection from the Archive of "*Jing Kyrsiew*", School Magazine of Ramakrishna Ashrama High School, Cherrapunjee.
5. Documents collected from the ex-students of the Ramakrishna Ashrama High School, Cherrapunjee.
6. Gambhirananda, Swami, "*History of Ramakrishna Math and Ramakrishna Mission*", Advaita Ashrama, 1983.
7. *Journal of the Indian Anthropological Society*, Volume 29, Issue 3, Indian Anthropological Society, The Society – 1994, p. 215.

8. Miri, Mrinal, *Linguistic Situation in North-East India*, North-East Council for Social Science Research, Concept Publishing Company.

9. Mukherjee, Jayasree, *The Ramakrishna Vivekananda Movement: Impact on Indian Society and Politics (1893-1922)*, Firma KLM Pvt. Limited, 1997.

10. Nag, Jamuna, *Social Reform Movements in Nineteenth Century India*, RBSA Publishers, 1988, p. 175.

11. Natarajan, Nalini, *The Missionary among the Khasis*, Sterling Publishers Pvt. Limited, New Delhi, 1977, p. 87.

12. *Prabuddha Bharata* or *Awakened India*, Volume 77, Published by Swami Smarananda for Advaita Ashrama, 1972, p. 8.

13. Prakash, Col Ved, "*Encyclopaedia of North-East India*, Atlantic Publishers and Distributors (P) Limited, p.1663.

14. *Proceedings of the North East India History Association Session*, 1983, p. 143.

15. *Ramakrishna Math and Ramakrishna Mission: Tribal welfare services*, Published by The General Secretary, Ramakrishna Math and Ramakrishna Mission, Belur Math, Howrah, West Bengal, 26th December, 1993.

16. Sen, Anindya, Ramakrishna Mission and community service in Eastern India (1922-1962): A qualitative and quantitative analysis, *Readers Service*, p. 164.

17. Sen, Siba Pada, *Social and religious reform movements in the nineteenth and twentieth centuries*, Institute of Historical Studies (Calcutta, India), 1979, p. 481.

18. Sharma, Suresh Kanta, Sharma Usha (ed.), *Discovery of North-East India*, Mittal Publications, p. 154.

26

Valedictory Address

Saroj Chaudhury

Respected Mr. President, dignitaries on and off the dais, learned participants and friends. Allow me to express my heartfelt gratitude to the organisers for such perfect organisation of the seminar. I convey my gratitude to the Sanskriti people for conferring on me the honour of Fellowship and the special honor of inviting me to deliver the valedictory address. I thank the learned participants whose deliberations have enriched me during all these three days. I have no presumption of being regarded as a scholar of any sort, except that, I have a will to learn. Thank you all for providing me the scope. One sad thing about all good things is that, they always end very quickly; but I know that such ends assure another beginning. With this belief I wish you farewell: "Punardarshanayacha."

For the last three days we have been listening to illuminating discourses on a rather uncommon topic: Concept of God and Religion: Traditional Thought and Contemporary Society. Many important things have become unusual and uncommon today, because our lifestyle and our thought process have become unusual. We have divided our lives into cubicles. We have lost the ability to look, even to think beyond the walls of the cubicle at the moment. Shut in the cubicle of material pursuit, we have relegated our thoughts, even our relationships to other hands. We feel comfortable to presume that others will do the thinking about matters that we consider do not concern us immediately. This is self-imposed intellectual imprisonment. It results in blindness about the future. Even if we fail to see its immediate necessity, such seminars are at least occasions for intellectual deliverance.

Papers presented in the different sessions have given idea about growth and development of religion and about the different dimensions of the concept of God and Religion, examples have been provided new Religions contributes to the growth of ethno-socio-cultural identity; how it moulds and is moulded by the conditions of life, and how it develops even the local ever remained intertwined. It is no burden of deadwood, as a living force it accommodates syncretism. It assimilates diverse elements.

Religion has a functionary dimension as well as a cultural dimension. In its functionary dimension it contains in it the process of socialization. It is the source of ethical codes and morals. Religion originates from the core of culture; it is a social construct. It aims at manifestation of highest humanitarian attributes. It is a framework through which innate human spirituality can find expression – although more religiosity may not generate spirituality. Its power depends on how closely it is related to real life. Religion as a concept is simple and at the same time complex. In its development also it moves from simple to complex. Simple sense of discrimination between good and bad may develop into the philosophical opposition of sacred and profane. At the core it is basic human sense of good and the will to do good; The more developed is human intellect, the more subtle the inquisitiveness, more complex dimensions are revealed. Religion is a social phenomenon set in the cultural matrix of a community.

If religion is a social phenomenon, why do we here septic voices questioning its relevance in contemporary society? Father superior has broached the question directly. He has observed that modern society shuns religion and religious people. He has rightly identified the probable causes like Exclusives, Bigotry, Politicalisation and Authoritarianism. I would humbly add one more probable reason: the usual practice of dressing up all religion-related discussions in straight-jackets of scholastic parlance. Such expressions like "It is unknowable essence" are sufficiently intimidating; Father has also suggested some very practical ways out: The aberrations are to be removed; the spirit of generosity in religion has to be made perceptible and priorities are to be determined on the basic of rationality. The religious leaders have to be pre-active.

Concept of God also came with the dawn of man's observation and understanding. He observed and realized existence of power, mostly natural forces, more powerful taken himself and his community. Question about his own source also must have troubled him, which resulted into the concept of the supernatural. This supernatural took shape into a Supreme doing : benevolent, Creator, maintaining his creation and controlling all spirits/phenomenon. Early man imposed anthropomorphic attributes on him, with his limited imagination. Gradually, qualities of the Supreme were speculated upon and newer attributes were added, leading almost to abstraction. This abstraction might have suggested the earliest seed of atheism in some cases. In others, hierarehies were constructed to accommodate the idea of spirit in different objects. The process was longer and much more complex than stated. However, God remained in the supreme position, whether one and only or the head of a troop. Though benevolent, the attribute of judgement also was added as one aspect of supremacy over the whole creation. He remained the ultimate and supreme.

There should not be any difficulty in accepting such benevolent supreme, but in contemporary society God suffers some degree of indifference. The reasons are difficult to be identified, but it is a fact that the present day world is a world of mediocre, and mediocre are averse to admit superior. Our scientific and technological progress has gifted us with quite some power (mostly negative) which were previously the purview of the supernatural. We suffer from a feeling of self – sufficiency. In some circles the Guru has substituted God (*Guru Brahma gururvishnu, guru deva Maheswar* etc.). only a deeper probe to social psyche probably can reveal the causes.

Like other human possessions, religion also can be used or misused. The fault lies not with the object, but with the user. Yet, in contemporary society religion or anything related with it is often held at a safe distance. If it is a wrong, confronting it squarely is the social attitude. Even denial is best effective when rationally and directly done.

Everything said and done, I remember a talk with Prof. Yashpal, the eminent physicist and educationist. He was talking about meaningful education of children. He told of drawing attending of the children to the variety and symmetry in the world around. If the child asks about the cause of the symmetry, will the reply of coincidence suffice? And again the Large Adorn Collider has found the Creator particle. The band of famous scientists has given it a name. what is that? God particle! Is God completely banished from our contemporary minds?

Friends, this is not a scholarly discourse. It is just an expression of personal feelings. In my comprehension of the matter, I have drawn upon your wisdom. I believe this seminar is a beginning - beginning of exploration of other areas like the social psyche.

Thanking you all, once again.

Editors & Contributors

K. Jose SVD (b. 31st January, 1963) is the Founder Director of *SANSKRITI* – North Eastern Institute of Culture & Religion, Guwahati. This institute is the anthropological research wing of International Society popularly known as SVD. Jose is a Life-time member of this Society which has a number of Anthropological and Folklore Research Institutions World-wide including Institute of Indian Culture, Mumbai. He has presented several research papers in various International, National and Regional Seminars and has organized the National Seminars on Tribes of North-East India consecutively from 2007 - 2010 and is the Director of the National Seminar on Anthropological Research in India: Retrospect and Prospect (2011) to be held at Guwahati. He is currently guiding various research projects in Arunachal Pradesh, Tripura, Meghalaya and Assam. He has jointly edited 5 volumes on themes specific to North East India. His areas of special interest are studies in cultural continuity & change, indigenous knowledge systems and resource management for sustainable development, and Peace initiatives and Governance in North East India.

Dr. Gautam Kumar Bera (b. 7th August, 1958), graduated in Science with Honours in Anthropology, passed his Master's degree in Anthropology with specialization in Social and

Cultural Anthropology securing First position in First Class, received his Ph.D. Degree in Anthropology. Recipient of National Scholarship for Advance Studies, University Gold Medal and Research Fellow Gold Medal (U.S.A.), and several other distinguished awards and honours at both national and international levels, he was elected a FELLOW of the prestigious Royal Anthropological Institute, London, in 1992, ADVISOR to the Research Board of ABI (U.S.A.) in 1996, *SANSKRITI* Foundation Fellow, and Stephen Fuchs Memorial Awardee, in 2009 of NEICR, Guwahati. He also received the Mother Teresa Centenary Award in 2010. Credited with authorship of seventeen books and edited volumes, more than ninety scientific research papers and about twenty five book reviews in scientific journals and books of international repute of both India and abroad, and over five dozen articles of common interest and popular science in different periodicals, newspapers and web site he is attached to four international scientific journals as CA Associate, *Current Anthropology* (U.S.A.), Assistant Editor, *Journal of the Anthropological Survey of India* (Kolkata), Book Review Editor, *The Oriental Anthropologist* (Allahabad), and Consulting Editor, *Contemporary Who's Who* (U. S. A). He is the Life Member of the Indian Anthropological Society, Kolkata and the Oriental Institute of Cultural and Social Research, Allahabad.

Prof. Birinchi K. Medhi, by profession is an anthropologist. Being a social anthropologist he penetrates into the hidden aspects of human cultures of the world with special reference to North-East India. He is also a novelist, poet, columnist, and lyricist in Assamese language. In 2009, he was selected as *SANSKRITI* Foundation Fellow. Medhi sees humans not as an anthropological subject only; as a novelist and short story writer he tries to understand the agonizing and devastating impacts of modernity on life and cultures of North-East India. Medhi has a number of publications in Anthropology, both in Assamese and English, to his credit. At present he is a Professor of Social and Cultural Anthropology in the Department of Anthropology, Gauhati University, Guwahati, Assam.

Dr. R. P. Athparia is a well known Anthropologist in North East India. At present he is the Head of Office in the Anthropological Survey of India, North East Regional Centre, Shillong. In 2009, he was selected as *SANSKRITI* Foundation Fellow. He is the Executive Member of North-East India Council for Social Science Research, Shillong. He edited five volumes of publications including Renewable Energy Resource and Its Management. Many of his research papers on anthropological and social issues on North-East India are published in the well known research journals in the country.

CONTRIBUTORS

Prof. Birinchi K. Medhi, Professor, Department of Anthropology, Gauhati University, Guwahati. birinchimedhi@rediffmail.com

Prof. Saroj Chaudhuri is winner of *Sanskriti* Emeritus Life Time Achievement Awardee 2010.

Prof. Vijoy S. Sahay, Professor and Head, Department of Anthropology, University of Allahabad, Allahabad- 211 002, E-mail: vijoysahay@gmail.com

Dr. Gautam K. Bera, "Upanishadam", 147/1, Jaigirghat Road, Thakurpukur, Kolkata – 700 063. gautam58kb@yahoo.co.in, 09477942184.

Dr. Paul Puthussery CSC, St. Joseph's Church, Agartala, is the director of Holy Cross Higher Education Ministry in North East India. pudusseryp@gmail.com

Dr. Ravi Khangai, Asst. Professor and HOD, Department of History, Ambedkar College, Fatikroy, Dt. North Tripura – 799 290. E Mail: ravikhangai@gmail.com

Dr. Surojit Sen Gupta, Assistant Professor, Department of Sociology, Maharaja Bir Bikram College, Government of Tripura, Agartala – 799004. meghaboy@yahoo.com

Dr. Arifur Zaman, Asst. Professor, Department of Anthropology, Dibrugarh University, Assam - 786004. Email : arifurz1@yahoo.com, Mobile : 94351 45920.

Dr. Binita Basu, Lecturer, Department of Anthropology, Nara Sinha Dutt College, Howrah. West Bengal – 711 102. binita_2006@sify.com

Dr. Joy Thomas SVD, Director, Ishvani Kendra, Pune, India; Tel: 9403185214; E-mail: joythomassvd@gmail.com

Dr. Luke Daimary Senior Lecturer, Department of History, Nehru College, Pailapool, North Cachar Hills, Assam. lumsram@yahoo.co.in.

Dr. Samita Manna, Professor, Department of Sociology, University of Kalyani, Nadia, West Bengal. samita.manna@gmail.com

Dr. Francis Pereira SVD, Professor, Comparative Religions, Regional Theological College, Sambalpur, Orissa. francispereira2@rediffmail.com

Dr. Pushpa Anbu SVD, Professor, Department of Philosophy, Khrist Premalaya Philosophate, Bhopal, M.P. anbusvd@gmail.com

Dr. R.P. Athparia, North Eastern Social Research Centre, Kharghuli, Guwahati- 4. rpathparia@yahoo.co.in

Lincoln Reang, Assistant Professor, Department of History, Tripura University. Suryamaninagar, Agartala, lreang@rediffmail.com.

Nishikant Kolge, Assistant Professor, Department of History, Tripura University, Suryamaninagar, Agartala. kolge270477@gmail.com.

Roshani Rai, Assistant Professor, Department of History, Tripura University, Suryamaninagar, Agartala.

Paulami Chattopadhyay, chatterjeepaulami26@rediffmail.com.

Rajib Chatterjee, Senior Research Fellow, Centre for Himalayan Studies, University of North Bengal, Darjeeling – 734013, West Bengal, Email: rajibanth@gmail.com

Bikash Bhargab Sarma, Asst. Professor and Head, Dept. of philosophy, Ambedkar College, Tripura(N) bbhargab@rediffmail.com

Tom Mangattuthazhe, Secretary, Diphu Citizens Peace Forum, Karbi Anglong, Assam. tmangatt@gmail.com

Janet Tellis, SSpS, Research Scholar, Department of Anthropology, Gauhati University, Guwahati, Assam – 781 014. janettellis@rediffmail.com

Sumitabha Chakraborty Research Associate, Anthropological Survey of India, Eastern Regional Centre, Kolkata, EN-79, Sector- V, Salt Lake City, Kolkata – 700 091. chakru4_su@yahoo.com.

Manoj Antony SVD Assistant Director, Sanskriti-NEICR, Guwahati – 781 014, Assam

K. Jose SVD, Director, Sanskriti-NEICR, Guwahati - 781 014, Assam, kjosesvd@gmail.com

John Bosco SVD, Research Associate, Sanskriti, Guwahati, 781 014 – Assam.

Lt. Col. Kinsuk Dutta, President of the Seminar, Agartala.

Hon'ble Advocate Shri Arindhom Lodh, Standing Council, Govt. of India & Editor of *Tripura Times*

Most Rev. Bishop Lumen Monteiro CSC, Bishop of Agartala Diocese

Mr. Babhatosh Dey, Eminent Educationist, Agartala

Bikshu Akshayanada, Secretary Tripura Rajyo Bikshu Sangho, Agartala

Rev. Fr. Cyprian Pinto SVD, Formerly Chairperson, Sanskriti, Guwahati

Dr. Debdas Singha, secretary Bahai Faith, Agartala

J. L. Chakraborty, Secretary, Indian Association for Religious Freedom, Agartala.

■■■